东亚文明的历史与展望
——东亚文明交流国际研讨会论文集

北京师范大学人文宗教高等研究院 ◎ 编

中国社会科学出版社

图书在版编目(CIP)数据

东亚文明的历史与展望：东亚文明交流国际研讨会论文集／北京师范大学人文宗教高等研究院编．—北京：中国社会科学出版社，2019.7

ISBN 978-7-5203-4371-8

Ⅰ.①东⋯ Ⅱ.①北⋯ Ⅲ.①文化交流—东亚—国际学术会议—文集 Ⅳ.①G131.5-53

中国版本图书馆 CIP 数据核字(2019)第 081904 号

出 版 人	赵剑英
责任编辑	任　明
责任校对	沈丁晨
责任印制	李寡寡

出　　版	中国社会科学出版社
社　　址	北京鼓楼西大街甲 158 号
邮　　编	100720
网　　址	http://www.csspw.cn
发 行 部	010-84083685
门 市 部	010-84029450
经　　销	新华书店及其他书店
印刷装订	北京君升印刷有限公司
版　　次	2019 年 7 月第 1 版
印　　次	2019 年 7 月第 1 次印刷
开　　本	710×1000　1/16
印　　张	23
插　　页	2
字　　数	381 千字
定　　价	128.00 元

凡购买中国社会科学出版社图书，如有质量问题请与本社营销中心联系调换
电话：010-84083683
版权所有　侵权必究

目 录

推动文明交流互鉴　实现亚洲合作共赢
　　——外交部部长助理孔铉佑在东亚文明交流国际研讨会
　　　开幕式上的讲话 ………………………………………………（1）
在东亚文明交流国际研讨会开幕式上的致辞
　　——北京师范大学党委书记、校务委员会主席　刘川生 ………（5）
在东亚文明交流国际研讨会闭幕式上的总结发言
　　——北京师范大学人文宗教高等研究院常务副院长
　　　朱小健教授 ……………………………………………………（7）
在东亚文明交流国际研讨会A组研讨对话会上的发言
　　——第九、十届全国人大常委会副委员长、人文宗教高等研究院
　　　院长　许嘉璐教授 ……………………………………………（10）
许嘉璐院长在东亚文明交流国际研讨会闭幕式上的致辞 …………（14）
民族文化的扩散和内省 ……………………………………许嘉璐（18）

An Account of The Development of Philippine Labor Unionism
　　（Pre-War Period） ……………… Emmanuel Jeric A. Albela（23）
Historical Aspects to Sino-Sri Lankan Contacts through the
　　Indian Ocean ………………………… Ramla Wahab-Salman（32）
Assimilation of Indian Culture in East Asia ……………… Sandhya Jain（37）
21st Century Challenges and Opportunities for Modernity
　　in East Asia ……………… Senuri Samalka Samarasinghe（72）
朝鲜儒者李栗谷的《老子》解 ……………………………蔡振丰（87）
先秦诸子对战争与和平的看法 ……………………………陈鼓应（104）
东亚的表达 …………………………………………………韩东育（112）

东亚近世思想交流中概念的类型及其移动 …………… 黄俊杰（121）

East-Asian Civilization Exchange: The relationship between
　　Chinese civilization and Khmer civilization ………… Khlot Thyda（134）

阳明学的东亚传播实态考：以朝鲜朝中期为例 …………… 李学堂（153）

中国典故在越南喃籍中的接受与改变 ………………… 吕明恒（176）

Indian Civilizational Literature in East Asia and the India-China
　　Cultural Synergy: The Forgotten Perspectives in the Works
　　of Probhat Kumar Mukherji and the Untold Facts in the
　　Course of India-China Cross-Cultural Communications
　　………………………………………… Prof. Priyadarsi Mukherji（188）

你翻译什么？
　　——《诗经》《宋词选》翻译工作的反思（散记）
　　…………………………………………………… 松冈荣志（213）

"一带一路"推动形成文明秩序
　　——在"东亚文明交流国际研讨会"的演讲 ………… 王义桅（218）

汉字与东亚近代的启蒙思潮
　　——梁启超与潘佩珠的《越南亡国史》 ……………… 王志松（223）

高等教育与东亚文明的未来 ………………… 吴清辉　伍鸿宇（240）

Tarok hnit Japan: The Personal Collections of Professor Ashin U
　　Ottama about China and Japan ……………… Zaw Lynn Aung（253）

人权儒学与文明的对话 ……………………………………… 辛正根（272）

预言还是教学？——胡适的儒教解释学 ………………… 绪形康（291）

近二十年来台湾的"东亚儒学"研究取向与发展特色 …… 张崑将（306）

Will China Sinicize and Confucianize the World? Case Study:
　　Malaysia ……………………………………… Peter T. C. Chang（333）

中国的国学（孟子学）能热到马来西亚来吗 …………… 郑文泉（346）

东亚文明中朱子文化的传承与实践 ………………………… 朱茂男（360）

推动文明交流互鉴　实现亚洲合作共赢

——外交部部长助理孔铉佑在东亚文明交流
国际研讨会开幕式上的讲话

尊敬的许嘉璐主席，
尊敬的刘川生书记，
女士们，先生们，朋友们，

大家上午好！

很高兴出席东亚文明交流国际研讨会。首先，我谨代表中国外交部对研讨会的举行表示热烈祝贺，对尼山世界文明论坛组委会、北京师范大学人文宗教高等研究院为举办本次研讨会所做的周到安排表示诚挚感谢。

文明是人类智慧的结晶，社会进步的产物，每一个民族的发展，每一个国家的进步，每一个人的成长都离不开文明的滋养。中国国家主席习近平在2014年亚信峰会以及2015年博鳌亚洲论坛上提出召开"亚洲文明对话大会"的重大倡议，反映出中国领导人对亚洲文明交流的高度重视，对人类美好未来的不懈探索。今天，亚洲各国学者齐聚北京，举行东亚文明交流国际研讨会，可谓恰逢其时。

当今世界，随着经济技术的发展，千里之遥变成咫尺之邻，人类的文明交流从未像今天这样便利。但世界并不太平，冲突与纷争并未停止，傲慢与偏见依然存在，文明冲突论、西方中心论以及针对特定国家、文明的威胁论层出不穷。民粹主义在一些地方大行其道，反全球化、反移民、反自由贸易的声音抬头，极端主义思潮活跃。中东冲突不断，欧洲难民危机发酵，恐怖袭击事件频发。与之相比，亚洲局势总体稳定，经济持续增长，是世界公认的发展高地。面对动荡纷扰的世界，亚洲应该如何应对？我们能否对症下药，提出化解对立、弥合冲突的"亚洲方案"，为世界和平与人类进步贡献"亚洲智慧"？我想这是要深入讨论、值得大家认真思考的重大课题。

朋友们，亚洲是人类文明的重要发祥地，东亚中华文明、南亚印度文明、西亚两河文明等世界三大古文明都发源于此。璀璨夺目的文明之花在亚洲大陆上竞相绽放，不仅在绵延不息的岁月长河中留下无数感人至深、千古传诵的历史佳话，也照亮了亚洲人民筚路蓝缕求发展、栉风沐雨谋幸福的漫漫征程。抚追今昔，我们应当为亚洲文明备感自豪。

亚洲文明形态丰富，多元共生。多样性是亚洲文明的基本特质。亚洲各国人民走过了不同的发展道路，有着不同的文化背景、社会制度和价值观念，形成符合自身特点的文明样式。习近平主席指出，一切文明成果都值得尊重，一切文明成果都要珍惜。不同文明只有姹紫嫣红之别，没有高低优劣之分，不能简单用一把尺子来评定。大自然的精彩源于生物的多样性，人类的生机源于文明的多样性。不同文明相互尊重、平等相待，才能创造出多元共生的活力亚洲。

亚洲文明开放包容，互学互鉴。文明因包容而多彩，因互鉴而丰富。早在数千年前，亚洲各国就在思想、艺术、宗教、科技等领域开展交流。佛教、制糖术、阿拉伯数字、各种农作物等从印度、西域、东南亚传入中国，中国的四大发明、丝绸、瓷器等也传至亚洲各地甚至欧洲。亚洲文明的开放性、包容性，不同文明的互学互鉴、深度融合，是亚洲各国共同提高、共同进步的不竭动力。

亚洲文明博大精深，以和为贵。亚洲文明汇聚了各国的历史精神和人文传承，积淀了各民族最深层的精神追求和行为准则。中国儒家提倡"天人合一"，强调"致中和，则天地位焉，万物育焉"，将"和"视作天地万物相生相长的源泉，人与自然、与社会相交往的最高准则。道教、佛教、伊斯兰教、基督教、印度教等宗教以及亚洲各国的本土文化中，都有不同形式对和平、和谐的追求。正如时间酿造美酒一样，伟大深邃的智慧在漫漫历史长河中慢慢沉淀，最终形成了"以和为贵"的文明精华。

朋友们，亚洲有辉煌的过去，但我们的文明不仅仅是在博物馆里供人们欣赏瞻仰的。亚洲更有发展的机遇、灿烂的未来，亚洲文明是照亮人类发展进步的耀眼灯塔。我们对亚洲文明的自信，源于对亚洲发展合作的自信。

第一，亚洲是世界经济发展的潮头。据经济史学家麦迪逊测算，近代以前，亚洲的国民生产总值长期占据人类的三分之二。近代亚洲的落伍只是历史的一个插曲,今天的亚洲正在迎头赶上、发展复兴,恢复她在人类文明中应有的高度。2008年国际金融危机以来,亚洲成为拉动世界经济复苏和增长的引擎,对世界经济增长的贡献率超过50%。2015年亚洲发展中国家经济增速达6.5%,对世界经济增长的贡献率为44%。今天,占世界人口总数三分之二的亚洲人,生产着世界上五分之四的产品。亚洲的发展离不开外部资金科技,但相较于外因,内因是决定性的,亚洲文明造就了人民的勤劳、智慧与无限创造性,内部潜力的释放将托起新的"亚洲世纪"。亚洲国家应当凝聚文明的自信、发展的自觉,推动世界经济复苏,引领全球化潮流,力争上游,后来居上。

第二,亚洲是地区合作共赢的典范。亚洲的区域性合作源远流长。在西方开启大航海时代之前,东亚就已经形成发达的"海上文明交流圈",中国、日本、朝鲜半岛、东南亚以及印度、阿拉伯的商人建立了密集的贸易网络。今天,亚洲各国交流与区域合作再次进入黄金时代。2015年中国与东盟十国互访人数超过2300万人次,中日韩等东北亚三国人员往来近2400万人次。亚洲区内贸易额从8000亿美元增长到3万亿美元,贸易依存度超过50%。地区国家已签署实施自贸协定近150个,其中40%为区域内自贸协定。东盟共同体宣告成立,澜沧江—湄公河合作机制正式启动。明年是东盟成立50周年,东盟与中日韩建立合作机制20周年,东亚区域合作面临新的机遇,各方应携手共进,实现2020年建成"东亚经济共同体"的目标。

第三,亚洲是"一带一路"建设的重心。数千年来,中国与亚洲各国克服高山大海的阻隔,开辟出连接彼此、横跨欧亚的陆上、海上丝绸之路。丝绸之路上驼铃声声、帆影重重,带动了亚洲文明前进的步伐。2013年,习近平主席着眼于世界发展大势和亚洲各国需求,本着共商、共建、共享原则,提出"一带一路"重大倡议,得到了沿线国家和人民的广泛支持。"一带一路"建设实施3年多来,取得丰硕成果。一批道路交通、港口、电站等基础设施建设项目启动。中国与东盟发表产能合作联合声明,加快建设港口城、临港工业园区、跨境合作区,为地区国家工业化、现代化提供强大助力,也为提高本地区国家与人民民生福祉,增进人民间的互鉴交流注入新的动力。"一带一路"正在续写历史、再造辉煌。亚洲各国应当通过文明对话促进民心相通,加强战略互信与发展对接,共同谱写亚洲文明的新篇章。

朋友们，

亚洲文明复兴的历史大幕正在拉开，这是一个精彩纷呈的舞台，充满希望的田野。中国作为亚洲文明古国，在五千年不间断的历史传承中，形成了讲仁爱，崇正义，尚和合，求大同的价值追求，秉持兼善天下的情怀。今天，中国正致力于实现中华民族复兴的中国梦，愿与各国人民携手实现合作共赢的亚洲梦、世界梦。"一花独放不是春，百花齐放春满园。"我们愿意与亚洲各国加深文明对话，促进相互理解，增进友好感情，实现共同发展，为亚洲文明的和谐进步不断注入"正能量"。期待各位专家学者通过此次研讨会相互学习借鉴各自文明的优长之处，围绕如何更好推动亚洲文明和谐共生、各国合作共赢畅所欲言，各抒己见，探讨交流，在历史与未来、文明与发展的对话中激荡思想、启迪智慧。预祝此次研讨会取得成功。

谢谢大家！

在东亚文明交流国际研讨会开幕式上的致辞

——北京师范大学党委书记、校务委员会主席　刘川生

尊敬的许嘉璐先生、孔铉佑部长助理，
女士们、先生们，朋友们：

　　大家上午好！今天，我们相聚在北京师范大学，隆重举行东亚文明交流国际研讨会，与来自东亚各国的专家学者共同研讨"**东亚文明的历史与展望**"这一主题。首先，我代表北京师范大学，对研讨会的召开表示诚挚的祝贺！对来自海内外的各位专家学者和嘉宾表示热烈的欢迎！

　　东亚是人类文明的重要发祥地之一，东亚各国有着源远流长的历史联系，孕育了丰富多彩的东亚文明。 在长期的历史进程中，东亚各国积极开展文化交流互动，共同走向发展与繁荣。东亚文明成为联系各国思想文化、推动各国共同发展的重要纽带，奠定了今天东亚经济重新崛起与文化复兴发展的精神基础。**去年的博鳌亚洲论坛和今年的亚信外长会议上，中国国家主席习近平提出要"构建亚洲命运共同体"，并倡议召开亚洲文明对话大会。** 就是希望推动不同国家、不同民族、不同文明间的交流对话，推动东亚各国各地区增进理解、相向而行、和衷共济，共同铸就和睦相处、合作共赢的东亚发展之路。

　　中国是东亚大国，拥有五千年悠久历史和辉煌灿烂的文明， 中国的儒家文化、汉字典籍、思想宗教等曾对东亚各国产生重要的影响，东亚各国的文化传统也对中华文明的发展起到积极的促进作用。今天，**我们在这里举行东亚文明交流国际研讨会，就是要**秉承和而不同、兼容并蓄的文化理念，尊重和理解东亚地区民族、宗教、文化的多样性和差异性，**大力弘扬**东亚各国文明的历史传统与文化精神，**大力发掘**东亚各国文明的理论内涵与思想精髓，**深入研究**东亚各国文明的互补交融与内在联系，**深入探讨**东亚各国文明的时代价值与现实意义，**以此促进东亚优秀文化的传承与发

展，推动不同文化间的相互理解、包容互鉴，使文化的多样性成为扩大交流合作的动力，使文明的交流互鉴成为增进彼此友谊的桥梁，为加强东亚文明对话、构建亚洲命运共同体提供有益的思想资源和文化支撑。

大学是传承文明、创新文化的重要殿堂，也是推动国际文化交流的重要力量。北京师范大学是中国最早成立的国立大学，拥有百余年丰富的历史积淀。我校的教育学、心理学、中国史、地理学、生态学五个一级学科排名中国第一，诺贝尔文学奖的首位中国获奖者莫言是我校校友。**我校高度重视国际化发展，**从20世纪60年代起就开始招收留学生，韩国、日本、蒙古等东亚国家是我校重要的留学生生源国。目前，学校已经与30多个国家和地区的近300所大学、研究机构签署了合作协议，在校留学生人数超过4000人，具有海外学习经历的学生有2000余人。我校还牵头举办了金砖国家大学校长论坛，金砖国家大学联盟的秘书处就设在北师大。**近年来，**我校开设了东亚文化与教育、东亚文学比较研究、东亚区域研究等一系列课程，建立了"一带一路"研究院、G20反腐败追逃追赃研究中心等一批国际化研究平台，成立了汉语文化学院、中国文化国际传播研究院等一批文化研究与传播机构，有力促进了与东亚地区相关的教育合作、学术研究和国际文化交流。

我校人文宗教高等研究院自 2012 年成立以来，积极整合各方优势资源，致力于打造高端的学术研究与文化交流平台。**研究院院长许嘉璐先生是我校的杰出校友，**是海内外著名的文化学者、教育家，为中华优秀传统文化的传承创新和国际文化交流倾注了大量心血。在许先生的带领下，研究院已经成功举办了北京尼山世界文明论坛、儒释道融合之因缘研讨会等一系列高端学术论坛，在学界和社会上产生了广泛影响，为推动不同文明和信仰间的对话与交流做出了积极贡献。

本次东亚文明交流国际研讨会，在中国外交部的指导支持下，邀请了来自中国、日本、印度、韩国、斯里兰卡、缅甸、柬埔寨、巴基斯坦、马来西亚、菲律宾、蒙古等东亚国家的专家学者齐聚一堂。相信大家一定会从东亚各国的历史文化中发现其现代价值，推动各国传统文化的创造性转化和创新性发展，为东亚文明的繁荣发展和交流互鉴贡献智慧和力量！

祝愿本次研讨会圆满成功！

谢谢大家！

在东亚文明交流国际研讨会闭幕式上的总结发言

——北京师范大学人文宗教高等研究院常务副院长 朱小健教授

尊敬的许嘉璐先生，
各位专家，各位来宾，各位朋友：

我们"东亚文明交流国际研讨会"经过一天半的大会和分组研讨，已经完成了学术讨论，受会议委托，我对会议略作小结。

我们在昨天的开幕式上提出过四个问题：东亚各国文明的交流走过了怎样的历程？东亚各国文明在当下具有怎样的现代性？包括中华文化、儒学在内的东亚各国文化将会走向哪里？东亚文明可以为构筑亚洲命运共同体，为人类的和平与发展做出什么贡献？经过讨论，从刚才两位小组总结的报告可以看出，这些问题已经有了一些结论。

我们的会议有四个明显的特色。

一 会议规模不大而参与的国家地区广泛多元

参加本次研讨会的有来自日本、韩国、蒙古、印度、巴基斯坦、柬埔寨、菲律宾、马来西亚、越南、缅甸、斯里兰卡以及中国内地与香港和台湾等14个国家和地区的27位知名专家，虽然人数不算多，但既有高校和科研单位的学者，也有政府机构的高官和高参，还有成功的企业家，具有广泛的代表性。

东亚是世界上人口分布最稠密的地区之一，其独特的文化也因此对人类社会有着巨大影响。这么多的国家代表出席我们的会议，参与者的广泛多元带来了对话的层面、领域、范畴的多样，也使得我们的论坛站在了东亚文明交流研究的制高点，更加有利于研究的针对性和深刻化。

二　学术探究专门深入并皆与文化交流相关

我们的讨论既有宏观层面对东亚文明政治经济的思考，也有着眼微观对某个文化现象、某部文献流布、甚至是某种游戏传承的考订。专家们的行业专攻不尽相同，但无论讨论的问题如何具体，都在从不同角度探究东亚不同国家地区文化的演变是如何互鉴创新，生生不息。

各位专家具体讨论的问题各异，而在自己的报告中都把研究对象置于东亚文明的大背景下进行观察，分析这些文化现象由产生到发展曾经从其他文明其他文化中得到何种营养从而发生了变化。这样的研究视角和方法，本身就是文化交流的成果和体现。

三　深邃的理论思辨与文化交流的实践并重

深邃的理论思辨贯穿在我们研讨会的全程，无论是许嘉璐先生的主旨演讲还是各位专家的对话研讨，都对东亚文明的特点与本地区文化交流体现的规律和价值进行了深入的思考。这种思考又与我们如何解决当下面临的各种社会问题紧密关联。

不少专家在报告中介绍了自己个人或所在地区单位传承、传播文化，尤其是在对青年学生以及社会民众的人格养成、道德修行等方面进行的实践。这些实践大多跨越国界，在东亚地区以及更广的范围中实施，取得了喜人的成效。这也从一个方面印证了文化、文明的对话交流在当下比以往更为重要。同时，也可以看出，我们的专家都身处文化文明传承、传播工作的第一线，正因为大家共同关注东亚文明的交流发展，我们才聚集于此，共话交流。

四　历史反思与对未来之路的设想相辅互证

我们会议的主题是"东亚文明的历史与展望"，回顾历史当然是为了借鉴经验，而我们研讨面向的是东亚各国不同的文明、文化，这就使得我们的借鉴既有时间纵向的回望，又有不同国度民族的横向对照，从而成为立体的互鉴。

由于上面第三点体现的实践特征，我们对未来的展望又是立足在坚实的实证基础之上。在专家们的报告中，我们看到了东亚国家之间既有共同的普遍价值伦理，也有各自独具的异彩，更有你中有我、我中有你的互促共荣。我们认识到，任何文化都不是绝对封闭独成的文化。既往的东亚文明正是经由本地区以及与世界其他地区文明的交流融合而形成特色，今后的东亚文明也必将由内部和外部的交流而发展并哺益全球。

许嘉璐先生昨天提到文明文化的交流有政府、民间、学者三大板块，并寄望于学者们的先觉导引。我们的研讨已经理性地认识到不同民族文化彼此之间互学、相融是各方共赢的需求。各民族、各文化的差异是弥足珍贵的，东亚的过去因为各国、各民族交流而精彩，而在当下和将来，正像许嘉璐先生指出的："在互学、相融问题上，东亚诸国有着其他各大洲诸多地区所没有的、甚或为其所排斥的条件；因而我们在21世纪，乃至更远的未来，在重建人类丧失殆尽的道德体系过程中，负有比其他地区更重的责任。"我们愿意负起这个责任，为己而学，为人而行。我们期待着亚洲文明的和谐共生，亚洲各国的合作共赢。

我们的研讨会得到了外交部、北京师范大学的指导支持，北京师范大学的志愿者付出了辛勤的努力。谢谢他们。

我们是第一次举办这样的研讨会，我们还会继续推动这样的研讨，期待能与大家再聚。祝各位在京愉快，旅途平安。谢谢各位！

在东亚文明交流国际研讨会 A 组研讨对话会上的发言

——第九、十届全国人大常委会副委员长、人文宗教高等研究院院长　许嘉璐教授

谢谢各位专家，各位朋友：

我之所以到这一组来听，是因为觉得在这组的议题里有着对历史遗产的丰富的思考，对现实生活，对亚洲未来，都有举足轻重的意义。刚才听了各位专家的发言，很受启发。我访问过很多国家，但是几次与斯里兰卡失之交臂。① 我感到各位对自己民族的文化，以及和别的文化的交流，无论在文献研究上，还是对现实生活，都有非常丰富的知识和深入的思考。感谢大家给了我这么多的营养。

听了前面各位专家的发言，我想谈谈自己的感触，大致有以下几点：

第一，在亚洲（不限于东亚），不同文化之间的交流给亚洲人民、亚洲繁荣，以及亚洲的未来，做出了很大贡献。但是，现在对各个民族及其交流的史料挖掘得还不够，今后需要加强，东亚学应该成为国际性学术，而不只是本民族的人或东亚人才去研究自己的历史。因为我们的祖先有很多智慧——我所说的"智慧"不是"知识"，他们没有火箭、卫星等——而是处理主客体关系的方法。古今亚洲人的智慧都值得开掘、研究，在研究中要相互合作。

第二，在"东亚文明的历史与展望"这一主题下，我们这个小组重点研究东亚，并进而扩展到亚洲的现代化问题。我们是不是还应该考虑，结合本民族的实际和 21 世纪的时空，来思考"现代化"，以及由"现代化"衍生的"现代性""现代主义"等问题，这样，我们的讨论会更加深

---

① 此组有来自斯里兰卡的专家。

入，对社会实践的指导意义也会更大。

我在今天上午的主旨讲演里用了"殖民时代"这个词。在我看来，直到现在，"殖民时代"并没有过去，只不过换了形式。殖民者不见得必须通过国家武装的形式，也可由凌驾于国家和国际条约之上的跨国垄断寡头，以国际化贸易、支持不发达国家（基本上是前殖民地）的形式开展。不同于以往殖民者经常以枪炮开路，把本国人移民到殖民地的做法，现在则是通过输出科技、产品、资金和管理经验，攫取资源和超额利润，同时造成目的国的环境破坏、社会不平等。与此同时，生产方式、贸易方式的演变，交通设施的空前便捷，信息传输技术的急速发展，在给人类带来空前方便的同时，也为寡头们提供了对他国进行新型殖民更加隐蔽、更加有效、降低自身损耗的途径。亨廷顿认为，人类文化分为西方文化和非西方文化。他的结论是：文化应该是多元的，而西方文化将是引路人。如果仔细想想就会发现，他对"西方文化"的界定是狭隘的，局限于希腊·罗马—盎格鲁撒克逊—希伯来文化，甚至只指美国文化。这一文化随着殖民运动、工业化、经济全球化，已经遍布世界所有有人的地方。现在就要发展到没人的地方了。没有人哪里来的文化？比如开发、占领南极、北极，我认为就是掌握了现代科技者的入侵。这是"现代性"的组成部分之一。

非洲、南美，以及亚洲，原来不是现在的样子。我们祖先的智慧不同于西方。像郑和下西洋完全是例外。一位英国教授写了一本书，假设哥伦布早生七八十年，他的船队可能在太平洋、大西洋遇到郑和，那么人类历史就可能会改写。我不赞成这一观点。一者，他用的是二元对立的思考方法：对异于己者必兵戎相对；二者，历史不能假设。历史是对已然的叙事，当然其中存在很多迄今仍无法验证的假设。而我们能做的、需要做的，是对"现代社会"这一"实在"进行深入的思考。

第三、跨国公司的权力已经超越了国家：不仅超越了本国的法律法规、技术标准，也超越了目的国的法律法规和技术标准，成为凌驾于所有国家之上的更庞大的帝国。正是因为看到这一点，自 20 世纪 60 年代开始，欧洲国家就开始酝酿成立欧盟。其后的东盟也是如此。但是，欧盟和东盟走了两条不同的路。东盟的所有成员国都保持着自己的主权，只在合作上协商，不见得大家对每件事情都意见一致，但都会坐下来谈。欧盟则不同，它把成员国的很多权力集中到布鲁塞尔的大厦里。英国要脱欧，这是原因之一。基于对欧洲史的研究，我推测第二个脱欧的很可能是意大利，2017年就可能发生。

我为什么做出以上推断？因为在当代，"现代""后现代""民族国家"仍然具有重要意义。人们好不容易从殖民地挣脱出来成为独立的国家，还没有把国家建设好，内部还有很多矛盾，跨国公司一来，应有的权力就被拿走了，一切都要听其指挥，生态被破坏了，不平等加剧……这样下去，人们是不能接受的，是要起来捍卫自己的权利的。我们不妨从这个角度看待东盟现象和亚洲国家之间的关系。

第四、我觉得现在思想界还应该注意一个很重要的问题，就是"民族文化中心论"。各个文明是平等的，每一种文化都是适应它生长的那片土壤的，不能评优劣，评优劣就需要以某种文化为标准，于是"中心"就要出现。有"中心"，就有歧视。这种现象在世界多处存在，包括中国一些人也有这种要不得的想法；而在美国尤为突出的个人主义极端化以及自我中心论又当别论。民族是复数，是若干人组成的，其主张是集体意志，不是"自我"说了算。

另外，我们在研究中还要考虑是不是应该去掉二元对立论。非白即黑、非此即彼，在市场和职场上就表现为零和游戏，犹如拳击，一定要KO到对手才能得到金腰带。这是原始人的遗留，不应该变成现代生活的一部分，更不应该变成赌博的内容。还有搏击，虽然是在做戏，但是刺激人的感官，激发人的残酷。这些都是二元对立在游戏当中的体现。在现实生活中，哪有非白即黑的事情？全人类自有地理学之后，就命名地球的南端为南极，北端为北极。"极"就是顶头。这是二元对立的副产物。地球上最大面积的地方是北极、南极呢，还是寒带、亚寒带、亚温带、温带、亚热带、热带呢？是后者。中间地带或灰色地带永远是多数。开个玩笑说吧，特朗普当选就是赢得了灰色地带的选票。

因此，在处理国际关系时，特别是知识精英进行文化交流的时候，一定要记住：世界上的万事万物都不是二元对立的，二元之间有着广阔的地带，在这个广阔地带中唯有合作、协商、妥协，才能携起手来一起前进。有不同意见，继续讨论、讨论、再讨论，总会找到于各方有利的出路。"一致"是暂时的、相对的，只要目标一致，取人之长，去己之短，人类就能够长久地和平共存、永续发展。

以上，是我对本组讨论的建议和补充。

刚才李学堂先生谈到退溪先生对阳明学的痛斥，我不是十分赞成。我很尊重退溪先生,他是朝鲜的"朱子"。他的二元对立并非来自西方。其实,在王阳明书上说得很清楚,大概意思是说,我之不同意朱熹是有根据的,我跟朱熹意见一样,那也不是假装的。其实二人最主要之异不过就是格物致知问题,是尊德性还是道问学的问题。这些都不是根本的分歧,根本在于心。

我想,我们的研讨会是拒绝二元对立的,希望大家都觉得今年开得圆满,作为主办人,希望大家明年再来。

许嘉璐院长在东亚文明交流国际研讨会闭幕式上的致辞

我戴着这个软钢的腰围本来是想站着讲，这样才能表达对远道而来的学者们为亚洲文化建设和复兴所做巨大贡献的敬意，但是工作人员非常关心我，为我摆放了桌椅，那我就恭敬不如从命。

刚才，由两位教授分别报告了 A 组和 B 组讨论的情况。朱小健教授在这个基础上避开了讨论的具体情况而归纳出我们这次论坛的四个特点。这些对我都有很好的启发。

我不仅要就着文化的本体谈谈体会，也要谈谈我自己。

首先袒露我的求知之路。社会学、哲学、人类学、考古学，这些学科都不是我的专长，我出身于在中国也是很冷僻的学问——训诂学。它是中国传统语言学的终结或者归宿，文字学、声韵学都是为它服务的，因此也必须在这些方面下大力气。现在我不仅仅在实践，成立了人文宗教高等研究院、中国文化院，过些天我还要到吴清辉教授担任校长的联合国际学院参加由中华炎黄文化研究会主办的论坛，因为我是该会的会长。我怎么做起了文化领域的事情呢？道理很简单，就是因为我看到中国社会和世界社会早已违背了轴心时代伟人们给我们所立的道德和价值标准。作为一个"公共知识分子"我应该为重建人类道德尽我之力。

我曾设想，如果轴心时代有现代交通和通讯的工具，那时的伟人们之间一定不会因理念不同而大打出手，他们会认真地倾听、交流。因为无论是在柏拉图那里，摩西、亚伯拉罕、婆罗门那里，还是在孔子那里，讲的都是包容、友爱和慈善。须知，现在人们所说的"真善美"，本是西方文化，出自《圣经·旧约》。但是，真善美不但对人类好，而且和中华文化所追求的相近，于是我们就吸收了，以至现在很多人已经不知道它来自西方文化了。与此相对，塞缪尔·亨廷顿的"文明冲突"论就不为大多数人所接受。可见，轴心时代的伟人们为后世所做的贡献、他们所立的标准带有普适性，而且影响久远，至今未绝。

人类正在朝着自己挖掘出的深渊走去。中国内地是我生长的地方，像每位专家一样，我不但爱着自己的祖国，还爱着自己生长的地方。但是，现在我们所耳闻目睹的许多社会情况却可以用与从朱子、陆九渊到陈献章、王阳明思想极为矛盾的一句话来概括："满嘴仁义道德、一肚子男盗女娼。"当然不能说人人如此，但是也不得不承认这样的人虽少，却搅乱了人心，毁了一锅汤。在中国内地，曾经有一段时间，在一些人眼里是笑贫不笑娼啊！这是什么问题？这是民族的沦落。难道只有中国如此吗？我去过82个国家，透过繁华的或贫穷的表面，看到了其背后的价值混乱、道德沦丧，看到这是世界性的社会现象。于是我想，这是怎么造成的？

我在拜读了哈贝马斯、德理达等法兰克福学派或者后现代主义的著作，才醒悟到为什么出现了"后现代"。原来所谓"现代"还有昨天我提到的"现代性""现代主义"，就在三百年之内，与科学进步、工业化同步，置利益、欲望于苍天之上，并且凭着高效杀人武器，推广到全世界神、佛、大梵，甚至天皇，地位下降了，一降再降。

现在很多国家看起来是独立自主的，还是联合国的成员国，但实际上这些国家政府的权力，人民委托的权力，已经并将继续迅速丧失，有的丧失得很厉害。为什么？世界"500强"，跨国公司，巧妙地绕过联合国和各国法律，享有种种特权，不但在肆无忌惮地鼓动人的物欲，同时又严重毁坏自然。可不可以说，现在的经济是时尚经济、模特经济、诱惑经济、虚荣经济。种种欲望造成远远超过需求的消费，资源能不枯竭吗？违背道德的事能不毁掉人类吗？

于是，我从训诂学向前跨出了五百里。但是一进入文化领域，吓了一跳！原来，如果没有哲学、社会学、人类学、民族志等方面的基本知识，就寸步难行，于是我又埋头于这些领域，一方面苦读，同时勾连起从年轻到垂老的积累，又向前走了五百里。这样，我就从北京走到了首尔、东京、华盛顿、巴黎、南非……也稍稍接近了柏拉图、耶稣、释迦牟尼……暂时疏远了原来比较熟悉的专业，我并不后悔。我感到高兴的是，通过自己的一点点努力，沟通了很多国家的很多学者，大家在一起超越时空和信仰来谈自己民族的文化和人类的前途问题。我所遇到的各国朋友都是勇敢的担当者，为了改变世界，都在行动着。而本次研讨会又给了我新的启示和鼓舞。

刚才李学堂老师说日本学者治学严谨，是的。这是中华文化传到日本，带上日本的特色又返还到中国，而在近代中国"严谨"却淡化了。我们应该向日本同行学习。例如，任何一个概念都是一部叙事，有它的产生、演变的历史，它就是一个本体所有特征的凝聚。可是，我们用概念的时候常常很随意，特别是中国内地的学者。因此，虽然我们书店里学术和文化著作琳琅满目，但是绝大部分却走不出国门。什么原因？就像刚才朱小健教授提到的我昨天所说的文化三大板块，中层是知识精英板块。各国的知识精英无法接受粗糙、疏漏的学术著作，翻译家也不愿意翻译。这样的学风使我不能不怀疑治学的目的是什么？

发过了一通"牢骚"后，下面我就要谈一下我们的论坛了。

朱小健教授说，他希望这样的论坛能够让我们再相聚。这可以叫"举棋不定"。我首先希望能够举办第二次论坛，在本次论坛四个特性的基础上，再多介绍一些本地区或者本国政府、学校，如何把民族文化传统撒播到老百姓心里的故事。这是我的一个期待。

其次，把我们这次论坛的会风延续下去。这种会风就是不分地域，不分国籍，真诚交流，为的是我们这个地区、自己生活的地方安宁、幸福。例如我每次去日本和韩国，如果心里总认为他们讲的是"韩国的儒学""日本的儒学"，而不是儒学"正宗"，我就错了。任何事物一进入社会生活就要产生变异，就像进步孕育着后退一样，"变异"意味着保护"正宗"。因此，只要其基础一样、核心不变，那么它就是它。你不能拿着自己中学时的照片说这不是我，或者只说这是哪一年的我，而只能说这是我中学时候的照片，抽象一点说，这就是"理一分殊"的道理。这需要从我们自己做起。比如最好不说"印度的佛教""中国的佛教"，而说"释迦时代的佛教""原始佛教""中国化的佛教"。佛教因传承文本不一样，教义也有所异。在我看来，原始佛教是无神论，只是在释迦灭度以后五百年，弟子们聚起来整理他的教导的时候开始把他神化了，中国所接受和本土化的，主要是释迦身后的佛教。大乘佛教，禅宗的出现，实际上又在向着无神论走。

我们这次研讨会涉及很多种信仰，表面看去彼此差异很大，其实你和我和他之间只隔着一层纸一般的帷幕，如追溯到根——为什么人类创造了宗教信仰？人类是从哪里来的？将走到哪里去？宇宙的终极又是什么？——越深究彼此的思想就越近，总有一天人们会大悟：你我他都是一母之同胞。

总而言之，如果我们能再一次在东亚文明国际交流研讨会上相会，我希望讲演更严谨一些，心胸更扩大一些。既向下看，人口最密集的大洲亚洲的老百姓需要我们的成果；也向旁边看，互相学习，彼此交融，在理论的深度上、扩散的广度上比这次有所提高。

现在我宣布："东亚文明交流国际研讨会"圆满结束！谢谢大家的合作！

民族文化的扩散和内省

许嘉璐[*]

文化，是个极其复杂、宽泛的领域。我今天在这里所说的文化则专指民族文化。"民族"是一个并不简单的概念。例如，日本国民就并不全是大和民族，韩国亦如是；"中华民族"一词并不是一个民族或种族概念。孙中山先生在高举"中华民族"大旗时，同时号召汉、满、蒙、回（即伊斯兰信仰者）、藏"五族共和"（当时聚居于国家西南、西北等地的许多少数民族尚未得以识别、确认族名）。如果我们要脱离开"民族"这个词语，只有两个可供选择的说法：一是以国家论，如日本文化、韩国文化；二是按信仰分，如基督教文化、儒家文化等。我总觉得民族、国家、信仰之间有着纠缠不清的关系，所以在此特别声明，我只好混用这几个概念了。

一　任何民族文化都要与"他者"发生关联

任何民族文化，都不是孤立地存在于地球上，因而或早或晚都要与"他者"发生关联，双方或多方关联的路径无论是什么样的，在发生和发现过程中总要含有以下这些选择：接触、了解、理解、发现、自省、欣赏、学习、相融。

任何民族文化都有扩散与收敛这样相反相成的两个方面。"他者"扩散过来的文化，给予"自我"（即民族文化主体）以刺激，是民族文化发

---

[*] 许嘉璐，第九、十届全国人大常委会副委员长，北师大人文宗教高等研究院院长，教授。此文为开幕式上所作主旨演讲。

展演变的外动力。勇敢地接受他者的刺激，把它转化为促进自我前行、创造的动力，这就是现在人们常说的"革新主义"；反之，如果没有了或拒绝了这一外动力，任何文化都要停滞甚至萎缩、衰落，这就是今之所谓"保守主义"。所谓民族文化的"收敛"，我是指对于外来文化的自发而生的惧怕、蔑视、疏远或拒绝。扩散与收敛是文化"天性"所有。同一民族，在不同时期，对待同一外来文化可能出现不同的趋向，或者以其中一个趋向为主。

如果以上述规律观察中华文化与东亚其他民族文化的往来，则大体如是。

日本传入中国古代儒学，大约是在5世纪初（《古事记》），中国的《论语》贡奉于应神天皇，也是日本开始接触域外文化的开始。自8世纪起，中华经师陆续赴日，传授中国"经学"，或为"中国古典儒学传入日本遂成定局"；"自8世纪中期起中国儒学在日本以超越'经学'本体的形态，而以'史学'和'文学'作为'明经'的两翼传入日本，从而使儒学进入扩散阶段"（严绍璗：《日本中国学史稿》）。至于中国儒学传入朝鲜半岛的具体起始点，则尚无定论。多数中、韩学者认为在中国汉代已经传入。

儒学及其经典的传入，与我们今天所说的文化之扩散并不等同。因为文化是有层次的。文化经典所要传达的，是民族文化的核心或底层，是历经若干代人创造、丰富而成的民族之魂。从古至今，从东到西，社会中真正能够把握经典知识及其内涵的永远是很少数人。"百姓日用"、直接接触的，则是与己不同的风俗习惯、衣食住行。因此我认为，最初传入日本和朝鲜半岛的，只是儒学，是文化的底层，还并不是严格意义上的中华文化。从这一角度看，多年来人们（特别是中国人）常说的"汉字文化圈"或"中华文化圈"等概念应该是不存在的，甚至可以说是个伪命题：使用同一文字并不一定能被视为同一文化圈，何况在东亚只有日本还保留了少数汉字，其他国家都已改为拼音文字了。

二　从文化的扩散和收敛来观察东亚文化交流的情形

不同文化之间的交往，从来不是单向的。当一种民族文化传入另一民族时，双方各自成为对方的"他者"，受益的绝不只是接受方，传入者一方同样可以得到在自己民族生活圈里得不到的启发。例如，当朱子之学传到朝鲜国后，经朝鲜大儒（如李滉退溪、李珥栗谷）结合自己的国情和环境，创建了具有自己特色的性理学，其成就对中国学者也有所启发。又如日本幕府时代末期和明治维新初期的社会状况和思想动态与明代中叶相近，诸藩侯和武士们正在寻找一种思想理论作为反对幕府、以天皇为"一尊"的武器，充分发挥藩侯和武士作用，达到"尊王攘夷"的目标。王阳明的事迹及其学说传到日本，他的文武兼备之才、平乱赫赫之功，既继承又不盲从朱子学说，提出的人生价值和奋斗目标简要而透彻，并且亲身履践，这些都引得日本欲革旧图新的研究者蜂出；王阳明的知行合一、致良知、倡功夫，以及人人即凡而可圣的道德平等思想，显然对想在国事上有所作为的下层武士们是很大的启示和鼓舞（张崑将：《阳明学在东亚：诠释、交流与行动》）。

但是，王阳明去世后，其传人对王阳明某些语焉不详处或未有明确定论的言辞产生分歧，本不为怪，中外历史上几乎所有"宗师"级人物莫不是如此的身后；有意思的是，这一分歧以及其末裔深陷空疏、支离、玄虚之病，也传到了日本和韩国。进入20世纪，阳明学在日本显著地被重经济、科技、物质的风气所压倒，不能引领国家适应工业化趋势的心性之学自然遭到冷遇。即使如此，在日本学界一直有不少学者和官员在坚守阳明之学，辩护之，捍卫之，有时中日两国学者遥相呼应。日本对阳明学的不离不弃也影响了中国学界，直待又一个世纪到来，阳明学才在其故国呈现复兴之势。

我之所以简略地回顾阳明学在日、韩传播、研究的大致过程，是因为认为从中可以体味到，不管三国的情况如何不同，其间的文化交流始终符合民族文化扩散与收敛的规律。日、韩由中国引进朱子学与阳明学，是符合"礼有来学，不闻往教"（《礼记·曲礼》）的传统的。这里面包含着学者和教者的相互尊重以及对于学习者主动性的鼓励，日本多次派遣"遣唐使"，就是显例。附带说一句，在《奥义书》时代，婆罗门们也秉持这一原则。儒学传入朝鲜半岛的历史久远，但对于是通过什么途径传入的问题，至今还缺乏一致的结论，也许永远得不出让所有人满意的结论。从总体上看，是中华古老的文献典籍促成了高丽王朝制度和礼仪制度的形成，由此推测，朝鲜半岛和中华文化的交流，也应该是以"来学"为主。

自 16 世纪始，西方的炮舰负载着誓把基督福音传播到全世界的传教士来到东方，同时也带来西方的一些科学技术知识。这就是明显的"往教"了。这种"往教"一个显著的特点是，西方强势国家自以人类文化领袖、权威自居，利用现代化手段、以援助发展为外衣，把自己也并不再尊奉的价值伦理、风俗习惯"教给"众多国家、民族的人民；而在现代，又常常受到当地政府和人们的欢迎，因为它可能给当地带来"现代化"和繁荣；当然在"来教"或"支持"面孔的背后却有着可以攫取超额资源和利润的目的。

三 "往学"或"来教"所传输的内容必须符合对方的国情和历史

我把中国古代所提倡的"来学"和殖民时代的"往教"连在一起，逻辑上未必严谨，而我主要的意思并不在此。我要强调的是，无论是"往学"还是"来教"，所传输的内容必须符合对方的国情和历史。

许倬云先生认为，日本原本没有自己的"原创文化"，"没有经历过枢轴时代的突破而发展为文明"。（许倬云：《历史大脉络》。枢轴，大陆通常称之为轴心。）在我看来，许倬云先生所说的"文化"和"文明"是同义词，二者所指并非泛泛意义上的文化或文明，而是指有传世文献和代表人物，并形成了关注人生、社会和宇宙的比较系统的思想遗产。如果我们就此意义而言，那么儒学传入日本，正是其在轴心时代之后跻身于世界民族之林所急需的。

但是，日本的儒学毕竟是从"他者"土地上移植过来的，难以完全服其水土，所以大约于 9 世纪日本提出"和魂汉才"的指导思想。在此后的一千年中，两国交往时断时续，有益于日本的中华文化仍在被吸收着，但是也并不是完全照搬，这对于中华文化来说，也是一个自省的机会。众所周知，以儒家为代表的中华文化，重内敛，重反诸己，而每次的反思自身几乎都有外界的刺激，包括"他者"的启示和挑战。这也是中华文化朝着多样化不断发展的一个源头，一种形式。即如日本参考汉字创制了假名，对保留下来的汉字做了一些简化，这无意中启发了中国人曾经做过的汉字拼音化的探索，在海峡两岸几乎同时进行简化汉字的工作时，也参考了假名（台湾则因政治原因而两度中辍）。又如前面所谈到的朱子之学和阳明心学，传入日、韩之后，两国历代的学者都做了精深的研究，其中有些足以补充中华之不足。韩国学者对王阳明后学的批评，日本学者在明治维新时期对刘宗周（蕺山）的重视（牟宗三：《从陆象山到刘蕺山》），都给了中国学界重要启发，其影响所及，直至辛亥革命前后。例如，孙中山先生在其题为"社会主义之派别及方法"的讲演中就说："强权虽合于天演之进化，而公理实难泯于天赋之良知。故天演淘汰为野蛮物质之进化，公理良知实道德文明之进化也。"此乃孙先生以心学破社会达尔文主义之论也，在全球亦应属于先发其声者。孙先生在距其辞世不到一年时（1924年6月）有"训词"云："要做革命事业，是从什么地方做起呢？就是要从自己的方寸之地做起。要把自己从前不好的思想、习惯和性质，像兽性、罪恶性，和一切不仁不义的性质，一概革除。"（《孙中山全集》）孙中山先生此语，实际上突出了刘宗周所强调的"慎独"功夫，因为"自性"唯自己最为了然（"良知"），既往之事须经反省，都是在无人处得之（"慎独"）。这两个例子是否足可证明日本阳明学对近代中国之反哺？这种情形，也是任何民族之间进行文化交流所必有的。

　　总而言之，东亚的文化是多彩的，东亚几个国家和众多民族的内部，文化也是多彩的。文化之同或异，都是普遍存在，常常也是相对的。不同民族文化之间的交流，在蒙昧时代已经发生，人类在历史长河中反反复复品尝了隔绝、对抗和对话的不同味道。现在，人类已经深陷无尽的风险之中，在人文思想领域所急需的，是要去除"文化中心主义"，理性地认识到彼此之间虽然可能时有摩擦，但互学、相融应该永远处于主流地位。（附带说一句：我之不敢苟同"汉字文化圈"之类的说法，也是因为其中带有一定程度的中华文化中心主义色彩。）在互学、相融问题上，东亚诸国有着其他各大洲诸多地区所没有的、甚或为其所排斥的条件；因而我们在21世纪，乃至更远的未来，在重建人类丧失殆尽的道德体系过程中，负有比其他地区更重的责任。

An Account of The Development of Philippine Labor Unionism (Pre-War Period)

Emmanuel Jeric A. Albela[*]

Abstract

The study provides an account of the roots and development of Labor Unionism in the Philippines before the emergence of Second World War in the country, showing the efforts done by our leaders to improve the condition of the workers, farmers, etc. in our country, as well as the personalities that made drastic changes in our government and society, paying attention to the rights and privileges of the workers.

This purports that the labor movement at that time is composed of organizations such as trade unions, farmers' associations, cooperatives, and other sectoral and people's organizations, with their traditional leaders composed of communists, socialists, nationalists, etc. The history of Philippine trade union movement reveals three (3) major features – communist infiltration and influence, government intervention and management domination.

This paper shows how labor movements followed the tenets of communism and socialism after the *Union Obrera Democratica*'s (UOD) demise, as the result of spreading the ideas of Marx and Lenin in Russia. With the efforts of Crisanto Evangelista and Pedro Abad Santos, labor unions were bent to ideologies that are most concerned to the society and the majority of the people. With this proliferation, President Quezon at the start of the Commonwealth, dealt

---

[*] Emmanuel Jeric A. Albela, Instructor of Department of History, Faculty of Arts and Letters, University of Santo Tomas.

with these groups just to win their support to the government. Laws were then passed in favor of the labor sector, for the security of their rights.

Introduction

The Philippine labor movement before the emergence of the Second World War is a social movement of workers and farmers led by middle class *illustrados* and socialist intellectuals. (Sibal, 2004) The rise of labor unions during the prewar period provides an interesting part of our nation's history, as it provided the celebration of Labor Day and the formation of many human organizations.

Such took place during the American occupation, particularly during the time of the Commonwealth, where there was a little space for the assertion of freedom despite the recurrence of colonization and the threat of Imperialism. With the rise of the labor movement in the Philippines, efforts were exerted by our leaders to improve the condition of the workers and farmers, leading to a drastic change in our government and society, particularly in the protection of human rights and privileges.

The labor movement at that time is composed of labor organizations such as trade unions, farmers' associations, cooperatives and other sectoral and people's organizations. Traditional leaders from these movements include communists, socialists, nationalists, etc. The history of Philippines trade union movement reveals three (3) major features – communist infiltration and influence, government intervention and management domination.

The Different Labor Movements established in the Philippines

a. The Early Days (1870–1903)

At the year 1870, in Manila, the workers from printing, tobacco and stevedoring industry, woodworkers, clerks, carpenters and barbers formed an organization called "gremios" or guild or community-based crafts unions. As they do not belong in one union, they were classified into four as documented: *Gremio de Escultores del Barrio de Santa Cruz*, *Gremio de Obreros de Sampaloc*, *Gremio de Litografos*, and *Gremio de Carpenteros*. (Scott, 1984)

Labor unions emerged during the early days of the Americans in the archipelago, as documented, in the year 1899. These were separate organizations for barbers, cigar-makers, tobacco workers, clerks, carpenters, woodworkers, printers, lithographers, and others. Scott and Sibal noted that the following must have been among the gremios that existed before the Americans arrived in 1898: *Litografos y Encuadernadores* (bookbinders), *Impresores*, *Carpenteros*, *Escultores*, *Obreos de Varadeo de Yangco*, *Tabaqueros and Cocineros* (chefs) (Scott, 1984, Sibal 2004).

In June 1901, leaders by the names of Timoteo Anzures, Melanio de Jesus, Nazario Pasucolan, and Arturo and Leopoldo Soriano organized a unit of larger entity with the name of *Union de Impresores*. On the same year, August 17, Juan Geronimo and Luis Santos established a 40-member "unit" in Carmelo & Bauerman, and obtained four women as members. Then, on Rizal Day the meeting was held by the printers in which—according to the labor lore of a later generation—they decided to incorporate all their craft unions in one organization called *Union de Impresores de Filipinas*. Two days later, ten workers from the house of Camelo, Lithographers, approached Isabelo de los Reyes for assistance in forming a sari-sari cooperative in which they could invest their savings. The connection of the above events is not clear, but the results were historic, because it led to the formation of the *Union Democratica de Litografos, Impresores, Encuadernadores y Otros Obreros* (Democratic Union of Lithographers, Printers, Bookbinders and Other Workers) which quickly snowballed the first Philippine labor federation that had been known by the popular press as *Union Obrera Democratica*. (Scott, 1984)

It was on February 2, 1902 when the first labor union in the Philippines was established by Isabelo de los Reyes. That was the time when Don Belong just returned from his exile in Barcelona, Spain, loaded with socialistic and liberal ideas that he learned from Spanish labor leaders (Dalisay and Gacayan,

1992). Such also paved the way to the foundation of the Philippine Independent Church (Aglipayanism).

Trade unionism membership rose to 20,000 in Manila and environs (Sibal, 2004; Scott, 1987). They organized strikes-often against American employers but neither against the British or Spanish. These massive actions threatened American business interests in the Philippines. Naturally, a colony could provide them with affordable labor which they could even exploit. (Scott, 1987) And for that, the Americans decide to eliminate Isabelo de los Reyes. And they are able to take a while there was a strike in Malabon of the UOD in August, he was arrested and incarcerated.

Isabelo de los Reyes was replaced by Dr. Dominador Gomez, of whose selection the Americans were very pleased. Since he has been known as a gentleman and dependable person, they believed that he is capable of keeping workers in their proper place. But these Americans did not have much time to abuse even the thought of Gomez' sense of propriety. (Scott, 1987) Gomez initiated demonstrations and strikes, led a UOD rally in Bocaue, condemned the killing of General Licerio San Miguel on March and organized the celebration of the First Labor Day on May 1, 1903.

On May 29, Dominador Gomez was arrested for fraud and subversion, his house and press were raided, all Union accounts were seized, and the UOD went into receivership. Lope K. Santos succeeded Gomez and tried to legitimize UOD with the American colonial government by affiliating UOD with the American AFL-CIO. This resulted to the weakening of the trade union movement.

b. The American Period (1905-1920)

Because of previous encounters with UOD, the Americans legally recognized labor unionism through the creation of Bureau of Labor in 1908. Because of this, labor union repression ended. Trade unionism swerved towards political unionism where the leaders of the previous lobbied for nationalism, early independence and elections.

Lope K. Santos organized the *Congreso Obrero de Filipinas* (*COF*) in 1913 but unsuccessful because majority of its membership consist of agricultural workers who were not qualified to vote. (In 1906, voting rights were granted only to

Filipinos who are literates and property owners.) At this time, De los Reyes and Gomez were elected to the legislative position but not for labor movement but because they are members of the Filipino upper class elites. William Henry Scott, however, defended de los Reyes by describing him as, "educated but not elite, bourgeoisie but not aristocratic and always have his sympathy with the less fortunate people." (Scott, 1984) Reading between the lines may help us infer some of the reasons that the Americans may have just chosen not to reveal. And most likely, such is about taming de los Reyes' political and religious influence to the Filipinos, most specially to the labor force.

c. The Expansion of Trade Unionism and Communism (1920-1934)

The growth of trade and related industries resulted by free trade policy imposed by U. S. led to growth of trade unionism. *Crisanto Evangelista*, a member of the COF, also belonged to the Nacionalista Party sent to a mission to the United States for the cause of Philippine Independence in 1919. He established ties among labor groups in America, and in 1925 was contacted by an Indonesian Communist Tan Malaka, as the emissary of Red International of Labor Unions (which belongs to Communist International), inviting him to a trade union conference in Canton, China. This resulted to the affiliation of a Philippine labor party to the Red International Labor Unions. The Labor Party was founded in 1928 where Communism flourished in trade union movement, strongly influenced by Moscow's Marxist-Leninist philosophy. It is also in the same year when Evangelista, Jacinto Manahan and Cirilo Bognot attended another trade union conference in Berlin and Moscow, building further linkages.

As early as 1927, members of Partido Obrero (under COF) have been pushing some progressive stances that appeared radical to some groups. These include: 1.) the establishment of industrial unions in place of craft unions and mutual benefit societies, 2.) the inculcation of the concept of "class struggle" instead of "labor-capital harmony", 3.) better linkages with the Chinese labor force and fight against Filipino chauvinism, 4.) rejection of American economic principles and the *ilustrado* morality, and 5.) to seek for the support of the Red International of Labor Unions through the Profintern. These were presented to the members of the COF in a convention in May 1929, which led to the divide of the group between the leftists and the rightists: the communists and the non-communists. Cristobal, Paguia and Tejada led the conservative wing. Crisanto Evangelista, on the other hand, pushed the communist ideals calling for a second convention and established the *Katipunan ng mga Anakpawis* in 1929. In November 30, 1930 and in commemoration of the November 1917 Russian Revolution, *Partido ng Komunista ng Pilipinas* (PKP or Communist Party of the Philippines) is finally launched (Sibal, 2004). Its leaders are Evangelista, Jacinto Manahan, Juan Feleo, Guillermo Capadocia, Lazaro dela Cruz and Felix del Rosario. With more concrete clamours, the following are the party's goals: 1.) to unite the labor force for the elimination of the Imperialist Americans, 2.) to establish a Philippine government patterned under the Soviet system, 3.) to develop living and working conditions of the laborers, and 4.) to support all revolutionary movements all over the world. With such radical advocacies, this is when laborers started to hold weapons and involve themselves in armed conflicts applying a highly socialistic mechanism.

After a while, the communist group leaders headed by Crisanto Evangelista were arrested and incarcerated for illegal assembly. The party continued to fight for its cause calling the masses to emulate the patriotism of Andres Bonifacio.

Meanwhile, a person named Pedro Abad Santos, a Katipunero Major jailed by the Americans during the Filipino-American War, organized the Philippine Socialist Party in the midst of peasants and workers in Central Luzon, particularly in Pampanga and fought for land reforms through radical and violent means. The social unrest posed by Abad Santos prompted President Manuel Quezon to create a social justice program in 1935 with the establishment of the Commonwealth government.

d. Commonwealth Period (Pre-War, 1935-1941)

d.1 Social Justice Program

The Social Justice Program was calculated to win the support of labor since it included an eight-hour labor law, the extension of workmen's compensation, minimum wage legislation, the establishments of GSIS and legal protection of members of legitimate labor unions.

President Quezon sought to achieve social justice by protecting the rights of laborers through legislation and personal projects, and by creating more jobs for the common man. He believed that work is the measure of a man therefore man must be allowed to improve his lot and the government must help him.

From this program, there were laws created and enacted for the labor sector. It led to the regulation of trade union activities and work stoppages were minimized.

d. 2 Labor Laws under Social Justice Program

Commonwealth Act No. 103

AN ACT TO AFFORD PROTECTION OF LABOR BY CREATING A COURT OF INDUSTRIAL RELATIONS EMPOWERED TO FIX MINIMUM WAGES FOR LABORERS AND MAXIMUM RENTALS TO BE PAID BY TENANTS, AND TO ENFORCE COMPULSORY ARBITRATION BETWEEN EMPLOYEES OR LANDLORDS, AND EMPLOYEES OR TENANTS, RESPECTIVELY; AND BY PRESCRIBING PENALTIES FOR THE VIOLATION OF ITS ORDERS

Compulsory arbitration was institutionalized as the mode of setting labor disputes. The Court of Industrial Relations was given the jurisdiction over labor disputes which were likely to cause a strike or lock-out which more than 30 workers.

Commonwealth Act No. 213

AN ACT TO DEFINE AND REGULATE LEGITIMATE LABOR ORGANIZATIONS

This was enacted to provide greater legal protection to legitimate labor organizations. CA 213 provided for the following:

o1) made punishable intimidation or coercion with the intent of preventing a worker from joining a 'legitimate labor organization';

o2) the regulation of a 'legitimate labor organizations' requires the investigation by the Constabulary of its activities.

d. 2. Other Events

President Manuel Quezon wanted to win the support of the labor force. He gave pardon to Crisanto Evangelista in 1938. In the next year, 1939, the PKP of Crisanto Evangelista merged with the Socialist Party of Abad Santos in order to have a bigger group with the coming of the Second World War. Because of this, communist activities reappeared in the Philippine labor movement.

The communist revolutionary intellectuals achieved peasant base in Central Luzon where the *Hukbong Bayan Laban sa Hapon* (HUKBALAHAP) was eventually launched during the Japanese Period. The communists founded a national labor organization, the *Collective Labor Movement* but later split into two groups—the *Conference Worker's Alliance* (*Communist Wing*) and the *National Federation of Labor* (*conservative wing*).

There were then two progressive elites leading the labor movement – the communist revolutionary intellectuals and the nationalists. The aim of the communists was to change the social order towards socialism, while the nationalists were completely independent from America. The communists led the labor movement because they were more skilled in agitation and mass-organizing which contributed to the strengthening of trade union movement and labor movement. But labor activities were suppressed when the Japanese Forces finally occupied the archipelago in 1941.

Conclusion

The development of Labor movement in the Philippines before the Second World War was greatly unprecedented. The efforts of leaders Isabelo de los Reyes and Crisanto Evangelista are found influential probably because their causes are not about the simple wants of the workers. More than just compensation and better benefits, these leaders fought for liberation from a colonizer and emancipation from an economic system that they find unfitting for the Philippines.

It was very evident that after the demise of UOD, the succeeding labor movements became mostly influenced by communism and socialism. This was the result of spreading the ideas of Marx and Lenin that are mostly concerned on the society and the majority of the people. Through the combined efforts of Crisanto Evangelista and Pedro Abad Santos, the philosophies were concretized into real human and Filipino concerns that the labors continued to fight for.

What could be interesting at this point is the response of the Philippine government. Knowing that some resolution could be arranged by dialogue, President Quezon at the establishment of Commonwealth government in the Philippines, dealt with these groups just to win their support. Laws were then passed for labor sector just to secure their rights and minimized the work stoppages and other form of demonstration that can deteriorate or had a great effect in our economy. This must have led to the divide of the labor movement during the pre-war period-the communists that aim to change the social order and the nationalists that aims for total or complete independence from USA. Nonetheless with such divide, the movements, although no longer with a common voice, have their most radical demands in common-and these are freedom from the colonizers and a life of social justice that every Filipino deserves.

References

Dalisay, Jose Jr. and Gacayan, M. D. Isabelo Delos Reyes: *Father of RP's Labor Unions*. Philippine Labor, Volume 18, No. 4, April 1992.

De Leon, Lilia R. *Isabelo Delos Reyes: The man who made Filipinos aware of labor unionism*. Mr. and Ms. Publication, May 6, 1986.

Lopez, Salvador P. *Does the Filipino Worker Have a Future*? Mr. and Ms. Publication, January 22, 1985.

Salanga, Alfrredo N. *The Founding of the Labor Party*. Philippine Panorama, October 30, 1983.

_____. *The Unavoidable-and inevitable-question*. Weekend Book Review, May 29, 1983.

Scott, William Henry. *Historical Background of the Union Obrera Democratica, The First Filipino Labor Union*. Diliman Review, Volume 32, No. 1, Jan-Feb, 1984.

_____. *The Birth of Labor*. Diliman Review, Volume 35, no. 1, 1987.

Sibal, Jorge V. *A Century of the Philippine Labor Movement*. Illawara Unity Journal: Journal of the Illawara Branch of the Australian Study of Labour History, Volume 4, Number 1, 2004.

Historical Aspects to Sino-Sri Lankan Contacts through the Indian Ocean

Ramla Wahab-Salman[*]

Introduction

As an island, to Sri Lanka, the past, present and future is intrinsically connected to the Indian Ocean surrounding her. Following the Asia centric foreign policy of the H. E. Maithripala Sirisena, the President of Sri Lanka, the island has witnessed a renegotiation of its foreign policy since January 2015. Through this renegotiation with the aim of an Asia-centric foreign policy maintaining good relations with all, and as the island records over her ancient and modern political history, China has stands as an "all-weather friend" and trading partner through times of stability and change.

The visits over the last decade of Chinese President Xi Jinping, Indian Prime Minister Narendra Modi and various high level US officials to the country have indicated in no uncertain terms the rise of international interest and international gaze upon the island as a player in the Indian Ocean arena. The 21st century projects of the Maritime Silk Road in the case of Sino-Sri Lanka relations falls within the purview of the large scale Chinese One Belt and Road initiative which encompasses 6 economic corridors connecting over sixty sovereign nation states over land and sea. In an attempt to understand the formation of identity through a community of common destiny through a historical rela-

---

[*] Ramla Wahab-Salman, research fellow of Institute for National Security Studies Sri Lanka.

tion, my paper today seeks to approach the relations between the Indian Ocean island of Sri Lanka and China through its connected history and memory over the Silk Road of old, and, the reformulation of this shared memory in the context of the 21st century.

The Silk Road: Exploring the political geography of an Indian Ocean island

The Silk Road over land or sea was not a ribbon of highway or a single clear cut sea-lane spanning a continent. Thus, to say what lies or does not lie along this imagined community depends on how one approaches the history of the multiple routes within the wider Silk Road geographically and chronologically. The Silk Roads in a historical relation have been described by the global historian Peter Frankopan as wide and varied paths spanning land and sea as a Roads of faiths, Roads of fur (luxury goods), Roads of revolution, Roads of concord, A Slave road, The Road to Empire, The Road to War and finally and probably most befitting the theme of civilizational contacts in the 21st century, Roads of dialogue and The Road to compromise.

The island of Sri Lanka has through its recorded history experienced constant contacts and encounters with scholars, saints, ambassadors, travellers, merchants and pilgrims, among many others. Located at the southern extremity of the Indian Ocean, the island holds ports and port cities of varying historical importance through time along its coasts. These ports have contributed to shaping the island's policies in trade and diplomatic encounter with migrant populations into the island and the vast number to travellers through its ports. Described as the largest cultural continuum until the 15th century, the Indian Ocean Region presents a case of a community not of a common destiny in the centuries past. Instead it was a community of commonalities and contrasts in civilization which displayed elements of cohesion and unity over several aspects. Travel, movements of goods and people and economic exchanges created a distinct sphere of shared interests. Religion, social systems and cultural traditions on the other hand provided contrasts between co-existing civilizations along the Silk Road of the Sea.

The 1990 UNESCO and Central Cultural Fund publication titled Sri Lanka and the Silk Road of the Sea shed new light on the concept of Sri Lanka being located as a terminus and hub holding its own with its distinctive island character, location at the southern extremity of the South Asian subcontinent and position at the centre of the Indian Ocean. From the $1^{st}-15^{th}$ century AD China and Sri Lanka maintained prolonged political relations backed by economic interests paving the way for diplomatic and religious delegations in constant communication. This paper draws on civilizational contacts between China and Sri Lanka before the 1403 withdrawal of Chinese fleets from its Western routes.

Existing historical and archaeological research on ancient port-city relations including the 6th century Egyptian sailor Cosmas Indicopleustus's account of the ancient Sri Lankan port of Mantai described as a trading station between China and Sri Lanka. Analysing maritime commerce based diplomatic and civilizational relations it further explores the expeditions of Ming Admiral Zheng He and archeological findings to support these connections.

Memory and a tactile remnant of a shared past: Diplomatic Token to Museum At traction

Memory may be regarded as a strong factor in identity formation. The 21st century broad and wide ranging approach of Chinese foreign policy seeking economic, cultural and technological co-operation draws on one underlying memory of a glorious era past- the memory of the Silk Road. The Silk Road may arguably be understood as once a world system which connected Europe to the East affecting and influencing nations on land and sea along this route. To this memory, an example of a tangible tactile memory from the Silk Road is a trilingual inscription presented by the Ming Admiral Zheng He in the 15th century which was discovered along the southern coast of Sri Lanka. The Galle Trilingual Slab Inscription discovered in 1911 lists alms bestowed to the "Buddhist Temple in the Mountain of Ceylon" by the Emperor of the Ming Dynasty in Chinese, Persian and Tamil languages. This inscription discovered by a British colonial official is presently preserved at the Colombo National Museum is testimony to the importance of memory of a connected past in understanding the dynamics of civilizational dialogues in the 21st century arena.

The Port of Mantai

The Port of Mantai along the northwestern maritime frontier of the island was the most prominent entrepot of sailors from East and West travelling to and enroute Sri Lanka.

In an attempt to understand the Silk Road as a roads to concord and dialogue, prominent historian and editor of the volume of the Silk Road of the Sea, Senake Bandaranayake highlights: the quality of being courteous to visitors of people along the ports is attributable to the softening effects of the teaching of the Buddha, who advocated that one should 'be the first to receive the other with a smile' (pubbahasi) and also be the 'first to talk courteously to the other' (pubbabhasi). To me, this example cited by Bandaranayake may be a lesson in accord deeply rooted in philosophical belief which may be applied through time and space.

The port was dominated by Chinese and Persian merchants. The Chinese were best known for their luxury trade in ceramics and silk whilst the Persian dominated trade in horses. In using a glimpse from historical literature of the potential of the island, the Chinese writer Li Chao in his book mentioned the special technological ability of the people of the 'Lion Country (Sri Lanka)' and their skill in building strong ship to sail distant shores both East and West of the island. It was through this port city setting that Confucianism, Taoism and various threads of philosophical understandings reached the island and her kingdoms The port of Mantai which fell into decline is a constant reminder of the memory of the threads of civilizational, religious and technological links maintained through the Silk Road of old.

Conclusion

While historians, archaeologists, museologists as well as diplomats and policy makers are constantly reminded of the dangers of idealizing the past, it is certain that a shared heritage once did exist thus justifying the 21st century initiative of rebuilding a "community of shared shared future for mankind". In an age of terror and conflict, poverty and disease, the 21st century community of common destiny remains to conquer steep challenges in security and connectivity. Much like a memory may drive a global initiative such as the Belt and Road policy, actors must remain cautious in understanding the challenges a recreation of the Silk Road may face, yet work toward a once existent thriving global network- never underestimating the dynamics of dialogue across civilizations and the power of a shared memory.

Bibliography

Sri Lanka and the Silk Road of the Sea: UNESCO and Central Cultural Fund, Colombo. 2003

The Silk Roads: A New History of theWorld, Alfred A Knopf, New York. 2015

Mantai: City by the Sea, Linden Soft. 2013

Assimilation of Indian Culture in East Asia

Sandhya Jain[*]

India is one of the world's earliest civilisations with a history that goes back at least 8000 years, according to the latest findings in the Balochistan region, where traces have been found of the civilisation associated with Mohenjodaro, Harappa, and the Indus – Saraswati Valley. The Vedic hymns, which rank among the earliest lyrics in the world, are several millennia old, and reflect the profound thinking of those early ancestors in the proto-historical era. Later, Panini created a mathematically perfect treatise on grammar, whose structure permits an infinite addition of new words from existing roots.

This civilisation and culture spread from both sides of India's long coastlines; land routes that were trade routes also facilitated the movement of peoples and ideas. While Buddhism remains India's best known export to the world, the Hindu civilisation also travelled along the same trade routes and made a deep impact, especially in the east. This is an understated and relatively unexplored facet of Indian history, and our sources are still sketchy. Excavations in Central and Southeast Asia and China reveal peaceful cultural exchanges that occurred along the Silk Roads from China and Manuscript Roads from India.

Trade played an important but subordinate role in India's cultural commerce with her north, east and south-east neighbours, where, for over fourteen hundred years up to the end of the fifteenth century, India made sterling contributions to Asian civilisation. In their journeys outside India, both Hinduism and Buddhism were unaccompanied by political or military force, were never exclu-

---

[*] Sandhya Jain, Columnist of *The pioneer*, New Delhi.

sivist or intolerant of native beliefs and rather accommodated them into new syncretic traditions that stimulated the creative energies of the local populations in spectacular ways. The only known case of military conflict is between the Chola rulers of south India on Srivijaya in the tenth century A. D. , by which time the Indianisation of the region was already a millennium old.

The contemporary shift in global power from the West to the East makes this seminar on the *Histories and Development of East Asian Civilisations* very pertinent, especially the emphasis on the *Civilisational Exchange of East Asian Countries*. The old civilisations of the region have tried to maintain their civilisational and cultural continuity, inherent values and traditions, despite turbulent historical trajectories and economic and political upheavals.

East Asia is a vast terrain to the east of India and includes South East Asia. From the early centuries BC, large parts of the region shared religions, culture, ideas, knowledge systems, skills, people, trade and commerce, while creating a unique art and architectural heritage. Regions that showed up on the historical map from the early centuries of the Common Era include Java, Sumatra, Cambodia, Malaysia, Indonesia, Laos, Burma (Myanmar), Siam (Thailand), Korea, Vietnam, and even Philippines and Japan. India and China loomed large over the region, in different ways, and are once again actively engaged in reviving the old commercial links with the region.

Between the first to the fourth centuries CE, a host of urbanised coastal settlement and local polities sprouted in the region, copying Hindu forms of administration. These earliest Hindu kingdoms include Butuan, Champa, Dvaravati, Funan, Gangga Negara, Kadaram, Kalingga, Kutai, Langkasuka, Pagan, Pan Pan, Po-ni, Tarumanagara and Tondo. All were indigenous and independent of the Indian mainland. Later, powerful empires arose, such as Srivijaya, Majapahit and the Khmer.

Scholars like George Coedès believe these states were founded by Indian merchants who had the knowledge and ability to transmit Indian culture in other lands. This seems a reasonable surmise as the sailing and trading communities that would remain in foreign ports for many months until the changing winds facilitated the return journey home were well placed to disseminate Indian ideas abroad. They would have established colonies to live in and trade in during the interregnum between journeys and communicated their ideas at the court of the local ruler and among the native populations, including traders from other places. Rulers along the coasts of the Indian Ocean helped their port cities to prosper by providing facilities, infrastructure, and fair treatment to visiting merchants.

A merchant named Magadu (also Wareru) founded the Hanthawaddy Kingdom and invited Mon specialists in Indian traditions to compile the Code of Wareru, which remains the foundation of Burmese common law to this day. However, most scholars believe that these kingdoms were founded by native rulers who then imported Brahmins as advisers on *rajadharma* (rules of kingship). These kingdoms adopted and internalised Indian religious, cultural and economic practices without input from Indian rulers; the Hindu and Buddhist monks legitimised their rule and stabilised their dynasties.

The Indian Ocean provided its littoral states the opportunity to collaborate in commerce and mutual prosperity. The discovery by Hippalus (79 A. D.) that the monsoon winds could move ships and boats laden with merchandise across the open sea, twice a year, ended the inefficient and protracted system of hugging the coast, and boosted commerce. Besides linen, silk, spices, and much else, cultures and religions travelled via monks and spiritual texts, creating a civilisational unity.

In recent years, India has begun to take serious interest in her sea-faring past, retracing her footsteps in East and South East Asia, where she once enjoyed a long and distinguished history that was disrupted by the advent of Islam and European colonialists, successively. But from the early centuries CE, until the medieval disruption, India made immense contributions to the region. As a peninsular country with over 7,500 kms of coastline, India was destined to be a maritime nation. Indian ships dominated the vast ocean on both sides of the peninsula for centuries, which is how it came to be known as the Indian Ocean, the only ocean in the world named after a country.

India's extensive commerce and cultural exchangesin the East, as opposed to a migration of peoples or political or military conquest, occurred via ancient ports such as Tamralipti, Mahabalipuram (Tamluk), Palura near Gopalpur (Ganjam, Odisha) on the eastern seaboard, and Broach (Bharuch), Debal (near modern Karachi, Pakistan) and others on the western shore. Early French and Dutch scholars, to whom we are indebted for our knowledge of this era, called this exchange 'Indian colonisation' to explain the acceptance of an Indian ethos by Southeast Asian kingdoms that embraced both Hinduism and Buddhism.

The first millennium BC was a period of spiritual ferment in Asia: the Buddha gave his message of universal compassion, Mahavira of *ahimsa* (non-injury), and in China's Chow dynasty, Lao-tse and Confucius propounded the *Tao-kiao* (School of the Way) and *Ju-kiao* (School of the Knowers), which upheld the principles of non-interference, suppression of ego, and purification of heart. Simultaneously, Zoroaster preached in Persia (Iran), and the famous Behistun and Nakshi Rustam inscriptions of Darius the Great invoked the right path.

Emperor Asoka (273-242 B.C.) spread the teachings of the Buddha, sending his own son (or brother) Mahinda (Mahendra) and daughter Sanghamitra to Ceylon (Sri Lanka). His transition from a ruler driven by the desire for conquest to one grief-stricken over the scale of violence in the Kalinga war is immortalised in the Edict of Kalinga, which Kalidas Nag describes as the "noblest monument of repentance". For the next twenty years (201-242 B.C.) Buddhism travelled to the frontiers of the Hellenic world to the west and the Mongolian world to the east. According to the Rock Edicts of 257-256 B.C., Asoka sent monks to Syria (under Antiochos Theos), Egypt (under Ptolemy Philadelphos), Cyrene (under Magas), Macedonia (under Antigonus Gonatus), and Epirus (under Alexander). In time, Asoka's cultural imperialism developed its own momentum and spread across Tibet and China to Korea and Japan, and across Burma and Indochina (mainland south-east Asia) to Java and Indonesia.

The second wave of cultural colonisation occurred in the fifth century A.D., an era of great material prosperity and intellectual efflorescence in India. This was the epoch of Kalidasa, Aryabhatta, Varahamihira and Brahmagupta. The famous frescoes of Ajanta were painted, and Gunavarman and Vasubandhu propagated Buddhism. Around this time, Champa and Cambodge were thoroughly Hinduised and new Hindu colonies sprouted in the Malay Peninsula, in ancient Siam (Thailand), Laos, Borneo, Sumatra and Java. Indian writing systems were exported – the Pallava script of the south Indian Pallava dynasty to Southeast Asia, and the Siddham script to East Asia. Indian systems of administration and architecture dominated the region until the advent of Islam in the fifteenth century. By the time of the Hun invasions towards the end of the fifth century A. D. , Kumarajiva and Gunavarman (who died in Nanking in 431 A. D.) were en route to China to preach Buddhism, while Chinese pilgrims like Fa-hsien, Chih-Rong and Fa-moug started arriving in India.

Nepal

As India's closest neighbours, Nepal and Tibet imbibed much of their cultural traditions from India. Ancient Nepal had three capitals, Kathmandu, Patan and Bhatgaon, which lay in close proximity to each other. Siddhartha Gautam, Sakya Muni, the founder of Buddhism, was born in the Lumbini forest of the city of Kapilvastu, one of the ancient republics of India, which is now within the boundaries of modern Nepal. Like India, Nepal is a predominantly Hindu country; indeed it was until recently the only Hindu kingdom in the world.

It seems reasonable to surmise that like other republics of the Vrijji confederation, Nepal would have come under the influence of the Buddha in His lifetime. Tradition, however, credits Asoka with the formal introduction of Buddhism into Nepal; the emperor visited Lumbini and erected an inscribed pillar to commemorate the birthplace of Buddha. According to another tradition, Asoka's daughter, Charumati, married a Nepali prince and built several stupas and monasteries, some of which still survive. When the Gupta dynasty began to rule Nepal, the princely families of India and Nepal began to intermarry.

In the medieval era, Nepal became the refuge of many Rajput and Brahmin families, and also Buddhist monks from Nalanda and elsewhere. Nepal preserves the nine Sanskrit texts which are considered the original official scriptures of Mahayana Buddhism, including the *Prajnaparamita*. Many Buddhist manuscripts, sent to Tibet for safety, are still preserved there. In fact, Buddhist works lost in India are still available in Chinese and Tibetan translations.

The Gurkhas ruled Nepal in the eighteenth century and made it a Hindu kingdom with its own unique character, synthesising its traditions with those of neighbouring Tibet. Nepal's most famous temple is Pashupatinath (Siva) and its language is similar to Sanskrit. Nepal developed its sculpture and painting styles from Pala art in Bihar and Bengal, while Tibet adopted the Pala tradition through Nepal and Kashmir.

Tibet

Tibet's recorded history begins with King Songtsan-Gampo (Srong-btsan-Gampo 630 – 698 A. D.), who brought the country out of its deep isolation when he married the Licchavi princess Bhrikuti, a daughter of Nepal king Amsuvarman, and princess Wen Ch'eng, daughter of Chinese emperor Tang Tai-sung. The Nepali princess introduced the Hindu-Buddhist cult of Tara and other occult practices to the kingdom and also brought an image of the Buddha with her. The Chinese princess brought Chinese Buddhism and an image of the Buddha, originally from Magadha in India; both were housed in a grand temple build by Songstan at Jokhang in Lhasa. However, despite its easy entry into the kingdom, Buddhism had to struggle with the native traditions and it was only in the eleventh century that Atisa (Dipamkara Srijnana) succeeded in entrenching it as the national religion of Tibet.

Songtsan-Gampo sent his minister, Thummi Sambhota, and sixteen scholars to study in India and create a Tibetan alphabet and grammar. Thonmi Sambhota composed eight independent treatises on Tibetan writing and grammar, and the first Tibetan translations of Sanskrit texts of Buddhism. The Tibetan script and grammar were based on the Sanskrit of the Gupta period.

Songstan-Gampo ruled for thirty years and began the construction of what became the grand palace of the Dalai Lama, at Potala. Tibetan scholars began to visit India to study Buddhism, and Sanskrit texts began to reach Tibet. Indian and Chinese scholars visited Tibet to help in the translation and interpretation.

Under King Khri-Srong-de-blsan (740-786 A. D.), savants who came to Tibet included Santarakshita from Nalanda University and Padmasambhava and his disciple Pagur Vairochana. Padmasambhava introduced Mahayana Buddhism tinged with Tantric ideas and absorbed many native gods as Tantric guardian deities; he laid the foundations of Lamaism. The Tibetans did not develop a separate Buddhist sect, but translated classical works like *Amarakosha* and *Meghaduta* of Kalidas, the grammar of Chandragomin, and the treatise on painting and iconography, *Chitralakshana*. They were attracted to the mystical texts of later Buddhism: *Vajrayana*, *Kalachakrayana*, which led to the rise of Lamaism, and preferred the alchemist-philosopher Nagarjuna to the Buddha himself.

Dipamkara Srijnana or Atisa (1038 A. D.) hailed from Vikramsila monastery of Bihar and was nearly 60 years old when he went to Tibet, where he lived and preached in all parts of the country for nearly fifteen years till his death in Nyethang monastery, where his *samadhi* still stands. Atisa based his teachings on the Yogachara tradition, took a synthetic view of the tenets of Hinayana and Mahayana Buddhism, enforced celibacy on monks and discouraged magic practices.

Tibetan Buddhism reached its pinnacle when the conquest of China and Central Asia by Chengiz Khan (d. 1227 A. D.) and his successor Kubilai Khan (d. 1260 A. D.) led to the spiritual ascendancy of Lama Phagspa, Kubilai's Tibetan ally. His disciples translated the Tibetan Buddhist canon into Mongolian.

Other Indian influences on Tibet include its medicine system based on Ayurveda; its tantric forms; painting based on the Buddhist art of the Pala period and Ajanta art. Some Tibetan art forms were later adopted by China in the Ming and Ching periods. Tibet took the arts and crafts of India and Nepal (especially bronze casting) to the Buddhist Mongolian emperors of China. Phagspa

(d. 1280 A. D) was succeeded by Lama Dharmapala as Imperial Chaplain of the Mongol emperors of China. Besides the Tibetans and Mongols, Buddhism spread among the Tunguse and Ouigur Turks in the frontiers of Siberia and other Samoyed races.

Gandhara to China

After the retreat of Alexander and Seleucus Nikator, the Greek converts to Buddhism who settled in the region along with the native Hindus developed the Graeco-Buddhist art (Gandhara School) which influenced the art of Central Asia and the Far East.

Mahayana Buddhism (the doctrine of the Grand Vehicle) deeply influenced the Eastern Asiatic world. The doctrine of Sarvastivada, which asserts that everything external and internal is real, was conceived at Gandhara. Katyayani-putra, teacher of Asvaghosha, composed the *Vibhasa* and the *Maha-Vibhasa*, the classical works of this new school of philosophy. The Vaibhasika sect of the Sarvastivadins flourished in north-western India, in Kashmir, in Gandhara and entered China through Udyana, Kashgar, Khotan and Persia.

Many traditions proclaim China's attempts to reach India. In the reign of Emperor Tsin Shih Huaung-ti, in 217 B. C., 18 Buddhist monks were reputedly brought to the capital. By the beginning of the Christian era, Yue-chi (Kushan) ambassadors to the Chinese court reputedly brought some Buddhist scriptures, which suggests that Buddhism had already reached parts of Central Asia. Buddhism was officially introduced into China in 67 AD, under Emperor Ming-ti, with the arrival of Buddhist scriptures, images, and two Indian monks, Kasyapa Matanga and Kasyapa Dharmaraksa. The former translated the first Chinese Buddhist text: "*The* 42 *Saying of Buddha*". In the then capital Louyang, the Pai-ma (White Horse) temple was built in Henan province and many Taoist and Confucian nobles converted to Buddhism by 71 AD..

Kumarajiva (344-413 A. D.), a monk from an Indian family living in Karashahr (Kucha, along the Taklamakan desert), taught Buddhism and

Indian culture to China when captured by a Chinese general. His translations are considered classics of Chinese literature; the most highly regarded being the "Lotus of the Good Law" (*Saddharma - pundarika*). Kumarajiva briefly reunited the Northern (Turco-Mongolian) and Southern (Indigenous) schools of Chinese Buddhism which had become popular among the people. Most early Sino - Buddhist texts of the Loyang School were translated by Yueh - chi, Parthian or Sogdian converts to Buddhism, in collaboration with Chinese Buddhists. Most of these translations were not directly from Indian classical languages like Sanskrit and Pali, but from popular dialects (Prakrits) from various parts of India.

Fa-hsien, the earliest known Chinese Buddhist pilgrim to India, crossed the formidable Taklamakan (Gobi) desert, Khotan and the Pamir ranges around 399 A. D. in order to reach India; he paved the way for direct traffic between India and China. For nearly fourteen years, he studied at Pataliputra (Patna) under Revati, master of Buddhaghosha, who took the faith to Ceylon, and returned home via Ceylon and Java, bearing many manuscripts, on an Indian ship around 415 A. D.

Other important Buddhist missionaries to China include Buddhabhadra, who founded the Shan-no (Dhyana, Zen) school of Chinese philosophy and poetry in concert with the monks of the Mount Lu Shan monastery associated with the great Hui - yuan (416 A. D.) Prince Gunavarman of Kashmir renounced his throne and propagated the *dharma* via his brilliant paintings and erudite translations of scriptures. In 400 A. D., he went to Ceylon and Java, where he founded the first Buddhist monastery and converted the King and Queen-mother, before moving to Canton (424 A. D.) and Nanking, where he founded two Viharas, introduced the strict *Vinaya* system of ordination, and organised the first monastery of Chinese nuns. After his death in China (431 A. D.) two groups of nuns arrived from Ceylon and organised the Chinese nunneries after the Sinhalese model.

Buddhaghosha went to China from Ceylon. He translated (472 A. D., from a now lost Indian original) the *"Lives of Twenty-three Indian Patriarchs"*, recording the lives of great Buddhist teachers like Kasyapa Matanga, Asvaghosha, Nagarjuna, Vasubandhu and others. Many names are now lost, but Edouard Chavannes and Sylvain Levi rediscovered many, viz., Chih-mong and Fa-mong (contemporaries of Fa-hsien, 400 A. D.) from China, and Sanghasena and Guna-vriddhi from India (492 A. D.).

In the sixth century, the sea route between India and China improved via the Malay Archipelago, and Bodhidharma took the first voyage to south China in 520 A. D. The second voyage was made by Paramartha, biographer of the Buddhist philosopher Vasubandhu (420-500 A. D.) Paramartha arrived in China in 540 A. D. and was invited to Nanking in 548 A. D. He translated the works of Asanga and Vasubandhu, and taught the Yogachara school of thought before Hiuen-Tsang.

The Tang Dynasty unified the North and South (617-910 A. D.), took control of Central Asia, and presided over a glorious period of Asian art and philosophy, most notably in the grottos of Dunhuang, whose polyglot library and stunning treasures are a legacy of the thriving trade and cultural exchanges of this era. Dunhuang is located on the highway to the Mediterranean, overlapping the main routes from Mongolia in the north and Tibet and India in the south.

Indochina, Funan

Indochina lacks a uniform history as the region is divided into several interlinked regions with frequent changes of boundary and much foreign domination. The Tonkin delta (northern Vietnam) had direct sea contact with India and helped take Buddhism to China. The Dong-son culture developed in Annam (southern Vietnam), but the earliest and most splendid Southeast Asian civilisations developed at Champa. Laoslies west of Tonkin, and to its south is Cambodia. The states of this region kept contact with China and India by sea, as the land routes posed formidable obstacles.

The Chinese and later the Indians arrived in the area at the beginning of the Christian era. The Dong-son culture thrived in the coastal belt of Annam between the fifth and second centuries B. C. , when China was expanding her frontiers and soon dominated Tonkin. But Indochinese civilisation got a real fillip with its brief contact with Indian culture, which ended around the fifth century, but proved so inspirational that the peoples of Indochina embraced it eagerly and crafted new civilisations of great originality. Paul Pelliot found traces of Indian culture in Funan (ancient Cambodia) as early as the third century A. D. , with big ships crossing the seas. Indians influence was evident in Pegu, Burma, Champa, Cambodge, Sumatra and Java.

Funan, which roughly covers modern Cambodia and South Vietnam, was the oldest and most important of the Indianised states and occupied the lower valley of the Mekong river. It had early contact with India and scholars are generally agreed that its civilisation began with the advent of Indian traders. Funan was rich in goods desired by India merchants and a useful halt en route to China.

A third century Chinese writer, Kang Tai, states that an Indian Brahmin, Huen-Chen of Ho-fu, went to Funan inspired by a dream, married a local princess, Lien-Ye, and founded a kingdom in the first century A. D. Funan's four oldest Sanskrit inscriptions date to the third century. Cambodian chronicles have a version of this story. A seventh century inscription from Champa identifies the Brahmin as Kaundinya of the Somavamsa. His successors extended their power over neighbouring lands and established diplomatic relations with India and China. Around 200 A. D. , the dynasty was overthrown by its military commander, Fan-cheman, who took Funan to great heights.

What little is known of Funan's history shows growing Indian influence. In the mid-fourth century, an Indian was ruling Funan. Sanskrit inscriptions, and the *History of the Liang Dynasty* which contains dates and facts, record the arrival of another Indian, Kaundinya-Jayavarman, who ruled between 478 and 514 A. D. An Indian monk, Nagasena, helped him establish ties with the Chinese emperor, from whom he sought help to defeat the neighbouring kingdom of Chenla. Funanese monks were Sanskrit scholars and some went to China to translate Buddhist texts into Chinese.

Kaundinya-Jayavarman's son, Rudravarman, succeeded his father and ruled for twenty-five years; he was the last great king of Funan. He sent six embassies to China. An ardent devotee of Vishnu, he patronised some of the great sculpture of Indochina. Funan later fell to its Indianised neighbour, Chenla. Funan enjoyed great material prosperity; Chinese annals aver that the country was overflowing with gold, silver, pearls, and spices. As Indians were already adept in irrigation and land reclamation, they possibly contributed to the region's agricultural prosperity.

Archaeological finds at Oc-eo have revealed a Roman gold medallion (152 A. D.) with the likeness of Antoninus Pius, and Hindu intaglios and seals with Sanskrit inscriptions of the same and subsequent periods. The medallion proves thriving Indo-Roman trade, which prompted Indian exploration of Southeast Asia. Statues of Buddha and Hindu gods (Vishnu, Siva, Harihara, Ardhanarisvara), gold ornaments, tin amulets with symbols of Vishnu and Siva, and merchant seals with inscriptions in Sanskrit, have been recovered from sites in Funan.

Funan's buildings reflect the influence of Gupta and post-Gupta architecture. The content of Funan inscriptions, executed in flawless Sanskrit, reveal that Indian religion, philosophy, and mythology were widely understood, and that secular knowledge of subjects such as phonetics (*sabda*), logic (*nyaya*), and political theory (*arthasastra*), were studied there.

Champa

The earliest inscriptions of Champa (south and central Vietnam) bearing evidence of Indian (Hindu and Buddhist) influence go as far back as the 3rd century A. D. Located on the coast of Annam, at the foot of spice-bearing mountains, this Indianised state lasted from 192 to 1697 AD.

The Chammost likely hailed from the same Indonesian stock as the founders of the Dong-son culture further north. Lying on the main sea routes from India and Java to China, Champa played a significant role in transmitting Indian culture in eastern Asia. Sri Mara was its first Hindu king (circa 200 A. D.), and it had close ties with Funan. A ruler, Bhadravarman according to Sanskrit inscriptions, was a good commander and scholar; he dedicated a temple to Siva at Mison, the Bhadresvarasvami, which became the royal temple in the centuries that followed. Champa became a Chinese tributary in the sixth century.

Excavations in the ancient capital of Tra-Kieu, reveal Sivaite and Vaisnavite shrines and bas - reliefs; the Chams were Sivaites. The earliest inscription, possibly the earliest in Southeast Asia, is the Vo-canh inscription written in a South Indian script, dating from the second or third century. The most ancient bronze statue found in Champa is a lovely Buddha of Dongduong, in Amaravati style; indeed, a principality in Champa was named Amaravati. Bhadravarman's inscriptions in Sanskrit and Cham, dated 350 A. D. are the earliest inscriptions found in Champa proper. I-tsing notes the presence of Buddhism in Champa.

Chenla

Towards the end of the sixth century, Chenla, an Indianised kingdom, defeated Funan and grew into the Khmer Empire. Though held by some to be the original home of the Kambuja people, the Kambuja royalty claim descent from Rishi Kambu Svayambhuva, king of Aryadesa (India) and the *apsara* Mera, reflecting a popular quest for elite genealogy by newly-minted royal families.

King Bhadravarman (d. 598 A. D.), who began the liberation from Funan, is recorded in a Sanskrit inscription as having consecrated a Sivalinga named Tryambaka (three-eyed); another inscription calls him King of Kings, strong as Mount Meru. He was succeeded by his brother, Chitrasena, who took the royal name Mahendravarman. He built many Siva temples and all his known inscriptions resemble Pallava inscriptions of the early seventh century. He sent Chenla's first embassy to China in 616-617 A. D. .

Chitrasena's son, Isanavarman, ruled over the whole of Cambodia, Cochin China, and the valley of the Mun River up to the Dangrek Mountains. He founded a new capital city, Isanapura, at Kampong Thom on the

Mekong River, which was the capital of the Kambuja kingdom until the ninth century.

Chenla's art, known as the Sambor style, and the early phase of Khmer art developed here. An inscription celebrates the consecration of a statue of Harihara (a fusion of Shiva and Vishnu) and of an *asrama* for *Pancaratra* priests. Sivaism appears to have been the state religion; Sanskrit the language of most inscriptions, and the literary culture derived from the *Ramayana*, the *Mahabharata*, and the *Puranas*.

Kambuja

The Khmer kingdom emerged from a fusion of Chenla and Funan, and became the most powerful state in Indochina, enjoying nearly seven centuries of glory until overcome by the Thais in the fifteenth century. The Pyu kingdom of Burma, Mon kingdom of Siam, and Srivijaya empire in Indonesia also bloomed in the seventh century.

At the turn of the ninth century, the whole country came to be ruled by Jayavarman II (802–854 A. D.) who launched the Angkor period and era of classical Khmer art. Jayavarman and his Brahmin teacher, Hiranyadama, introduced the cult of the Deva Raja (God-King) and redesigned the state around seven capital cities. Excavations on the ruins of Phnom Kulen by Philippe Stern and Henri Mouhot reveal several temples overrun by dense foliage, whose style bridges the gap between pre-Angkor and classical Angkor art.

The Khmer rulers commissioned grand temples, most notably the complex of Angkor Thom. Yasovarman I (889–901 A. D.) built the city of Angkor, which was much larger than Angkor Thom, founded by Jayavarman VII at the end of the twelfth century. Yasovarman erected the Siva temple of Phnom Bakeng and issued several Sanskrit inscriptions, written in Kavya style. Mahayana Buddhism began to dominate the kingdom in the reign of Jayavarman V (968–1001 A. D.)

Suryavarman (1002–1050 A. D.) from Siam (Thailand) initiated a new dynasty of great kings. Though a Buddhist (he was posthumously named Nirvanapada), he built temples of Siva and Vishnu. But it was Suryavarman II (1113-1152 A. D.), who took Cambodia to the pinnacle of its glory with the breathtaking splendor of Angkor Wat, justly called an epic in stone. The largest temple complex in the world, it was dedicated to Vishnu. Lost for centuries, it was discovered by Henri Mouhot, who called it unparalleled in the whole world.

Jayavarman VII, also a Buddhist, created Angkor Thom around the Hindu concept of the world comprising of a circular, central continent (Jambudvipa, ancient name of India) surrounded by seven ring-shaped continents, nestled in oceans and enclosed by a huge mountain range. Mount Meru is at the centre of Jambudvipa, surrounded by the stars and planets, and at its summit is the city of the gods, bounded by heavens of *Lokapalas* (guardian deities). At Angkor Thom, the central mountain is the Bayon, temple of the Bodhisattva Lokesvara, Lord of the Universe; the city is surrounded by a wall and moat forming a square almost two miles on each side. By the time Jayavarman VII (1181-1220 A. D.) died, the kingdom was in decay and fell to the advancing Thais.

The Khmers patronised all branches of Indian learning, and all royal princes were educated in Indian philosophy and literature. As a result, many educated Brahmins came to the kingdom to teach. They in turn influenced the marriage customs, social customs, and funerary rites. Though Hinduism remained the dominant faith, Buddhism also thrived and in the ninth century, King Yasovarman erected a monastery for the monks.

The Thai dynasty possibly mentored Cambodia's transition to Buddhism. Gradually, the Hindu gods were absorbed into Buddhismand even in the great temples like Angkor Wat, were substituted by images of the Buddha.

Malaya

The Malay Peninsula, which includes modern Malaya and southern Thailand, played a crucial role in Indian sea trade with East Asia and in diffusion of

Indian culture throughout Southeast Asia. Takkola, modern Takua Pa is southern Thailand, was the first halting place for traders and settlers from India, from where they dispersed in different directions. Indian influences pervade the region in the form of ruins of shrines, images, Sanskrit inscriptions, *et al.*

Malaya's wealth attracted outside powers and she came to be dominated by Funan, the Thai kingdom, and later the Srivijaya and Majapahit Empires. Ancient Indian literature contains few references to Malaya, but Chinese chronicles mention Indianised cities in the peninsula, which are difficult to identify today.

In the first or second century, the kingdom of Langkasuka was founded on the east coast near Patani. In 515 A. D., King Bhagadatta (Po chi-ieh-ta-to) dispatched an envoy, Aditya, to China. At least three more embassies were sent to China in the sixth century. The state of Pan Pan, neighbouring Langkasuka, received Brahmins from India, and the second Kaundinya travelled from here to Funan.

Kolo (Kolo-fu-sha-lo) was another state that George Coedès believed was near Kedah or Kra; in the sixth and seventh centuries it received envoys from China. Chinese annals state that diplomats came from Malaya to China in the sixth century and Indian kings ruled there and used the Sanskrit language.

The kingdoms of Kalasapura and Kamalanka, mentioned in Indian literature, could have been in the Malay Peninsula, Kala (Kedah), and Pahang. The *Puranas* and other Sanskrit dramas and stories mention Katahadvipa (Kataha), which figures amongst the nine divisions of the world across the seas, to which regular voyages were made from Tamralipti (an ancient city on the Bay of Bengal). The Tamil epic, *Silappadikaram* (second century) mentions huge ships entering a city in South India laden with goods and spices from a Malayan port called Tondi. Indian and Chinese sources contain references to Kedah, the most important Indianised principality in Malaya proper. I-tsing was the first Chinese scholar to mention Kedah (Chieh-cha), which he visited in 671 A. D..

Though the Sanskrit inscriptions discovered so far do not pre-date the fourth century, the emerging evidence supports literary references that hint at a much earlier date for the Indianised states of the Malay Peninsula. Possibly an Indian ship brought an Attic vase of the fifth century B. C. to Perlis. Roman beads found at Kota Tinggi in Johore likely came with Indian traders at the beginning of the Christian era. The remains of a Siva temple excavated by Quaritch Wales at Kedah Peak link the transition from the funereal shrines of South India to the *Chandis* or tomb shrines of Java. Eight of the sites excavated by Wales are Buddhist, twelve are Siva, and three are secular monuments. Malacca was also likely to have been an Indian mart.

Pallava settlements have been found in Kedah, on the Bujang river; images of Ganesa and other statuary linked to the Siva sect have been found in temple ruins. Over centuries, it became a centre of Indian art styles and cultural traits, mostly from South India, though Indians came from other parts of the country as well.

Kedah was home to both Mahayana and Hinayana Buddhism in the fourth century. Important relics, including bronze images of the Buddha, have been excavated from Perak, Pangkalan, and Tanjong Rambutan. In Province Wellesley, a total of eleven Sanskrit inscriptions of the fourth century were discovered by James Low at Cherok Tokun. A statue of the Bodhisattva Avalokitesvara with tantric emblems in the Pala style (eighth century) was recovered from Bidor, among other sites.

Among the profusion of sites, mention must be made of Ligor, possibly the most important Indianised state of the Peninsula, now called Nakhon Srithammarata, in southern Thailand. Though a Buddhist colony with almost fifty temples around a stupaof a very early period, there are still Brahmins of Indian origin at Patalung. Hindu relics have been found in the area.

In the eighth century, Malay came under the control of the Indonesian Empire of Srivijaya and the Sailendras; this lasted till almost the end of the thirteenth century; remnants of this period are scattered all over the Peninsula. In the fourteenth century, the Indianised Majapahit Empire displaced Srivijaya and influenced Malaya culture.

Though Islam and the European colonialists brought about profound changes in Malaya culture, many social ceremonies retain marks of Hindu culture and some Sanskrit words are still used in important rituals. Malaya's literature and folklore are deeply influenced by the epics, *Ramayana* and *Mahabharata*, and her language contains many Sanskrit loan words. Until the introduction of the Arabic and later Roman script, Indian scripts were used in Malaya and the Archipelago.

Indonesia, Java

Indonesia figures in the annals of Han Emperor Wang Mang who ruled China at the beginning of the first century. Chinese ceramics of this era, found in Sumatra, indicate regular contact between the two countries. King Devavarman (Tiao-pien) of Yavadvipa (Java Island) sent a mission to China in 132 A. D., which suggests that Indian influence in the region began in the pre-Christian era.

Fa-hsien, who visited Java about 414 A. D. for five months, observed that the country was a Hindu bastion; he proceeded to Canton in a merchant vessel with 200 Hindu traders on board. Two decades later, the Buddhist monk, Gunavarman, visited Java en route to China and introduced Buddhism to the island. Chinese annals are replete with accounts of Indianised Java. Ptolemy in the second century mentions *labadiou* (Prakrit form of Sanskrit Yavadvipa) and refers to several places in the Archipelago and Peninsula under their Sanskrit names.

Local legends say Rishi Agastya (Bhatara Guru) came from India and settled there; his image is popular in art and sculpture. Javanese sources add that 20,000 Indian families came to Java from Kalinga in the second century; prince Kano rose from their ranks a century later. Several tales link the original settlers and their leader, Aji Saka, with heroes of the *Mahabharata*. The Javanese era commences from Aji Saka 78 A. D., a tradition refers to a Hindu state in 56 A. D..

Archaeological finds across the country refer to much later eras. Sanskrit inscriptions of a King Mulavarman from Kutei in Borneo, undated but possiblyof the fourth or early fifth century, have a script close to early Pallava inscriptions of South India and early inscriptions of Champa and Kambuja. Inscriptions from West Java mention a King Purnavarman, possibly of the mid-fifth century.

Indonesia's first Indianised kingdom was Srivijaya with its capital at Palembang, in Sumatra (Chinese, Fuche). Most scholars believe it was founded in the seventh century, though R. C. Majumdar feels it was founded around the fourth century and peaked towards the end of the seventh. However, it is only in the last quarter of the seventh century that the kingdom is mentioned in epigraphy and literature.

Srivijaya was a large kingdom, covering Java to the Malay Peninsula and southern Siam from the seventh to the twelfth and possibly the thirteenth, century. Inscriptions found at Palembang, some dated 683–686 A. D., refer to the conquest of Jambi (Malayu) and the island of Bangka. An inscription dated 775 A. D., from Nakhon Srithammarata, lauds the power of the king under whose command several Buddhist temples were erected.

By the eighth century Srivijaya ruled the whole of Sumatra, West Java, and the greater part of the Malay Peninsula. Its hold over the two straits added to its wealth as Indian traders had to pass through either strait; those who took the land route to Indochina and China had to pass through the northern part of the Malay Peninsula. Coedès states that Sri Vijaya succeeded to the commercial hegemony of Funan and control of the southern area.

This immense wealth triggered the quest for knowledge and arts. I-tsing spent six months in Palembang (671 A. D.) learning Sanskrit grammar, and on returning from India after 14 years, devoted four years to copying and translating Sanskrit texts into Chinese. He returned to Palembang again with four monks from Canton and wrote his *Memoirs* there. Buddhism was the most popular religion in Indonesia from the seventh to the eleventh century; monks from India, including the renowned Dharmapala of Nalanda university, came to Indonesia in the seventh century. Atisa (eleventh century), who became head of Vikramsila university and presided over the second epoch of Buddhism in Tibet, studied there in his youth.

In the fourth and fifth centuries, there were many Indianised states in Java, two of which sent embassies to China in the fifth century. Early archaeological finds in West Java include four stone inscriptions in Sanskrit of a king Purnavarman of Taruma who reigned in the fifth century; they speak of his grandfather as a *rajarshi*, and another ancestor as a *rajadhiraja*, which suggests an Indianised society flourished in Java during in the fourth and fifth centuries. Chinese annals refer to several kingdoms in the Java islands, including Ho-ling in the Tang period, which could be the Indonesian Kaling or Kalinga, named by immigrants from India's east coast.

In the eight century, the Sailendras emerged as an independent power in central Java. Nilakanta Sastri believes they could be a branch of the South Indian Pandyas; they presided over an era of unparalleled cultural achievement. Arab writers, such as Ibn Khurdadhbih, Abu Zayd Hasan, Al Masudi and Al Biruni extolled their immense political, commercial, and cultural accomplishments. At some stage in the ninth century, a Sailendra prince became ruler of Srivijaya at Palembang; this dynasty lasted up to the thirteenth century.

The Sailendras were a mighty naval power, and maintained close ties with the Buddhist Pala Kingdom of Bengal. Kumaraghosha of the Pala Empire was royal preceptor of the Sailendra kings (782 A. D.). A copper plate inscription found at Nalanda, dated about 860 A. D., chronicles the building of a monastery there by King Balaputradeva of Suvarnadvipa, for visitors and scholars from Indonesia. A Chola inscription from South India records that two Sailendra kings, Chudamanivarman and his son, Sri Maravijayottungavarman, constructed a Buddhist monastery at Nagapattana (Negapatam) and granted lands and villages for their upkeep.

The Sailendras were friendly with the Chola rulers of South India, who were also a great naval power. At the opening of the eleventh century, Rajaraja the Great (985 – 1014 A. D.) and his more eminent son, Rajendra Chola (1014–1044 A. D.), were the greatest power in southern India. But some conflicts arose and two Chola inscriptions (1024, 1030 A. D.) mention Rajendra Chola's military conquests of several countries in Southeast Asia including Srivijaya and the Sailendra Kingdom. Another Chola king, Virarajendra (1063 –

1070 A. D.), also attacked the Sailendra successfully, but the century-long warfare between the Cholas and the Sailendras ultimately weakened both.

Under the Sailendras, Buddhist art attained new heights. The dynasty introduced the north Indian Devanagari script, rechristened Malaysia as Kalinga, and built spectacular monuments such as the stupa at Borobudur, which Ananda Coomaraswamy described as a ripe fruit matured in breathless air. Borobudur is the largest Buddhist monument in the world and is shaped like a giant stone mandala, a fusion of Buddhist ideas and native megalithic tradition of step pyramid.

Eastern Java came to the fore in the tenth century. Prior to the rise of the Sailendras in central Java, a powerful dynasty was ruling eastern Java with its capital at Mataram; its king, Sanjaya, led successful expeditions to Sumatra and Cambodia. An inscription found at Changal in district Kedu, records Sanjaya erecting a monument for a Sivalinga in 732 A. D. After his death, the Sailendras conquered central Java and pushed his successors eastward. By the ninth century, Mataram broke free of the Sailendras in eastern Java, which became a bastion of Indian culture for the next five hundred years.

Mpu Sindok, ascended the throne of Mataram in 929 A. D. under the title of *Sri Isana Vikrama Dharmottungadeva*. Princess Mahendradatta, his great granddaughter, married Udayana, a prince from Bali. Their son, Airlingga, ruled the Mataram kingdom from 1010 to 1049 A. D. and brought all Java under his dominion. An inscription notes that he built a dam to stop the Brantas River from flooding. Revered as an *avatara* of Vishnu, an image of Vishnu on his mount, Garuda, has been erected at Balahan, where he was cremated. He patronised literature; Kanva wrote an epic poem, *Arjunavivaha*, in this era. Sindok divided his kingdom between two sons, and the states of Kadiri and Djanggala lasted till the opening of the thirteenth century, when the Singhasari dynasty emerged.

Close to Borobudur are a group of six Hindu temples in two lines of three each, known as the Prambanan group. The largest and most exquisite, Lara Djonggrang, is a Shiva temple erected by King Daksha of Mataram about 860 A. D.; the two smaller ones are dedicated to Vishnu and Brahma. The Lara

Djonggrang is the local name of Durga Mahisasuramardini, whose image it contains. On the opposite side are *chandis* of the mounts of the three gods of the Trimurti; 45 bas reliefs on the Rama story are carved on the inner wall of the gallery, which are far more beautiful than those at Borobudur. The gate arches and entrances have elaborate ornamentation, with the head of Mahakala in the centre. The inspiration is obviously Indian.

Singhasari was founded by Ken Angrok, but the dynasty peaked under Kritanagara (1268–1292 A. D.), a devout Buddhist and adept in Yoga. Marco Polo visited Java at this time and described Singhasari as a rich kingdom ruled by a great king. Kritanagara conquered Sumatra, Bali, parts of Borneo, and the Malay Peninsula. He challenged Kubilai Khan, but before the latter's army could reach Java he was overthrown by the governor of Kadiri.

In the unrest that followed this coup, in which Kubilai Khan's army participated, the kingdom of Majapahit arose in central Java under Vijaya, a son-in-law Kritanagara; he declared kingship over the whole of Java in 1294 A. D., taking the name of Kritarajasa Jayavardhana. The kingdom's commander, Gajah Mada, became the prime minister (1331–1364 A. D.) and brought Sumatra under the empire, along with Bali and other islands.

The gigantic Panataran temple complex are the largest and most important monuments in eastern Java and were possibly begun during the Singhasari period, but were completed under the Majapahit. The main temple is dedicated to Siva and is built in the form of a stepped pyramid, considered the pinnacle of Majapahit art.

Rajasanagara or Haym Wuruk (1350–1389 A. D.) took the kingdom to the height of its glory, ruling over the main islands in the Archipelago and most of the Malay Peninsula. He built trade and cultural relations with neighbouring countries, such as Kambuja, Champa, China, Siam, and India, and patronised many Brahmins and Sramanas in his capital. The empire collapsed after his death and Ming China assumed suzerainty over Sumatra and the Archipelago.

Formally, the Majapahit Kingdom continued until 1520, by which time Islam had made considerable inroads into Java and soon overcame the Indianised kingdoms in Java and Indonesia. Only tiny Balambangan (Bali) managed to protect its Hindu identity. Bali's most important temple is that of Pura Besaki which lies at the foot of the mountain Gunung Agung, and is dedicated to the Hindu Trinity, was possibly built by Wira Dalem Kesari (Warmadeva Keshari) at the opening of the tenth century.

Indian culture profoundly influenced Indonesian language, art, social customs, legal and political systems, literature, folklore, and philosophy. The Kawi language is replete with Sanskrit loan words, and the language of the oldest extant script, the Pallava script, is Sanskrit. Another Indian script used there was an early form of Devanagari, possibly introduced in the eighth century during ties with the Palas and Sailendras. Madurese, Sundanese, and Balinese scripts also derive from the Pallava, as does the Batak writing in central Sumatra. People in other parts of the archipelago also used alphabets and scripts derived from India, until the coming of Islam and the Europeans.

The great empires patronised literature and stories from the *Mahabharata* and *Ramayana*, translated and adapted in Javanese, became the basis of the rich corpus of Indonesian literature, along with other Sanskrit works such as Kalidasa's *Raghuvamsa*. Sri Rama is the role model for the Indonesian concept of chivalry, while Sita is the role model for girls. Java's main river, Sarayu, is named after the river on whose banks Rama's capital, Ayodhya, was situated in India. The *Mahabharata* is even more popular, and Arjuna is the national hero of Indonesia. Works like *Panchatantra* and *Hitopadesa* influenced Indonesian writing. Indian puppet theatre, *kathaputali*, became an integral part of the local culture. Indian impact is discernible on Javanese music, village organisation, rural economy and customary laws regarding property.

Chandi Kalasan on Volcano Merapi in central Java, built around 778 A. D., is the oldest shrine and its inscription is the first Javanese record of the Sailendra kings. The temple is dedicated to the Buddhist goddess Tara and may have been a tomb for the king's consort.

An Indian connection with Borneo survives in the form of seven inscriptions at Maera Kaman in Kutei (East Borneo), inscribed on stone pillars in the Sanskrit script of the fourth century. They refer to King Mulavarman and his ancestors and a sanctuary called Vaprakesvara, dedicated to Siva or

Agastya. Many relics and inscriptionsare scattered across the region, but overall knowledge of the region is sketchy.

Korea

From Central Asia and China, Buddhism spread to Korea, Japan and Mongolia. It reached Korea in the second half of the fourth century, at a time when the region was divided into three kingdoms, viz., Koguryu in the north, Pekche in the southwest, and Silla in the southeast.

It is said that a Chinese monk, Shun Tao (or Sundo), came to Koguryu in 372 A. D., by royal invitation; another Chinese monk, A Tao, followed soon after. In 375 A. D. the king built two temples, one for each monk. An Indian or Tibetan monk named Marananda took Buddhism to Pekche in 384 A. D.; other monks followed from China and it soon became the state religion. Silla converted last, after a Buddhist monk, Mokucha, cured the royal princess of illness by offering prayers to Buddha and persuaded the king to invite monks from China.

In 668 A. D., the Silla dynasty (lasted 935 A. D.) united Korea, and monks were sent to China to study Buddhism; some went to India. Kyongnu, the capital of Silla, became a flourishing centre of Buddhist culture and trade, attracting merchants from India, Tibet and Iran. I-tsing notes that five Korean monks visited India during the seventh century. The Korean monk, Yui-shih, propagated the "consciousness-only" doctrines of Yogacara Buddhism in the country. Early Sillan art was also influenced by India.

By the eleventh century, Buddhism was flourishing in Korea, but a series of invasions created a feeling on insecurity in the land. At the turn of the century, the crown prince became a monk and went to China to study; on his return he taught the T'ien-t'ai school of Buddhism. The faith spread from the aristocracy to the masses through the efforts of Pu-chao, who introduced Korea to Son (Dhyan, Zen) Buddhism; he edited the catalogue of the Chinese *Tripitaka*, called the *Taejang* in Korean. Buddhism declined towards the end of the fourteenth century when Korea came under Chinese domination. But with its annexation by Japan in 1910, Korean Buddhism recovered ground though Japanese Buddhists attempted to recast Korean Buddhism in conformity with their own version.

Under the Silla Empire, Korean culture made great strides, with the construction of grand cave temples at Sokkulam, southeast of Kyongnu, around the eighth century. Of the 34 Buddhist monasteries in the Diamond Mountains, the greatest is Yu Chomsa, whose unique sculptures depict 53 miniature Buddhas in sitting and standing pose, placed on the roots of an upturned tree. It is said the edifice honours 53 Indian monks who came to Korea centuries ago and pacified hostile dragons (enemies?) by placing an image of Buddha upon each root of the tree.

Koreans excelled incasting bronze bells, embellished with relief decorations of figures and ornaments. Migrants took this art to China and Japan. The temples in China's Shantung province were built on the Korean model. Buddhism broke the aristocracy's monopoly over education by publishing religious literature with explanations, in local languages.

While China gave her language and ideographs to Korea, India contributed Sanskrit and phonetic letters from which syllabaries or alphabets were constructed. The Korean syllabary, *nido*, was a collection of syllables and not a true alphabet; it gave a phonetic value to some of the more common Chinese characters. The Korean alphabet, *unmum* (common language), was invented by the Buddhist scholar monk, Syel-chong. Under the kings of the Yi dynasty, a large number of Buddhist scriptures were translated into Korean.

Japan

Korea introduced Buddhism to Japan sometime in the sixth century when a diplomatic mission from Pekche presented a gold-plated statue of the Buddha, some scriptures and banners to the Japanese court with the message, "Buddha dharma the most excellent of all laws which brings immeasurable benefit to its believers... had been accepted in all lands laying between India and Korea."

Japanese culture is a rich amalgam of Shinto, Confucianism, and Buddhism. Prince Shotoku Taishi (593–621 A. D.) called them parts of the tree of Japanese culture, Shinto being the root or native traditions, Confucianism the trunk and branches of legal and educational institutions and ethical codes, and Buddhism the flower of religion and fruit of spiritual life. He made Buddhism the state religion and invited Korean monks to teach writing, and sciences like astronomy and medicine, and sent students to China to study Buddhism.

The first known Buddhist in Japan is Shiba Tachito, who went as a refugee in 522 A. D. In time, eminent Buddhists emerged from the same family, including the first nun, Tori. She was the greatest artist of the seventh century and cast the main image of the Horyuji Temple at Nara.

The first Buddhist pagodas were built during the regency ofPrince Shotoku (593 – 621 A. D.), along with seminaries, hospitals, dispensaries, and homes for the aged and destitute. The temple of Kokoji was built in 596 A. D. and the temple of Horyuji in 607 A. D.. At Horyuji, the Prince himself explained the Mahayana *sutras*, especially the *Saddharma pundarika* (Lotus of the True Law), the *Vimalakirtinirdesa* and *Srimala – devi – simhanada – sutra*. Horyuji Temple became an important centre of the Yogacara School.

Buddhism triggered the creativity of Japaneseartists and artisans who, patronised by devotees and philanthropists built asylums, hospitals, dispensaries and sponsored painting, sculpture and architecture. The Chinese missionary Kan–jin (754–763 A. D.) organised medical missions and founded botanical gardens. Bodhisena, a Brahmin of Bharadwaja *gotra*, came to Japan in 736 A. D. with Cham and Chinese disciples, and lived there until his death in 760 A. D..

In the Kara Period (708–794 A. D.), Buddhism spread from the capital city to the provinces where devotees endowed religious and philanthropic institutions which soon brought all of Japan under Buddhism. Japanese sculpture and painting flourished and China regularly exported the ideas of different schools of Buddhist thought. The mystic Mantra sect, introduced into China in the eighth century by Subhakarasimha and Amoghavajra, reached Japan in the ninth century and even esoteric sects like the Dharma-lakshana of Asanga, which vanished in India and China, were preserved in the Japanese school of Buddhist philosophy.

Over the next two hundred years, the Japanese developed new and wholly indigenous sects and schools of philosophy and art. In the ninth century, Saicho founded the Tendai sect, and Kukai founded the Shingon sect; both influenced Japanese aristocracy deeply; the military class and populace developed their own schools. In the 12th century, Horen (1133-1212 A. D.) expounded the doctrine of *Sukhavati*, whereby anyone could be saved by faith in the grace of Bodhisattva Amitabha. The Buddha-Amitabha cult spread across temples, accompanied by the image of the Indian saint, Pindola Bharadvaja.

Shinto was transformed when Chika-fusa (1339 A. D.) declared that all Shinto divinities were *avataras* of Buddha. The samurai class embraced the philosophy of Zen (Dhyana), which entered Japan in 1250 A. D. through followers of China's Shan-no (Dhyana) sect.

Japan's encounter with Buddhism made her keen to study the original texts; the Japanese began to study the Sanskrit language and literature. Some very ancient Sanskrit manuscripts are preserved intact in Japanese temples, many of which are much older than those preserved in India. Japanese scholars believe that the arrangement of the Japanese syllabary into fifty phonetic sounds is actually an adaptation of the Sanskrit alphabet, probably by the Buddhist, Bodhisena. Had the Chinese language and script not taken deep roots in Japan before the Indian alphabet could reach her, Japan would have found the Indian script more suitable than the Chinese ideographic characters, as Japanese characters are phonetic like the Devanagari letters. Still, the development of writing led to the blossoming of Japanese literature which was also influenced by Indian stories from epics like the *Mahabharata*.

Several Buddhist deities entered Japan and are still immensely popular, including some Hindu gods who were absorbed in the Buddhist pantheon. These include Indra, god of thunder and king of gods, worshipped in Japan as *Taishakuten* (great King Sakra); Ganesa, worshipped as Sho - ten (holy god). The *naga* is worshipped as a sea-serpent called Ryujin; Hariti and Dakini are also worshipped; and Kubera, god of wealth, is revered as Bishamon. Other Indian deities revered in Japan include Siva; Varuna, the sea god; Sarasvati, the goddess of speech; Viswakarma, the divine architect; and Yama, the god of death. Japanese customs of cremation and ancestor worship were influenced by India and even today many citizens prefer the ceremonies to be performed by Buddhist priests.

Painting, music, dance, including the masked dance, Gigaku, the famous tea ceremony, and popular game, backgammon, are further instances of India's impact on Japanese civilisation.

Ceylon

Ceylon (Sri Lanka) has enjoyed long cultural and political ties with India. Though not geographically part of Southeast Asia, Ceylon was an important transit point for the eastward movement of Indian culture and religions. The country is renowned for its role in the great epic, *Ramayana*, wherein Rama, Prince of Ayodhya, battled and defeated Ravana, King of Lanka, and rescued his wife, Sita.

Historiansconcur that the earliest settlers in the island came from India. The *Mahavamsa* narrates the story of Prince Vijayasimha who came from northern India in the sixth century B. C. , which is generally considered accurate. The early settlers created settlements, introduced the use of iron, created a system of government, and spread Hindu doctrines. Other faiths such as Jain and Ajivika arrived. In the third century B. C. , Asoka sent a mission headed by Mahinda (Mahendra) to Ceylon. The *Mahavamsa* narrates that the King, Devanampiya Tissa (247-207 B. C.), embraced the new faith along with his people. By the time Mahinda left after preaching for twenty-six days at the capital, Anuradhapura, there were already sixty-two monks. Mahinda devoted the next forty-eight years of his life to the island and was responsible for the creation of Sinhalese culture as we know it today.

Later, Asoka later sent his daughter, Sanghamitra, to ordain Queen

Anula and other women who wished to take monastic vows. She brought with her a sprig of the Bodhi Tree under which Gautama Buddha had attained enlightenment; the sacred tree exists to this day. Later, other sacred relics were acquired. A Ceylonese mission returning from Pataliputra brought the alms bowl of the Buddha, which was housed in the Thuparama Dagoba; one of the Buddha's teeth was enshrined in a specially built temple, Dhammachakka. The tooth was in Ceylon when Fa-hsien visited the country in the fifth century.

During the reign of Vattagamani (*circa* 29-17 B. C.), the sacred Pali canon, the *Tripitaka*, till then committed to memory, was written down, a gigantic task involving hundreds of reciters and scribes. The canon survives to this day in Sri Lanka, though the original has been lost to India as a result of medieval upheavals; this gives Ceylon a special status in the Buddhist world.

Until the disruption caused by Portuguese rule in the fifteenth century, Ceylon was closely integrated with India; there were matrimonial alliances with ruling south Indian dynasties, and the Ceylonese alphabet is undoubtedly of Indian origin. Art, iconography, and architecture bear the imprint of India's Amravati, Ajanta, Gupta, and Pallava styles. The country also hosts several important Hindu shrines; Vishnu is popular in Buddhist shrines and is considered a protector deity.

Burma

India and Burma (Myanmar) maintained trade and cultural ties mainly by sea as the land route, though extant from very ancient times, involved highly difficult terrain across the Assam and Manipur hills and the Arakan hill ranges. It is not clear when Buddhism entered the country, but Ceylonese chronicles state that Sona and Uttara, two Asokan missionaries, were dispatched by the Third Buddhist Council to Burma to revive the faith.

Burmese tradition asserts that Buddhism was brought to the country by two Mon merchants, Tapussa and Bhallika, whom Buddha had graced with some hair from his head, which they enshrined on the top of Singuttara Hill, where the famous pagoda, Shwe Dagon, now stands. Chinese chronicles of the third century mention a Buddhist kingdom of over one hundred thousand families and several thousand monks in Lin-Yang in central Burma.

Burmese acknowledge that the foundations of their civilisation and culture were laid through contact with India, specifically with Sakyan migration. Their legends state that Taganng, their first capital, was founded in Upper Burma by Sakyan princes from Kapilavastu; this is also recorded in Chinese chronicles which observe that Buddhism was strong in central Burma and Hinduism in southern Burma.

The *Periplus* mentions Sino-Indian trade with the Sesatai tribes of the north of Burma, between China and Assam. Ptolemy in the second century mentions place names in Sanskrit that have been identified with places in Burma; the ports of Takkola and Vesunga could be Takola and Besynga. He describes the Irrawaddy Delta and mentions Kirrhadia, beyond the mouth of the Ganges, which grew the finest cinnamon; nearby dwelled the Tiladai, identified as the Kiratas mentioned in an inscription at Nagarjunakonda, who lived in Arakan and Lower Burma and were converted to Buddhism by monks from Tambapanna. As cultural contacts matured, Burma derived her script, literature, art, thought, religion, and many material goods from India.

The Burmese people fall into three broad racial categories, viz. the Mon, the Burmese, and the Shan. The Mons made contact by sea with the Telinganas of the Andhra-Pallava region in the first century; Burmese writing and religion is their legacy. The earliest Mon inscription found on a pillar at Lopburi in Thailand is in the Pallava script of the fifth century.

Archaeological discoveries have been slow in Burma as only the Pyu capital site near Prome has been seriously excavated. The earliest relics are fragments of Pali scriptures dating from 500 A. D. and written in a script resembling the Kadamba script of South India of the same period. Later finds at Hmawza include a manuscript of twenty gold leaves and stone statues of the Buddha in Gupta style, with inscriptions in Pyu and Sanskrit. The findings suggest ties between Buddhism from the Andhra-Pallava centres of Amaravati, Nagarjunakonda, Kanchipuram, and Kaveripattinam, all of which are linked to the Buddhaghosa tradition. Theravada Buddhism dominated in Burma though Mahayanism, probably from eastern India, also existed.

The kings of the Pyu dynasty and others bore Indian titles of Varman and Vikrama. Their capital, Sri Ksetra, replicated Indra's city, Sudarsana (also called Amaravati) on the summit of Mount Meru, with 32 main gates and a golden palace at the centre. Conforming to this plan, the Pyu kingdom was divided into 32 provinces. Chinese scholars Hsüan-tsang and I-tsing observed that Pyu was a Buddhist kingdom in the seventh century.

The Hmawza ruins reveal many Buddhist objects along with images of Vishnu, Siva, Ganesa, Brahma, and other Hindu gods. In Prome, ruined stupas dating to the sixth century have been found, some showing influences of contemporary Pallava art of South India and some of the Gupta style of the north. Hinduism and Buddhism thrived in the Mon kingdoms of Pegu (Hamsavati) and Thaton (Suddhammavati); a Hindu dynasty, Sri Dharmarajanujavamsa, ruled Arakan from 600 to 1000 A.D..

Burma's most spectacular monument is theAnanda Temple at Pagan. On its external walls are 1500 plaques illustrating the *Jataka* tales, each with an inscription in Pali or Mon; the inner aisles contain 80 niches with sculptures of the early life of the Buddha, made by Indian artists or artists following Indian styles. Another great temple at Pagan is the temple of Thatbyinnyu, which reflects the style of contemporary temples in North India.

Near the end of the twelfth century, a schism occurred as monks of Capata established an independent Ceylonese order (Theravada) and controlled Burmese Buddhism for the next two hundred years. Commercial ties with India remained brisk; an inscription at Pagan alludes to a Vishnu temple built by Nanadesi merchants and to a gift made to the temple by Malabari merchants in the thirteenth century.

As Buddhism came under stress in India, several Buddhist monks migrated to Burma, taking Pala art and Tantric Buddhism with them. The Indo-Burmese link became feeble after northern India fell to Turki-Afghan rulers. By the end of the thirteenth century, the Mongols captured Pagan and threw Burma into prolonged anarchy. Stability returned under Dhaddacedi in the second half of the fifteenth century; he restored the Sangha to its former prestige and power and Buddhism's ascendancy in Burmese society was never again challenged.

Thailand

Siam (Thailand) is an ancient land which came under the Thai people after they were driven out of their kingdom, Nanchao, in Yunnan in southwestern China, by Kubilai Khan's army in 1253 A. D. . Nanchao was open to Indian influences from early on, as it lay on a well-travelled route between India and China. Two bells with Buddhist inscriptions in Chinese and Sanskrit, dated around the eleventh century, have been found at Nanchao. There were Indian settlements at Nanchao and Thai folklore mentions Brahman advisers to the government.

Siam received its first civilisation from the Brahmins of India and then from the merchants of the Malabar and Coromandel coasts. Archaeological remnants of its Hindu past survive in its former capitals, Savankhalok, Sukhokai and Lopburi. Later, it received the Ceylonese or southern Pali Buddhism from Cambodia, and remained within India's cultural sphere of influence until the arrival of the Portuguese in the 16th century. It derived its sacred language, civil institutions, writing, arts, and literature from India. In the 13th century, Brahmin teachers adapted Indian scripts in use in the land to develop the Thai alphabet, which became the prototype of the present alphabet.

The most important Thai kingdom in Yunnan was called Gandhara, a part of which was also known as Videharajya (name of the capital of King Janaka, father of Sita, of the epic *Ramayana*). The capital was called Mithila (name the Janaka's kingdom), and the king, addressed as "Maharaja," claimed descent from Asoka. Nanchao's alphabet is of Indian origin and its folklore states that Avalokitesvara came from India and brought the people into the Buddhist fold. Southeast Asian rulers often assumed lengthy Sanskrit titles and founded cities, such as Ayutthaya in Thailand, after Ayodhya of the epic, *Ramayana*.

Thailand's most popular temple, the Erawan shrine, is dedicated to Brahma. In the year 2016, Thailand celebrated the god Ganesh's birthday festival at eight places in the country (5-11 September) along with the 70th anniversary of the accession to the throne of His Majesty the King (who passed away shortly thereafter), and commemorated its historical, social and cultural ties with India.

The Philippines

The Philippines and Formosa (Taiwan), which were once parts of the Srivijaya empire, also came under the sway of Indian culture; for The Philippines this continued under the Sailendras. In the fourteenth century, the Hinduised Majapahit empire included Formosa and New Guinea in its dominion.

Indian cultural influences possibly reached The Philippines around the first millennium B. C. The country was near the sea route between India and East Asia, and was likely visited by Indian sailors and traders. Excavations in the late 1920s suggest that all artifacts found, including pottery, iron implements and capons such as knives and axes, glass beads and bangles and beads of semi-precious stones (carnelian, agate, amethyst), came from India over long trade ties pre-dating the Christian era, and match objects found in prehistoric South India. American anthropologist Alfred L. Kroeber observes that even the remotest tribes in The Philippines bear traces of Indian culture.

The worship of *Bathala*, supreme god of the ancient Tagalog, shows Indian influence as the term originates from the Sanskrit *Bhattara* (honourable, noble lord); such inputs permeate the religion and culture. Many religious relics found in the island of Mactan and in eastern Mindanao show Indian influence; two images of Hindu deities have been unearthed. One image of solid gold reflects the influence of Hindu – Javanese art of the tenth century. Indian influence is visible in the alphabet of the major languages of the country, and lingers in the scripts and vocabularies of the more remote tribes.

Philippine literature, mythology, and folklore bear traces of Indian culture. The Maranaw epic, *Darangan*, is based on the *Mahabharata* story of Arjuna extracting water from a rock with an arrow, for the dying Bhishma.

Indian influence permeating through Sumatra brought the calendar, Buddhist folklore, and the syllabic alphabets to The Philippines; Java contributed the advanced arts of metal work, jewellery, and weaving. Modes of dressing, such as the *sarong* and *putong* (turban), personal ornamentation, and old names for money (*salapi*, *siping*, *gatang*, *tanso*, *pilak*, and *bakal*) are reputedly of Indian origin. The lotus design on Philippine weapons clearly derives from India.

Emerging world order

There is little doubt that the emerging world order is distinct from the New World Order once passionately strategised by American neo-cons, who were certain that the collapse of the Soviet Union in 1991 would result in the linear rise of American hegemony. America did enjoy a brief period of unipolarity during which it wreaked havoc on Yugoslavia and much of the Middle East, till the global financial crisis of 2008 exposed the hollowness of the Western economic model, and the rise of a multipolar Asia, accompanied by a weakened Europe took the sheen off the universal hegemon. Washington's master strategist, Zbigniew Brzezinski, who wrote the blueprint for U. S. supremacy in his book *The Grand Chessboard: American Primacy and Its Geostrategic Imperatives* (1997), recently conceded that the imperial vision has failed. America will no longer prevail across the Middle East and Asia.

India under Prime Minister Narendra Modi is paying special attention to East Asia as part of its Act East policy, an extension of former Prime Minister Atal Bihari Vajpayee's Look East policy, for increased trade and connectivity. While China pursues the Belt and Road and Maritime Silk Route projects, India is invigorating its sea and land links with the region via Project Mausam and the BIMSTEC grouping (Bangladesh, Myanmar, Sri Lanka, Thailand, Bhutan and Nepal, besides India).

In recent years, the Ocean has become a major and even a contested resource, whether in terms of fishing rights or in terms of each nation's share of continental shelf and undersea resources in the Exclusive Economic Zone under the UN Law of the Seas. Meanwhile, the Indian Ocean is of even more critical importance than in the past. Transportation by water is the cheapest form of transport, particularly for bulk freight and oil. As much as 90 per cent of global commerce and 65 per cent of all oil travels by sea. Nearly 50 per cent of the world's container traffic and 70 per cent of the traffic in petroleum products transits the Indian Ocean.

India uses oil for over 33 per cent of her energy needs, of which 70 per cent is imported; she imports coal from ten countries, (including Mozambique, South Africa, Indonesia and Australia). China, Japan, South Korea and the rest of Asia-Pacific rely on oil supplies that come via the Strait of Hormuz and transit via the Malacca Strait into the region. The security of these sea-lanes is vital. Even in the crucial arena of cyberspace, 95 per cent of internet traffic is transmitted via underwater cables.

India holds the strategic position in the Indian Ocean and can help ensure open access to the maritime corridors which are critical for trade on both sides of the ocean. The Indian ethos of peaceful commercial and cultural exchanges is relevant at a time when some nations are trying to impose inequitable terms of trade on other parts of the world. What the world needs for mutual material prosperity is a stable multi-polar world in which the main non-Western powers – Russia, China, India and Iran – have a place of honour. Attempts to distort the balance of power via economic sanctions on some nations have the potential to disturb world peace and are likely to be resisted. At the same time, trade in multiple currencies must be encouraged. Finally, the major Asian powers must ensure that their bilateral disputes are not exploited by other powers.

21ˢᵗ Century Challenges and Opportunities for Modernity in East Asia

Senuri Samalka Samarasinghe[*]

Introduction

Though its origin cannot be traced to a static point of time in history, modernity is a concept which became prominent in international politics after the end of the Second World War. States with communist economic systems and democratic political structures experienced the characteristics of modernity such as urbanization, sexual freedom, standardized education system, technological development, communication advancements and employment of women in all levels of businesses. Along with these characteristics, modernity penetrated into other regions across the globe too from its Western birthplace. Consequently, East Asia today has become the non-western region with the highest levels of development and modernization to compete with the West. Industrialization, urbanization, globalization, advancements of community and technology, and capitalist expansion were the main factors that contributed to the spread of modernity in East Asia. Meanwhile, world's regions are in a state of change. Similarly, East Asia's modernity is neither static nor unchallenged. Within that context, this research would analyze the opportunities and challenges that affect the face and character of modernity in East Asia in the

---

[*] Senuri Samalka Samarasinghe, Research and Lecturer in International Relations Bandaranaike Centre for international Studies (BCIS), Colombo, Sri Lanka.

twenty-first century, in an International Relations theoretical and conceptual framework.

Part 1　Opportunities for modernity in East Asia

1. Regional cooperation

Regional cooperation is a sphere through which East Asian modernity could be enhanced. Association for South East Asian Nations was formed in 1967 during the Cold War. Even though the Cold War period witnessed the regional states split into two polarized power camps, end of the Cold War lifted the barriers to regional cooperation. Therefore, ASEAN membership was further enlarged. The signing of Bangkok Declaration in 1967 (also known as the ASEAN Declaration), Declaration of the ASEAN as a Zone of Peace, Freedom and Neutrality in 1971, ASEAN Free Trade Area in 1992, formation of the ASEAN Regional Forum in 1994, East Asia Summit in 2005, ASEAN Charter in 2008, ASEAN Community in 2015 are among the milestones in the development of regional cooperation efforts under ASEAN.

ASEAN can be considered a model for regional cooperation. Functionalism, a major approach in International Relations advocates the benefits for countries that could be gained of integration and regional cooperation. While Realism advocates military security and focuses on high politics like balance of power and maintaining hegemonic stability, Functionalism advocates maintaining cooperative and collaborative relations while focusing on low politics such as economic security and social progress. Realists assert the fact that conflicts are inevitable, whereas Functionalists believe that peace could be achieved through consensus. ASEAN was formed in 1967 in this backdrop of functional integration. The major aim of ASEAN at its inception was to establish multilateral regional cooperation to reach common consensus in order to prevent regional conflicts and to establish peace, security and stability.

Apart from regional organizations like ASEAN, parallel sub-regional and trans-regionalcooperation mechanism too have been successful in East Asia. For example, APEC (Asia Pacific Economic Cooperation) was launched in early 1990s and The Greater Tumen Initiative was launched in 1991 (Zhenmin 2012). The latter serves as a platform for North East Asian sub-regional economic cooperation. The Greater Mekong Sub-regional Cooperation (GMS), launched in 1992, ensures cooperation in fields such as telecommunication, transportation, tourism, environment protection, human resource development, energy, trade and investment (Zhenmin 2012). Furthermore, Asia-Europe Meeting launched in 1996 ensures dialogue and cooperation between Asia and Europe (Zhenmin 2012).

2. Geo-economic vitality and high economic growth

Geo-economic vitality of the region, constituted by relatively high financial growth and economic stability serves as an opportunity through which Eats Asian modernity can be enhanced. ASEAN has proved to be an economic powerhouse. If all the ten ASEAN member states are taken together, ASEAN constitutes the world's seventh largest economy and the fourth largest economy by the year 2050. The total population is above 600 million and it is more than the population of the United States, North America and the European Union taken together. (Thompson & Tomby et al 2014). The vast population is an asset as it serves as the region's dynamic labour force. Most importantly, half of the ASEAN population is young and educated.

East Asia is neither a monolithic market nor the economic capability of the regional states is monolithic. The contribution of each individual regional state to the overall GDP of the region is not the same. For example, Indonesia is contributing 40% to the ASEAN GDP, whereas Laos, Brunei and Cambodia remain as the smallest contributors (Thompson & Tomby et al 2014). Singapore's economy is thirty times larger than that of Laos and fifty times larger than that of Cambodia or Myanmar. Also, Singapore's economy is considered more mature than the sophisticated Western economies like Canada or the United States of America (Thompson & Tomby et al 2014). Even though the East Asian states have different developmental phases, all of them do possess immense economic growth potential. As a result, the region has shown a steady economic growth especially after the year 2000.

East Asia's economic and financial stability is well proven in the strong vitality which the region has shown in both Asian Financial Crisis of 1997 and the International Financial Crisis of 2008. Asian Financial Crisis was a negative effect of globalization. East Asia is a region highly exposed to globalization because it heavily relies on global economy for resources, technology and markets. This heavy dependence on external global trade has proven the regional vulnerable to effects of globalization. Nevertheless, East Asia successfully responded to the challenges of global financial crises. In response to the crises, China, Japan, Republic of Korea, and ASEAN led Chiang Mai Initiative (CMI) which later became a multilateral mechanism (Zhenmin 2012). CMI is an initiative which proved regional integration as a defensive measure against the challenge of globalization.

3. China's influential role in East Asia

China's influential role in East Asia as an active advocate and contributor is another area through which East Asia's development and modernity can be advanced. China's East Asian policy is of three major aspects; politics, economy and military (Sørensen 2010). China's role in the region can be explained in light of Neo-liberal Institutionalism in International Relations. Neo-liberal Internationalists argue that even though the international order is anarchic, international politics involve not only conflict but cooperation too. States with identical desires join together for cooperation. Even the states with competing interests and desires try to make room for compromise and adjustment. As a result, politics involve both friendly as well as hostile relationships (Dyke 1966). The validity of this claim made by Neo-liberal Institutionalism is well visible in China's foreign policy principle of "common development". As stated in the book "*Xi Jinping: the Governance of China*", China tries to maintain a peaceful foreign policy based on the shared development goals and interests of its neighbors, in order to achieve sustainable cooperation in economic development with mutual benefits among all (2014).

In order to promote the principle of "common development", China has deepened its economic and trade cooperation with East Asia. China supported East Asian countries to overcome their financial difficulties by maintaining its currency stable during the 1997 Asian Financial Crisis (Zhenmin 2012). The nation is also currently the biggest trading partner of ASEAN since the inception of China- ASEAN Free Trade Agreement. China in fact is the first country to initiate a free trade agreement with ASEAN. It is hopeful about a trilateral free trade agreement between China, Japan and South Korea. China has further initiated large scale multilateral projects in East Asia such as the Greater Meckong River sub-region project, Tumen River Regional Development Initiative and the Bohai Economic Circle in North-East Asia (Mingjiang 2010).

Meanwhile, China's role in East Asian cooperation does not limit only to trade and economic sphere. Yet China is a deep advocate of the region's security cooperation. It is the first country to support South East Asia Nuclear Weapon Free Zone Treaty and the first country to join Treaty of Amity and Cooperation in South East Asia (Zhenmin 2012). China also has an active plan in promoting regional cooperation in non-traditional security. For example, in 2000, China signed an action plan with ASEAN to counter drug trafficking in the region (Mingjiang 2010). Also in 2004, China and ASEAN signed a MOU on non-traditional security cooperation (Mingjiang 2010).

Different theoretical schools have different perceptions on China's influential role in East Asia. Neo-liberalists argue that China's rise is an opportunity rather than a threat for the region (as quoted in Sørensen 2010). Similarly, Social Constructivists, who focus on cognitive process of China's socialization in East Asia, hold the view that China's role in East Asia is positive and proactive as China has changed its previous negative attitude towards the region through the process of social learning (Mingjiang 2010). However, Realists argue that China's rise in the region signifies the nation's aspiration to gain regional hegemony by enhancing its political economic and military strength as well as by exercising an intervening role in regional issues and conflicts.

4. Soft power potential of regional states

The potential for soft power projection and public diplomacy is a great asset for regional states. With the relatively stable increasing economic might of the region, East Asian countries look forward to build and enhance their soft power projection. Soft power is a way of achieving and promoting national power through cultural attractiveness, both intentionally and unintentionally by states (Lee & Melissen). Joseph Nye, in his book "*Soft Power: The Means to Success in World Politics*", states that soft power is the means by which countries win via attraction rather than coercion (as quoted in Thinking Taiwan). Accordingly, soft power is to get the world's attention by non-military means. Joseph Nye further gives prominence to soft power as he argues that it is one of the three main sources of national power which are relevant in different degrees in different relationships. According to him, the three main sources of national power are military, economic and soft power (Lee & Melissen). Wang Hunning, who has published the first article on China's soft power, identifies main resources of soft power. They are culture, foreign policies, political values and ideas (Glaser & Murphy). China, Japan, South Korea and Taiwan are among the countries that have strong soft power capabilities in East Asia.

There are two schools of thoughts that hold views on China's soft power. One school of thought, including the Chinese leaders believe culture as the core of China's soft power (Glaser & Murphy). Accordingly, Taoism, Confucianism and Buddhism are promoted within the country and across the borders. Confucius institutes are established overseas with the aim of disseminating Chinese culture and language. International exchanges and cultural events such as China Year in France in 2003, China Year in Russia in 2007, Beijing Olympics in 2008 and Shanghai Expo in 2010 are examples (Glaser & Murphy). Under the twenty first century Maritime Silk Road and Silk Road Economic Belt, China invests in infrastructure development of countries of Asia, East Asia, Middle East, Africa, Central and Eastern Europe. Multilateral projects across the Maritime Silk Road such as Asian Infrastructure Investment Bank (AIIB) and Free Trade Area of the Asia Pacific are China's efforts on soft power projection.

On the other hand, the second school of thought believes that the core of the country's soft power is politics. Within this context of reinforcing the nation's political power, soft power can be used as a tool of foreign policy. Among the political means of achieving soft power lie in China's strengths of international institution building, agenda setting, mobilization of coalitions and participation in multilateral diplomacy, overseas assistance programs, and peacekeeping operations (Glaser & Murphy).

Japan as a nation has a strong soft power might in East Asia. The closing ceremony of Rio Summer Olympics in 2016, which was named as the Tokyo Show was a great showpiece of the country's soft power projection. (Foreign affairs) Modern Japan's art, pop culture, technology, cinema are considered major sources of Japan's soft power.

Taiwan too competes with the other regional giants in order to gain the attention and the attraction of the rest of the world. Taiwan is a country in diplomatic isolation due to "One-China" policy. The country has diplomatic relations with only 22 countries and it is represented only in 57 countries in its consular service (Thinking Taiwan). Therefore, Taiwan finds soft power as the alternative to achieve significance in global affairs, to maintain a distinct identity in the Asia Pacific region and to confidently compete with China. Taiwan promotes its soft power by commercially important globally recognized brands such as Giant, Din Tai Fung and HTC Corp (Thinking Taiwan) Taiwanese arts and culture have spread across Asia via TV, music and movies; including the famous Cloud Gate Dance Theatre (Thinking Taiwan).

South Korea is a country that has set the example that hard power only is not adequate for a country's growth and prosperity; yet soft power too should be developed to further patrol a its growth. The nation's cultural exports are highly consumed all over the world (The Economist). Amidst South Korea's hard military capabilities, which have the potential to compete with the world's leading military powers, the nation promotes its soft power via dramas, movies, pop music and food. Scholars believe that South Korea will surpass Japan in the near future as the trendsetter of soft power in Asia (Nye 2009).

Part 2   Challenges for modernity in East Asia

1. Institutional deficiencies

Institutional deficiencies of ASEAN are a major challenge for the region's modernity in the twenty first century. One deficiency is that ASEAN Secretariat is understaffed and underfunded. It is due to the reason that all the member states have to pay a similar amount of payment. So the amount which is affordable to the slowest growing economy is the amount for all the other states too. Meanwhile, scholars argue that ASEAN member states give priority to keep ties with China rather than ensuring their sustainable contribution to ASEAN. As a result, a division has taken place within the regional organization between the member states that have pro-Chinese standpoints and those who do not have pro-Chinese standpoints. Moreover, Ambassador Liu Zhenmin argues that ASEAN cooperation mechanisms such as East Asia Summit, ASEAN 10+1 and ASEAN 10+3 are informal in nature, so they need to be more binding and efficient in order to effectively carry out the provisions of these initiatives (2012).

2. Intra-state conflicts

Intra-state conflicts are another major present day challenge in East Asia. The global trend of world politics is the gradual decline of inter-state conflicts after the end of the Cold War and the increase of intra-state conflicts. Internal conflicts take the form of violent civilian power struggle, ethnic conflicts, civil wars, revolutions, insurgencies, military coups and militarized ideological campaigns (Brown 1996). East Asian region is not an exception to this trend of increasing conflicts within states. As an area highly affected by modernization, the region remains vulnerable to internal conflicts. Samuel P. Huntington, in his book Political Order in Changing Societies, argues that modernization and economic growth cause a dramatic increase of internal conflicts (1968). Factors like urbanization, literacy, education, and mass media add better life standard to the lives of people and that lead people to develop more aspirations about life (Huntington 1968). If those wants are not met, people express their protest to the governing bodies through violent uprisings.

The main conflict affected regional states in the twenty first century are Myanmar, Laos, Philippines and Thailand. Conflicts in Myanmar are mainly characterized by communist insurgencies from the Burmese communist party and separatist disputes from ethnic and territorial groups living in the country. Laos has been affected by the conflict between the government and the United Laos National Liberation Front (ULNLF) since 1989. Large scale illegal drug trade is further patrolling the internal conflict. As a result, Laos today remains one of the world's poorest countries. With a per capita GDP of US $ 11.75, it is considered the world's fourth poorest country (Bercovitch & Derouen 2011). Internal conflicts in the Philippines too take the form of protracted conflicts. They are mainly between the Filipino government and the extremist religious groups. Extremist religious groups include Moro National Liberation Front (MNLF), who fight to establish the Islamic state in Mindanao and Sulu Archipelago, Huk group, who carry out guerrilla warfare, and New Peoples' Army (NPA), who carry out Maoist style communist insurgencies (Bercovitch & Derouen 2011). Conflicts in Thailand are mainly by extremist separatist groups operating in Southern Thailand. They are Pattani United Liberation Organization (PULO), Barison Revolusi Nasional (BRN), and Gerakan Mujahideen Islam Pattani (GMIP) (Bercovitch & Derouen 2011).

3. Territorial disputes

A main discourse in the current international politics is that inter-state conflicts have disappeared and intra-state conflicts have emerged to the forefront in the international politics after the end of the Cold War. It is true that inter-state conflicts have become less frequent as states have slowly but surely resolved outstanding boundary disputes (Zartman 2009). Yet, they have not totally disappeared. William Zartman identifies four types of resource oriented conflicts; territorial disputes, allocation disputes, access conflicts and internal asset struggles (Zartman 2009). Twenty first century East Asia mainly witness territorial disputes out of these conflicts.

Territorial disputes take two forms. They are competition over the ownership of contested border zones and offshore areas. An example for the dispute over contested border zones is that between Cambodia and Thailand. Though in the less violent form, the dispute still continues. Even though there is a decline in the boundary disputes, conflicts over offshore territories still remain prominent. A conspicuous example is the South China Sea Conflict. Tensions are growing between China and other countries of the South East Asia and the risk of it becoming a military clash is escalating. The South China Sea is rich with oil, gas reserves as well as it serves as a maritime exclusive economic zones (EEZs) with valuable fisheries and undersea resources. As a result, maritime disputes have evolved due to the clashing territorial claims made by China, Vietnam, Taiwan and the Philippines over the South China Sea islands such as Spratlys, Paracels, Scarborough, Kurils and Natuna islands.

Furthermore, tensions between Japan and China over the contested islands of Senkaku/Diaoyu in the East China Sea are escalating. The conflict has historical and resource related roots. It has been building steadily since 2010. If unresolved, the conflict has the scope to develop into a direct military clash between the two Asian giants. Therefore, the view held by Realists that international politics involve a completion for power to promote national interests within the context of anarchic international order can be well applied to the backdrop of East Asia's territorial disputes. These tensions hinder the economic growth and prosperity of East Asia while building mistrust and lack of cooperation among the neighbors.

4. Extra regional power influence

The United States of America is considered the main extra regional power that has hegemonic aspirations in East Asia. The U.S. foreign policy towards East Asia mainly focuses on strengthening traditional alliances with the regional states, working with the multilateral regional mechanisms, building up trade relations and enhancing trade ties trough Korea-U.S. Free Trade Agreement and the Trans Pacific Partnership (Council on Foreign Relations). However, Choi Kang, president of the Institute of Foreign Policy and National Security (IFANS), Korea National Diplomatic Academy, states that the U.S. has no comprehensive policy towards the East Asian region its policies are rather selective and issue based. This has aggravated the skeptical attitude of the regional states towards the U.S. policy. Scholars argue that China hold the view that the U.S. has a policy of encirclement to achieve hegemony in the region. This has led the regional states to make a strategic choice between China and the United States. (Council on Foreign Relations)

5. Non-traditional security threats

Threats posed by non-military sources are called non-traditional security threats (NTS). Their main characteristics are they are transnational in nature, therefore cross sovereign states borders. They cannot be countered by military means like conflicts and wars. Traditional security threats give birth to non-traditional security threats and vice versa. Non-traditional security threats are posed mainly by non-state actors. Neo-liberal Institutionalists argue that the impact of globalization is not only on states, but on all the societal actors including non-state actors such as organized groups and individuals (Sørensen 2010). This hyper-globalist approach gives the rationale for the reasons as to why transnational organized groups are active and dominating in the East Asian region. The other major transnational threat phenomenon which challenge the peace and stability in the region are drug and narcotics trafficking, infectious diseases, environmental degradation, natural disasters, human trafficking, piracy, terrorism, arms trafficking, money laundering, international economic crimes, and cyber-crimes.

Conclusion

It is not adequate to consider the future of East Asian modernity only in terms of economic development and industrial advancements. Yet, opportunities and challenges of non-economic and non-military nature should be taken into account as decisive determinants of East Asian modernity. It is noteworthy that opportunities and challenges are interlinked with each other and each have a causal effect on the other. For example, even though high economic growth and modernization seems to be an opportunity, it does cause a dramatic increase in internal conflicts. Scholars also see the potential of China factor in the region to be a cause to hinder regional cooperation in the long run even though it is considered beneficial in the short run. Moreover, the face and character of each opportunity and challenge will not remain static or unchanged. The impact which each factor has on the region is changing and broadening. The role of each factor becomes dynamic and complex. For example, even though Japan has a strong soft power potential to affect world politics, its inability to project military power due to post-war restrictions limits the country's capability to aspire a much larger role in global affairs. Within this complex context, present day challenges are crucial and they need to be addressed cooperatively to determine the future stability of the region. A common approach to combat non-traditional security threats is timely and needed. A common regional policy towards extra regional power seekers in the region like the Unite States should be geared towards economic cooperation and security cooperation via a common pledge among all the member states to minimize security dilemma between the U. S. and regional giants like China. Meanwhile, East Asia's scope and ability to achieve dispute settlement though peaceful means should not be ignored or underestimated. For example, Conflict in Aceh, Indonesia was settled with a peaceful resolution in August 2005. Despite a four month dispute between the Indians and Muslims, Malaysia has not experienced a major conflict since the end of the Cold War. Thus, challenges of East Asia can be developed into opportunities, and prevailing opportunities should be further strengthened to prevent the deterioration of their potentials. East Asia will face larger opportunities and greater challenges in the future due to rapid modernization. The most pragmatic recommendation should be to gear the East Asian regional community achieve not a less competitive regional environment, due to the validity of the Realist arguments that conflicts and competition are inevitable, yet to achieve a less violent, less dangerous regional environment based on mutual cooperation and mutual benefits on their journey along the path of modernity in the twenty first century.

References

Argerich, J. A. Study of Modernity, [Online], Available from: http://www.immi.se/tidskrifter/invandraren/inva982/ modernity.htm. [Accessed 06th October 2016].

Bercovitch, J. & Derouen JR, K. (ed.) (2011) *Unravelling Internal conflict in East Asia and the Pacific*, UK: Lexington Books. [Online], Available from: https://books.google.lk/books? id = aFrp−X73BrwC&printsec = frontcover&source=gbs_ ge_ summary_ r&cad = 0#v = onepage&q&f = false. [Accessed 08th October 2016].

Brown, M. E. (1996), *Internal Dimensions of Internal Conflict*, Cambridge: Centre for Science and International Affairs, Massachusetts.

Business dictionary, *What is modernity*, [Online] Available from: http://www.businessdictionary.com/definition/ modernity.html. [Accessed 15th October 2016].

Council on foreign Relations, *A Changing East Asia and U. S. Foreign Policy*. (2012) [Online], Available from: http://www.cfr.org/south−korea/changing − east − asia − us − foreign − policy/p28385. [Accessed 07th October 2016].

Council on Foreign Relations, *Foreign Affairs journal*, [Online], Available from: https://www.foreignaffairs.com/articles/ china/2015 − 06 − 16/china−s−soft−power−push http://thediplomat.com/2016/08/tokyo−2020−and−japans−soft−power/. [Accessed 01st October 2016].

Dyke, V. V. (1966), *International Politics*, 2nd ed, New York: Meredith Publishing Company.

Glaser, B. S. & Murphy, M. E. Soft Power with Chinese Characteristics, *Chinese soft power and its implications for the United States*, [Online] Available from: https://csis − prod. s3. amazonaws. com/s3fs − public/legacy _ files/files/media/csis/pubs/090310_ chinesesoftpower_ _ chap2. pdf. [Accessed 04th October 2016].

Huntington, S. P. (1968) *Political Order in Changing Societies*, New Haven: Ayel University Press.

Lee, S. J. and Melissen, J. Public diplomacy and soft power in East Asia, *Palgrave Macmillan Series in Global Public Diplomacy*, [Online], Available from: http://www.palgraveconnect.com/pc/doifinder/ view/10.1057/9780230118447. [Accessed 13th October 2016].

Lowly institute for international policy, *South China Sea*, (2016), [Online], Available from: https://www.lowyinstitute.org/issues/south−china−sea. [Accessed 09th October 2016].

Minjiang, L. (2010) Cooperation for Competition: China's Approach to Regional Security in East Asia, *Security Politics in East Asia and Europe* [Online], Available from: http://www.kas.de/upload/dokumente/ 2010/06/PolDi-Asien_ Panorama_ 02-2010/Panorama_ 2-2010_ SecurityPolitics_ Li.pdf. [Accessed 8th October 2016].

Nye, J.S. (2009) South Korea's Growing Soft Power, *Project Syndicate*, [Online], Available from: https://www.project-syndicate.org/commentary/south-korea-s-growing-soft-power? barrier = true. [Accessed 03rd October 2016].

Smith, S.A. (2013) April 08, A Sino-Japanese Clash in the East China Sea, *Council on Foreign Relations*, [Online] Available from: http://www.cfr.org/japan/sino-japanese-clash-east-china-sea/p30504. [Accessed 05th October 2016].

Sørensen, C.T.N. (2010), China's Role in East Asia, *University of Copenhagen*, [Online], Available from: http://www.eascdu.org/eascdu-content/uploads/2014/07/China%E2%80%99s_ Role_ in_ East_ Asia.pdf. [Accessed 04th October 2016].

The Economist, *South Korea's Soft Power*,(2014) August 09, [Online], Available from: http://www.economist.com/news/books - and - arts/ 21611039- how - really - uncool - country - became - tastemaker - asia - soap - sparkle-and-pop. [Accessed 09th October 2016].

Thinking Taiwan, *Taiwan's Soft Power: A Hard Sell.* [Online] Available from: http://thinking-taiwan.com/taiwans-soft-power-a-hard-sell/. [Accessed 02nd October 2016].

Thompson, F. and Tonby, O. (2014) Understanding ASEAN: Seven things you need to know, *McKinsey & Company*, [Online], Available from: http://www.mckinsey.com/industries/public - sector/our - insights/understanding-asean-seven-things-you-need-to-know. [Accessed 06th October 2016].

Xi Jinping: The Governance of China, 1st ed, 2014, China: Foreign Languages Press, Beijing.

Zartman, I.W. (ed.) (2009), *Imbalance of Power*, USA: Lynne Rienner Publishers.

Zhenmin, L. (2012), October 24, East Asia Cooperation – Challenges and Opportunities [Online] Available from: http://www.china-un.ch/eng/hom/t982239.htm. [Accessed 20th October 2016].

朝鲜儒者李栗谷的《老子》解

蔡振丰[*]

一　前言

李珥（1536—1584），字叔献、见龙，号栗谷、石潭、愚斋，后世称为栗谷先生，是畿湖学派的宗主，也是朝鲜朱子学"主气论"的代表人物。李珥著有《醇言》[①]一书，是朝鲜时代（1392—1910）第一本《老子》注解书。由于朝鲜以朱子学为立国的精神依据，且将佛、老视为异端的思想，因此《醇言》的成书就具有耐人寻味的意义。为了说明《醇言》在朝鲜时代学术发展上的意义，本文尝试由朝鲜王朝何以视佛、老为异端以及李珥以何种诠释观注解《老子》、希望达成何种学术目的等问题出发，论述《醇言》一书的传世意义。

二　朝鲜初期将老子与佛氏等同看待

朝鲜王朝是由高丽守门下侍中李成桂（1335—1408）推翻高丽王朝所建立的国家，而高丽后期的腐败也与佛教势力庞大阻碍政治、经济、文化发展之因素有关。如执政阶级崇信佛教，除了在政治上受到佛教僧侣的影响外，免除佛寺的租税劳役，又赠予大量的土地，也造成财政的恶化；而庶民阶级在接受佛教的果报思想后，也增长了"现世求福"的迷信倾向。[②]

---

[*]　蔡振丰，台湾大学中国文学系教授。
[①]　以下所论《醇言》文本，主要依据서울시:지식 을 만드는 지식，2010 年之《醇言=순언》。
[②]　参见최영성著：《한국유학통사韩国儒学通史》（上）（首尔，심산출판사，2006 年），页310。

针对高丽王朝因崇信佛教所造成的政经困局，朝鲜建国的规划者郑道传（三峰，1342—1398）有《佛氏杂辨》之著作，借批判佛教而企图以儒教作为新国家的意识形态。

郑道传的《佛氏杂辨》以佛教的"虚无""寂灭""悟修"对照儒教的"虚有""寂感""知行"，①认为佛教是无根之学，儒教所论的"太极"或"理"才能解释天地的创造本源。②这种说法与朱子（1130—1200）颇有相合，③而其《心问天答》《心气理》也吸收了《朱子大全》及《朱子语类》中程朱理学的说法而展开了斥佛论述。由于郑道传是主道政变的一等功臣，他在朝鲜初期掌握政权，尊崇朱子学且严格地排斥佛释之说，使朝鲜士人在讳言佛释之外，也避讳老庄思想，以免遭受朝廷安以"斯文乱贼"的罪名。如活动于成宗（1457—1494）和明宗（1534—1560）的李彦迪（晦斋，1491—1533）论及异端时，即将佛、老连言，而论及儒者所言的"太极"乃强调"太极"是"道之本体"，"非若老氏之出无入有、释氏之所谓空也"。④

李彦迪之后，李珥的《栗谷全书》也反对"惑世之术"的异端之教，⑤但其所谓"异端"似乎并不包括老子之学，而将重点放在以禅伪儒的陆九渊（象山，1139—1193）之学上。故《栗谷全书》卷20《圣学辑要·修己第二·穷理章第四》于《论语》"子曰：攻乎异端，斯害也已"条下，引真德秀（西山，1178—1235）"老氏所该者众，无为无欲，近理

---

① 郑道传《三峯集》卷9〈佛氏杂辨·儒释同异之辨〉言："此之虚，虚而有；彼之虚，虚而无。此之寂，寂而感；彼之寂，寂而灭。此曰知行，彼曰悟修。此之知，知万物之理，具于吾心也；彼之悟，悟此心本空，无一物也。"

② 《佛氏杂辨·儒释同异之辨》言："盖未有天地万物之前，毕竟先有太极，而天地万物之理，已浑然具于其中。"

③ 如《朱子语类》卷126"释氏"言："释老称其有见，只是见得个空虚寂灭。真是虚，真是寂静处，不知他所谓见者见个甚底？"

④ 李彦迪《晦斋集》卷5《答忘机堂第一书》言："夫所谓太极者，乃斯道之本体、万化之领要，而子思所谓天命之性者也。盖其冲漠无朕之中，万象森然已具。天之所以覆，地之所以载，日月之所以照，鬼神之所以幽，风雷之所以变，江河之所以流，性命之所以正，伦理之所以著，本末上下，贯乎一理，无非实然而不可易者也。周子所以谓之无极者，正以其无方所无形状：以为在无物之前而未尝不立于有物之后；以为在阴阳之外而未尝不行于阴阳之中；以为通贯全体，无乎不在，则又初无声臭影响之可言也。非若老氏之出无入有、释氏之所谓空也。"

⑤ 见《栗谷全书》卷3《疏箚一·谏院陈时事疏》。

之言，虽君子有取焉"、"皆吾圣人之所有也"之言，① 以表明老子之学非不可取，而论及禅学、陆学则有"佛氏之害，如外寇之侵突；陆氏之害，如奸臣之误国"之断语。② 崇尚朱子学的李珥对异端的看法为何偏离了朱子佛老并称的脉络，而对老子抱有好感？这可能与他的学术兴趣及对《老子》的诠释观点有关。

三　李珥的学思历程及其对《老子》"无为"的解释

李珥在师从李滉（退溪，1501—1570）之前，曾于十九岁在金刚山习禅一年，其后省悟而专精正学。③ 李滉知其"读释氏书而颇中其毒"，虽然以程颢（明道，1032—1085）、张载（横渠，1020—1077）、朱子皆有类似的经历而勉励之，但仍然忧虑其"新嗜靡甘，熟处难忘"，而希望他加强"穷理居敬"之工夫。④ 李滉所谓的"新嗜"是指"儒学"，而"熟处"指"禅学"，这也说明了在李滉的眼中，李珥并未完全放弃对佛

---

① 《栗谷全书》引真德秀言，曰："老氏所该者众，无为无欲，近理之言，虽君子有取焉。养生之言，为方士者尚焉；将欲夺之，必固与之，此阴谋之言也，言兵者尚焉；其以事物为粗迹，以空虚为妙用，清谈者效之。自其近理者言之，固在所可取，然皆吾圣人之所有也。下乎此，则一偏一曲之学，其弊有不胜言者。"此段文字出自真德秀《大学衍义》卷13《明道术·异端学术之差》，然文字多有删改。
② 《栗谷全书》卷20《圣学辑要·修己第二·穷理章第四》言："禅学虽足以惑人，其言非儒、其行灭伦，世间稍知有秉彝者，固已疑阻，又经程朱之辟，宜乎其迹若埽矣。陆学则不然，言必称孔孟、行必本孝弟，而其用心精微处，乃是禅学也，辟之之难，岂不十倍于佛氏乎？佛氏之害，如外寇之侵突；陆氏之害，如奸臣之误国。此不可不知，故并著焉。"
③ 《朝鲜王朝实录》，《宣祖修订实录》卷18，宣祖17年1月1日，己卯一则中，有关于李珥的生平记载云："因丧母悲毁，误染禅学，十九岁入金刚山，从事戒定，山中哗言：'生佛出矣。'既而省悟其非，反而专精正学，不待师承，洞见大原，剖析精微，笃信力行。"
④ 《退溪文集》卷14《答李叔献》言："前书深以往时失学为叹，足下行年甫弱冠耳，而颖脱如许，不可谓失学，而尚且云然者，岂不以所学有差，同于未学也耶？悟前非而思改，又知从事于穷理居敬之实，可谓勇于改过，急于向道，而不迷其方矣。圣远言湮，异端乱真，古之聪明才杰之士，始终迷溺者，固不足论矣。……惟程伯子、张横渠、朱晦庵诸先生，其始若不能无少出入，而旋觉其非。……往闻人言，足下读释氏书而颇中其毒，心惜之久矣。日者之来见我也，不讳其实，而能言其非，今见两书之旨又如此，吾知足下之可与适道也。所惧者，新嗜靡甘，熟处难忘，五谷之实未成，而稊稗之秋遽及也。如欲免此，亦不待他求，惟十分勉力于穷理居敬之工。"

学的喜好。除了李滉之说外，朝鲜晚期的宋时烈（尤庵，1607—1689）在《进文元公遗稿仍辨师友之诬又乞许孙畴锡归田读书疏》也论及李珥"泛览佛老诸书，而于其中最好《楞严》一书"，并以之"说心说性"。①李珥之不避佛老，使现代的韩国学者论及其思想时，多指出他的"理通气局说""气发理乘"说受到华严哲学"理事"说的影响。② 由历来学者对李珥的评述，可知李珥虽以朱子学为宗批判佛教，但于佛、老之学也未必全然不取，这种对学问的态度，使他在《醇言·后序》中对《老子》作如下的评价：

> 大抵，此书以无为为宗，而其用无不为，则亦非溺于虚无也。只是言多招诣，动称圣人，论上达处多，论下学处少。宜接上根之士，而中人以下则难于下手矣。其言克己窒欲、静重自守、谦虚自牧、慈简临民之义，皆亲切有味，有益于学者。不可以谓非圣人之书而莫之省也。

上段引文说明了李珥所以作《醇言》以作为《老子》注解的用意。李珥何以能说《老子》所言的"无为"非如朱子或其他理学家所言是与佛、释类同的"虚无"之学、权谋法术之学、③长生巫祝之学④的源头？这与他对老子"无为而无不为"的诠释息息相关。

李珥认为老子以"无为"为体，以"无不为"为用，在"无不为"

---

① 宋时烈《宋子大典》卷19《进文元公遗稿仍辨师友之诬又乞许孙畴锡归田读书疏》言："窃惟文成公臣李珥，……，年才五六岁已知为学之方。逮及十岁尽通经书，而曰：圣人之道只此而已乎。于是泛览佛老诸书，而于其中最好《楞严》一书。盖其为说，内之则说心说性，十分精微，外之则锚天铢地，极其宏阔，若非珥之高明，则童稚之年，何以能知之？"

② 以李珥之理气观恰似华严哲学之理事二门者，如李丙焘《韩国儒学史略》（首尔，亚细亚文化社，1986）第167页。又，崔英辰《韩国儒学通史》（首尔，심산출판사，2006），第755页。

③ 如《朱子语类》卷125《释氏》言："关机巧便，尽天下之术数者，老氏之失也。故世之用兵算数刑名，多本于老氏之意。"又，《二程遗书》卷18《刘元承手编》载程子言："老子书其言自不相入，处如冰炭，其初意欲谈道之极妙处，后来却入做权诈者上去，如'将欲取之，必固与之'之类。老子之后有申韩，与老子道甚悬钜额，然其原乃自老子来。"

④ 《朱子语类》卷125《论道教》言："老氏初只是清净无为，清净无为却带得长生不死，后来却只说得长生不死一项。如今恰成个巫祝，专只理会厌禳祈祷，这自经两节变了。"

的作用下,《老子》之书实即传达了"克己窒欲""静重自守""谦虚自牧""慈简临民"的思想,可以与儒学的"治己治人"之道相互补充,故《醇言》对《老子》第48章"为学日益,为道日损,损之又损,以致于无为",以及第10章"爱民治国,能无为乎"作如下的注解:

> 学以知言,道以行言。知是博之以文,故欲其日益;行是约之以礼,故欲其日损。盖人性之中,万善自足,善无加益之理,只当损去其气禀物欲之累耳。损之又损之,以至于无可损,则复其本然之性矣。①

> 修己既至,则推以治人,而无为而化矣。②

在上两章的注解中,将老子之"无为"视同于性理学之"复性",因而以为老子所说的"损之又损"即是性理学的"去其气禀物欲之累"。而且李珥也认为"无为"与"无为而化"乃就"治己"与"治人"两面而言。由"治己"而能去欲、复性达致"无为"的境界,则可以推己而"治人",不拘执于礼法形式而完成"无为而化"的目的。在此解释下,李珥将"无为"与"无为而化"("无不为")作为儒道交涉会同的关键语,从而与儒家所论的"治己"与"治人"结合起来。③

四 《醇言》之赋予《老子》性理学的意义

《醇言》既以儒学的"治己治人"解《老子》之道,则其解释,亦多将《老子》之语言转为性理学之语言,以下兹举数例说明之。

(一)"道"与"太极""理"

理学家周敦颐(濂溪,1017—1073)的《太极图说》以"太极—阴

---

① 见《醇言》第六章。
② 《醇言》第五章。
③ 此亦可参见金洛必《栗谷李珥"醇言"所内涵的儒道交涉:以经世理念为主讨论》(圆光大学圆佛教思想研究院,《圆佛教思想》第20号,1996),第453页。

阳—五行—万物"解释万物化生的过程,而朱子的理气论则将"太极"视为"理",作为"气"之本体,将"阴阳"视为"气",作为"理"之作用。故朱子言:"天地万物之理""万物中各有太极"。① 《老子》中虽无"太极"之说,然而南宋董思靖在其《道德真经集解》中,引用朱子之说,解《老子》42章"道生一,一生二,二生三,三生万物",而言:"道即《易》之太极,一乃阳之奇,二乃阴之耦,三乃奇耦之积。其曰二生三,犹所谓二与一为三也。其曰三生万物者,即奇耦合而万物生也"。②是以"道"为"太极","一"为"阳","二"为"阴","三"为"阴阳之积变"。李珥《醇言》全依董氏之说,而将《老子》中的"道"视为具有"太极"及"阴阳两仪"之变化,如此而将《老子》之道视为是性理学之"太极"与"理"。

(二) 道德与理气、体用

理与气在程朱理学中是一组体用的范畴,依气中有理或理堕气中之说,则有"万物中各有太极""万物莫不有理"之说。李珥既以性理学的理气、体用观解释《老子》,则其视《老子》中的"道"与"德"也同样以理气、体用的关系来解释。如《醇言》第二章云:"道即天道,所以生物者也;德则道之形体,乃所谓性也。人物非道,则无以资生;非德,则无以循理而自养,故曰道生德畜也。物之成形,势之相因,皆本于道德,故道德最为尊贵也。"于此,李珥以《老子》之"道"为"所以生物"之"理",以《老子》之"德"为"理"堕于"形体"之中,而为"性"。然而,李珥论《老子》之"道德"与"体用"的关系,也有偏于"气"之一面,而言"气"自身亦有"体"有"用"者,如他解释《老子》42章"万物负阴而抱阳,冲气以为和"时,引董思靖与司马光(温公,1019—1086)之言,而有"万物莫不以阴阳为体,以冲和

---

① 《朱熹文集》卷37《答程泰之》言:"道生一,一生二,二生三。熹恐此道字即《易》之太极,一乃阳数之奇,二乃阴数之耦,三乃奇耦之积。其曰二生三者,犹所谓二与一为三也。若直以一为太极,则不容复言道生一矣。详其文势,与列子'《易》变而为一'之语正同。所谓一者,皆形变之始耳,不得为非数之一也。"

② 见于〔宋〕朱鉴《朱文公易说》卷1《太极》"程大昌问"条。

为用"之说,① 以"阴阳"为"气之体",以"冲气"为"气之用"即以为"气"本身亦可以"体用"关系论之。故李珥在解释《老子》时,有将"体用关系"应用于"理气本体论"与"气化现象论"的不同用法。②

(三)"无为而无不为"与"寂然不动,感而遂通"

在"太极/阴阳"与"理/气"的体用架构下,前节所述的"无为/无不为"亦可统属于此理论架构之下。③ 李珥认为"无为"即是《诗经·大雅·文王》所谓的"上天之载,无声无臭",而《周易·系辞上》所言"《易》无思也,无为也,寂然不动,感而遂通天下之故"中的"无思无为""寂然不动"即是老子所言之"无为","感而遂通"即为老子所言之"无不为"。如此,老子的思想中的"虚无""无为"只是对"本体"之无思、寂然不动的描述语,而不是指"虚无之本体";"无不为"只是对"本体之用"能感通无方的描述语,不是指"消极无为的生命态度"。④

(四)"啬"与"敬"

李珥于程朱理学最重"敬"之义,故有"敬者,圣学之始终也"之言。⑤ "敬"作为"圣学之始"意谓:"未知者,未敬无以知"故须"以持敬为穷理之本";作为"圣学之终"意谓:"已知者,非敬无以守",故

---

① 《醇言》第一章:"董氏曰:'凡动物之颣,则背止于后,阴静之属也,口鼻耳目居前。阳动之属也。植物则背寒向暖。故曰负阴而抱阳,而冲气则运乎其间也。'温公曰:'万物莫不以阴阳为体,以冲和为用。'"

② 此可参见宋恒龙《栗谷李珥的老子研究和道家哲学》(收入《韩国道教的现代的照明》,首尔:亚细亚文化社,第143—153页。

③ 《醇言》第三章解"道常无为而无不为"言:"上天之载,无声无臭,而万物之生,实本于斯。在人则无思无为,寂然不动,感而遂通天下之故。右第三章,亦承上章,而言道之本体无为而妙用无不为,是一篇之大旨也。"

④ 此亦可参见琴章泰《〈醇言〉和栗谷的老子理解之说》,见《东亚文化》第43辑,页190—191。

⑤ 《栗谷全书》卷20,《圣学辑要·修己上》载:"臣按:敬者,圣学之始终也。故朱子曰:'持敬是穷理之本',夫知者,非敬无以知。程子曰:'入道莫如敬,未有能致知而不在敬者',此言敬为学之始也。朱子曰:'已知者,非敬无以守'。程子曰:'敬义立而德不孤,至于圣人,亦止如是',此言敬为学之终也。"

须"以敬义为立德之本"。《老子》中并未有"敬"之说法,然而李珥认为《老子》中的"啬",其义类同于"敬"。"啬"的主要意义虽是"爱惜""收敛",但是《醇言》却从"治己(自治)、治人"两方面论"啬"。在"治己"方面,"啬"意味"防嗜欲养精神""慎言语节饮食""居敬行简"的工夫;在"治人"方面,"啬"则是"谨法度简号令""省繁科去浮费""敬事爱人"的作为。① 如此,"啬"字贯穿了治己、治人二者,其义同于"居敬行简"与"敬事爱人"之"敬"。此外,《醇言》第 13 章以"守道克己""不自矜伐""常知止足"三者,解释《老子》67 章"我有三宝,持而保之,一曰慈,二曰俭,三曰不敢为天下先"。其所谓的"守道克己""不自矜伐""常知止足"亦可看出是由"啬"之"爱惜""收敛"义或由"敬"之"居敬行简""敬事爱人"义所延伸出来的意义。

(五)"故有之以为利,无之以为用"与"君子以虚受人"

《老子》11 章言:"三十幅共一毂,当其无,有车之用。埏埴以为器,当其无,有器之用。凿户牖以为室,当其无,有室之用。故有之以为利,无之以为用。"《醇言》第 4 章以"外有而成形"解"有",认为这是"身"之譬;以"中无而受物"解"无",认为这是"心"之譬。② 如此,他所说的"无/有""心/身"也即是"理/气""体/用"的关系。在此关系下,李珥所谓的"非身则心无所寓"可转译为"非气则理无所寓,非理则气无可行",这是就理气关系而言;所谓的"心不虚则理无所容"可转译为"不持敬虚心而穷理,则无法复性命之本然,求造圣贤之极致",此是就体用之工夫而言。如此,《老子》所谓的"有之以为用",在《醇言》中转为"以虚明无物之心而得本体之用","虚明无物"一方面

---

① 《醇言》第七章:"董氏曰:'啬,乃啬省精神,而有敛藏贞固之意。学者久于其道,则心广气充,而有以达乎天德之全矣。'愚按:事天是自治也,孟子曰:'存其心养其性,所以事天也。'言自治治人,皆当以啬为道。啬是爱惜收敛之意,以自治言,则防嗜欲养精神,慎言语节饮食,居敬行简之类,是啬也。以治人言,则谨法度简号令,省繁科去浮费,敬事爱人之类,是啬也。"

② 《醇言》第四章:"外有而成形,中无而受物。外有,譬则身也;中无,譬则心也。利者,顺适之意。利为用之器,用为利之机也。非身则心无所寓,而心不虚则理无所容。君子之心,必虚明无物,然后可以应物。如毂中不虚,则为不运之车;器中不虚,则为无用之器;室中不虚,则为不居之室矣。"

可连贯于《大学》的"格物致知",一方面也可连系于《周易·咸卦》《象传》的"君子以虚受人",① 故《醇言》言:"三章以上言道体,此章以后始言行道之功,而以虚心为先务。盖必虚其心,然后可以舍己之私,受人之善而学进行成矣。"

五 《醇言》所呈现的诠释观点

《醇言》可以将道家的经典文字作儒学的解释,这说明李珥对于文字或对文字的诠释有特殊的看法。司马迁的《史记》将老子与庄子、申不害、韩非的传记合写在一起,这说明他认为庄子、申不害、韩非的思想,与他们对《老子》的文本的不同诠释不无相关。换言之,《老子》作为一种"深远"的文本,不必然只有一种诠释的结果,这种想法若为李珥所接受,则《醇言》所欲展示的,也只是对《老子》文本的另一种诠解,而兵家、道教的长生之学也是如此。

以道教的长生学而言,《老子》本有"长生久视"之说,59 章言:"有国之母,可以长久,是谓深根固蒂,长生久视之道",东汉末的河上公《老子章句》据此章文本,因而可将《老子》的"道"解释为"自然长生之道"。② 朝鲜初期的郑道传对道教的长生颇有讥讽,而有"不义而寿,龟蛇矣哉"的说法,认为真正的君子应当是"可死则死,义重于身"。③ 郑道传批判了长生之说,也连带地否定了《老子》的价值。然而《醇言》在价值观上虽然延续了郑道传"从义不从身"的观点,但李珥也看到道教长生学之诠释方向并不完全决定于《老子》的文本本身,而在于诠释者对其诠释向度的取舍。因之,《醇言》第 23、24 章对《老子》55、56 章作如下的解释:

> 含怀至德之人,诚一无伪,如赤子之心也。董氏曰:"全天

---

① 《周易·咸卦》:"《象》曰:山上有泽,咸。君子以虚受人。"明代来知德《周易集解》解《象传》言:"虚者,未有私以实之也;受者,受人之善也。"
② 河上公《老子章句·体道第一》注"非常道"言:"非自然长生之道也。"
③ 见《三峰集》卷 10《心气理篇·理谕心气》。

人，物无害者。"①

善摄生者，全尽生理，故所遇皆正命，必无一朝之患也。或疑圣贤亦有未免祸患者。曰："此只言其理而已，若或然之变，则有未暇论也。"②

李珥明显地看到《老子》55 章所言的"蜂虿虺蛇不螫，猛兽不据，攫鸟不搏"是象征的说法，不能如道教徒般质实地看待。故李珥以"善摄生者"取代"善养身者"，而其所谓"善摄生者"是指"全尽生理"，而不是养其身体寿命者。李珥言"全尽生理"，事实上也在于表明他对《老子》文本所抱持的诠释原则。

李珥所说的"生理"非"全身之理"而指为性理学家所论的"天地之理"，有关此点也可以参看李珥《神仙策》一文。③《神仙策》言：

天地之理，实理而已。人物之生，莫不依乎实理，则理外之说，非格物君子之所可信也。

天地不可以长春，故四时代序；六气不可以独运，故阴阳并行。日往则月来，寒往则暑来，有盛则有衰，有始则有终，莫非天地之实理也。禀气于天，受形于地，囿于是理之中，而欲逃于理数之外者，岂不谬乎？

夫有所为而然者，人也；莫之为而然者，天也。智者，修其在人而任其在天；愚者，求其在天而忽其在人。是故，吾儒之所谓怡神养性者有异于此，内不汨于嗜欲，外不牵于物诱，方寸虚明，恬淡无为。心广体胖，晬面盎背，不忧不惧。故孟子曰：养心莫善于寡欲。至于死生则在天而已，吾何与焉？

盖闻天地万物，本吾一体。吾之心正，则天地之心亦正矣；吾之气顺，则天地之气亦顺矣。是故，圣王正其心以正朝廷，正朝廷以正天下；和其心以和朝廷，和朝廷以和天下。夫如是则天地位而万物育，日月以之顺其度，四时以之顺其节，阴阳调、风雨时，天灾时

---

① 《醇言》第 23 章。
② 《醇言》第 24 章。
③ 见《栗谷全书》《拾遗》卷 5。

变、昆虫草木之妖，莫不销息，诸福之物，可致之祥，莫不毕至。

由上列《神仙策》的四段文本，可以看到李珥对"生理"或"天地之理"的看法。在李珥眼中，所谓的"实理"或"天地之理"可以从二方面说明。其一，李珥言："理外之说，非格物君子之所可信也"，可见"实理"是指"可格物而知之理"。依此而论，长生学所论"三清真人、八种行仙"皆不可格物而知，可知其为"假设""虚妄"之言。其二，"实理"是指能阐发性命自觉之理，此即所谓"正命"之理。能正命者不求其所不能掌握之事，故"修其在人而任其在天"，故能正命者必能"恬淡无为""不忧不惧"而可参赞天地之化育。

李珥以此"实理"作为诠释《老子》文本的原则，因而在面对《老子》中有关长生的文字，也能由价值生命的角度去理解。不仅仅把《老子》视为是道教长生学的源头。如《老子》33 章"死而不亡者寿"，道教徒注意到的是生命上的"长生"，而努力探求延长生命之法，而李珥却认为《老子》所追求的"长生"不是身体上的"长生"，而是道德上的"长生"，故《醇言》第 9 章以"孔、颜既没数千载，而耿光如日月，岂非寿乎！"说之。[①]

六 《醇言》的编排结构及其对儒、道差异的意识

在"实理"的诠释原则下，栗谷或许为了使读者脱离对《老子》所生的刻板印象，因而重新编辑、削减了《老子》的篇章，且在《醇言》40 章中，对其结构作如下的说明：

> 首三章言道体。四章言心体。第五章总论治己治人之始终。第六章以损与啬为治己治人之要旨。自第八章止十二章皆推广其义。第十三章因啬字，而演出三宝之说。自十四章止十九章申言其义。二十章言轻躁之失。二十一章言清静之正。二十二章推言用功之要。二十三章四章申言其全天之效。二十五章言体道之效。二十六章至三十五章

---

① 见《醇言》第 9 章。

言治人之道及其功效。三十六章言慎始虑终防于未然之义。三十七章八章言天道福善祸淫亏盈益谦之理。三十九章四十章叹人之莫能行道以终之。

为了讨论上的方便，兹将《醇言》的篇章排列与《老子》原有的次序作成表格如下：

《醇言》	《老子》	主题	《醇言》	《老子》	主题
1	Ch. 42, 5	道体	22	Ch. 56	用功之要
2	Ch. 51		23	Ch. 55	全天之效
3	Ch. 37		24	Ch. 50	
4	Ch. 11	心体	25	Ch. 34, 63	体道之效
5	Ch. 10, 12	总论治己治人之始终	26	Ch. 54	治人之道及其功效
6	Ch. 48	以损与啬为治己治人之要旨	27	Ch. 81	
			28	Ch. 27	
7	Ch. 59		29	Ch. 49	
8	Ch. 22, 24	推广损与啬之义	30	Ch. 29	
9	Ch. 33		31	Ch. 57, 58	
10	Ch. 44		32	Ch. 43	
11	Ch. 47		33	Ch. 30	
12	Ch. 46		34	Ch. 31	
13	Ch. 67	因啬而演出三宝之说	35	Ch. 60	
14	Ch. 76, 78	申言"慈、俭、不敢为天下先"三宝之义	36	Ch. 63, 64	慎始虑终防于未然
15	Ch. 9		37	Chs. 72, 73	天道福善祸淫亏盈益谦之理
16	Ch. 39		38	Ch. 77, 79	
17	Ch. 8, 66		39	Ch. 70	叹人之莫能行道
18	Ch. 68				
19	Ch. 41, 45		40	Ch. 53	
20	Ch. 23, 26	轻躁之失			
21	Ch. 45	清静之正			

在上表中，明显可以看到李珥先以"理/气""道/心"的结构定位《老子》的根本思想，再由"心之体道""体道而用心"论"治己治人之始终"。在治己治人方面，李珥认为《老子》的特色在于提出"损"与

"啬"的要旨，这即是"无为而体道"，体道用心而无不为的表现。由"损"与"啬"而有"慈、俭、不敢为天下先"的三宝之义，以及清静与轻躁之得失，这些概念可谓简要地概括了治己治人之道。故《醇言》之第1章至21章，可谓尽《老子》之底蕴，而第22章至40章只是引伸之论。

在上述李珥所建立的诠释纲领中，所不取于《老子》文本者，有《老子》第1、2、3、6、7、13、14、15、16、17、18、19、20、21、28、32、35、36、38、40、52、61、62、65、69、71、74、75、80等章。从大的方向看来，李珥所避开《老子》文本，主要是道家原有对"道"与"德"的说明，如第1章"道可道，非常道。名可名，非常名。无名天地之始，有名万物之母。故常无欲，以观其妙；常有欲，以观其徼。此两者同出而异名，同谓之玄，玄之又玄，众妙之门"及第38章"上德不德，是以有德；下德不失德，是以无德。上德无为而无以为；下德为之而有以为。上仁为之而无以为；上义为之而有以为。上礼为之而莫之应，则攘臂而扔之。故失道而后德，失德而后仁，失仁而后义，失义而后礼。夫礼者，忠信之薄，而乱之首。前识者，道之华，而愚之始。是以大丈夫处其厚，不居其薄；处其实，不居其华。故去彼取此"。其他未收录于《醇言》者，多与此《老子》原有的"道""德"概念有关。而且，《醇言》中所录的《老子》篇章有些也是断章而取之，非取全章之义，如第37章"道常无为而无不为。侯王若能守之，万物将自化。化而欲作，吾将镇之以无名之朴。无名之朴，夫亦将无欲。不欲以静，天下将自定"只取"道常无为而无不为"，第5章"天地不仁，以万物为刍狗；圣人不仁，以百姓为刍狗。天地之间，其犹橐籥乎？虚而不屈，动而愈出。多言数穷，不如守中"，亦不取"天地不仁，以万物为刍狗；圣人不仁，以百姓为刍狗"。除此之外，《醇言》亦有取《老子》数章合为一章者，如《醇言》第一章言："道生一，一生二，二生三，三生万物。天地之间，其犹橐籥乎？虚而不屈，动而愈出。万物负阴抱阳，冲气以为和"即删省《老子》42章、5章而重编为一章。

由《醇言》之结构及对《老子》篇章之取舍，可知李珥在意识上仍然存有儒、道差异的意识。此外，由《醇言》多取董思靖及司马光之说，亦可推测李珥所见的《老子》注解本应该只有董思靖的《道德真经集解》，《醇言》所引司马光《道德真经论》（又名《老子道德论述要》）的意见，应该也是间接引自《道德真经集解》。董思靖为南宋泉州圭山天庆观道士，其书《道德真经集解》约成于宋理宗淳祐六年（1246），书有四卷，其说解"采撷诸说，间出己见"，所采撷者除先秦韩非，汉魏严遵、河上公、王弼外，对唐玄宗、宋徽宗御注，彭耜、陈景元、司马光、苏辙、王安石、王雱、陆佃、刘概、刘泾、曹道冲、马蹄山、达真子、了一子、李文愁、陈象古、叶梦得、刘骥、朱熹、黄茂材、程大昌、林东、邵若愚等诸家的说法皆有引述。《道德真经集解》虽然采撷诸家之说，但《醇言》于此书，仅采用董思靖、朱子及司马光之说，由此可推测李珥所以用此书为理解《老子》的基本书，主要在于此书反对以炼丹升仙之说解释《老子》，且认为其所引《朱子语类》卷125《老子书》《朱文公易说》等四条，引司马光《道德真经论》之说二十三条，皆合于性理学之旨。

七 《醇言》之写作目的

李珥既意识到《老子》文本中不可抹去的儒道差异，则其重新改编注解《老子》的目的何在？是否可以宋翼弼（龟峰，1534—1599）所批评的"非老子之本旨，有苟同之嫌"视之？[①] 有关此一问题，或许可有两个思考的方向。其一，与李珥的学问兴趣有关；其二，则与其特有的政治思维有关。[②]

关于李珥之学问兴趣的部份，在本文的前论中已略有述及，除了李珥

[①] 《醇言》书后所附洪启禧《跋》言："当先生之编此也，龟峰宋先生止之曰'非老子之本旨，有苟同之嫌'。"

[②] 如韩国学者金学睦认为李珥以"虚心（无）"和"啬"为主旨编辑、注释《老子》，是为了使朝鲜士人反省党争所形成的政治冲突。参见金学睦《渊泉洪奭周注释道德经的目的》（《哲学研究》第60辑，2003年，第5—24页），第13页。又，李锺晟在《〈醇言〉与养生——对其政治哲学养生论的可能性摸索》（大同哲学会论文集，第40辑，2007年9月，第21—47页）一文中，也讨论了栗谷养生论和政治思想之间的关系。

早年的学思多元外,也可猜想而其改宗儒学之后,或许曾将佛、道的经典视为是格物的对象,而以"实理"的角度探求其中的奥义,或者采取其中合于"实理"的见解。这也是《醇言》后所附洪启禧(1703—1771)《跋》文所说"昔韩愈以荀氏为大醇而少疵,欲削其不合者附于圣籍,曰:亦孔子之志欤","至若先生之范围曲成,虽异端外道,尚惜其可用者混归于不可用,必欲去其驳,而俾归乎醇"的意思。

在政治思维上,首先可以注意的是李珥曾深入参与东西党人分裂的过程。① 1565 年,仁宗(1515—1545)继母文定王后薨逝,明宗(1545—1567)仁顺王后之弟沈义谦(1505—1565)联合尹元衡(文定王后之弟,1509—1565)的门客金孝元(1532—1590)等人,发动政变将尹元衡赶下台,朝廷大权落在以沈义谦和金孝元为首的两股士林派的手中。宣祖(1568—1608)即位之初,仁顺王后以王大妃的身份垂帘听政,沈义谦因而得以培养政治势力,这引起另股势力金孝元等人的不满。中枢府事李浚庆(1499—1572)对于这两股势力深表忧虑,曾上疏力陈破朋党之论,果然到了宣祖八年(1575)出现了乙亥党论,起因于兼任吏曹正郎的金孝元反对兼任吏曹参议的沈义谦推荐其弟沈忠谦(1545—1594)担任吏曹铨郎。由于沈家在汉城西边,而金的家在汉城东边,故以沈义谦为首的一派被称为西人,以金孝元为首的一派被称为东人。当时右议政卢守慎(1515—1590)和副提学李珥出于公心奔走于金孝元和沈义谦之间,劝说他们放弃政争,建议将沈、金二人调补地方官。宣祖虽然同意将金孝元调任庆兴府使,将沈义谦调任开城府留守,但并未平息党争,且西人中有许多李珥的门人和亲友,所以东人认为李珥偏袒西人。② 之后,东人党共奉许晔(1517—1580)为领袖,而西人党共奉朴淳(1523—1589)为领袖,东人党的宋应溉、朴谨元、许篈等不断陷害李珥,致使他于宣祖十六年被流放(癸未三窜),一年后(1584)李珥逝世,享年四十九。

---

① 参考姜周镇《李朝党争史研究》(首尔大学出版部,1971);李离和:《朝鲜朝党争의展开过程과그系谱》(《韩国史学》8);金学睦《朝鲜儒学者〈道德经〉注释和时代情况》,第 119 页。

② 《朝鲜王朝实录》《宣祖实录》卷9,宣祖10年5月27日,甲寅四则中:"初沈义谦以外戚用事,一时名疏皆附之。金孝元为铨郎,始斥之。其出入时辈恶之,朋类渐分,始为东西之说。李珥言于大臣,请两出之,以杜厉阶。于是孝元为三陟府使,义谦亦为监司,而用事之辈,引进私党,排摈正士,自是朝廷多故矣。时李珥退居海州,金宇顒亦引疾还乡里。"

在上述东西分党的过程中，李珥心中对政争所持的立场为何？这可以由《栗谷先生全书》卷4《疏箚·论朋党疏》略知一二。《论朋党疏》所针对的是李浚庆向宣祖所进言的破朋党论。李珥对李浚庆破朋党论深不以为然，① 并且主张宣祖在面对朝廷公论时，不应在意其议论是否为朋党所为，而应留意于判断是君子或小人之言，若是君子为朋，应当多多益善，若是小人为朋，则一人也不能容忍。② 由《论朋党疏》，可知李珥认为朝廷并无朋党可破，真正的要务在于"当审其举错，务得其实"破除廷臣的虚伪之风，使"上有道揆，下有法守"。③ 由《论朋党疏》可知李珥不愿将廷臣的议论直接视为是朋党之私，而主张用"道""法"来面对公论，这种看法虽然陈义甚高，但李珥可谓亲身实验之，希望以超然中立之立场，打破东西的壁垒，以保合廷臣，使之一心徇国。

由李珥的《论朋党疏》及其面对东西党人分裂的态度，可以推测他在面对政争时，特别能感受《老子》所论"争"与"不争"的意义，因而他在诠释"损""啬"与三宝时，特别将此主题凸显出来。如《醇言》第13章解《老子》67章"舍其慈且勇，舍其俭且广，拾其后且先，死矣"言："矜勇则必忮，矜广则必奢，矜先则必争，皆死之徒也"；《醇言》第8章解《老子》22章"不自见故明；不自是故彰；不自伐故有功；不自矜故长；夫唯不争，故天下莫能与之争"言："愚按：《书》云'汝惟不矜，天下莫能与汝争能'与'汝惟不伐，天下莫能与汝争功'即此意也。"可以注意的是：李珥在突出"损""啬"与三宝之义时，特别举《尚书·大禹谟》"汝惟不矜，天下莫能与汝争能"，"汝惟不伐，天下莫能与汝争功"为说，这或许也可以看出在李珥的意识中，《老子》"夫

---

① 《栗谷先生全书》卷4《疏箚·论朋党疏》言："小臣离京日久，顷者入城，察见风色，殊异平昔。有志之士，深怀隐忧，入则仰屋窃叹，出则骇目相顾，顿无治世气象。窃怪其故，徐询厥由，则盖以卒领中枢府事李浚庆将死，进言以破朋党为说，殿下深信其说，疑朝廷已乱，朋党已成，而朝臣之疏箚，皆诿以自辨之辞，莫之深省，故臣邻之惶惑如此。"

② 《栗谷先生全书》卷4《疏箚·论朋党疏》言："朋党之说，何代无之，惟在审其君子小人而已。苟君子也，则千百为朋，多多益善；苟小人也，则一人亦不可容也，况于成党乎！"

③ 《论朋党疏》言："今日之朝廷，殿下固以为已乱，而臣亦不敢以为已治也。第未知殿下之所谓已乱者指何事耶？臣之所谓未治者，臣请言之。夫所谓朝廷之治者，上有道揆，下有法守，纪纲整肃百度俱贞，发政施仁黎民皞皞之谓也""今殿下既恶虚伪之风，则当审其举错，务得其实，不可只形于语言而已也。若殿下不务好贤之名，而惟务好贤之实，则虚伪之人安敢仰干天威乎？"

唯不争，故天下莫能与之争"的想法也是三代"无为而化"之政治理想的体现，也符合于他所追求的"复古"之道。①

八 结论

李珥《醇言》虽然是朝鲜时代第一本《老子》注释书，但《醇言》并未给予《老子》独立的地位，而只能视为是性理学的附庸书。因此，《醇言》只能是李珥儒学世界观下的产物，很难说其内容具有"儒道同源"或"会同儒道"的意义。在此情形下，《老子》对于李珥的意义，应在于：以"实理"观异端之学，则异端之学必有可观之处，有可补充于儒学之处。《醇言》所呈现的儒道互补之道何在？除了《老子》所论的"无为而无不为"也有"治己治人"之义外，本文以为李珥在党争的纷扰下或许也反省了儒教积极用世的精神观，因而认为《老子》所论"夫唯不争，故天下莫能与之争"可补救积极用世在道德及政治上所形成的盲点。因此可说：《醇言》是李珥"实学"思想的展现，也是他对于士人深入性理学，却无法逃脱计算政治利害之现象的反省。

---

① 如《朝鲜王朝实录》《宣祖实录》卷9，宣祖8年10月25日，己丑一则载："予观往史，时代渐变，夏不及唐、虞，商不及夏，周不及商矣。今代固难复三代之治也。珥曰：'世道固渐降矣。虽然，若行古道，则岂无复古之理乎？程子有言曰：虞帝不可及已，三代则决可复也。盖唐、虞之时无为而化，后世不能及也。若三代之治，则苟行其道，必可复也，只是不为耳。'"

先秦诸子对战争与和平的看法

陈鼓应[*]

不了解中国的历史，就不能认识中华民族的苦难；不认识中华民族的苦难，就不能体会中国人民的坚忍和中国文化的深厚面。

我们阅读前人留下的记录，为的是要从那血泪的长河中吸取教训。《夏潮杂志》的总编辑苏庆黎说："历史是为现代人而写的。"这是从过去经验的学习中朝前发展的一种态度，是古为今用而非为古所泥的态度。

今天我们来谈先秦诸子对某些问题的看法，为的是看看当时思想家们是如何面对现实提供解决之道的。

先秦诸子触及的问题范围很广，从宇宙论到人生观，从认识论到政治学，都提出了许多发人深省的慧见。那是个百花齐放的时代，他们在多层问题上激辩着，诸如：人治与法治的问题，公天下与私天下的问题，复古与变革的问题，人身崇拜与反偶像的问题。他们还讨论了许多哲学上的问题。虽然我是研究哲学的，特别是先秦哲学，但我和学生会的同学初步交换意见时，似乎感到大家对纯粹哲学史上的问题兴趣不大，因此来谈谈先秦诸子对现实关怀的态度与观点，我们把范围缩小到"先秦诸子对战争与和平的看法"这一个问题上。

回顾"春秋战国"，我们关切到一个重大的问题，那就是长期割据战乱，给人民带来了深沉的灾难。如何结束分裂的局面而重建家园，正是各家所热烈讨论的一个焦点。

春秋时期所发生的战争，少则数日，多则数月，到了战国时期，就扩延到少则月，多则"旷日持久数岁"。《战国策》说，一次大战仅以兵甲车马的损失，就"十年之用而不能偿也"。这庞大的战费都由人民负担，

---

[*] 陈鼓应，北京大学哲学系教授。

而农民的牺牲最为惨重。徭役、贡赋、征发，要他们无休止地供应。农民"解冻而耕，暴背而耨"，却"无积粟之实"，弄得"父母冻饿，兄弟妻子离散"，有的借债度日，甚至"嫁妻卖子"。战争死亡的惨景，正如《战国策》所描绘的："刳腹折颐，首身分离，暴骨草泽，头颅僵仆望于境。"这种情况，促使先秦诸子纷纷提出如何解救世乱的主张。

孔子："和为贵"

在诸子中，孔子是较为保守的一位。其他各家之所以比他要激进，和时势的演变也有关。虽然我们不欣赏《论语·乡党篇》孔子那种战战兢兢地遵守贵族礼制的态度，但他对时局的主要看法，却提供了宝贵的意见。

孔子说齐桓公主持诸侯盟会，停止战争，都是管仲出的力，《宪问篇》："桓公九合诸侯不以兵车，管仲之力也。"从孔子称赞管仲"不以兵车"召集盟会来看，他是不赞成执政者用武，而赞成用和平谈判方式解决问题，古时所谓"盟会"，就是各方停战举行媾和会谈。再从卫灵公问阵，孔子回说："军旅之事，未之学也"，也可能他是不主张使用武力来解决时局的。

"和为贵"是孔子人生哲学的一个要旨，主张人际关系应和睦相处，这意义延伸到当前国家的处境，则为"和平统一是可贵的"。

孔子的统一思想，在下面的两段话里表现出来。他说："天下有道，则礼乐征伐，自天子出，天下无道，则礼乐征伐，自诸侯出。"所谓"礼乐征伐，自天子出"自然是处于国家去维持统一的局面下，"礼乐征伐，自诸侯出"，则是国家处于分裂的状态。孔子肯定前者而谴责后者，他的观念若用现代的语言来表达，乃是认为：领导阶层、政治措施及国防军事制度化，则国家情势将会上轨道。

孔子评论管仲时说："管仲相桓公，一匡天下，民到如今受其赐！微管仲，吾其被发左衽矣！"在这里，孔子明白地指出国家统一给人民带来的好处。国家分裂，则易为外族所乘，外强势力的进入，更加深国家的分裂，国家分裂的激化，则导致同胞自相残杀。觅观当代的历史，南北韩战争与南北越战争的惨痛经验，历历在目。孔子这话应用到今天，其意则为：国家统一，免于被帝国主义所侵害，这对人民有极大的好处。"民到如今受其赐！"这正是饱尝国家分裂痛苦的历史见证者深刻体认到国家给人民带来的好处所发出的心声!

孟子:"定于一"

孟子谴责当时的割据战争:"争地以战,杀人盈野,争城以战,杀人盈城,此所谓率土地而食人肉。"对于贫富的两极化,他也提出沉痛的抗议:"庖有肥肉,厩有肥马,野有饿兽而食人也。"

孟子的政治思想,在反映民情,主张"民为贵"及"定于一"这方面,在中国历史上起了进步作用。

战乱加上为政不良,使人民生活"乐岁终身苦,凶年不免于死亡","凶年饥岁,老弱转乎沟壑,壮者散之四方"。这种景况,促使孟子十分关切如何"保民"和促进国家的统一。如何才能"安定于统一":孟子要求统治集团首先应停止武力的竞争,他说:"以力服人者,非心服也","威天下不以兵革之利"。一场仗打下来,死伤的都是自己的同胞,打仗就是杀人,所以他说:"如有不嗜杀人者,则天下之民皆引领而望之矣。"结束军事争战的行动,是人民"引领"盼望的,所以他说:"不嗜杀人者能一之。"

孟子还提到进行或停止军事行动,应取决于民意:"取之而(燕)民悦,则取之。""取之而(燕)民不悦,则勿取。"孟子基本上是主张和平统一的,但是当时的中国正处于武力剧烈对峙的阶段,所以孟子又提出统一的军事行动要取决于"民悦"与否。

孟子主张停止用武,而后进行道德性的政治竞赛。在这方面,虽然儒家说了不少迂阔的话,不过孟子提出内政改革的纲要中,有关"省刑罚,薄税敛""深耕易耨,勿夺民时"等主张,确是当务之急。孟子认为:有固定产业收入的人才有一定的道德观念和行为准则。《滕文公》:"有恒产者有恒心"。安定人民生活,给民众以教育,"谨庠序之教""保民"则达成统一的基本前提("保民而王")。

老子:"师之所至,荆棘生焉"

在"定于一"的问题上,道家并没有正面触及。但对现况,他们是强烈地批评。老子和庄子,可说是先秦诸子中抗议性最大的知识分子。老子提出少私寡欲、知足不争等观念,都是针对当权贵族无餍欲求而提出的。有位内地学者说:"老子的无为论在当时是有一定的积极作用,它在反对统治人民的各种苛繁的法律、兼并战争及沉重的租税负担等方面，反映了被压迫的人民群众的要求。"（胡寄窗，《中国经济思想史》）这看法比一般学者笼统说老子是代表没落贵族发言为确。

老子对于处理世务的态度，固嫌不够积极，但对社会之不平是勇于抗击的。他批评贵族统治者们"服文彩，带利剑，厌饮食，财货有余"简直是强盗头子。他还反击"民之饥，以其上食税之多，是以饥，民之轻生，以其求生之厚，是以轻死"。

对于战争的恶果，老子说了好些精辟的话。他描述说："师之所处，荆棘生焉，大军之后，必有凶年。"因而他呼吁："不以兵强天下。"又说："兵者不祥之器，不得已而用之。恬淡为上。胜而不美，而美之者，是乐杀人。夫乐杀人者，不可得志于天下。"老子对逞气用武者还说："兵强则灭，木强则折。""天下有道，却走马以粪，天下无道，戎马生于郊。"

老子曾提到防御性的备战。"用兵有言：吾不敢为主，而为客，不敢进寸，而退尺。""行无行，攘无臂，扔无敌，执无兵。"这些话都是表示虽然储备对敌的力量，但不轻易使用，这些话也可引申为反对挑衅及发动侵略性战争。所谓"国之利器，不可示人"。准此而推，对外，老子是反对霸权的；对内，是反对向强国购武器对付自己同胞的。

墨子："诸侯相爱，则不野战"

墨子站在"维护国家百姓之利"的立场，主张兼爱非攻。

在《非攻》篇，他说："今有一人，入人园圃，窃其桃李，众闻之则非之。以其亏人自利也。至攘人犬豕鸡豚者，其不义，又甚入人园圃窃桃李，以亏人愈多，其不仁兹甚，罪益厚。……至杀不辜人也，扡其衣裘，取戈剑者，其不义，又甚入栏厩，取人马牛。"他进而描述割据战争之"虐万民"。他说："夺民之用，废民之利"，"春则废民耕稼树艺，秋则废民获敛"，"竭天下百姓之财用，不可胜数"。尤有甚者，"刭杀其万民，覆其老弱"，"饥寒冻馁疾病而转死沟壑者，不可胜计"。这里，他控诉了战争导致生产停顿，耗费民财，弄得"百姓离散"，乃至战事一起，"杀人多必数于万，寡必数于千"。因而墨子谴责："杀一人，谓之不义，必有一死罪矣，数十人，十重不义！必有十罪死矣，数百人，百重不义，必有百死罪矣！"这和孟子所抨击的"……杀人盈城，罪不容于死。故善战者服上刑"观点一致。

在解决统一所使用的方式上，法家的观点，和儒、道、墨各家正相对立。

当时的情况是各地的权力集团正在进行决战，强则存、弱则亡，所以法家认为当前最重要的问题就是如何富国强兵。

以商鞅、韩非为代表的法家，首先强调在内政上要作彻底的改革。当时各国为形势所逼不得不进行改革，但改革最大的阻力来自统治阶级内部。商、韩在推行改革政策时，立即与贵族集团的守旧派发生冲突，首先在改革现状与保持现状的论点上引起激辩。商鞅认为："世事变而行道异。"他说，"三代不同礼而王，五霸不同法而治"，不同的时代有不同制度，要灵活应变，"不法古，不修今"，他批评说："法古则后于时，修今则寒于势。""修今"是拘泥于现代，总之客观情势之不同（"异势"），必须要制定相应的办法。韩非也从人类历史的发展观点，论述"不期修古，不法常可"的道理。他说："古今异俗，新故异备"，墨守成规无异守株待兔。

鉴于战争为害人民至巨，墨子提倡"非攻"，呼吁大家要"兼相爱，交相利"。他提出"兼以易别"的口号。所谓"兼"，扩大来说，要求世界大同，国际互相合作，落实到中国的政局来讲是求同胞发挥友爱互助精神，所谓"别"，即是政治集团间搞分裂。"兼以易别"，就是促进中华民族的大团结，以消除分离敌对的局面。"诸侯相爱，则不野战"，正是期望执政当局停止军事对峙之意。

商鞅："勇于公战而怯于私斗"

改革派的主张在秦国获得有力的支持，于是开始推行法治。（1）建立高效率的官僚体系，商鞅批评当时的贵族集团："虱官"充斥，"禄厚而税多"。因此规定：凡宗室非有军功不得列入贵族籍。取才以能，提高行政效率。商鞅说："无宿治，则邪官不及为私利于民，而百官之情不相稽。""无宿治"就是不推脱积压公事的意思。（2）进行经济制度的改革：开封疆阡陌就是其一项重大的改制。这是"废除领土贵族割据的占有土地形式"的一种措施（见杨宽《战国史》），它承认新开垦的土地所有权，这刺激人们去垦荒，在赋制方面，按照人民实际耕种的田地面积来规定赋税，所以开阡陌对农民是有利的。（3）全国总动员。商鞅建立了一个严密的户口制,将全国人民整编起来,并调动劳动方积极从事生产,严禁阔家子弟优游闲荡,此外商鞅还进行其他方面的重要改革,例如推行郡县制、统一度量衡制等。

商鞅是领主贵族的最大克星,他认为"法之不行,自于贵戚","法之不行,自上犯之"。太子犯法,他也不留情,因而《史记》本传说:"商君相秦十年,宗室贵戚多怨望者。""宗室多怨鞅",但老百姓的反应却不同,《史记》记载法治的实施:"行之十年,秦民大悦,道不拾遗,山无盗贼,家给人足。民勇于公战而怯于私斗,乡邑大治。"商鞅的命运虽然很悲惨,但他的理论与治绩却奠定了统一事业的基础。"民勇于公战而怯于私斗"的精神,用在今天,"公战"可指反对"霸权主义","私斗"就是同胞相残,自己人打自己人。"怯于私斗",此其时矣!

结束分裂,"无战争之患"

现在,总结一下。从先秦诸子的言论里,我们可以得到不少的认识与启示:

①分裂局面太久,战争给人民的损失太大,正如《吕氏春秋》所说的:"以兵相残,不得休息","黔首之苦,不可加矣"。又如《史记》所描述的,"天下共苦战斗不休","兵革不休,士民罢敝"。这种境况下,结束分裂,"无战争之患",正是亿万人民共同的愿望。

②先秦诸子多属统一运动者。孔、孟为首的人是和平统一运动者,商、韩为首的人则是武力统一运动者。这期间,孔子"一匡天下"的观念,孟子"定于一"的主张,以及商鞅等人统一度量衡制度,在中国历史上对中华民族的大结合都有重大的影响和贡献。

③先秦诸子竞相建言,呈现百家争鸣的情况,创造了中国思想史上的黄金时代。当时各家的见解虽然有分歧,但都有关怀民瘼的心怀。

对现实态度的积极程度虽有差异,但都能本于社会良知,指陈时政缺失,对国内政治改革起了巨大的推动作用。只有少数"巧言辩说"者"其术长于权变"而且只知依靠外国势力,这班人"随从外权,上可以得显,下可以求官爵",正是今日买办官僚的写照!

④先秦诸子多属人道主义者,而且有深厚的时代使命感。各家之中,墨子的社会意识最强。但在老子和孔子的言论中,可以发现到他们不满社

会财富分配不均的现象。老子抨击人间社会："损不足以奉有余。"而主张高者抑之，下者举之，有余者损之，不足者补之。并譬喻说："天地相合，以降甘露，民莫之令而自均。"以示理想的社会为分配均等。孔子也说道："有国有家者，不患寡而患不均。"他们都看出财富分配悬殊不平所呈现的社会危机，由之而产生均等的意识。这均等主义的观念，对历代中国知识分子及社会人士产生深远的影响。

⑤在权力分配方面，特别对于权力过分集中的现象，道、墨、儒各家都不同程度地表达了意见。墨子抨击贵族的政治集团的政治垄断，指责"亲亲"政治，仅凭"骨肉之亲"就可以"无故而富贵"。他将理想中的治者改造而为具有服务心的劳力生产者。老子主张"治大国，若烹小鲜"尽量减少对人民的干扰，让人民享有充分的自主、自由。老子说："爱国治民，能无为否！"孔子也接受"无为而治"的理想（"无为而治，其舜也与！"），这也就是说领导人主意不要太多。可惜在我们这封建意识笼罩下人身崇拜之风仍盛的社会，这种理想始终难以实现。此外，各家还触及政权转移方式的问题，他们虚构"禅让"之说，实含有和平转移政权，并认为政权的转移非一家一姓所私有之意。同时，居于"爱民"与"以百姓心为心"的观点，对于政治权力的运作，也都不同程度地希望在消极方面减少其危害性，而积极方面在"政治道德"的使命感下多做有益民众的事。

⑥战国时代，经济社会结构有巨大的改变，冶铁技术的进步，使铁制生产工具获得广泛使用，荒地的开垦，水利事业的开发，牛耕的推广，提高了农业生产水平；手工业技术的发展，城市的兴起，货币的流通都加强了各地人民的来往。《荀子·王制篇》写到了商业交易的繁盛：北方的走马、吠犬，南方的齿、革，东方的织物、鱼盐，西方的皮革、文旄，都出现在中原的市场上。《礼记·月令篇》上也说："易关市，来商旅，纳货贿，以便民事。四方来集，远近皆至。"这里说到的"易关市"，就是开放关市。孟子也曾极力主张开放关卡，他说："古之为关也，将以御暴，今之为关也，将以为暴。"这里，他陈述关卡作用的变化，并批评现在关卡的设置是不利通商的。总之，社会经济的发展，需要建成一个统一国家。反之，割据的情况，不仅关卡太多，不利商业交通，从水利的观点，"雍防百川，各以为利"，危害性也很大，正如《战国策》所说的："东周欲为稻，西周不下水"，甚至在大水时决堤放水，"以邻为壑"。可见分歧

的局面之不利于人民。而战争之为害尤烈，所以结束分裂而朝向统一，是有益全体人民的。

战国时代，中国虽处于战争对峙状态，但人民之间仍可相互往来，孔子周游列国可以为证，既不需"签证"，也免于户口检查，那时自由度及社会的开放性，值得"口谈仁义"者学习。

东亚的表达

韩东育[*]

东亚世界有许多根本性问题往往被熟视无睹：(1)"东亚"是"欧洲人"所给定的区域指代，还是曾经有过的文明圈域？(2)"欧洲一体"是事实还是假设？如果是事实，两次世界大战均引爆于欧洲的历史便无从得到解释；可如果是假设，"亚洲一体"说的前提，又当依何而定？(3) 在东亚率先完成"国民国家"改造任务并试图领导邻国一道去实现这一近代化指标的日本，何以会招致东西方力量的双向排斥和联合反对？(4) 历史和现实是否已给未来的东亚关系走向提供过足够的暗示？

亚细亚，古希腊语作"Aσία"，拉丁语作"Asia"，通常被视为新航路开辟后欧洲人给东方世界所赋予的区域名称。正如"日本"的国名只能出自日本以西的国度一样，Asia 原意的"太阳升起处"，在比利时学者奥特里乌斯（Abraham Ortelius, 1527—1598）绘制于 1570 年的 Typvs Orbis Terrarvm（《世界地图》，黄时鉴：《早期欧洲世界地图上的远东海域及其名称》）中，也当然被措置于世界的最东端。不过，这一纯粹的地理方位指代，却在意大利耶稣会士利玛窦（Matteo Ricci, 1552—1610）绘制的《坤舆万国全图》（下略称《全图》）中，被注入了有机内涵。因考虑到古来自称"中华"或"中国"的明廷感受，利玛窦还"有意抹去了福岛（指西班牙的加那利群岛）的第一条子午线，在地图两边留下一条边，使中国正好出现在中央"（《利玛窦中国札记》），然后将朝鲜、日本、吕宋、安南等地按照其与明朝的传统关系附以图注和说明："大明声名文物之盛，自十五度至四十二度皆是。其余四海朝贡之国甚多。"利玛窦或许将明朝"声教"所及地区与"朝贡国"混作一谈，但该圈域与

---

[*] 韩东育，东北师范大学副校长，历史学教授。

朱元璋早年划定的"十五不征国"范围（《皇明祖训》），基本叠合。

然而，这两幅地图上的亚洲，却成为引发近代东亚地区百余年震荡的直接触媒。山室信一教授指出过一个事实，即近代日本的自我认识史总是与亚洲"言说史"作一体观瞻。为此他认为，有以下四点认识需要提及：（1）对日本而言，亚洲毕竟是来自欧洲人的地理区域指代，而绝非亚洲人自我发现和创造出来的概念。（2）日本人了解欧洲人世界划分下的亚洲，是通过利玛窦的《坤舆万国全图》（1602年做成，1606年传入日本）从外部得知。（3）亚洲虽是一个被强加的概念，但日本人曾试图通过某种框架或基准将其实体化，哪怕其中含有极明显的政治意图。（4）日本对亚洲的认识不是确立于对亚洲实体的认知，而是用事先形成的思想基轴对实体本身所做出的切割。在这个空间中，人们可能会通过对"文明"与"人种""文化"与"民族"的相近认识来寻出某种具有同一性的统括式共同社会，并由此而形成某种"集结化"和"境域化"的意识（山室信一：『思想課題としてのアジア』）。

早年，西嶋定生曾探讨过构成前近代"东亚世界"的实际内涵，认为近代以前的"东亚世界"曾拥有过完整和自律的历史，并且也只有内陆的历史才是包括日本等邻国在内的"东亚世界"的历史。以中国为核心的"东亚世界"，包括朝鲜、日本、越南以及蒙古高原、青藏高原之间的西北走廊东部地区；而构成"东亚世界"的文化要素，则主要是汉字、儒教、律令制和佛教（西嶋定生：『中国古代国家と東アジア世界』）。这表明，无论是前近代自生的"东亚"，还是近现代被给予的"东亚"，这两个"世界"应该是相互叠合的同一个"世界"。可山室教授的观察，亦同时为人们提供了某种相反的事实，即到了近代，前近代东亚各国的上述共通点，不但不是区域联合的"纽带"，反而成为"绝对没有现实有效性"的"观念上的东西"。这意味着，由欧洲人所创造的"国民国家"理念，已彻底切断了前近代"超国家"地缘结构的一切连接纽带，即便有所痕迹，也只能保留在观念的层面上，想想而已。（同前揭）

然而，相对于"欧洲"这一"他者"，"亚洲"又经常被理解为能够与"欧洲"相抗衡的区域单位。日本汉学家冈千仞的邻国连带倾诉（岡千仞：『藏名山房文初集』中卷）、"兴亚会"创始人曾根俊虎的"联合兴亚"主张（「法越交兵記」）以及李鸿章所言"我们东方诸国，中国最大，日本次之，其余各小国须同心和气，挽回局面，方敌得欧罗巴住"

等提携愿望（《照录李鸿章与森有礼问答节略》），似乎都在讨论这一问题。如此敌礼欧洲的心态，还集中凝结为冈仓天心的"亚洲一体"（Asia is one）论（『東洋の理想』，1903年）和"欧洲的光荣便是亚洲的耻辱"（『東洋の覚醒』，1902年）诸命题。至于蜡山政道用来对抗欧美的所谓"东亚协同体"，则有意从理论的角度来否定西方的国际秩序，并代之以日本为主导的世界秩序构想。然而山室教授认为，这种"虚妄的想法"，与其说确立于"东洋"固有要素之基础上，不如说是刺激于近代欧洲地缘政治的产物："那时曾把同文、同种、同教、同州、同俗即文字（汉字）、人种、宗教（儒教）、区域（亚细亚洲）、风俗等同一性视为纽带，认为联合是可能的。不过大家都知道，这种纽带只不过是观念上的东西，它绝对没有现实的有效性。"（山室信一：《近代日本的东北亚区域秩序构想》，徐兴庆译）

在东亚，欧洲国际法虽最早传入中国，但日本反应的快捷程度，却远速于中国。丁韪良（W. A. P. Martin）所译《万国公法》，曾提到过"恒例"之外的"变例"（上海书店出版社2002年，第18、59、72、73、90页）；而日本对那些"变例"，似乎表现出了更大的兴趣。1872—1873年，"岩仓使节团"赴欧美访问。其间，他们从普鲁士宰相俾斯麦（Otto Von Bismarck）的直露表述中，不仅了解到"国际公法"的弱肉强食"变例"（『岩倉公実記』中卷「具視外務卿『ビスマルク』ノ招宴ニ赴ク事」），而且后来的事实证明，日本在东亚政策的实施过程中，还逐渐掌握了"变例"的运用技巧。然而，俾斯麦产生于欧洲"铁血"经验的"变例"言说，意味着"欧洲一体"论所反映的并不是欧洲的实情；其由相互仇杀所造成的历史裂痕，使欧洲国家之间并不是像日本人所描述的那样犹如"一块铁板"（费正清（John King Fairbank）：《中国：传统与变迁》；王韬：《普法战纪》）。两次"世界大战"主战场均为欧洲的事实意味着，"欧洲一体"的说法，其实是不成立的；而没有"欧洲一体"的事实，"亚洲一体"论，也就当然失去了存在的前提。若详审王韬的分析还会发现，在当时的中国"大战略"上，似乎只考虑过"联英法以御俄"，而并无与日本联手的想法。时势如此而日本却执意坚持"联亚抗欧"论，说明这类提倡的目的并不单纯，即："亚洲"是一个由欧洲人所给出的空间概念，并且还是一个与"欧洲"相"对置"、"对立"甚至"对决"的空间概念。欧洲人的思想"暗示"及其日益东扩的"殖民"行动，使率先在东亚地区实现近代化改造任务并完成了"国民国家"组建工作的日本，敏锐而强烈地感受到了区域担当意识，于是乎，一种舍我其谁的责任感和使命感，开始把自身推向世界舞台，并从此展开了以日本的思想和行动为核心的"实体化"亚洲的全过程。但是，由于日本在声言促进亚洲各国"近代文明"化和"国民国家"化的同时，又先后将"殖民主义"和"大东合邦"等构想强加给区域内各国，加之其"第三种国际关系体系"的构想必然要与欧美列强发生冲突，因此，近代而来的日本全部工作，最后以"太平洋战争"的失败而走向终结（山室信一『思想課題としてのアジア』）。

表面上看，无论是"文明开化"还是"国民国家"，也无论是"反帝反殖"还是"第三种体系"，日本所欲实现的每个单一目标，在那个时代的原则和文脉上似乎均不失历史和逻辑的可行性。可是，事情的走向并不会遵循内容单纯的线性原则和人为设计，而日本的体量和能量又决定了它明显缺乏整体运作能力，因此，近代以来日本所提出的全部个案式构想，只能以其自身难以驾驭的交叉互动式网状格局被立体推出。正是在运转、应对和调整这部高度复杂的"世界机器"的过程中，日本的"正面意义"和"负面效果"，几乎从一开始便无法摆脱孪生并至、善恶交织的命运。就中，"反帝反殖"意义上的"联亚拒欧"舆论，或许有可能调动起东亚甚至全亚洲的"合力"，部分中、韩人士的感慨和感动，证明了这一点。可是，空间意义上的区域捍卫能否取得成功，当取决于时代意义上的东亚是否进化。这就使"近代化"价值和"国民国家"原理，被赋予了思想和行动的前提意义。但是，这也就注定会导致日本言行上的逻辑混乱：既然代表"近代化"和"国民国家"的欧洲逻辑具有自明的正当正义性，那么，嗣后日本在亚洲所采取的系列行动，至少在文明进步的意义上是成立的，尽管这些行动会在亚洲当地普遍遭到抵制。于是乎，那些看似"不得已"的行为在世界大势面前却仍不乏"近代"意义的观点，遂逐渐流为"二战"后日本知识界的部分看法，如梅棹忠夫（「文明の生態史観序説」）、沟口雄三（《创造日中间知识的共同空间》）和船曳健夫（『右であれ左であれ、わが祖国日本』）。他们的言说，把日本在"地域"上属于亚洲而在"时代"上属于欧洲的身份表达，和盘托出。然而，对于想通过"欧洲秩序＝世界大势"之构图去竭力捕捉日本行动意义的舆论家来说，一个更直白的观点，似乎也应该成立：亚洲既然是外来的区域世界观，那么如果日本要"实体化"亚洲，其援用外来的标尺即欧洲的原则和逻辑来测量并规划亚洲事务的想法和做法，便不应该受到"欧洲"以外标准的过多指责。

可是，日本不久便发现，在东亚的精英阶层中，反对欧洲的保守派，未必甘于被日本所领导；而倾向于近代化改革的人，却未必反对欧洲。这就要求日本必须着手以下两大要务：一是如何渲染欧洲列强灭绝亚洲的危险度和东亚列国联合御侮的紧迫性；二是如何在亚洲树立起足以让邻国痛感其落差的近代"模范国"形象。前者让人想起了曾根俊虎的声泪俱下："夫日韩与清固同文同教，所宜唇齿相依者也。若安南一地，约计纵横二万三千五百余方里。土地肥沃，物产繁殖。户口殆不下二千万人，与我同文同教。且同隶亚洲，盖亦亚韩之一国耳。……余夙忧欧洲人之凌辱我亚洲也，于是兴同志会者谋，创立兴亚会。其意在挽回亚洲之衰颓，而压欧洲之强暴。此事也，余所日夜关心，辄常卧不安席，食不甘味，抚膺太息，血泪沾襟。竟至落魄中原，结燕赵之士，讨论古今，悲愤满怀。或怒发冲冠，或挥剑斫柱。呜呼，欧亚强弱之势，何至今相反之甚耶！"（『法越交兵記』）而后者，则让人忆及大隈重信那段足以令东亚人自叹不如的倨傲式训导，"国之兴也，非兴于兴之日，必有所由；业之成也，非成于成之日，亦必有所自。我之文华致今日者，岂朝夕之故哉！清人乃观其既成之迹为可袭而取，亦已过矣。苟欲取则于我，莫如审我实势；欲审我实势，则莫如考其沿革；欲考其沿革，则如此书者，亦必在其所取也"（『日本開国五十年史』序），当然，也不乏康有为式的吹捧与附和："泰西以五百年讲求之者，日本以二十余年成之，治效之速，盖地球所未有也，然后北遣使以开虾夷，南驰使以灭琉球，东出师以抚高丽，西耀兵以取台湾，于是日本遂为盛国，与欧州德法大国颉颃焉。然论其地，不过区区三岛；论其民，不过三千余万，皆当吾十之一。然遂以威振亚东，名施大地。迹其致此之由，岂非尽革旧俗，大政维新之故哉！"（《日本变政考》序）

然而，日本人的努力，却让东亚地区陷入了兵连祸结的乱局。对此，需要研究者第一关注的是，型塑于前近代东亚体系"自解体"过程中的内部关系特征——彼此"警觉"和"防范"；而与此相密结的第二点是，日本"联亚拒欧"构想所必需的空间占据，在很快被有识者窥破的同时，西方的"条约体系"反而逐渐为中国人所认可。这意味着，日本的"联亚拒欧"倡导，至少面临着两重不可逾越的障碍：一个是历史的，另一个是现实的。就历史而言，无论日本怎样以"同文同种同教同俗"的宣传尝试与东亚各国联合，近世以来东亚的内部争执和分离局面，都不可能因为早已背离这一体系者的几句动听言辞就会有所改变，何况日本的说法和做法之间又总是南辕北辙呢！就现实而论，当近代国际关系体系被东亚人接受后，几乎很少还有人想回到不乏伦理但缺乏平等的家长制国际关系格局中（王韬：《华夷辨》），自然也就不会轻信在东亚历史上很少树立过良好道德形象的日本及其所主导的所谓"大东亚体系"。然而，这并不意味着"亚洲"的概念真的就与前近代东亚区域无关，也不意味着日本在"实体化"亚洲过程中利用东亚既有关系资源的做法便全无根据。日本的"大亚洲主义"之所以会速兴速灭，很大程度上乃根源于前近代东亚体系的"自解体"格局及其彼此分立的准"国民国家"性质，也决定于在东亚近代前夜，金字塔式的区域支配关系已经成为名存实亡的话题。森有礼以"属国"概念诘问李鸿章时李的频频语塞，证明了这一点（《清季外交史料》卷4、卷5）。尤为重要的是，那种类似于前近代"华夷秩序"的"大东亚体系"，还会毫无悬念地招致来自欧美世界之近代平等理念和国民国家体制的"警觉"与"防范"。换言之，当看清日本对周边邻国以欧美价值之名、行武力并吞之实的行动轨迹后，西方列强才终于了解到其东亚行动的目的——一个以摧毁中国中心"华夷秩序"的方式去建立新的、以日本为中心的"大东亚共荣圈"这一不啻否定"条约体系"的非平等区域关系体系。实际上，日本在处理东亚事务时与欧美各国所签订的全部条约和条款，都不过是为完成上述任务而与之进行的敷衍、欺瞒、迂回和周旋。由此而引发的最后对决——"太平洋战争"，终于使日本的全部"东亚理想"在东西方力量的双向围堵和并力反击中，走向悲剧。美国的日本史专家霍尔，曾矛盾地表达过他的感受，"在19世纪中叶，当欧美的旅行者注意到日本这些与世隔绝的岛屿的时候，他们很难想象在一个世纪之内这个神秘的'帝王之邦'将把自己变为现代世界的主要国家之一"，"但是今天日本是世界第三工业国，而且曾经试图搞军事扩张，结果把自己的城市变成核战争的最早目标"（霍尔（John Whitney Hall）：《日本：从史前到现代》）。

近代以来的日本行动，笔者以为至少给东亚世界带来了三种后果：一是"大日本帝国"的崩溃及其"大东亚共荣圈"的速兴速灭；二是连接过东亚内部的显隐纽带遭到了毁灭性的破坏；三是"亚洲"仿佛回到了奥特里乌斯地图的单纯地理指代，"东亚共同体"从原理到形式已经从世界舞台上消失。然而，当我们将前近代和近现代合而观之时不难发现，"东亚世界"还因此而形成了两个"长期"不易改变的局面：一是东亚各国的长期"不和"；二是东亚各国的"想和而不能和"。

东亚各国长期"不和"的原因，当根源于一个"不易消逝"和一个"彻底消逝"。所谓"不易消逝"，是指在国家独立、主权平等的现代国际格局中，前近代固有的"非平等"区域关系规则，仍若隐若现地存在于东亚人的内心深处。换言之，欧洲的"国际法"所带来的"国际关系"新格局虽然在形式上取代了东亚固有的"区域关系"框架，但东亚人在思考和处理地区问题时，总不免会带上传统的高下等级视角（马丁·雅克（Martin Jacques）：《当中国统治世界》）。对此，丸山真男在分析日本民族主义时所揭示的前近代东亚非平等"基因"，十足令人瞩目。他认为，该基因当中并没有现代国际关系中的对等性意识，相反，它是拿国内阶层统治（金字塔式）的眼睛来看待国际关系的。它观察问题的方法只能是"二者择一"，即不是征服或吞并对方，就是被对方所征服或吞并。它足以导致这样的结局，即一旦出现 1945 年"大日本帝国"战败等情形时，日本全体国民会突然出现整体性"虚脱"现象并陷入意义迷失和自暴自弃的泥淖中，难以自拔（丸山真男：『日本におけるナショナリズム』）。而本来在前近代即已松弛不堪的区域伦理感觉，经由近现代日本的无边界"恶用"，则已然从东亚人的记忆中"彻底消逝"。明治天皇对琉球、朝鲜的强行"册封"和昭和时代的"王道乐土"欺骗，毁灭了东亚两千年来息脉仅存的伦理暖意，以至于今日中、韩人士一听到"同文同种"和"东亚共荣"这些"和制汉语"时，心里的感受则不是恐惧，就是排斥、厌恶甚至愤怒。即便有欲通过那些旧日纽带试图恢复一点往昔情愫的努力，也不过仅停留在"乡愁"的水平上，说说而已。

然而，这并不意味着东亚各国从此就不想合作。"二战"后，随着相互间经济依存度的加深和恢复邦交后人员往来的频密，一个新时代的"东亚共同体"轮廓，曾几何时还仿佛给区域内民族和国家带来了再度联合的憧憬（魏志江等：《日本学界关于东亚共同体构想的基本观点》）。只是当人们想顺着这一方向去努力时却发现，无论是历史的远因还是现实的近忧，环绕东亚的国际关系格局，似乎都很难允许区域内还会发生真正意义上的联合。如果把传统东亚地区依经济版图大小和文化水平高低而结成的"朝贡体系"与"大东亚共荣圈"时日本军国主义所带来的东亚劫难合而观之，还会令人沮丧地发现，缠绕于东亚各国和地区之间"剪不断、理还乱"的恩恩怨怨，事实上已无法在短时间内得到真正的化解。而这两大东亚人难以逾越、由历史情结所带来的睦邻壁垒，却极大地便利了美国霸权对东亚的控制和支配。重要的是，由于GHQ（驻日盟军总司令部）对日占领所带来的影响已远非日本一国，所以这不但意味着几千年来东亚国际关系体系中第一次体制性地植入了代表世界强势的西方力量，而且由于美国在日本等国策应下所提出的"重返亚洲"战略已无人知晓会持续多久，因此，东亚各国"想和而不能和"的局面，就成了人们必须长期面对的现实。吊诡的是，美国对东亚内部恩怨关系的谙熟，还注定了它对东亚的控制和支配行为会十分得心应手：只要它想让东亚"热闹"一下，这里的国家和地区就会瞬间"沸腾"（韩东育：《东亚的病理》）。

然而，当我们搞清了东亚往日冲突的根本原因后，历史的旧页总需翻过的意义才能获得切实的凸显。一是，不这样做东亚便注定没有未来；二是，既然要面向未来，便没有必要重启那些有可能再度引发冲突的负能量。这或许意味着，有三个参考性指标可能会有利于对上述尴尬的摆脱：一是以利玛窦的《坤舆万国全图》去提示前近代东亚各国的区域连带感和亲缘伦理关系，但这种提示显然不是为了以联手的方式去对付哪个结盟的敌人。它的全部意义，只在于让亲缘者知道，东亚纠纷的本质其实不过"内争"，而从此不再将把伙伴间的竞争恶变为寇仇间的战争，哪怕彼此间存在着再大的差异和不同。二是用奥特里乌斯的《世界地图》，把东亚的邻里关系进行自然地理和生态意义上的还原和新诠。在这一前提下，东亚各国应完全按照威斯特伐利亚的国际平等规则行事，而无需重启那些有可能再度引发冲突的伦理恩怨及其他负能量。然而，除非我们硬要回到前近代充满温情却摒弃对等的伦理世界或者完全没入近现代平等至上却了无爱意的利害原则中，否则，历史和现实、东方和西方的复杂纠葛，大概最终只会把我们推向能够融汇并抽取出这两种构图中最优部分的中间值，并创造出能够引领人类未来的"新文明体系"。这将是一个以熔铸东西文明优长为特征的观念模式、行为模式和制度模式。它既包含东方的发展论原理，又融汇了西方的现代化价值；既能克服自文化中的惰性因素，亦堪抵制异文化中的负面影响。它不需追问纯然的自我，因为自我与外来已无法拆分；也无须苛察体用的畛域，因为体和用已融为一体（韩东育：《第三种传统》）。而且事实上，这已经不再是人们想与不想的问题，而是只能如此的问题。它要求未来的政治制度如此，价值取向如此，而国际关系规则，将尤其如此。

东亚近世思想交流中概念的类型及其移动

黄俊杰[*]

一 引言

东亚地域自古以来是许多文化与政治权力互相遭遇、冲突、协商与融合的所谓"接触空间"（contact zone）。[①] 在19世纪中叶以前的东亚世界里，中华帝国是区域中最大的强权，在权力不对等与文化不对等的状况下，与周边国家进行交流。

在近三百年来东亚的思想交流中，许多重要概念如"道""仁""仁政""中国""革命"等均起源于中国，而向周边地区传播。东亚概念移动与传播的过程，呈现如萨义德（Edward W. Said, 1935—2003）从近代西方文学理论之移动经验所归纳的四个阶段：（1）起源点，（2）时间之距离，（3）接受之条件，（4）新时空之中新用法与新地位之形成，[②] 但是在东亚交流史中概念的移动过程中，外来概念与移入地的本土因素之间的协商与冲突颇为激烈，值得深入观察。

本文以东亚思想交流史所见的四个概念，包括"道""仁政""中国""汤武革命"作为具体例证，分析概念的类型及其移动之效应，指出在东亚思想交流中，概念之"普遍性"（Universality）愈高者，愈容易被异域人士所接受并融入异时异地之文化氛围与异域人士之思想脉络。反之，概念之

---

[*] 黄俊杰，台湾大学讲座教授兼人文社会高等研究院院长。

[①] "接触空间"一词用 Mary Pratt 的定义，参见 Mary L. Pratt, *Imperial Eyes: Travel Writing and Transculturation* (London: Routledge, 2000, c1992), p. 6。

[②] Edward W. Said, *The World, the Text, and the Critic* (Cambridge, Mass.: Harvard University Press, 1983), pp. 226-227。此书有中译本，爱德华·萨义德著，薛绚译《世界·文本·批评者》，台北立绪文化事业有限公司2009年版，第344—345页。

"特殊性"（Particularity）愈高者，愈容易受到传入地知识分子之排斥，愈难以融入传入地之文化或政治氛围。"普遍性"高的概念之"超时空性"较强，而且多半属于"文化认同"（cultural identity）领域；"特殊性"高的概念则深具"时空性"，常涉及"政治认同"（political identity）问题。

为了论证上述论旨，本文第二节先讨论东亚思想交流中的接受者主体性问题，及其在概念移动中所产生的作用。本文第三节分析在思想交流中概念的类别及其移动之效果。第四节则提出结论。

二　东亚思想交流中的接受者主体性问题

在进入思想交流中接受者的主体性这个问题之前，笔者想首先指出：任何抽象概念一旦经由起源地形成或由开宗立范之思想人物提出之后，就取得了相对于思想接受者之自主性而言的自主性，因而也具有流动性，可以移动于不同的时间与空间。虽然后来参与思想交流的人物，会运用各种譬喻而将抽象概念予以具体化，但这只是为了阐明抽象概念之内涵，概念本身并不会因为被具体化而被固定化，因而阻碍其跨域之流动性。

由于直到19世纪中叶以前，中华帝国一直是东亚交流活动中的强权，也是诸多思想或概念的起源地，所以过去学术界许多有关东亚文化交流史的研究论著，常常过度聚焦于中国作为"中心"，而致力于研究"中心"对周边的"影响"。[①] 此类研究论著对于中国文化之向外传播之研究，有其贡献，但因常假定作为"中心"的中国文化与思想是最高的标准范式，所以常致力于检核周边国家的文化与思想，距离最高标准尚有多远。此种研究或可称为"忠诚度研究"（fidelity studies）。

这种研究视野虽有其操作上的方便，也累积了相当的研究成果，但是这类研究最大的障蔽在于过度忽略文化或思想交流中的接受者实有其主体性。诚如东晋（317—420）郭璞（景纯，276—324）所说："物不自异，待我而后异"，[②] "自我"主体性必须先建立，才能在文化交流中真正认识

[①]　例如：朱云影《中国文化对日韩越的影响》，黎明文化事业公司1981年版；朱谦之：《中国哲学对欧洲的影响》，河北人民出版社1999年版。

[②]　（晋）郭璞注《山海经》，台北台湾商务印书馆，1965年景印《四部丛刊初编缩本》，页1，上半页。

"他者",并与"他者"互动。思想或概念的接受者身处他们特定的时间与空间之中,面对境外传来的新思想或新概念,他们自主决定接受或拒斥,他们也决定如何接受或进行何种转化。在东亚思想交流史中,概念的接受者并非毫无自主意志地等待被外来思想洗礼,他们正是在与外来思想冲突、协商、融摄的过程中,建构并彰显他们的主体性。

但是,什么是"思想接受者的主体性"呢?这个问题可以从两个角度来思考。第一个角度是"主客对待"意义下的"主体性"。所谓"主"是指文化交流中思想或概念的接受者而言,"客"则是指域外传入的文化或思想而言。相对于概念的创始者或起源地之作为"他者"而言,概念的接受者绝不屈己以从人,反而致力于改变来自"他者"的概念或重新解释"他者"的思想,以适应"自我"思想风土,从而彰显概念接受者的主体性。

第二个角度是:相对于外来概念移入后所可能产生的社会、政治、经济效果而言,只有作为外来概念之接受者的"人"才是"主体"。这是"主副对待"意义下的"主体性"。《六祖坛经》云,"一切修多罗及诸文字,〔……〕皆因人置",① 在概念的移动过程中,首先撞击的是文本的阅读者,只有阅读者才是解读外来概念的主体。

在以上两种意义下的"接受者主体性"照映之下,源自境外的概念的移动,常常经过以下两种调整方式:

第一种调整方式是"挪用"(appropriation)。在思想交流或概念移动之中,所谓"文本"并不是只依原样而被理解,实际上,"文本"因应解读者的情境而对异域的解读者敞开、说话。② 在"文本"与解读者对话的过程中,"文本"的含义就必然会被解读者所"挪用",并创造新的含义。

在东亚的概念移动中,日本对"中国"这个概念的"挪用",最具有代表性。我过去曾说:"中国古代经典所见的'中国'一词,在地理上认为中国是世界地理的中心,中国以外的东西南北四方则是边陲。在政治

---

① 参见(唐)释慧能《六祖坛经》,台北善道寺佛经流通处,未著日期,《般若品第二》,第25—26页。

② 参见 Gerald L. Bruns, *Hermeneutics: Ancient and Modern* (New Haven and London: Yale University Press, 1992), p. 76。

上，中国是王政施行的区域。"① 11世纪上半叶北宋石介（字守道、公操，学者称徂徕先生，1005—1045）所撰的《中国论》这篇以"中国"为题的论文中，更将"中国"提升为居宇宙之中心位置的国家。石介说:②

> 夫天处乎上，地处乎下，居天地之中者曰中国，居天地之偏者曰四夷。四夷外也，中国内也。天地为之乎内外，所以限也。

这样定义下的"中国"概念，从17世纪以后随着中国典籍东传日本，难以获得日本知识分子的认可，他们站在"日本主体性"立场，将"中国"一词挪用来指称日本。17世纪的山鹿素行（名高兴、高佑，1622—1685）说:③

> 以本朝〔指日本〕为中国之谓也，先是天照大神在于天上，曰闻苇原中国有保食神，然乃中国之称自往古既有此也。〔……〕愚按：天地之所运，四时之所交，得其中，则风雨寒暑之会不偏，故水土沃而人物精，是乃可称中国，万邦之众唯本朝及外朝得其中，而本朝神代，既有天御中主尊，二神建国中柱，则本朝之为中国，天地自然之势也。

三十年后的浅见絅斋（名安正，别号望南轩，1652—1711）撰写《中国辨》一文，解构"中国"概念在地理上的固定性，他强调日本与中国"各是天下之一分"，并无贵贱之分。浅见絅斋说:④

---

① 黄俊杰：《东亚文化交流中的儒家经典与理念：互动、转化与融合》，台大出版中心2010年版，第86页。
② （宋）石介：《中国论》，收入石介著，陈植锷点校：《徂徕石先生文集》，中华书局2009年版，卷10，第116页，并参看本书第7章。
③ 〔日〕山鹿素行：《中朝事实》，收入广濑丰编：《山鹿素行全集》，东京岩波书店1942年版，第13卷，上册，第234页。
④ 〔日〕浅见絅斋：《中国辨》，收入吉川幸次郎等编：《山崎暗斋学派》，《日本思想大系》，东京岩波书店1980年版，卷31，第416页上。原稿系古日文，感谢工藤卓司教授与池田晶子女士指导并协助解读，中文译文如有欠妥之处，由本文作者承担责任。

中国夷狄之名，久行于儒书之中。因此，儒书盛行于吾国，读儒书者即以唐为中国，以吾国为夷狄，甚至有人后悔、慨叹自己生于夷狄之地。〔……〕夫天包罗地，地往往无所不戴天。然则各受土地风俗的约束之处，各是天下之一分，互无尊卑贵贱之嫌。

德川时代日本知识分子站在"日本主体性"立场，将"中国"这个概念中的"中国中心主义"（Sino-centrism）予以"去脉络化"，并将"中国"概念"再脉络化"于日本的社会政治情境之中，可以说是最典型的在"脉络性转换"之中，①"挪用"外来概念的一个个案。

第二种调整方式是"新诠"（re-interpretation）：对外来的概念提出新的解释，赋予新的意涵，使外来概念易于被移入地的人士所理解并接纳，而融入当地的文化风土之中。

中国的"仁"这个概念东传日本的经验，是说明这种融旧以铸新方式最恰当的例证。在先秦儒家"仁"学论述中，"仁"既是私领域的私人道德，又是公领域的社会伦理与政治原则，诚如萧公权（1897—1981）先生说："孔子言仁，实已冶道德、人伦政治于一炉，致人、己、家、国于一贯。"② 孔子之后，"仁"成为东亚各国儒家学者共同的核心价值，古代中国多以"爱"言"仁"，到了南宋朱子（晦庵，1130—1200）撰《仁说》这篇论文以"心之德，爱之理"阐释"仁"，将"仁"提升到宇宙论与形而上学层次，大幅提高了人之存在的高度与广度。

自从朱子提出"仁说"之后，德川时代一些日本儒者也以"仁说"为题，写了多篇论文，伊藤仁斋（维桢，1627—1705）、③ 丰岛丰洲

---

① 关于中日儒家思想交流史所出现的"脉络性转换"，参见 Chun-chieh Huang, "On the Contextual Turn in the Tokugawa Japanese Interpretation of the Confucian Classics: Types and Problems," *Dao: A Journal of Comparative Philosophy*, Vol. 9, No. 2 (June, 2010), pp. 211-223, 收入 Chun-chieh Huang, *East Asian Confucianisms: Texts in Contexts* (Göttingen and Taipei: V&R Unipress and National Taiwan University Press, 2015), chapter 2, pp. 41-56。

② 萧公权师：《中国政治思想史》，台北联经出版事业公司1982年版，上册，第62页。

③ ［日］伊藤仁斋：《仁说》，《古学先生诗文集》，收入《近世儒家文集集成》，东京株式会社ぺりかん社1985年版，册1，卷3，第60—61页。

（1736—1814）、① 赖杏坪（1756—1834）、② 浅见絅斋（1652—1711）③ 都撰有以"仁说"为题的论文。大田锦城（1765—1825）撰有《洙泗仁说》。④ 朱子的"仁"学论述东传日本之后，引起日本儒者激烈的批判。我曾研究德川时代日本儒者回应朱子的仁说，主要表现在以下两条思路，第一是对形而上学的解构：日本儒者言"仁"，多不取朱子以"理"言仁之说，伊藤仁斋中年以后所撰的论著如《语孟字义》《童子问》就完全摆脱朱子学的影响，而走先秦孔门以"爱"言"仁"的道路，强调在具体的"人伦日用"之中实践"仁"的价值理念。⑤ 荻生徂徕（物茂卿，1666—1728）则以"安民之德"释"仁"。不论是采取阐朱或反朱之立场，德川日本儒者都致力于解构朱子学的形上学基础。用传统的语汇来说，他们都在"气"论的基础上反对朱子仁学中的"理"学思想。日本儒者释"仁"的第二条思路是：在社会政治生活中赋"仁"以新解。日本儒者既反对朱子以"理"言"仁"，也反对以"觉"言"仁"，他们主张"仁"只能见之于并落实于"爱"之中。伊藤仁斋说"仁者之心，以爱为体"，在人与人相与互动的脉络中言"仁"。荻生徂徕说"仁，安民之德也"，是在政治脉络中释"仁"。⑥

在德川日本儒者重新解释来自中国儒学的"仁"这个概念中，我们看到了"日本主体性"在东亚概念移动中所产生的主导作用，也看到了外来的概念必须经过重新解释，才能适应移入地的文化氛围与社会环境。

总之，虽然我们可以在方法上区分"挪用"与"新诠"两种不同的方法，但是在东亚概念移动的实际历史进程中，"挪用"与"新诠"常常

---

① ［日］丰岛丰洲：《仁说》，收入关仪一郎编《日本儒林丛书》，东京：凤出版1978年版，第6册，第1—8页。

② ［日］赖杏坪：《原古编》，收入井上哲次郎、蟹江义丸编《日本伦理汇编》，东京育成会1903年版，第8册，朱子学派の部，卷3，《仁说》，第449—454页。

③ ［日］浅见絅斋：《记仁说》，收入《絅斋先生文集》，收入《近世儒家文集集成》（第2卷），东京ぺりかん社1987年版，卷6，第124—125页。

④ ［日］大田锦城：《仁说三书三卷》，收入井上哲次郎、蟹江义丸编《日本伦理汇编》，东京育成会1903年版，第9册，折衷学派の部，第452—472页。

⑤ 《论语·颜渊》"樊迟问仁，子曰：'爱人'"，见朱熹《论语集注》，收入朱熹《四书章句集注》，中华书局1983年版，卷6，第139页。

⑥ 黄俊杰：《朱子'仁说'及其在德川日本的回响》，收入锺彩钧编《东亚视域中的儒学：传统的诠释》（第四届国际汉学会议论文集），台北"中央研究院"2013年版，第409—429页。

是同时进行、同步完成的。

三 东亚思想交流中概念的类别及其移动之效果

以上所说的在概念从原生地移入接受地之后，常出现的"挪用"与"新诠"这两种现象，与概念的类型密切相关。我在此所说的概念的类型，常常也表现为概念的层级性（hierarchy）。

大致说来，我们可以将在不同地域之间移动的概念，以"普遍性/特殊性"加以区分：概念的"普遍性"愈高者，异域的思想人物之接受度愈高。举例言之，中国古典常见的核心概念如"道""仁"等，具有超时空性之"文化认同"或"价值认同"，常能对异域的文本解读者发出强烈的"召唤"（calling），使他们身心投入、生死以之。相对而言，概念的"普遍性"低而"特殊性"高者，常是特定时空交错下的思想产物，深深地浸润在原生地之特殊的政治与社会氛围之中，如中国经典中常见的"中国"或"革命"之类的概念，多属"政治认同"之范围。

我们举例阐释以上所说这两种类型（与层级）的概念及其移入异域之效果。首先，在东亚思想交流史上，"普遍性"最高而成为东亚知识分子核心价值的概念之一，就是"道"这个概念。孔子毕生慕道，志于"道"、据于德、依于仁、游于艺，欣夕死于朝闻，体神化不测之妙于人伦日用之间。《中庸》第一章："道也者，不可须臾离也。可离，非道也。"[1] 孔子以"一以贯之"说明他毕生抱道守贞的坚忍志业。"道"这个概念在中国儒家传统中既具有"内在性"，又有其"超越性"之内涵，所谓"极高明而道中庸"[2] 者是也。日本儒者虽然都同意儒者必须求"道"、行"道"，但是，他们对来自中国的"道"这个概念的内涵，也提出新的诠释。大致说来，日本儒者都强调"道"的"日常性"。山鹿素行就说孔子的"道"就是"日用所共由当行"之"人道"。[3] 17世纪古学

---

[1] （宋）朱熹：《中庸章句》，收入朱熹《四书章句集注》，中华书局1983年版，第17页。

[2] （宋）朱熹：《中庸章句》，收入《四书章句集注》，第35页。

[3] ［日］山鹿素行：《圣教要录》，收入井上哲次郎、蟹江义丸编《日本伦理汇编》，东京育成会1903年版，第4册，卷中，第20页。

派大师伊藤仁斋说孔子的"道":"不过彝伦纲常之间,而济人为大。"①仁斋解释孔子所说"朝闻道,夕死可矣"(《论语·里仁》)一语说:"夫道,人之所以为人之道也。"② 18世纪古文辞学派大师荻生徂徕说:"盖孔子之道,即先王之道也。先王之道,先王为安民立之,〔……〕"③又说:"大抵先王之道在外,其礼与义,皆多以施于人者言之。"④ 德川时代日本儒者浸润在"实学"的思想氛围之中,他们虽以"道"作为价值认同之对象,但是,他们在解释"道"时最常用的是"人伦日用"四字,他们所强调的是"道"的日常性。他们在新诠释之中解构中国儒学中"道"的超越性,并展现他们的社会文化"主体性"。

在东亚思想交流史中,"普遍性"略低于"道"的则有"仁政"这个政治理念。东亚各国知识分子都同意:统治者的道德责任在于实施"仁政",而"仁政"以统治者之"仁心"为其基础。我在上节已说明:德川日本古学派儒者大多采取以"爱"言"仁"的进路,他们都拒斥朱子之以"理"言"仁"的中国宋学的旧典范。古代中国的"仁政"概念东传日本以后,日本儒者判断统治者所施行的是否为"仁政"(例如管仲是否可称"仁"者)时,所采取的是一种"功效伦理学"而不是"存心伦理学"的立场。⑤ 朝鲜时代(1392—1910)不论是儒臣上疏或是君臣在宫廷的对话,以及传统中国儒者对"仁政"的探讨,均重视落实"仁政"之具体的政治或经济措施,而不在于对"仁政"作为统治者的道德责任之理论分析。⑥

---

① [日]伊藤仁斋:《论语古义》,收入关仪一郎编《日本名家四书注释全书》,东京:凤出版1973年版,第3卷,第230—231页。

② [日]伊藤仁斋:《论语古义》,第50—51页。

③ [日]荻生徂徕:《论语征》,收入关仪一郎编《日本名家四书注释全书》,东京:凤出版1973年版,第7卷,第83—84页。

④ [日]荻生徂徕:《辨名》上,收入井上哲次郎、蟹江义丸编《日本伦理汇编》,东京育成会1903年版,第6册,第65页。

⑤ 笔者采取李明辉的定义:"功效伦理学主张:一个行为的道德价值之最后判准在于该行为所产生或可能产生的后果;反之,存心伦理学则坚持:我们判定一个行为之道德意义时所根据的主要判准,并非该行为所产生或可能产生的后果,而是行为主体之存心。"参见李明辉《孟子王霸之辨重探》,收入氏著《孟子重探》,台北联经出版事业公司2001年版,第47页。

⑥ 另详:黄俊杰:《东亚儒家政治思想中的"仁政"论述及其理论问题》,收入《东亚儒家"仁"学:内涵与实践》(待刊)。

从"仁政"这个概念在古代中国由孟子（前371—前289）提出之后，在帝制时代的中国、朝鲜时代的朝鲜以及德川时代（1603—1868）的日本之所以被理解为"政术"而不是"政理"，[①] 主要原因是"仁政"概念经过了专制王权的权力网络的筛选与淘洗。"仁政"这个概念虽然是东亚各国知识分子共同的政治核心价值，但是，因为"仁政"这个概念之政治性远高于"道"这个概念，所以，异时异地的概念接受者常常必须因应他们所处的时空条件而有条件地接受。

与"道"或"仁政"这两个概念比较之下，"中国"与"革命"这两个概念的"普遍性"更低，不是受到概念移入地之知识分子的拒斥，就是必须加以大幅度地进行意义重组或创新。在上一节的讨论里，我们已经看到日本儒者挪用"中国"一词以指称日本，以新酒入旧瓶，偷龙转凤，极具创意。

"中国"这个概念在中国古典中将"政治认同"与"文化认同"熔于一炉而冶之，而且主张"中国"是宇宙之中心，与"边陲"之疆界不可逾越，是一种二元对立之关系，并由二元对立关系而衍生"中心"与"边陲"之"道德二元性"，这种"中国"论述在11世纪北宋的石介所撰的《中国论》一文中完全定型。

中国的"中国"概念东传日本，受到强烈的挑战。18世纪的浅见絅斋所撰的《中国辨》一文，就主张所谓"中国"并不是地理上固定不变的概念，依据"《春秋》之旨"[②]，任何一个国家都应以自己作为主体，任何国家都可以说是"中国"。从"中国"概念的移动及其在异域所获得的新解释，我们看到了"中国"概念中的"政治认同"因素被剔除，而"名分论"的因素则被强调。经过这种"去脉络化"与"再脉络化"的过程之后，日本知识分子就可以"挪用""中国"一词，并强有力地宣称日本才有资格称为"中国"。本书第七章对石介《中国论》与絅斋的《中国辨》有深入的探析与比较。

在东亚交流史中，比"中国"这个概念，更具有强烈的政治性而在移动过程中激起论辩的则是"汤武革命"这个概念。这个概念源于古

[①] 萧公权（1897—1981）先生说"中国政治思想属于政术之范围者多，属于政理之范围者少"，其说甚是。见萧公权师《中国政治思想史》，台北联经出版事业公司1982年版，下册，页946。

[②] ［日］浅见絅斋：《中国辨》，第418页上，并参见本书第七章。

代中国经典《易经·革卦》彖曰:"汤武革命,顺乎天而应乎人",① 孟子说:"贼仁者谓之贼,贼义者谓之残。残贼之人,谓之一夫。闻诛一夫纣矣,未闻弑君也。"(《孟子·梁惠王下》)② 孟子主张贼仁贼义的统治者已失其合法性,称之为"一夫"。荀子(前298—前238)也称许汤武革命是"夺然后义,杀然后仁,上下易位然后贞,功参天地,泽被生民"。③ "汤武革命"这个概念形成于封建邦国林立互争雄长的古代中国,到了公元前221年大一统帝国出现在中国历史的地平线上之后,这个政治理念与专制政体之间的紧张性就完全爆发。宋代中国批判孟子的知识分子如李觏(泰伯,1009—1059)、郑厚叔(叔友,约1135年)及司马光(君实,1019—1086)等人,莫不聚焦于孟子之肯定汤武革命、不尊周王之言论,视孟子的君臣观如毒蛇猛兽,对孟子展开激烈的攻击。④

这个在中国引起极大争议的"汤武革命"概念,东传朝鲜与日本之后,也与不同的权力关系互动而获得不同解释。朝鲜国王仁祖(在位于1623—1649)推翻其兄光海君而取得王位,1641年(仁祖十九年,明崇祯十四年)7月10日甲申的《仁祖实录》就记载延阳君李时白上劄"光海罪恶,不啻如桀、纣,反正之举,有光于汤武。臣闻诛一夫纣矣,未闻以桀、纣为逊位也",⑤ 显然为了讨好仁祖而肯定孟子的"汤武革命论"。

除了上述这个个案之外,朝鲜儒臣对"汤武革命"基本上都持保留态度,主要原因如南孝温(1454—1492,字伯公,号秋江)所说:"君臣之分,如天地之不可易。革命之际,非君如桀纣,臣如汤武,则叛命逆命而已。"⑥ 许多朝鲜儒臣在"君臣之分"的权力结构之下,思考"汤武革

---

① (魏)王弼撰,楼宇烈校释:《周易注校释》,中华书局2012年版,下经,第183页。
② (宋)朱熹:《孟子集注》,收入《四书章句集注》,卷2,第221页。
③ 《荀子·臣道篇第十三》,引文见(清)王先谦撰,沈啸寰、王星贤点校《荀子集解》,中华书局1988年版,卷9,第257页。
④ 笔者在《孟学思想史论(卷二)》,台北"中央研究院"中国文哲研究所1997年版,第四章,第127—190页有所讨论。
⑤ 《仁祖实录》,收入国史编纂委员会《朝鲜王朝实录》,首尔东文化社1955—1963年版,第35册,第120—121页。
⑥ [韩]南孝温:《秋江集》,卷5,《命论》,收入民族文化推进会编《韩国文集丛刊》,第16集,首尔民族文化推进会1988年版,第107a—107d页。

命",常常在"常 vs. 变"或"经 vs. 权",① 或在"汤武革命 vs. 匹夫革命"的对比架构下,为"汤武革命"提出合理化的新解释,这是因为他们都承认"苟有一日君臣之分者,则君之无道,不能匡救,而又从而为利,则甚不可"。②

"汤武革命"这个政治理念在德川时代引起极大的批判,伊东蓝田（1733—1809）与佐久间太华（？—1783）都对"汤武革命"痛加挞伐。正如张崑将所说,③ 这是由于"汤武革命"理念与日本之"天子一姓,传之无穷,莫有革命"④ 之政治观如方凿圆枘,完全冲突,所以日本儒者对"汤武革命"攻排不遗余力。

综合本节所论,我们可以说:在东亚思想交流活动中,政治性较强的概念通常也是特殊性较强的概念,所以域外人士较难以完全接受或必须大幅注入新的意涵,以适应本地的社会政治氛围。以本节所探讨的四个概念而言,"道"的普遍性最高,最不受时空因素之制约。"道"源起于古代中国,但几乎已经成为东亚世界的普世价值。"仁政"作为一个政治理念,对统治者课以道德责任,亦广为东亚各国人士普遍接受,但是对于"仁政"的具体内涵及其落实措施,则因应各国之特殊社会政治背景而因时因地制宜。"中国"与"革命"这两个政治性最强的概念,东传日韩之后就引起强度不同的反应或拒斥。

论述至此,如果我们上述说法可以成立,那么,我们必须接着讨论一个问题:"自由""民主""人权""法治""自由贸易"等源起于近代西欧特殊时空条件的价值理念,何以能够成为20世纪以降所谓的"普世价值"（universal value）？

这个问题可以从两个角度思考。首先,"自由""民主"等概念各有其"内在价值"（intrinsic value）,是人类共同接受的价值观,是东西海人

---

① [韩]金诚一:《疏:请鲁陵复位。六臣复爵。宗亲敍用疏。辛未》,收入民族文化推进会编《韩国文集丛刊》,第48集,首尔民族文化推进会1989年版,《鹤峯集》,卷2,第186c—194a页。

② [韩]权得己:《汤武革命论》,收入民族文化推进会编《韩国文集丛刊》,第76集,首尔民族文化推进会1991年版,《晚悔集》,卷2,第015b—016c页。

③ 参见张崑将《近世东亚儒者对忠孝伦常冲突之注释比较》,收入潘朝阳主编《跨文化视域下的儒家伦常》（上册）,台北师大出版中心2012年版,第177—213页。

④ [日]伊东蓝田:《蓝田先生汤武论》,收入关仪一郎编《日本儒林丛书》,东京:凤出版1978年版,第4册,引文见第2页。

人心同理同者。但是，近代以前源起于中国文化的"道""仁""仁政"等概念，也是普遍性极高的价值理念，何以不能成为全球的普世价值？这项质疑，就引导我们进入思考这个问题的第二个角度——思想交流的外部因素。自从19世纪中叶以来，西方列强挟其强大武力与资本主义体系，侵略亚、非、拉等地的弱国、穷国与小国，将其源起于西欧特殊条件下的政治、经济、生活方式及其价值理念，在非西方世界推广而成为"普世价值"。相对而言，近代以前的中华帝国并未诉诸武力的征服，也缺乏以现代工业生产为基础的资本主义体系，所以，历史上中华帝国对周边国家的支配，文化的因素远大于政治经济的因素。[①] 东亚周边国家在思想交流过程中，可以因应各国的政治社会条件而对来自中国的诸多概念，进行选择、鉴别、重组，并赋予新的意涵。

四　结论

从本文所检讨近代以前东亚思想交流中概念的类型及其移动效果，我们可以获得以下三点结论：

第一，概念一旦形成或被提出之后，概念就取得了自主性的生命，而不再是概念的起源地或原创者所能完全掌控。具有自主性的概念必然具有移动的能力，而在思想交流活动中，随"时"更化、与"时"俱进，因"地"制宜，旧概念传入异域后，因与传入地的文化因素互动而不断更新其内容，获得崭新的诠释，发展新的生命。

第二，从东亚思想交流经验观之，概念的移动必经移入地的"中介人物"（intermediate agents）如儒家知识分子、官员（如燕行使）或僧侣

[①] 最近Ian Morris检讨西方国家在历史上主宰世界的原因，指出西方的霸权主要是靠四个因素：第一个是开发能源的能力；第二个是都市化的能力；第三是处理资讯的能力；第四个是发动战争的能力。参见Ian Morris, *Why the West Rules — For Now* (New York: Farrar, Straus and Giroux, 2011)。Niall Ferguson也指出，西方成为全球霸权的主要原因，在于它具备六个由制度、相关观念及行为具体构成的新复合体：1. 竞争，2. 科学，3. 财产权，4. 医学，5. 消费社会，6. 工作伦理。参见Niall Ferguson著，黄煜文译：《文明：决定人类走向的六大杀手级Apps》，台北联经出版事业公司2012年版，第38—39页。Morris与Ferguson所说的支撑西方霸权的这些因素，都是近代以前的中华帝国尚不具备或较不发达的因素。

等各种与文化交流有关的人物之主体性的照应、筛选、重组、新诠，才能完成其新生命的转化。如果我们将思想交流中的概念譬喻为光的话，那么，这些异域"中介人物"就可以被譬喻为棱镜（prism），对于外来的概念进行折射、屈光或反射。如果我们将概念譬喻为波，那么，概念之波在抵达传入地的海岸线时，必经"中介人物"的淘洗，并注入本地的源头活水，才能汇成新流。

第三，从东亚概念移动史的经验来看，概念移动史的研究不能以概念起源地之原始形态作为最高而唯一的"标准"模型，更不能取起源地的概念模型以检核移入地新发展的概念距离起源地的"标准"多远。相反地，我们应将概念在各地的发展，置于各地的特殊条件或语境中加以理解，而视为各地文化主体性成长的过程。总而言之，在东亚思想交流活动中，概念随时随地而移动，并更新其内容，并无一成不变的标准形态，因此，思想交流史中的"中心"与"边陲"的界限也因时因地而更迭。

East-Asian Civilization Exchange:

The relationship between Chinese civilization and Khmer civilization

Khlot Thyda[*]

What is civilization?

The tree of civilization:

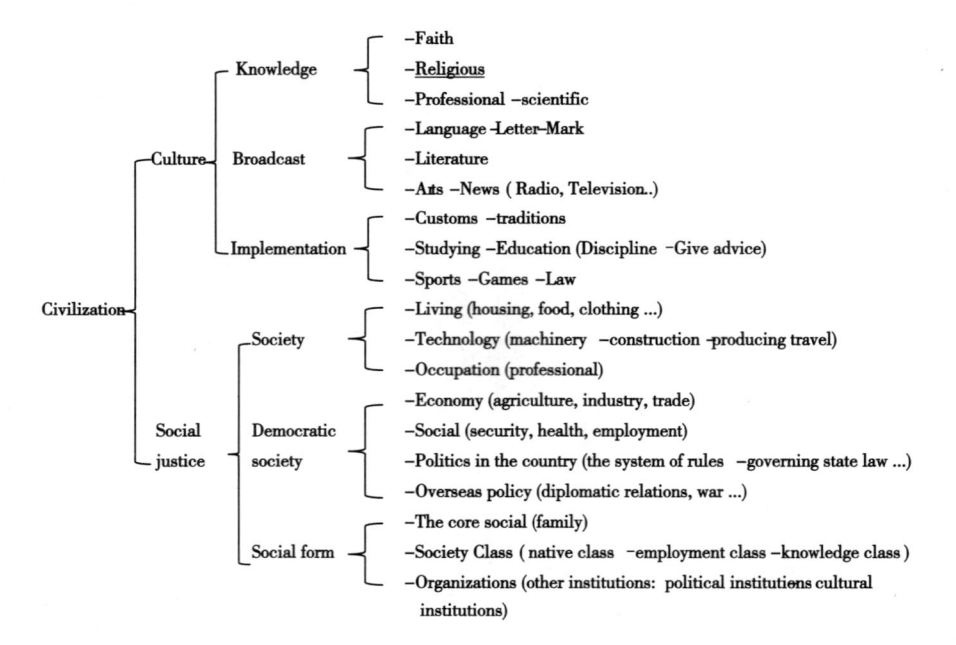

```
Civilization
├─ Culture
│   ├─ Knowledge
│   │   ├─ Faith
│   │   ├─ Religious
│   │   └─ Professional –scientific
│   ├─ Broadcast
│   │   ├─ Language -Letter-Mark
│   │   ├─ Literature
│   │   └─ Arts –News ( Radio, Television..)
│   └─ Implementation
│       ├─ Customs –traditions
│       ├─ Studying –Education (Discipline –Give advice)
│       └─ Sports –Games –Law
└─ Social justice
    ├─ Society
    │   ├─ Living (housing, food, clothing ...)
    │   ├─ Technology (machinery –construction –producing travel)
    │   └─ Occupation (professional)
    ├─ Democratic society
    │   ├─ Economy (agriculture, industry, trade)
    │   ├─ Social (security, health, employment)
    │   ├─ Politics in the country (the system of rules –governing state law ...)
    │   └─ Overseas policy (diplomatic relations, war ...)
    └─ Social form
        ├─ The core social (family)
        ├─ Society Class ( native class –employment class –knowledge class )
        └─ Organizations (other institutions: political institutions cultural institutions)
```

---

[*] Khlot Thyda, President of the Royal Academy of Cambodia (Minister), Personal Advisor of the Prime Minister HUN SEN.

Human civilization: when people have faced oppression, exploitation of others or were persecuted steal... People have always relied on faith to survive. But later, they still cannot win and live in suffered life, violence, so people seek something principles as necessary to protect themselves. With the search for peace, human has to create religious, traditions for a referral living in a good condition. Sometimes their struggles greatly exacerbated and voice call out for justice, moral, Dharma (God) humanitarian come together. We know that civilization is a philosophy of progress of human society, while I strongly favor holding civilization of resident religion and Buddhist.

The war happened, we heard the cries everywhere "justice" may be a rolling out look? Dharma has taken shape at the same time as the shape of human society. Society always raise these ethical for members of the legal, social but moral and rotate along with the evolutions of the society under the format of relations of production.

Primitive social morality is no less valuable. An ethic is universal for all members at the class and requires moral conformity with the interests of each class. Philosophers of ancient Greece raised moral views into consideration his education to the lives of people.

Boundless greed, greed of power, love of honor, prestige, gold and money is excessive loss of moral between individual, family and society. The war dragged on for some individuals the opportunity to use morally wrong direction or violate ethical conduct immoral to exploit. Terrorism and piracy whith are endless make people around the world suffer a horror.

Dharma is a commandment no one hates, not even animals are also pleased with the action of justice, but why does the world remain constant warfare? What war experience? Is the lack of critical thinking, moral, humanitarian, justice, understanding and tolerance, equity in legal terms?

1-The Khmer Civilization

Base on the main point of Khmer civilization was considered Women as a head family and society, we can say that the word Khmer likely from the word May (Leader), has evolved as follows:

— "May" refer to women as a mother in the family or women's leadership in society.

The Chinese society was marred Ancestor worship. Each family, husband is an important role in the responsibility to make this worship can take place without hindrance.

Old generation believe that the dead is not zero, its mean the soul is reincarnation. Khmer Loeu living on the plateau today also has great faith in this soul too. They has divided three types of the human soul is out of 6 months of a small dead souls go when dead and some soul died 6 months and then released. When people died, the dead were buried and individual vessels were used to bury with him to leave anymore. Khmer traditional nowadays, when people died we always preparing material donated to the monks to send to death body. According to the study's senior historian, Old generation buried death body in a jar or under a rock Gross (Dolmen or Menhir) by putting the body sitting. This habit endures until today: if the elite have died and they buried him in urns that might be derived from that jar and for ordinary people, they have put in urns and buried in the mausoleum.

The main consequence that occurred from the belief of the dead not zero, this is the belief in ghosts and spirits. Ancestor is the soul of the dead, and Ancestor still takes care of the welfare of their children. Khmer traditional nowadays, still have a lot of faith in Ancestor, especially among farmer: Ancestor's cottage was built in whole villages and also celebrate ancestor annually. Khmer Loeu also had the same faith, and they call ancestor 'God'. So we see that resident always practice ancestor worship a long time ago before India came. When Buddhist come, the belief of the dead not zero due to the spirit is born again, also similar with the resident's faith (soul and spirit are not precisely), and they accepted. Today, Phchom Ben ceremony is a random synthesis between Buddhist faith and resident's faith.

The early humans are also belief that a place for worship is on the height of the hill. Such is the faith of great an idea of building a temple: Eh No said: some historians such as Quarit Ches Wates, explaining that the temple is stand for the mountain and the penis placed in this temple is the ancestors.

Another notable resident is respect earth-gods because earth is basically offer rice as an every important food. This belief is shown in Chrot Prash Nangkal (Plugging) ceremony at the season of farming.

We have found that Buddhism has a very important function in the maritime trade routes between India and Southeast Asia, and they have observed that in many countries broadcasting the testimony of the oldest civilizations of India is Buddha caused to passengers by sea is very popular. Therefore, Buddhist seems to have opened the way to India to Southeast Asia. However, the United Kingdom, which was established in the region soon accept the idea of Shaiva of the monarchy, which is based on the relationship between Brahman and Princess and worship penis cult.

1. 1-Khmer civilization at Mountain Empire

The evolution of history has shown that Empire has greatly influenced Indian civilization twice, one is before 1st Century BC and other one is at the beginning of 5th Century BC. We will further test the mapping images Khmer society at that time based on China and inscriptions.

a- Social life: - Living, tradition

China said that people in the Mountain Empire were black skin, curly hair, not much beautiful. This information can tell us about the Anthropology of Khmer - Mon, and especially the anthropology of Khmer. Even China says Khmer have black skin, curly hair, not much beautiful is mean compared with the characteristics of China.

China document said people's wearing in Mountain Empire is: for ordinary people wearing silk Sarong and without shoes, rich man wearing Chorobab Sarong with shoes. Their house built from the ground cover on the top by Sloekcheak (kind of plan leaf) that grows in the sea and decorated. These houses are built from wood taken from the forest, have surrounds by fence and gathered as a village, have 50 to 60 houses and have a pool belong together.

In foreign policy, Mountain Empire is always alliances with countries such as India and China in particular.

There is also a commercial boom. Evidence is found port mark of a great friendship. Expert opinion that the port (Oh Kao port) is an international port because excavations at the site have found various objects from faraway countries such as the Roman Empire, from Iran to India. So that day locals Empire not only trade with the neighboring countries but also related business with China, India, Roman and Perks country. And the merchant can afford to travel so far because they are highly technical in construction big ship across the sea. China said the ship, about 30 meters in length, head and stern shaped head and tail like a fish. Many goods sold as gold, silver, Prae skirt and glass.

China said Mountain Empire is the place that great gold, silver, copper, lead, Somnor phahang, ivory and diamonds. This document also press that the diamond was diving toward the ocean and a solid iron is not broken, but broken iron. Also remarkable residents are good at doing gold or silver, like gold rings or bracelets or made dish from silver. Residents are also good at doing a mould, chorobab silk and glass refinery.

b- Culture

China document said: at the Mountain Empire have books and archives, but sadly because they may destroyed so that we have more difficult in the study of Khmer history in this era.

But even so, they knew that our first imported Buddhism is Yinayan Buddhist used Sanskrit language in India at Amaravatey esteem in 2nd and 3rd century of Christian era... VoKånh inscriptions and Ta Prohm Baty inscriptions can confirm this feature. Buddhism becomes prosperity, especially in 5th and 6th century under the control of King Kao Dern Jayavaraman and king Rudravaraman. We were sending monks of Khmer and India to China to bring other documents and Buddha to the king of Chinese cities, or help translate the scriptures from Sanskrit into Chinese. Buddhist monks stayed in China were around 16 years and have worked in 5 offices. King of China marvel at so much for the monks and regarded as his teacher.

When the Chēnlà armies make a war to get Mountain Empire, Yinayan Buddhist and Sanskrit lan guage may still prosperity. And when the early 7th century, Chinese Monk name Yi Xing who had to return from India to China said that "at the beginning Dharma is very prosper and advertisement everywhere but now a cruel king destroyed everything, even a monk he also did." So Yinayan Buddhist may lost at that time until the next century we can see Mahayana Buddhism came to advertise its doctrine.

And about Hinduism, there is respect for the Indian god (preash Eyso), preashVishnu, preashhariharak (Vishnu and Eyso together) and Brahma. In the earlier Mountain Empire, Eysoism Commission likely position as the official religion, because China documents show that, the king always went up on Motan Mountain to respect to Preash Morhasvarak. But then there is some imperial conversions Eyso and popular to Buddhist such as King Kao DernJayavaraman. And for Vishnu we saw the statues of Vishnu and his Avatars in Da Mountain, Kabas district, Takeo province. Besides this, the inscription of princess Kulbropearvetay and Preash Kunvaraman was also very popular in Vishnu too.

In the field of architectural, traditional temples built of clay. Therefore, we do not have any of these temples can endures to this day, but the castle was built by mountain cave. The temple stupa that we found at Oh Kao port and Angkor Borey are also building from clay. Art of statue we also found several Buddha and a lot of Tevakrop in Preykabas district Takeo province such as Buddha statue in Ramlok Pagoda, Reash Visnok, Preash Kalin, Preah Kovakrakthon. All these works are still in India style such as the statues has big built and has a bow or beam or caved letter on rock is not yet fully bas-relief style.

In conclusion, Khmer in Mountain Empire built a wonderful civilization is superior to neighbor's civilization in the same session. Although this civilization is not yet has real national style, but it is a very important heritage for new generation that of self-taken entry to foreign recycling by paired elements National to form a civilization which has strong style and reached the top at Angkor era.

1. 2-Khmer civilization in Chenla era

For Chenla era and Mountain Empire, the information related to cultural and civilization are almost from China. For Chenla era, we have relied on Switz (Souei) genealogy which records the story related to the reign of 1st Īśānavarman and Mr. Ma Guan Lin has copied completely in the book "The study of people outside China" in 13th century.

In religious field, inscriptions said the worship committee for the fellowship:

— Shiva: has position as official religion because all king since the 1st king Bhavavarman and his cousin King Citrasen are build "Leung (penis) of Preash Aysoh" as we have already seen. For some of the king such as King 1st Jayavarman, is likely to use death name already. However, the inscription in 713, which say that "The king who went to Sivaburak" maybe want to talk about this king. For the death name Intraklork that has record on stone number 803 seem want to talk about King Bos Skarak that we think he went to reign in Sampakburak when the royal throne is suite there and he used force. Besides worship in Leung (pennis), they also have other worship like Peash Eysoh is Basutaba.

— Vishnu: less popular. There is respect for the Phanchakrad.

— Hari Harak: They start to respect Hari Harak from Mountain Empire. There are a lot of illustrate Hari Harak Statue and good looking also such as Hari Harak Prasat Ondeth "Floating temple" (in Stong distric Kampong Tom Province). After this, there was no respect for Hari Harak.

— Buddhism: not lost, but is likely to fail gradually, especially in the 7th century, based on the testimony of the Chinese Buddhist, name Yi Sing. They see only one inscription descript about two monks. Mahayana Buddhism began to respect by some people.

In the field of architectural, the temple always make from bricks separate or together as a team. Flowers and the gate was made of sandstone.

The sculptures has India style, but mostly showed Khmer style and look so good also (Hari Harak Prasat Ondeth "Floating temple"). Decorative sculptures are luxury and will continue to its leverage until in Angkor era.

a. Religious Field

In Angkor era, religion has a very important function in politics, but there is no unified in leadership class, it is always changing according to each individual's preference: Some king's respect in Preah Eysoh, in Preas Vishnu, in Brahma and some respect to Buddhist. For this incident, Mr. Sylvain Levi said "it is derived from the social structure of Khmer. However, at that time, religion is consider as the goods they import or cultural dignity for the king and the nobles, and not mixed in the lower strata of society, that still maintain early faith is faith on Spirits. When visited Cambodia, Mr. Zhou Taguan observed that some people respect the rocks that Mr. Paul Pelliot thought that it was the "Leung (penis) of Preash Aysoh" in fact is just the rocks①.

State from 9th to 11th century, Shevakism commission have superiority on the other commission, because the king was mostly regarded as a religion for the state by respect Tevakreach, the king is consider as the god (Preash Eysoh) and have Sevak Leung placement in the mountian temple.

Then, we saw that Mahayana Buddhism imported since Chenla era (8th century).

b- Personalism Doctrine

From 9th to 12th century, we saw a lot of statue of divinity or Bodhisattva, but the statues were not representative of the divinity or Bodhisattva, they all representative of the king, royal relative, teacher in royal or the persons qualified for the national they exalted to the rank equivalent to divinity or Bodhisattva. Names of those statues were made by combining the name of the person they worshiped as divinity or Bodhisattva.

We should observe that personalization has very proper in last 12th century.

1. 3-The development of the E-Kuan Tao Dharma or vice champion justice in Cambodia

1. The E-Kuan Tao temple or Vice champion of Justice have come to spread dharma in Cambodia on January, 18, 1995 and registered in the Ministry of Dharma and Religion on 4 September, 4, 1995, the full name is "The Dharma E-Kuan Tao Association in Kingdom of Cambodia".

---

① Treung Nga "Khmer history" Part1-2, 1973 p. 62-66.

2. There are 30 churches and about 100 churches at home (home that consider as churches).

3. There are 30 Teacher, more than 100 seat, more than 60 human resource.

4. Partisan ask for Dharma has more than 10 thousand and other member is about 1000.

Then, because of this religion is become not so much popular, partisan become believe on magic things such as ghosts, they believe that ghost can have a lot of power so they started to respect and pray that l differences from origin doctrinal as we see today.

2. Chinese Civilization

2.1-Tao Doctrine in China has developed from the early medieval of China

China is one of the major religions such as Buddhism, Taoism, Islam, Catholicism and the Protestant religion.

Major respected by Wudoumi Tao Nig Taiping Tao, said that 5000 word of Taoism is the world of Laozi and Tai Ping Jing, principles of peace without end.

Tao which means "the way" is the basic belief of Taoism. Taoism believes that Tao is the unity and existence of the universe and make the magic for all living things. If a person decides to unite with him so he is as a person with virtue. The doctrine taught by the Scriptures to recognize and ethical farming and this doctrine believe that the implementation of the doctrine can be free from the pain of the world. For Taoism also believe that the doctrine can be leveraged to help living life and if have so many years of struggle will bring immortality.

The basic principle of Taoism is just like the Dao De Jing said, First: to have mercy. Second: Pure. Third: Do not be greedy (do not act in advance of other people). Mercy means to behave tolerance for things that are in it attention and support to the compatibility of the things that exist in the universe. Making pure means to eliminate excessive wealth and must clear in mind and body. Will not have the courage to take advantage or covet the wealth of others and that is humble, and its leadership in the truth instead of the expected behavior or characteristics of strength and overwhelming them. So Tao Doctrine show the way to peace and against war.

According to the Association of Chinese Taoism, no new laity and biologists are shown among the Chinese people during the many years ago. However, since the Tao doctrine, the multi-talented, became a long history, and it still has some influence in the countryside. This was true for both the areas inhabited by the Han people mostly lived a religious as well as ethnic minorities lived. In recent years, the actual results have implemented activities of Taoism. Taoism has researched the work and change with many foreign religious groups. The Chinese government has implemented liberal policies for religious believers. Means that religious believers can perform religious society can coordinate with construction. So it is not a difference thing and it is an optimistic future of Taoism in China better.

For recent evolutions, the study of Taoism and the meaning of the traditional of Taoism was emphasized more fully the strong influence of Taoism.

When there are more than 10 biologists and Buddha band participated in the concert. In 1989, Taoism Association of China celebrated for the members of the new pontiff (Quanchen) Tao. Baiyum church, White cloud church (White cloud Temple) wrote the 15 lyric tales, 1st Taoism selectively chosen from volunteers over a hundred①.

Soon there will be a creation of Chinese Taoism. With the development and the further expansion of Tao doctrine to development of China to the outside world, Taoism have analyzed and exchanged between the two countries and progress steadily. Sometimes Tao of China worried that Taoism is no alternative.

---

① Edited by Lu Yun "Religion in China, 100 questions and Answers", Beijing Review, Published by New Star Publishers, 24 Baiwanzhuang Road, Beijing, China, Zip Code: 100037, translated by: Dr. KHLOT THYDA, the People's Republic of China in 1994.

2.2-Buddhism in China

The first recorded in history books of China regarding the first arrival of Buddhism is in the 2nd century BC, when Yichun who is the ambassador of the King Dayuenhi, the kingdom which was established in Central Asia by a group of indigenous people who are resident in Gansu provinces in China, traveled to the Changan city, which currently is called Xiam. Teach neither Buddhist lesson, nor the law of Buddhism to his apostle is Jing Lu. It is also a possibility that could open the way to the diocese Western during the reign of Wudi of the Han in the 120 years, was a missionary of Dayenhi and Buddhism and those religion may come to China at that time as well.

Buddhism in China is developed into three branches: Han Language System, Tibetan System Buddhism and Pali Buddhism①.

Most believers of the Han Language System of Buddhism are the people of the Han. After Buddhism was introduced into China, the Scriptures of the sectarian Hindu of Buddhist has been reintegrated through the national culture of the Chinese as well as further development, especially in China today have 8 important region denominations: Sanlun region denominations, Yoga region denominations, Trantai region denominations, Huayan region denominations, Chan region denominations, Pure Land region denominations, Ritsugaku region denominations and Esoteric region denominations. Each region denominations develop in their own way.

Buddhism can be divided into two major sects, Mahayana and Theravada. Mahayana Buddhism has attached great importance to altruism doctrine when Theravada specified deviations personal pain. Both Han and Tibetan Buddhists in the vehicle are owned by the Great Buddhist Pali (Pali Buddhism), and also belong to the Theravada.

The earliest, Chinese people took to print an image of the Buddha that we found in the Preash Tribiaduk in China. However, the Buddhist art of China's

---

① Edited by Lu Yun "Religion in China, 100 questions and Answers", Beijing Review, Published by New Star Publishers, 24 Baiwanzhuang Road, Beijing, China, Zip Code: 100037, translated by: Dr. KHLOT THYDA, the People's Republic of China in 1994. p. 5.

steadfast with Chinese characteristics and can be considered as the heritage qualities the art world.

Chinese architecture and art images are mostly from Buddhism. The best of contemporary Chinese architecture is the pagoda of Buddhism. Nowadays, Long Hua pagoda is in Shanghai and local in Baoen temple, Suzhou district. Both pagodas were built up during the 3rd century and were built to continue thereafter. During the 4th and 6th century architectural of pagoda has been found throughout the country.

The pagoda of Buddhism is still well protected, which can be divided into two features is: India-China features and another is China features which is often shoots from China's cultural ideas. Buddha's statues of China change in subject matter according to its effects. Both art and pagoda have form and methods are valuable for the study of architecture history and cultural heritage of China because they are well protected their architecture too.

Meanwhile, China's musical, astronomy, pharmaceutical science and sports gymnastics spread with the introduction of Buddhist doctrine.

History document has shown that the Chinese Buddhists was given attention to public welfare for a long time. For example, some monk pharmaceutical operations and distribution of medicinal plants (herbs), some monks build bridges and build roads and some monks taught to read, write, or planting trees. Today there are many magnificent spectacles throughout China, which is testimony to the good work of monks in planting trees (Afforestation) and the building of luxury pagodas.

Today Buddhist China remains concerned about the welfare of the public concerned. This concerning is an evidence based on equality that their love toward faceted meditation and farming. The first philosophy is supported by meditation Baizhang (720-814); they still push public affairs such as forest cultivation repair bridges and roads, and the implementation of Medical Sciences.

The Chinese Institute of Buddhist Studies was established in Beijing in 1956 as a special high school for advanced training craft Buddhism. The Institute began to enroll students who learn awarded in 1961; the institute has provided the first Tibetan language courses in 1962. Students from the Institute of

Buddhist temple and presence across the country amounted to 384 have graduated from the institute before it was stopped temporarily in 1966. Beginning studies continued in 1980, nearly 100 students have graduated from the institute. Now the Institute has 70 students in the programs of 4 years and can be continue to study next level.

In 1987, the Institute for the training of researcher's Tibetan Buddhist system was established in the last king 10th Bainqen. Local Buddhist school and training courses have also been established, such as the Institute of Buddhist Shanghai, Sichuan School for Buddhist nuns, Fujian Buddhist Institute and southern Fujian Buddhist Institute.

Mr. Zhao Puchu director of the Buddhist Association of China think that Chinese Buddhism has a history of nearly 2,000 years to make China prosperous and rich culture as well. Within this meaning (Tems) has experienced and influential international Buddhist China must be recognized. Moreover, because of the perspective of religion or the display features of the study at any time that the level of thinking on cultural development and progress of human civilization.

2. 3-Tao Religious

Tao religion is a religion of Chinese nation that takes place in China in the modern era and nominal primitive.

Tao creator is a Chinese national hero whose name is Lao Chu and others called Loa Chun and others called Hleu En. This hero is born in Zhou Dynasty era before Confucius 51 years ago between Buddha time is in the year of Buddha go to stay in peace.

Tao's word has describe as dharma that mean for their condition, they can understand that Tao is God.

Tao doctrine is the doctrinal nature, doctrine that believe on nature or related with natural. In theory, this doctrine consider Tao as the construction and destruction of the world.

Lao Chu has been determined that all objects in the universe is born from Tao, all people who are born in this world is just a part of Tao and born from Tao as other objects. Tao has every power, including the power to order the coming season, flood, water go up and down, to fire, hot and cold etc. But nobody cannot see Tao or hear his sound. Conduct the mortal universe is simultaneously appointed as Tao is going to happen or zero mutual line of Tao. If realized this creature must give physical life of Tao.

a- About the death of Tao Doctrine

Tao Doctrine related with the death of Loa Chu performances that: death is cannot avoid, which cannot escape but should rejoice with death because it will return to the zodiac of the universe, which is the element simple as autumn, sadness as the property of scholars, death as the end of us. Accordingly in comparison when it comes, we only and must take to people who are terrified of death may not clearly understand that holiday the peace of death. Since about the time of death raconteurs a common human qualities, death is a peace place of all human.

b-Tao partisan and believe in magic things

Tao partisan, students of Lao Chu who believe on Tao called "Tao Zin" means "people of the Tao or Tao partisan" for clergy called Tao Sher "Tao clergy". Clergy Tao much enjoyed walking to wish for peace. Even Loa Chu also conduct himself as a clergy.

3. The Relationship Between the Khmer Civilization and Chinese Civilization

China's interested in the region of Southeast Asia is a long time ago and marched to get Tonkeung to take direct control since 111 befor Christian era. Until 939 of Buddhist era.

In the middle of the 3rd century of Buddhist era. Two Chinese envoys is Kang Tai and Tchou Ying has stay in the Mountains Empire for a while. When he returned Kang Tai has published a story related to his long journey. Then the king of Mountains Empire always has good relationship with China. So we have a diplomatic mission, commercial and cultural exchange are often mutual and all this even were recorded by Chinese historical thoroughly.

In addition to the document, we have a recorded history document which is relating to Chinese believe on Buddhist. All of Buddhists are high knowledge and have the utmost faith in Buddhism and used to travel to India to visit some of the sacred places and to increase religious knowledge. These trips have been deployed from 3rd—11th century of Buddhist era. Buddhists were traveling by sea and tie up in the state that has influenced by India. History book written by Hiuan tsang and Yi-Tsing have said about Cambodia in 7th century.

Among of China's documents, the most important document is recorded by Zhou Daguan which has title "Recording bout traditional of Chenla country". This document was described about Cambodia in latest Angkor era and has described about the capital, standard of living tradition of the locals and the other institution in that era. Achievement of Zhou Daguan have translate into French language for two time: 1st by Abel Rémusat in 1819 and 2nd by Paul Pelliot in 1902. In the final translation, all researchers of Khmer civilization always used as reference. But we should add that Mr. Lee Theam Teng, Khmer Writers' Association members who visited China in 1962 has copied the files of Zhou DaKuan in Chinese and then translated into English, published in 1971. Earlier Christian, most important state in Southeast Asia is Mountain Empire. China called Funan[①].

According to Mr G. Cœdès's thinking, Funan is come from Khmer ancient word is Vnum (Mountain) which is now becoming Phnum (mountain). He emphasized that the king at the time has function name is Sdach Phnum (King of Mountain), Khmer ancient word called KorongPhnum equally Sanskrit's word is Borvit Phobal or Shell Rech.

For the above routine Mr. E. Aymomier noted that in ancient China is no reason to separate the people from the country. They often use the same name for human, capital and for a whole country or the rank name of leadership.

For Mr. G. Cœdès opinion, this document should be noted that China has said clearly about Emperor of Mountain Empire name KorLong which means "king reigned". So "Funan" is called by China depend on the name of

---

① Treung Nga "Khmer history" Part1-2, 1973 p. 44-46.

Emperor of Mountain Empire. And the reason of having the name like that is probably from the mountains, where the emperor go to meet Preas Eysoh (his God). China said that the deities descended on Mo-tan Mountain, often came there to express his greatness emperor, all King received the blessings of God and people prosper because of it too.

First Dynasty Creating

Mr. Kang Tai, Chinese envoys who traveled to Funan in the middle of 3rd century, recorded first King of Funan name Hùn tián from India or from the Malayu or South Island. Hùn tián dream about angel gave magic bow and ordered him to board a large ship. In the morning, Hùn tián went to the temple and saw angels bow like a dream. After that, he traveled by the sea and landed Funan. In Funan have a queen named Liu Yee, when she saw the strange ship came back to fight an enemy but Hùn tián used his magical bow shot her ship leaked from side to side. She was very nervous and asked to surrender. Hùn tián took her to be his wife then become an Emperor in Funan.

Here's how storytelling (version) of China on the origin of Funan's dynasty.

According to royal genealogy (Lang genealogy) said that King Hùn tián have a children who go to manage a part of land which have seven city. Amount of reign King, has a king named Hùn Pang Huang. This king has used various tactics to separated army's unity until he got success. Then he sent his children and grandchildren to control them one by one. King Hùn Pang Huang died at the age of 90 years. His second son named Pan Pan was enthroned but gave states Centurion to Fan Cheng Mann charge. King Pan Pan reigned only 3 years old and died. People have agreed to Fan Cheng Mann reigned. This king had the courage and power, he came to take so many neighbor country to live in his controlling. He was announced that "the Emperor of Funan".

China document has confirmed to us further that King Fan Cheng Mann died when he lead army to fight the Qin Lin state (wall of gold), which

Mr. G. Coedès said "Suvarnaphumi" (Land of gold in the Bali article meaning) or Suvanakot (Rampart of gold in Sanskrit article meaning in South Burma or on the Malayu).

All the above events ranging from Fan Cheng Man's death, Fan Si Yun enthronement took place between the years of 225 – 250. In King Fan Chhan's reigned, mountain Empire has first associated with Marin royal in India and sent first emissaries to China. For relationship with China, G. Cœdès thought that it is because of business more than politically. However, at that time, during 3 United Kingdom – South China (Wu Kingdom) which cannot trade with Western country through land way (controlled by Wee), turn to buy luxury items they need in the way of the sea. Thus, as they come in contact with the Mountain Empire, in the middle way of the business on the sea, and which is place which they cannot avoid for those sailors going through Malaka or for who like to bring goods across Malayu.

King Fan Si Yun reigned in 289 until the middle of 4th century. There are no document mention about Mountain Empire. Sin and Lang Royal genealogy said: in 357 King of Mountain Empire named Tian Qu ChhanTan brought elephants as a gift for king of China. Tian Qu is the name called by China refer to India. So Tian Qu ChhanTan means that Indian name "ChhanTan".

King Rudravarman is the last of King Mountain Empire. He sent envoys to China several times in between 517 and 535 Christian era. Mountain Empire envoys who brought a rhinoceros to the king of China in 539 had said "in my country has a god head with 3 meter long hair". When heard it, King Lang Woo Ty ordered the monks name Thae Yun Pao come to Mountain Empire with that envoys, to bring the god head to China. Sanskrit inscription at Bati district said, he was on the throne, while they worked to build Buddhist that written in that document. According to Lang Royal genealogy, at that time Buddhist is very prosperous because has a China missions was sent to the Mountain Empire between 535 and 545 Christian era to suggest the imperial in this empire, sent a scholar and the Buddhism's document to China. At that time, has a Indian scholar name Boramathi or Kun Rothanak has stay in Mountain Empire, so the king decided to send him to China by brought so many Buddhism's documents in 546.

Mahayana Buddhism does not specify the timing of the importing into Cambodia, but if we examine the relationship between Cambodia and China, this relationship have since Funan era. Currently, there are many small denominations such as respect Mei Leuk god, Khong Meung denominations, Kong Si-em denominations ans Nakta Chin (Chinese ancestor) denominations. This religious has member more than 15 thousand[1]. In particular, current Confucianism has been a lot of progress beginning from 2009 in our Academy of Cambodia. H. E. Xi Jinping was the former Vice President, he was invited to inaugurate there also currently expanded in several places in the country to change the culture of each other.

Conclusion

To avoid overheating the enemy steal or vandalize laws or any documents and national culture, we have no way to solve but we must to study hard to get knowledge of any laws or history that our ancestors often instruct from mouth to mouth, from one generation to other generation that it a perspective of getting high knowledge. Moreover, in response to modern technology, we should modern synthesis of new knowledge and old knowledge to overcome.

After all, such as the operation of the Tao doctrine, Loa Chu has performances that the original state of the human is difference from the nature or the fact of nature, so just need to keep this state in pure by follow the law of the high maternal that mean the natural give us a birth so the natural always give justice to everyone, not biases. The natural is admissibility, not love or hate to any one and conduct themselves in accordance with the facts that base on, etc.

Buddhism's purpose is also not different to other religion, it only different some practicing and theories, but the same good intentions. What difficulties and conflict between one civilization and other civilization is due to the human

---

[1] Reporter of Paharak (other religion) religion's commission: "Religions in Cambodia", 2003, p. 3.

factor, when people do not understand, when people recognize that their favorite, at that time human will face a crisis between religion and religion as well as between civilization and civilization. Therefore on behalf of our researchers, as well as all partisan should do to be a model is: 1. does not fall in the wrong direction, 2. honored well, 3. Gratitude: know the gratitude they had done to yourself, 4. like to think good all the time, 5. prefer to speak good regularly, 6. progress knowledge and morality, 7. Keep manage your heart, 8. justice is the fun is near your school, pagoda that an easy way to give alms or listen to dharma, 9. All human who live around us are good people, have dignity and know how to respect each other (this is how dharma, civilization and religion are have the same purpose).

Reference

1. Edited by Lu Yun "Religion in China, 100 questions and Answers", Beijing Review, Published by New Star Publishers, 24 Baiwanzhuang Road, Beijing, China, Zip Code: 100037, translated by: Dr. KHLOT THYDA, the People's Republic of China in 1994.

2. Dr. KHLOT THYDA Buddhist wisdom.

3. Dr. KHLOT THYDA Buddhism financial trade and religion in society Khmer next day 7th January 1979 (1979- present), pages 259-260.

4. Treung Ngear "Khmer history" part 1-2, 2517 of Buddhist era, 1973 28-30 of Christian era.

5. Tang Vekhoung (director of Cambodian students and offering Christians) "contribute to maintaining peace and development".

6. Khmer society "intervention in a national seminar on "the religious situation in Cambodia today" July 31, 2002.

7. William Collins: "The Chams of Cambodia" 1996.

8. Bahai court of Justice religion in Cambodia: "Bahai religion" 1999.

9. Paharak religion Department (Cult and Religion ministry): Paharak religion's statistics in Cambodia, 2004.

阳明学的东亚传播实态考：
以朝鲜朝中期为例

李学堂[*]

一　绪论

　　作为东亚儒学重镇之一，韩国儒学按照其自身的发展规律，形成了有别于中国宋元理学的性理学特质和浓郁的民族特征。但不可否认的是，这种民族化儒学——朝鲜性理学的形成，是中国儒学自公元前3世纪前后传入朝鲜半岛以后，历朝历代在与儒学的源头国中国不断互动的过程中实现的，这种文化上的互动对东亚的儒教文化圈的形成起到了决定性作用。从新罗的遣唐使和宾贡科生的留唐学习，高丽国王和文臣的内服交流，一直到朝鲜朝每年定期和不定期的朝贡使节团朝天燕行，地缘政治的结果所导致的中韩关系使韩国历代知识阶层频繁地往来于中国大陆与朝鲜半岛之间，儒学思想随着历代学者对五经四书经典的悬吐解读逐渐被接受，其教化性内涵不断深入人心，本土化了的儒家政治典章制度和社会礼仪规范最终被确立并推广开来。

　　中韩历代儒学者间的互动交流，表现出通过批判性的研讨，在相互辩驳、诘难的过程中实现相互认可和文化交融的显著特征。这在壬辰倭乱前后的朝鲜中期表现得尤为明显，此时期已经通过前期学者如李穑、郑梦周、权进等人的经典解读和教化，李滉、曹植、李珥、李彦迪、奇大升等人的理气论、四端七情论、人物性同异论等主题的往复论辩，朝鲜特色的

---

[*] 李学堂，山东大学韩国学院教授。本研究得到了山东大学儒学高等研究院学术研究项目"韩国集部儒学文献萃编"（2012—2018）的资助。本文曾以"朝鲜朝中期的阳明学批判：以退溪、西厓、栗谷为中心"为题刊于2016年《韩国实学研究》第31号，收入本书时题目、绪论、结论部分略有修改。

性理学体系已经基本上得以确立起来。朝鲜性理学又称为朝鲜朱子学，是以接受程朱理学性即理思想和理气论为前提而确立起来的一种理论体系，尤其对朱子《小学》和《四书》注释的理论受容和社会实践上的奉行是主要的方式和途径。将朱陆之辩中的朱子思想视为不容置疑的定论，形成了朝鲜性理学内部的一种卫道论理念，此亦即朝鲜性理学的道统意识和门户之见，对陆王心学一边倒的批判和辩驳的理由和根据无不与此有关。

在王阳明《传习录》出版后的第三年（1521年），朝鲜就有了关于这部书的讨论，此后阳明心学一直受到以李滉为代表的朝鲜士人的尖锐批判。这种批判并未局限于朝鲜朝内部，而是蔓延到了阳明心学的源头国，积极主动地作用到了中原思想界。[①] 朝鲜儒学界不仅利用朝天、燕行的机会与朱王两派学者接触和交流，阐明其思想立场，还在壬辰倭乱时期与援朝而来的明朝将领、阳明学者宋应昌等就《大学》的朱王见解差异各陈己见，在戎马倥偬之场携手编纂了题为《大学将语》的著作，堪称东亚战争史上的奇观，在世界军事史上也是罕见的学术现象，具有特殊的历史和学术意义。[②]

从根本上说，程朱和陆王之争是儒学内部长期存在的矛盾的公开化，同样成为当时中韩两国学者间的论争焦点。程朱与陆王之间重伦理与重道德的差异，可以向上追溯至孔子重"道"与孟子重"志"的异时态差异，以及二程同时态下的道学、心学重心的偏移，正因为这个原因，双方论争不可能分出胜负输赢，最后只能走向思想理论上的包容和贯通。从朝鲜中期退溪、栗谷等人对王学的批判来看，中韩理学界共有的理论模式特征和话语表述方式决定了话题的相通性和有效性，使得批判性的话语过程反而成为促进相互理解和沟通的催化剂。在同属理学一脉的理念上并不相互排斥，尤其在诚敬慎独的治学方法论和实学指向的知行论上并无根本性的矛盾，形成了相当的理论共鸣，在一定程度上表现出让步和默契。但一些理论上的分歧还是得到了确认，如道学和心学的理念和治学方法的不同、"性即理"与"心即理"的不同、"为学之方"上的"易简"与"支离"

[①] 在壬辰倭乱前后，中韩儒学界发生了三次理论争鸣，辩论的主题均是针对阳明心学。即1566年尹根寿和陆光祖之间的"朱陆论难"、1574年的许篈与明朝士人之间的"卫朱斥王笔战"以及1593年李廷龟与宋应昌之的"大学讲语论辩"。

[②] 参见笔者指导的徐云飞硕士论文《洪大容实学思想研究》（2014年）、杨晓云硕士论文《月沙李廷龟的儒学思想研究——以〈大学讲语〉与〈筵中讲义〉为中心》（2014年）。

或"博览"与"守约"的不同、立言宗旨上的"心理为一"与"心理为二"的不同。

因此，这种理论上的辩驳和争鸣看似激烈，实则促进了朝鲜性理学者对阳明心学的理解，加速了在韩半岛的传播，其思想上的怀疑主义和重视实践的实用主义、行动主义特征在很大程度上推动了朝鲜后期实学的产生和发展。

二 退溪的阳明学批判

1. 退溪对阳明学学理性质的辨别与批判

退溪李滉（1501—1570）批判陆王心学的最重要的著述有两篇。一是《〈传习录〉论辩》，二是《〈白沙诗教〉〈传习录〉抄传，因书其后》，前者是退溪对阳明心学主张的举例辩驳，"《传习录》，王阳明门人记其师说者。今举数段而辩之，以该其余"；后者则通过对比白沙学与阳明学，指出阳明学的禅学异端性质及其危害。在退溪年谱中，也记述了退溪作这两篇文章的思想缘由，即"先生又尝患中国学术之差，白沙、阳明诸说，盛行于世，程朱相传之统，日就湮晦，未尝不深忧隐叹，乃于《白沙诗教》、阳明《传习录》等书，皆有论辩，以正其失云"①。

退溪的《〈传习录〉论辩》涉及了王阳明与弟子徐爱、郑朝朔之间有关"亲民"与"新民""格物致知""心即理""知行合一"说等对心学诸主要问题的解释与答疑。

对于王阳明的解释，退溪根据阳明师弟之间的问答内容予以辩驳，并下了结论。现将退溪由此得出的"王阳明论"内容，摘录如下：

① 阳明乃敢肆然排先儒之定论，妄引诸说之髣髴者，牵合附会，略无忌惮，可见其学之差而心之病矣。由是求之，种种丑差皆是此病。

② 本是论穷理工夫，转就实践工效上衮说。

③ 阳明徒患外物之为心累，不知民彝物则真至之理，即吾心本具之理，讲学穷理，正所以明本心之体，达本心之用，顾乃欲事事物物一切扫

---

① 李滉：《四十五年丙寅，先生六十六岁》，年谱，《退溪先生年谱》卷之二，第230页。《韩国文集丛刊》第31辑（本文所引用的原文资料均出自该丛刊，以后不再予以注明）。

除，皆揽入本心衮说了，此与释氏之见何异？而时出言稍攻释氏，以自明其学之不出于释氏，是不亦自欺以诬人乎。彼其徒之始明者，不觉其堕坑落堑于邪说，乃曰言下有省，亦可哀哉。

④ 阳明谓今人且讲习讨论，待知得真了，方做行的工夫，遂终身不行，亦遂终身不知，此言切中末学徒事口耳之弊，然欲救此弊，而强凿为知行合一之论。此段虽极细辩说，言愈巧而意愈远。……故《大学》，借彼表里如一之好恶，以劝学者之毋自欺则可，阳明乃欲引彼形气之所为，以明此义理知行之说则大不可。故义理之知行，合而言之，固相须并行而不可缺一；分而言之，知不可谓之行，犹行不可谓之知也，岂可合而为一乎。阳明亦自知其说之偏，故以不分知行为知行本体，以分知行为私意隔断。然则古圣贤为知行之说者，皆私意耶？

退溪认为，朱子释"亲民"为"新民"是在学字义上的串说，与养之亲之之意，初不相涉（①）；致知格物本是穷理功夫（②、③）；知行固相须但不可视为一事（④）。而王阳明"亦自知其说之偏"，为了自圆其说，"乃敢肆然排先儒之定论，妄引诸说之聱齾者，牵合附会，略无忌惮，可见其学之差而心之病矣。由是求之，种种丑差皆是此病"（①）。

从批判强度上说，与对白沙陈献章和湛若水的较温和批评不同，退溪直指阳明心学为纯禅学，考虑其异端危害性，主张必须极力排斥之。

这里退溪从"亲民"说"心即理""知行合一"等王学的重要主张出发，从学理和性质上指出了王学的弊端。虽然此处并未提及王阳明晚年定论"致良知"说，但并不能说明退溪对此没有了解。实际上退溪对王阳明的生平及心学上的重要主张，包括致良知说均有把握。《退溪先生文集考证》中记载："阳明，明儒王守仁，字伯安，浙江人。自幼聪明才辩，登进士，其学以致良知为说。嘉靖初，论功新建伯，既而削其爵，且斥其伪学，榜示天下。"① 这表明退溪学派内部对王阳明在世时心学在明朝的际遇状况也十分了解，并且对其晚年定论致良知之说也颇有研究，这与中国学界所知的退溪及退溪学派的阳明学批判情况有较大出入。②

---

① 李滉：《答洪应吉》卷13，书，《退溪先生文集考证》卷4，第350页。
② 如钱明（2006）认为，朝鲜中宗时期传入韩国的《传习录》为"不完整抑或不能代表真正阳明精神的阳明学，这就是何以李退溪批判王阳明仅涉及阳明早期思想中的'心即理'、'知行合一'、'亲民'说等，而从不提及阳明的晚年定论'致良知'说的根本原因"。他断定退溪对王阳明的"致良知"说并不了解。参见照第138—146页。

而且退溪对与阳明心学有密切关系的学者如甘泉湛若水、白沙陈献章的学说也深有研究，"湛氏之学，曾于《白沙集》，略见其病处，其格通一书，亦曾电披，见其好为异论，心固厌之"认为湛氏之学非程朱正学。

在《〈白沙诗教〉、〈传习录〉抄传，因书其后》中，退溪通过对比分析白沙学与阳明学的差异，提高了批判阳明学的强度。

从题目《〈白沙诗教〉、〈传习录〉抄传，因书其后》可以看出，退溪及其门下弟子把湛若水注释的陈献章《白沙诗教》和阳明弟子整理的王阳明《传习录》作为批判性资料作了广泛传抄。

《白沙诗教》又名《白沙子古诗教解》、《白沙先生诗教解》，是湛若水（1466—1560）注释其师陈献章（1428—1500）部分古体诗的著作。

退溪首先对白沙学和阳明学做了性质上的定义："按陈白沙、王阳明之学，皆出于象山，而以本心为宗，盖皆禅学也。然白沙犹未纯为禅，而有近于吾学"，即两者皆以本心为宗，故同属于禅学。退溪援用罗钦顺的评论认为白沙学虽为禅学，但与阳明学尚有区别，未纯为禅学，"不尽废书训，不尽铄物理"，而有近于儒学。阳明学则不然，"学术颇忒，其心强狠自用，其辩张皇震耀，使人眩惑而丧其所守，贼仁义乱天下，未必非此人也"①。即学术上错误，且以其雄辩而迷惑学界，终至"贼仁义乱天下"。这是相当强硬的评语，毫无妥协余地。

> 详其所以至此者，其初，亦只为厌事物之为心害而欲去之，顾不欲灭伦绝物如释氏所为，于是创为心即理也之说，谓天下之理只在于吾内，而不在于事物，学者但当务存此心，而不当一毫求理于外之事物。然则所谓事物者，虽如五伦之重，有亦可无亦可，划而去之，亦可也。是庸有异于释氏之教乎哉？持此而揆诸圣贤之训而不合，则又率以己意，改变经训，以从其邪见，乃敢肆为诐淫邪遁之说，畔道非圣，无所畏惮。欲排穷理之学，则斥朱说于洪水猛兽之灾，欲除繁文之弊，则以始皇焚书，为得孔子删述之意。其言若是，而自谓非狂惑丧心之人，吾不信也。使若人者，得君而行其志，则斯文斯世之祸，

---

① 李滉：《〈白沙诗教〉〈传习录〉抄传，因书其后》，《退溪先生文集》卷41，杂著，第419页。

未知其孰烈于秦也。邪说之陷人，一至于此，可胜叹哉。①

退溪从王阳明创立"心即理"心学的初衷出发，认为如按心学以本心主导认知天下的事物，则如无伦之重亦可以视为外物，极易误入佛教巢窟。退溪批判王阳明擅改朱子《大学》的格物致知以从己见，"敢肆为诐淫邪遁之说，畔道非圣，无所畏惮"，对朱子学说肆意非议，这是作为认程朱理学为正学的退溪所无法接受的。由于看到阳明学说如果得到朝廷认可，则必将像洪水猛兽一样，"斯文斯世之祸，未知其孰烈于秦也"，表示强烈担忧。

退溪在《〈白沙诗教〉、〈传习录〉抄传，因书其后》之后，又作了一篇《抄〈医闾先生集〉，附白沙、阳明抄后，复书其末》，显示在上篇文抄之后，又抄传了《医闾先生集》。

这里所谓的抄传，应该是退溪师弟范围内的学术研讨之用，可见在一段时期内，对有关陆王心学方面的学术研讨成为当时朝鲜程朱理学内部最大的现案。

贺钦为陈献章白沙学的传人，与湛若水同为白沙门下著名学者。其学专读《五经》《四书》《小学》，期于反身实践，主敬以收放心。退溪在论述作为修养功夫的"静坐之学"时，在阐述了"静坐之学"源于禅学、发之于二程，被李侗、朱熹师弟改造为理学修养方法的过程之后，对心学系统的"静坐"之学作了比较。

> 如白沙、医闾，则为厌事求定而入于禅，然医闾比之白沙，又较近实而正。至于阳明，似禅非禅，亦不专主于静，而其害正甚矣。②

退溪指出，贺钦的静坐方法"较近实而正"，与禅学保持了一定距离。而王阳明则"似禅非禅"，不主于静的功夫，反而更加有害于正学。在程朱理学看来，静即敬，静坐功夫实为诚敬之功，这是程朱理学有别于禅学的最大特征之一。退溪正是据此对心学系统的静坐方法与禅学的关系

---

① 李滉：《白沙诗教传习录抄传，因书其后》，《退溪先生文集》卷41，杂著，第419页。
② 李滉：《抄医闾先生集，附白沙、阳明抄后，复书其末》，《退溪先生文集》卷41，杂著，第420页。

作了判断，进一步彰显了程朱理学与陆王心学的区别。

此处退溪并未提及王阳明的静坐功夫论。在《传习录》下，王阳明说：

> 吾昔居滁时，见诸生多务知解，口耳异同，无益于得，姑教之静坐；一时窥见光景，颇收近效；久之渐有喜静厌动，流入枯槁之病，或务为玄解妙觉，动人听闻。故迩来只说"致良知"。良知明白，随你去静处体悟也好，随你去事上磨练也好，良知本体原是无动无静的；此便是学问头脑。我这个话头，自滁州到今，亦较过几番，只是"致良知"三字无病。医经折肱，方能察人病理。

可见王阳明教人静坐只为澄清心念，复于天理。但又恐流于寂静枯槁，故教人静坐以致良知。关于在事上磨炼之功夫，又说：

> 问静时亦觉意思好，才遇事便不同，如何？先生曰："是徒知静养而不用克己工夫也。如此临事便要倾倒。人须在事上磨方立得住，方能静亦定，动亦定。"

即在事事物物上克己以致良知。退溪指出在静坐功夫的方法论上，阳明心学与禅学虽有不同，但在目的论上，阳明所主张的"致良知"又流于禅学，正是在这一点上与理学的诚敬功夫有所不同。

退溪有论学理趣诗，专门对薛瑄（1389—1464）、陈献章、贺钦、王阳明等的学术倾向作了概括。

> 真知力践薛文清，录训条条当座铭。最是令人发深省，不为枝叶不玄冥。右，薛文清《读书录》。
> 屹立颓波陈白沙，名悬南极动中华。如何不重吾家计，极处终归西竺邪。右，《白沙诗教》。
> 医间生长裔戎方，一变因师勇退藏。况是青能自蓝出，逃禅归我尽端庄。右，《医间先生集》。
> 阳明邪说剧洪流，力遏罗公有隐忧。读到论心兼理气，令人又觉别生愁。右，《传习录》、《困知记》。

性理诸家皇极笺，天原二鲍复论镌。恨予得见奇书晚，一抚遗编一怅然。右，《性理诸家解》《皇极经世释义》，《天原发微》。①

作为"几与阳明中分"的中国北方"明初理学之冠"，薛瑄之学为朱子学传宗，"开明代道学之基"，与阳明学共同成为有明一代两大学脉之一。退溪在上述论学诗中，首先点明了薛学主张"笃实践履"、重视"真知实践"的实学性质。同时薛瑄修正并维护程朱的"道统"观念，主张"理在气中"和"复性"，所以退溪首举薛瑄，认为薛学发人深省。

对于白沙和医闾，退溪在警戒其近于禅学性质的同时，肯定了白沙"屹立颓波"、医闾"青出于蓝"。陈白沙以"宗自然""贵自得"的思想体系，打破程朱理学沉闷和僵化的模式，开启明朝心学先河，在宋明理学史上是一个承前启后、转变风气的关键人物。贺钦在继承白沙之学的同时，又强调反身实践，主敬收放心，与心学保持了一定距离。

诗中对王阳明的批判，退溪再次援用罗钦顺的观点。罗钦顺反对王学"心即理""致良知"之说："岂可谓心即理，而以穷理为穷此心哉？"（《困知记》卷上）同时又用理气为一物修正了朱熹理气二分的理气论。而罗钦顺对于心学有关心兼理气、统性情的主张并不完全否认。正是在这一点上，退溪作为"性即理"程朱理学的坚定维护者，表示了担忧。

退溪最后提及明嘉靖年间杨维聪编撰《性理诸家解》、余本所撰《皇极经世释义》、宋代鲍云龙所撰、明初鲍宁辩证的《天原发微》，其中第一本是性理学普及书，后两本书都与邵雍之学有关，是象数和古代宇宙论方面的书。

退溪对整庵罗钦顺的关注，主要是看重《困知记》的阳明学批判内容，并在门派内部将其作为重要的参考资料与《传习录》一起广泛传抄。

退溪早年在阅读《心经附注》时对元代学者吴澄（1249—1333）的学说有所接触，说："当时议者，以澄为陆氏之学，《困知记》以为其晚年所见，乃与象山合"，即采信了罗钦顺的看法。"整庵之论，案整庵与王阳明书，极论草庐说之非，以为儒释之分，正在毫厘之差云云。"② 罗钦顺批评吴澄为陆学，有禅学嫌疑。可见，退溪在批判陆王心学时，对罗

---

① 李滉：《韩士炯胤明往天磨山读书，留一帖求拙迹，偶书所感寄赠》，《退溪先生文集》别集卷1，诗，第43页。

② 李滉：《心经后论》，卷41，杂著，《退溪先生文集考证》卷7，第409页。

钦顺的观点多有援用。

2. 退溪学派内外对阳明学的体认与警戒

从退溪与弟子间的论学书内容来看，主要还是普及和宣扬程朱性理之学、批判陆王心学，确立朝鲜性理学的道统观念。

退溪在回答弟子李桢（1512—1571，字刚而，号龟岩）的问目时，对王阳明的观点随手拈来，与朱熹的观点进行对比，以加深对两者区别的认识。如："答江德功书，以物言者，挽而附之于己，如王阳明谓忠孝之理，不可求之于君父，只在此心之类，是也。以身言者，引以纳之于心，如此书上文所论有礼则安。《礼记》之意，本谓有礼则身安耳，德功必以为心安之类，是也。"① 李桢在研读朱熹《答江德功书》时，涉及朱熹对格物致知的认识，提出了如何分辨"以物言"和"以身言"的问题。退溪指出不可像王阳明一样，把物我身心合为一物，混为一谈，引用了《传习录》中王阳明说过的关于"忠孝之理，不可求之于君父"的观点，认为王阳明"挽而附之于己"，这里的"己"即"心"，以说明理学对格物认识与心学不同。

在退溪弟子中，洪仁祐（1515—1554，字应吉，号耻斋）是较晚及门的（1552年），而且是从奇大升门下转入退溪门下的。当时洪仁祐对阳明心学十分关注，并且向退溪借阅两书（指《传习录》和《困知记》）。此时，退溪十分担心洪仁祐会受到阳明心学影响。"两书皆呈，但禅学如膏油，近人则辄污，阳明又以雄辩济之，尤易惑人，诸公须戒之勿作。徐曰仁辈，始明终昏，而自以为得"②，直接把阳明心学指目为禅学，警戒弟子们小心戒备，不要受以雄辩见长的王阳明迷惑。

在给洪仁祐的信中，退溪对阳明学在朝鲜学界的传播情况作了陈述。"两书，案《耻斋日记》，因退溪闻阳明《传习录》，求见其学。大概务为好异，故罗钦顺著《困知记》，以攻其失云云。据此，则两书即《传习录》、《困知记》。徐曰仁名爱，曰仁，字也，阳明弟子。记其师说，为《传习录》。始明止为得见四十一卷传习录辨。"③ 退溪这里提及的《耻斋日记》是耻斋洪仁祐于1538年至1552年在花潭徐敬德和退溪门下读书时的日记，而耻斋于1552年6月第一次见到退溪，并转到退溪门下。两年

---

① 李滉：《答李刚而问目朱书》，《退溪先生文集》卷21，书，第18页。
② 李滉：《与洪应吉》，《退溪先生文集》卷13，书，第350页。
③ 李滉：《与洪应吉》，《退溪先生文集考证》卷4，卷13，书，第350页。

后因病离世。由此可见退溪得见《传习录》和《困知记》当在 1552 年以前。

该日记载于洪仁祐文集《耻斋遗稿》中,名为《日录钞》,记录了当时洪仁祐的思想和学问历程。从该日记所记内容中可以了解到,当时朝鲜学界纷纷研读从明朝像洪水一样涌来的新的理论书,如《心经附注》《延平问答》《传习录》《困知记》等,保存了可以了解 16 世纪中期朝鲜学界思想动向的珍贵史料。

退溪对整庵罗钦顺(1465—1547)对王阳明的批评十分关注,说:"《困知记》,这做学多有精到处,然其以人心为已发,道心为未发,最是错认了,岂辨倒阳明差路乎。"① 认为正是由于其人心道心说方面的错认,无法使王阳明心服。

在给洪仁祐的信中,退溪曾指出"整庵所见,于大头脑处错了",这是退溪针对罗钦顺不同意朱熹"理与气是二物"而提出"人犹物也,我犹人也,其理容有二哉?然形质既具,则其分不能不殊;分殊故各私其身,理一故皆备于我"而言,这就是退溪所说的"大头脑处错了"。但退溪也承认罗钦顺在与阳明本人及其后学的论辩中,在批判阳明心学的禅学性质方面所做出的特殊贡献,"犹能与阳明角立,以争禅学之非,是为整庵而已"②。可见作为程朱理学的绝对遵信和拥护者,退溪十分清楚中原学术论争的阵营分野及其学术主张性质。

退溪同时指出,罗钦顺《困知记》中主张的"人心道心说"割裂了道心与人心在已发时的联系,削弱甚至抹杀了道心的主导地位。他说:"若罗氏《困知记》,则又谓:道心,性也;人心,情也。至静之体不可见,故曰微;至变之用不可测,故曰危。此其为说颇近似,非湛氏之比,然其为害则为尤甚。夫限道心于未发之前,则是道心无与于叙秩命讨,而性为有体无用矣,判人心于已发之后,则是人心不资于本原性命,而情为有恶无善矣,如是则向所谓不可见之微,不可测之危,二者之间,隔断横决,欲精以察之,则愈精而愈隔断,欲一以守之,则愈一而愈横决,其视朱子说体用精粗工夫功效该贯无遗者,为如何哉?"③ 再次表明了道心在修养论上的主宰地位。

---

① 李滉:《答洪应吉》,出处同上。
② 同上。
③ 李滉:《答友人论学书,今奉寄明彦》,《退溪先生文集》卷 17,书,第 444 页。

卢守慎（1515—1590，字寡悔，号苏斋）由于生性温柔敦厚而深孚士望，并深受宣祖的尊敬和宠爱，但也因深入研究阳明学而受到退溪李滉、高峰奇大升等朝鲜朱子学者的攻击。苏斋早年在向国王经筵讲学时，对人心道心的说明与朱子说一致。但他此后流放珍岛时节（约1547—1568），看到了罗钦顺的《困知记》，此后便变更了以前的学说，解释为"道心未发，人心已发"。

退溪深信朱子，坚持朱子立场，主张道器分明。退溪认为理贵气贱，理尊气卑。理发于四端，流为道心；气发，发于七情，流为人心。基于修身养性成仁的需要，理必须主宰气，命令气。理命物而不命于物的这种特权是由理的极尊地位所决定的。人必须维持本然之性善，才能做到物我一理，天下为仁。此亦即退溪学派为代表的朝鲜理学对于理气关系的认识。退溪说："今按若理气果是一物，孔子何必以形而上下分道器？"① 在给许篈之父许晔（1517—1580，字太辉，号草堂）的信中，肯定了许晔对卢守慎的批评意见，说："人心为已发，道心为未发之非，所论甚善。大抵整庵，于大原处见未透，而寡悔，尊信整庵大过，故寡悔之论，亦有此误处，可惜。"② 他认为卢守慎过分遵信罗钦顺的主张，以至于认为"理气为一物"。

卢守慎遵信罗钦顺的"理气为一物"说，"人言寡悔颇悦禅味，中间，又闻其尊信《困知记》"，在当时朝鲜学界引起轩然大波，不仅退溪及门下弟子议论纷纷，奇大升、李恒、金麟厚等当代学者也都参与其中。李恒支持卢守慎的主张，认为理与气、太极与阴阳为一体，也受到了退溪的批评。退溪认为卢守慎"其见处乃不合于程朱，而反合于整庵也"，"似是从禅学中错入路头来"。③ 但退溪实际上对这种看法的根据也难以把握，"此病所从来处，思之不得"，希望奇大升予以批驳。

在丙寅年即1566年退溪致奇大升的信中，提及这次对卢守慎人心道心论的批评。"盖寡悔论人心道心，而主整庵之说。又以《朱子语类》及经书小注、《性理大全》，皆谓不足观云云。人心道心两绝（苏斋诗）：元来道与器非邻，可认人心是外尘。须就道心为大本，用时还用道乘人。此心无外

---

① 李滉：《非理气为一物辩证》，《退溪先生文集》卷41，杂著，第414页。
② 李滉：《答许太辉乙丑》，《退溪先生文集》卷15，书，第384页。
③ 李滉：《重答奇明彦》，《退溪先生文集》卷17，书，第441页。

强分邻,要着工夫入息尘。若道发时方致一,静中真个睡中人。"①

对于卢守慎的这两首人心道心关系的绝句,退溪似乎理解上有所失误。"寡悔既以理气为一物,则似亦当以道器为一物矣,而其诗曰:元来道与器非邻云云,是又判道器为二致,不相干涉,此病所从来处,思之不得,幸示破何如?"② 退溪认为第一首绝句即"元来道与器非邻,可认人心是外尘。须就道心为大本,用时还用道乘人"中的"道与气非邻"说明卢守慎并不把道与器视为一物,实际上应该是曲解了卢守慎的本意。应该把第二首绝句联系起来看。第二首即"此心无外强分邻,要着工夫入息尘。若道发时方致一,静中真个睡中人"。卢守慎对第一首绝句中所说的"道与器非邻"说作了批判,认为"此心无外强分邻",道心人心本为一物,不应该强行分为道心和人心两个心,而这正是卢守慎接受了罗钦顺见解的证据。退溪据第一首绝句就认为卢守慎主张"判道器为二致,不相干涉"应是误解,两首绝句的关系应该是第一首先提示程朱的人心道心之说,第二首则就此加以批判,提出自己的主张,即"道器为一物"、"道心人心非二"。

退溪曾在庚午年即1570年(退溪去世之年)回答许篈(1551—1588,字美叔,号荷谷)问目。在《退溪先生文集考证》对这封信的考证中,提及了许篈的生平和朝天时的朱陆学问论辩。"号荷谷,居京,大司谏晔子。生嘉靖辛亥,聪慧绝伦,十岁,诗文已成,游门下。弱冠登第。甲戌,以书状官赴京,与中朝士大夫,论朱、陆学问邪正。万历癸未,以典翰上箚,论斥栗谷,流甲山。乙酉,放还,放浪山水而卒,年三十八。"③ 可见许篈父子在朱陆之辩问题上,均受到了退溪见解的影响。

三 西厓、栗谷的阳明学批判

1. 西厓与阳明学

关于西厓柳成龙(1542—1607)与阳明心学初次交集的准确时间,

---

① 李滉:《丙寅答奇明彦》,卷17 书,《退溪先生文集考证》卷4,第359页。
② 李滉:《重答奇明彦》,《退溪先生文集》卷17,书,第441页。
③ 李滉:《庚午答许美叔》,卷33,书,《退溪先生文集考证》卷6,第398页。

西厓本人的记录最为可信。西厓在作于1593年的《书阳明集后》中说："右阳明文集。余年十七,趋庭义州。适谢恩使沈通源自燕京回,台劾不检罢,弃重于鸭绿江边而去,行橐中有此集。时阳明之文未及东来,余见之而喜,遂白诸先君,令州吏善写者誊出,既而藏箧笥中,忽忽三十有五年。壬辰秋七月,倭寇入安东,焚先庐及远志精舍,家藏文籍,荡然一空,惟此数卷,独全于林薄间,余得复见之,不觉泫然以悲,挟与俱行,到堤川,略记梗概,俾子弟宝蓄之,毋更遗失云尔。"① 文中标注的十七岁之年即1558年。据西厓所说,"时阳明之文未及东来",即此前阳明著作尚未东传朝鲜,此记录也成为学界定义朝鲜朝学者接触阳明学的初始时间的直接证据之一。关于阳明学东传的准确时间,尽管有人提出最早为朝鲜中宗十六年(1521年)的假说,但证据较为模糊。也有学者根据洪仁祐《耻斋日记》推定为1553年。② 笔者认为应该可以推定为至少在1553年之前,这是比较可信的。在前述引文中,从西厓获得其父同意,付诸誊写来看,不仅西厓本人喜好阳明著作并认真研读,而且在周边人物中当有传播,但似乎并未造成多大影响,因此"藏箧笥中,忽忽三十有五年",直到1593年才重新入手,并使子弟仔细保管。

西厓不仅仔细研读了阳明文集,对阳明的诗也极为喜好,并曾步其韵赋诗。③ 西厓读了王阳明的《纪梦并序》诗后,说"阳明幸阐幽,一歌同斧钺"。④ 历史上有名的晋代"我不杀伯仁,伯仁因我而死"事件已过去千年之久,多亏王阳明明晰是非幽微,假托忠臣郭璞的口吻,对历史事件和历史人物最终做出了公正评判。⑤ 借此可以洞悉权臣王导的奸雄真面目,认识到周伯仁的"有恩不市人,公义益精白"的真丈夫胸怀难能可贵。西厓赞赏王阳明明辨忠奸、秉笔直书的历史认知和读解方式,对此给予了积极评价。

---

① 柳成龙:《书阳明集后》,《西厓先生文集》卷18,跋,《韩国文集丛刊》第52辑,第347页。下文在引用该刊时,将只标注页码。

② 韩睿嫄(1998)参照。

③ 柳成龙:《次阳明韵,题玉渊壁上》,《西厓先生别集》卷1,诗,第419页。"幽居兴味与时深,尘事宁容一点侵。竹坞秋声闻戛玉,江台月色见镕金。行藏泪滴登楼眼,精一功惭望道心。浮世已知真梦幻,晚来长啸白云岑。"

④ 柳成龙:《咏王导》,《西厓先生文集》卷1,诗,第33页。

⑤ 参见王守仁《纪梦并序》,《王阳明全集》(中)卷20,上海古籍出版社,第856—857页。

西厓从学术上分辨阳明与朱子的意见相左之处，认为主要是由于对"致知格物"认识上的差异所致。王阳明认为"理在吾心，不可外索"，而朱子则主张"即物穷理，以致其知"。而西厓认为"捐去书册，瞑目一室，但事于本心良知之间，则虽一时凝定之力稍若有得，而所谓三千三百，致广大尽精微者，终不能如圣人矣"，不是适合中品以下人的治学修养方法，即并不认同王阳明的致良知方法论。

西厓对王阳明的"致良知"说和"格物致知"说的源头和性质也有所辩证。"如良知之说，亦求于《孟子》而得之；格物致知之说，求诸《大学》而得之。"即均从四书中来，其讨论的对象和依据依然是儒家经典的概念。但他并不同意阳明学主张的良知顿悟之法，"若使阳明，自初闭一室中，不识一字，则虽自谓有自足之心，必不知何者为良知，何者为格物致知，其名犹不能知，况于其义乎？"西厓认为良知与格物致知的知难以区分，良知不足以自足，于事物上亦不足以自明。王阳明"其所谓性命、心意、情志之辨，大概皆从先儒余论而得闻，以自开明其心知"，他由此得出结论王阳明是"以夫子之道，反害夫子"①，这正是阳明心学的可怕之处，西厓认为这种学问危害甚大。

西厓认为王阳明以良知为学，正是在学以致知问题上"不能察儒释之分"，从而走上了佛学"弥近理而大乱真，正以认心为理"之路，因此王阳明"专以致良知为学，而反诋朱子之论为支离外驰，正释氏之说也"②，这也是西厓通过研读佛经，最终发现了陆王心学与佛学联系和在立说过程中的援用。西厓认为王阳明"致良知"说是"见有困于火者，却教投水"，"阳明欲救宋末文义之弊，而专为本心之说，不知其流弊，反有甚于文义也"③，即矫枉过正。

西厓对王阳明的"知行合一"说作了专门研究。他首先考证了孔、孟关于知行关系的论述，提出圣学"虽重于行，而尤以知为贵"的主张④，并引用《周易·乾·文言》"知止止之，可与几也；知终终之，可与存义"的"一以贯之"之说，认为想要达到对圣贤之道"真知"的地步，必须持之以恒，不懈求知。在知行关系上，西厓认为"程朱说有来

---

① 柳成龙：《寄金溪读书处》，《西厓先生文集》卷12，书，第244页。
② 柳成龙：《王阳明以良知为学》，《西厓先生文集》卷15，杂著，第294页。
③ 柳成龙：《王阳明》，《西厓先生文集》卷15，杂著，第299页。
④ 柳成龙：《知行说》，《西厓先生文集》卷15，杂著，第289页。

历，有着落，断断乎不可易"。而王阳明之说有违圣人本义，有"新奇创立之病"。①

但西厓也承认王阳明的知行合一之说有其时代意义。"详王氏之意，盖惩俗学之外驰，于是一以本心为主，凡所着心讲求者，皆以为行，盖矫枉而过直者也。"② 这里所说的"俗学"即朱子学末流的口耳之学。

西厓认为王阳明之所以提出这样的主张，实际上是由于"嘉定以后，末学之弊，已极于口耳出入之间"，是为了矫正明朝嘉定以后的朱学末学汲汲于口耳之学的弊端，但"阳明其亦矫枉而过直者欤"③，认为王阳明在这个问题上矫枉过正。

西厓当时对王阳明的认识还是比较客观的，他认为王阳明创立心学的出发点在于纠朱学末学之偏。这代表了当时朝鲜学界的部分观点，这种观点已经注意到了朱学末学注重不切实用的口耳之学的弊病，而且对阳明学的历史意义有了一定认识。

尽管西厓从学术上承认阳明学的历史意义，但作为朝鲜主理派程朱理学的最重要的奠基人退溪的爱弟子，西厓从维护朝鲜理学的道统思想出发，坚定地选择并维护退溪学派视阳明学为禅学的朝鲜朝学界主流观点。

西厓于1569年十月（时年28岁），"以圣节使书状官兼司宪府监察赴京。时李青莲后白为正使，先生以书状辅行"。在燕京宣治门内，与太学生论学。"先生问近日中朝道学之宗为谁？诸生相顾良久曰：王阳明、陈白沙也。先生曰：白沙见道未精，阳明之学，专出于禅，愚意当以薛文清为宗耳。有新安人吴京者字仲周，喜而前曰：近日学术污舛，士失趣向，故诸生之言如此，而君乃发正论以斥之，可见深有意于辟异端矣。嗟叹久之。"④ 这就是退溪后来屡次提及的"西厓辟异端"。

郑经世在所撰《西厓柳先生行状》中详细介绍了这次使行中西厓与明朝新安人吴京（字仲周）的交游，重点提及西厓"以退溪先生圣学十图示之"。在次年三月返回朝鲜后，西厓曾"上退溪先生书，略陈在燕京时与诸生问答语。老先生覆书曰：陆禅怀襄于天下，公能发此正论，点检

---

① 柳成龙：《知行合一说》，《西厓先生文集》卷15，杂著，第289页。
② 同上。
③ 柳成龙：《读阳明集有感二首》，《西厓先生文集》卷2，诗，第46页。
④ 柳成龙：《年谱》，《西厓先生年谱》卷1，年谱，第495页。

其迷，诚不易得也"①，西厓的"辟异端"受到了退溪的称赞。这说明当时朝鲜朝主流学界已经定义阳明心学为禅学异端，西厓对此不但未表示异议，而且在与明朝学者的对话中，也阐明了朝鲜学界的这种看法。

西厓在1570年前后时提及，自己曾致力于象山之学，"因抄出警语作一册，出入自随，每疑朱子攻象山，未免太过，虽口不敢言，而心尝疑之"，对朱陆之辨中朱子攻忤陆学的禅学性颇不以为然。此后仔细研读佛经原理之后，发现佛学的"机轴运用，皆与象山学相出入，特象山改换头面，文以儒说耳"②，自此对朱子的持论深信不疑。

年谱中还记载了一件大事，1588年，"先生赴召，上引见论学，因问及王阳明致良知及心即理之说，圣意不甚以为非。先生剖析甚详，上倾听忘倦曰：学当以程朱为宗师，不可他求。又曰：闻卿久处林下，多读古人书，今见卿论议果然。后先生入经筵，又极陈阳明心术之非，学问之谬。盖圣学高明，不屑于章句训诂之学，天语往往有过高处，先生忧之，前后劝戒，极其深切"。③

可见此时国王宣祖"不屑于章句训诂之学"，对王阳明的致良知和心即理之说十分熟悉，"不甚以为非"，即认为有其合理之处。因此西厓对此感到担忧，以至于"前后劝戒，极其深切"。

西厓后来慨然以阐明程朱正学为己任，对当时朝鲜思想界的现状深表忧虑，"盖今世无向学人，虽有之，率多浅陋褊暗，于古人论学路径，全未有一斑之见，而虚诞骄傲，抗然欲下视程朱。此风日肆，而世无大人君子以救正之，儒道之厄，何以至此耶？"希望金昌远"勿为异说所挠"，这里的异说即指陆王心学。④

明穆宗隆庆六年（1572年），侍御谢廷杰汇集王阳明的各类著作，以及钱德洪编的阳明先生年谱、王正亿编辑的世德纪、王阳明友人所写的阳明先生墓志铭、行状、祭文等，定名为《王文成公全书》，编为38卷，予以刻印。主要包括《传习录》《文录》《文录续编》等。在与门人金昌远的信件中，西厓披露入手《阳明全书》并仔细研读。"近日有人寄示阳明全书，未免阅过。其论出鬼入神，惊天动地，使人震慑，因此亦颇有管

① 《西厓柳先生行状》[郑经世]，行状，《西厓先生年谱》卷3附录，第531页。
② 柳成龙：：《象山学与佛一样》，《西厓先生文集》卷15，杂著，第294页
③ 柳成龙：《年谱》，《西厓先生年谱》卷1，年谱，第495页。
④ 柳成龙：《与金昌远》，《西厓先生文集》卷11，书，第222页。

窥，但无与告语，未尝不怅然有怀于吾昌远也。"①

西厓与金昌远的通信大都在壬辰倭乱之后，这封信证明《阳明全书》（《王文成公全书》）在1600年前后已经传入朝鲜学界。西厓研读之后，认为王阳明的心学主张"出鬼入神，惊天动地，使人震慑，因此亦颇有管窥"，可见王阳明的心学主张对朝鲜性理学界已经造成了极大冲击。

2. 栗谷与阳明学

与退溪相比，栗谷（1536—1584）提及陆王心学尤其是阳明学的文章较少，但也表现出了强烈的维护道学正统的观点。

栗谷李珥于1581年对明人陈建（1497—1567）的《学蔀通辨》作跋，提出了几个观点。

一是学有正邪，异端害正，理势然也。"清澜陈建氏慨然以辟邪扶正为志，著《学蔀通辨》，博搜深究，明辨详言，指出象山、阳明掩藏之心肝，使迷者不被诳惑，其志甚盛，而其论甚正矣。"

二是对于学界认为陈建的性理未精，以及"过于张皇，而欠精约之义为疑"，栗谷认为"但因其言，深知陆王之邪术，则其功已伟矣，何必觅指疵累，以助党邪之口乎"。

三是对于阳明从祀之说的认识。"中朝之士，靡靡入于陆学，传闻王阳明得参从祀之列，然则邪说之祸，怀山襄陵，匹夫之力，难以救止。陈氏明目张胆，孤鸣独抗，其言不得不引以自高，而排难解纷，务在雄辩，果不能主于精约也，亦何伤哉。"栗谷认为中国王学泛滥，侵害正学，而陈建力挽狂澜，应该予以肯定。

四是对朝鲜当时学风的批判。"或问：中朝之士，多染陆学，而我国则未之闻也，岂我国人心之正，胜于中朝乎？答曰：不染陆学，而专用功于朱学，能知能践，则固胜于中朝矣。若专攻利欲，而朱陆之学两废，则其优劣何如哉？余尝叹中朝之士，犹有所事，不肯放心，故或朱或陆，终不虚老；邪正虽殊，犹愈于饱食终日，无所用心也。我国之士，不朱不陆，专务俗习者多矣，此与佣夫贩奴何别？以此求胜于中朝，无乃左乎？异端之言，岂专攻利欲，而朱陆之学两废必佛老禅陆为然乎？世之非先王之道，循一己之欲者，莫非异端也。若以俗习为是，孜孜求利，而非笑陆学，则何异于尊尚四凶，而讥刺杨墨乎？呜呼，世之为士者，其专务正

---

① 柳成龙：《与金昌远》，《西厓先生别集》卷3，书，第458页。

学，而无至于佣夫贩奴之归，可乎哉？"

可见栗谷对当时"专攻利欲，而朱陆之学两废"的朝鲜学风有着清醒的认识，虽然"非笑陆学"，但实际上"不朱不陆，专务俗习者多"，于圣学无补无益，"中朝之士，犹有所事，不肯放心，故或朱或陆，终不虚老；邪正虽殊，犹愈于饱食终日，无所用心也"，因此栗谷认为朝鲜当时的学风反倒不如中国。①

对于栗谷专门作跋的陈建的这篇《学蔀通辨》，据《退溪先生文集考证》记载，退溪亦有所提及。"《道一编》案篁墩《道一编》凡六卷，名以道一者，盖谓朱、陆之道，始二而终一也。《学蔀通辨》（陈清澜建自序）近世一种造为早晚之说，乃谓朱子初年所见未定，误疑象山，晚年始悔悟，而与象山合，其说盖萌于赵东山之对江右六君子之策，而成于程篁墩之道一编，至近日王阳明因之，又集为《朱子晚年定论》。建为此惧，窃不自揆，慨然发愤，究心通辨云云。"② 从《考证》内容来看，退溪提及了陈氏的该著作，但仅仅资料性地转录了陈建本人的序，借以强调对王阳明集编的《朱子晚年定论》的怀疑和不满，但并没有像栗谷一样作专门辩说。

此后，栗谷也获得了直接面对明朝阳明学者进行学术对话的机会。

1582年（万历十年）九月，因皇长子诞生，明朝以黄洪宪（1541—1600，浙江嘉兴县人，号葵阳）、王敬民（生卒年不详，江苏句容人，号敬吾）为正、副使颁庆，朝鲜方面远接使为李珥，馆伴使为郑惟吉，黄廷彧、许篈、高敬命为从事官，权擘为制述官。

朝鲜方面十分清楚明朝使臣的学术倾向，即"盖两使，主象山、阳明者也"，当两使"请先生讲克己复礼""以试先生"时，先生"著说以进"，"专主程朱之训"。尽管如此，仍然受到了两使的肯定，"两使曰：此说极好，当传布中国。回到江上，临分，恋恋不忍别，至于出涕，礼敬之至，前后所未有云"③。可见，当时明朝在学术争鸣方面，允许并尊重不同声音的存在，对朱子学在朝鲜的确固不动的地位表现出宽容和理解，并不强以己见加之于异国士人。

---

① 李珥：《学蔀通辨跋辛巳（1581）》，《栗谷先生全书》卷13，跋。《韩国文集丛刊》第44辑（下文引用栗谷原文时，将不再注明该刊。）第274页。

② 李滉：《别纸》，第二十一卷 书，《退溪先生文集考证》卷5，第371页。

③ 李珥：《墓志铭并序〇慎独斋金集撰》，附录四，《栗谷先生全书》卷36，第390页。

除此之外,在《栗谷先生全书》附录的《前后辨诬章疏》及宋时烈所撰《紫云书院庙庭碑》文中均提及,李珥曾明确表示陆王心学"尤为吾道之害":"尤严于辨异端明正学之说,尝曰:中朝之学,尊信象山,以至阳明之徒出,则尤为吾道之害。遂推穷源委,剖破诐淫,使之不惑。"①

栗谷作为主张理通气局的朝鲜性理学代表学者,在对待阳明学问题上与退溪学派保持了基本一致的观点。他极力抨击明朝学界遵信陆王心学的风潮,辨异端明正学,倡导程朱理学,为确立朝鲜性理学的道学正统地位而摇旗呐喊。

四 结论

在东亚交流史上,儒学交流是具有标志性特殊历史意义的学术现象。从历史资料来看,这种交流并非单纯地从源头国到接受国的单向传播,而是经过接受国自我的学术努力,经过甄别扬弃的消化吸收历史过程,形成了具有浓郁本民族特色的思想文化,并一定程度地反向作用于儒学源头国,呈现出复杂的双向传播样态。作为例证之一,阳明学在东亚各国的传播过程和学术命运与程朱理学纠缠交错,集中体现出各国精英学者在思想交流过程中的重要地位和作用。

明朝中晚期,以王阳明为代表的心学者出于纠朱学末学口耳之学之偏的需要,提出了心即理、知行合一、致良知等主张,从治学方法、知行论和修养论上形成了一股席卷学界的新思潮,其余波对朝鲜学界也造成了极大冲击。以退溪、西厓和栗谷为代表的朝鲜中期理学者们对这种思潮极为关注,不仅从学理上进行了深入研究和分辨,而且从性质上进行禅学异端定义,对其所造成的影响十分忧虑。在对待阳明心学的态度问题上,他们表现出了惊人的一致,几乎无一例外地予以极力排斥。

朝鲜学界之所以对阳明心学采取批判和抵制的态度,首先是出于确立和维护本国正统道学的需要。

---

① 分别参见李珥《紫云书院庙庭碑尤庵宋时烈撰》,《栗谷先生全书》卷37,附录五,第400页;《前后辨诬章疏》,《栗谷先生全书》卷38,附录六,第431页。

以退溪、栗谷等人为代表的朝鲜中期程朱理学家通过研读和悬吐儒家原始经典和宋代五子的著作,并主要通过研读《二程遗书》《四书章句集注》《朱子大全》《朱子语类》《近思录》等宋代代表理学家的著作体味天理天道、理一分殊、理气论、四端七情、人物性同异等理学范畴,从而构筑起了朝鲜程朱理学的总体框架和本国本民族的道统学统。

对陆王心学的批判,标志着自朝鲜朝中期开始,韩国儒学对道统和学统的正统性的自觉,韩国思想文化不再是天然无觉,而是有根据有源头的,有活生生的血脉流淌,已经开始活泼地开花结果,并且为了维护自我的纯粹性,开始对异己思想有了甄别和抗拒。

这种甄别和抗拒几乎与中国维护程朱理学正统的努力同步,不仅在朝鲜理学内部,而且对儒家文化宗主国发出自己的声音,这是前所未有的,具有特别重大的意义,同时对陆王心学的动向和流传,以及由此所导致的社会文化风潮的变化过程保持持续关注。这也就可以解释为什么朝鲜朝中期对中国思想界阳明学泛滥、甚至对陆王从祀文庙的举措表现出极度的困惑和不安。

明亡以后,朝鲜王朝朝廷上下以继承了中原文化的正脉,自居为"小中华",这种想法的根源之一,即是朝鲜朝思想界认为朝鲜学界抵制了陆王心学的异端思想,继承了程朱理学的正脉,从而保留住了中原儒学的正脉。

其次是朝鲜朝中期理学内部是非曲直的学理选择和伸张。

对陆王心学的批判,标志着朝鲜朝程朱理学已经确立起明确的是非判断和价值判断,从为道具体和具体而微两个角度确立了自己的评价依据。为了正人心熄邪说,提供维护道统传承纯洁性的保障,必须从学术上辨明异端邪说的虚妄。其主要的方法论,就是以圣人的"一以贯之"和"述而不作"精神,批判陆王心学的"不仁"和"妄作"。

在朝鲜朝中期,经过退栗为代表的性理学者的学术努力,程朱理学及其文化认知已经以某种方式和途径进入了社会成员的文化心理结构当中,形成某种特定的认知图式,产生了文化上的继承和同化过程。而这种文化心理又反过来影响了朝鲜朝对阳明心学的群体认知,形成了阻碍吸收和适应新学术思想的环境背景,从而影响整个社会成员的文化思维方式、传统及价值观等。这就可以解释为什么朝鲜朝中期阳明心学受到顽强抵制,未能在朝鲜土地上开花结果的原因。①

尽管如此,通过以上研究也表明,朝鲜朝中期,对阳明心学的认识并非全然骂倒,也有部分学者从学理上对阳明心学做了细致研究。退溪学派出于研究阳明学的需要,内部广泛传抄了《传习录》和《困知记》;西厓最早接触了《传习录》等阳明学著作,栗谷为明人陈建的《学蔀通辨》作跋,这说明从 16 世纪上半叶开始阳明学在朝鲜学界已经广泛传播并产生了相当的影响。西厓所主张的王学创立是为了纠朱学末学之偏的观点代表了当时朝鲜学界的部分视角,表明朝鲜学界已经对阳明心学的历史意义有了一定认识。

参考文献

《退溪先生文集》,影印标点《韩国文集丛刊》第 29—31 辑,民族文化推进会 1988 年版。

《西厓先生文集》,影印标点《韩国文集丛刊》第 52 辑,民族文化推进会 1989 年版。

《栗谷先生全书》,影印标点《韩国文集丛刊》第 44 辑,民族文化推进会 1989 年版。

《王阳明全集》,马昊宸主编,线装书局 2014 年版。

《王阳明全集》,上海古籍出版社 2011 年版。

[韩] 韩睿嫄:《韩国阳明学研究的历史和课题》,《国际儒学研究》第四辑,1998 年版。

[韩] 张炳汉:《以 19 世纪阳明学的礼学论的一特征为中心》,《韩国实学研究》第 30 号,2015 年。

[韩] 高桥亨:《朝鲜的阳明学派》,《朝鲜学报》第 4 辑,1953 年。

钱明:《朝鲜阳明学派的形成与东亚三国阳明学的定位》,《浙江大学学报》(人文社会科学版) 2006 年第 3 期。

陈代湘:《罗钦顺与王阳明学术论辩述评》,《湘潭大学学报》2010 年第 34 卷第 6 期。

---

① 在 2016 年尼山文明论坛组委会与北京师范大学人文高等研究院共同举办的"东亚文明交流国际研讨会"上,台湾大学著名学者黄俊杰先生就笔者的观点提出了珍贵的补充意见,认为阳明学在朝鲜中期的命运除以上两点主要原因之外,两班政治斗争所导致的学术门派利益之争也是不可忽视的重要因素。对此,笔者将在以后的研究中予以关注。

徐云飞：《洪大容实学思想研究》，硕士学位论文，山东大学，2014 年。

杨晓云：《月沙李廷龟的儒学思想研究——以〈大学讲语〉与〈筵中讲义〉为中心》，硕士学位论文，山东大学，2014 年。

中文概要

在朝鲜朝中期，经过退栗为代表的性理学者的学术努力，程朱理学及其文化认知已经以某种方式和途径进入了社会成员的文化心理结构当中，形成某种特定的认知图式，产生了文化上的继承和同化过程。而这种文化心理又反过来影响了朝鲜朝对阳明心学的群体认知，形成了阻碍吸收和适应新学术思想的环境背景，从而影响整个社会成员的文化思维方式、传统及价值观等。

出于确立和维护本国正统道学的需要，以晦斋李彦迪和退溪李滉为代表的朝鲜道学者们一方面从学理上积极研究程朱理学理论，探讨并选择性地继承其心性理气的性理学观念，从而从朝鲜性理学内部形成了一整套概念系统和价值伸张体系。这就可以解释为什么朝鲜朝中期阳明心学受到顽强抵制，未能在这块儒家思想成为精神文化支柱的异国土地上开花结果的原因。

尽管如此，通过本论文的研究也表明，在朝鲜朝中期，对阳明心学的认识并非全然骂倒，也有部分学者从学理上对阳明心学做了细致研究。退溪学派出于研究阳明学的需要，内部广泛传抄了《传习录》和《困知记》；西厓柳成龙最早接触了《传习录》等阳明学著作，栗谷李珥为明人陈建的《学蔀通辨》作跋，这说明从 16 世纪上半叶开始阳明学在朝鲜学界已经广泛传播并产生了相当的影响。西厓所主张的王学创立是为了纠朱学末学之偏的观点代表了当时朝鲜学界的部分视角，表明朝鲜学界已经对阳明心学的历史意义有了一定认识。

关键词：阳明心学，退溪李滉，西厓柳成龙，栗谷李珥，文化心理，朝鲜性理学

Criticism on School of Wang Yang-ming in Mid Joseon Dynasty —Focused on Toegea, Soae and Yulgok

Li Xue-tang

[**Abstracts**] In Mid Joseon dynasty, by academic endeavor of scholars, represented by Toegea and Yulgok from Korean rational Confucianism, the Neo-Confucianism and its cultural cognition has been in the cultural psychology of Joseon community members in some ways, formed a specific cognitive schema with cultural inheritance and process of assimilation, which influenced the group cognition on School of Wang Yang-ming in Joseon dynasty, thereby hindered them to absorb and adapt new academic thinking and affected their mode of thinking, tradition and values.

In order to establish and preserve the native orthodox neo-Confucianism, scholars of Joseon dynasty, represented by Hoejae and Toegea, researched on the theory of neo-Confucianism while inherited its concept of heart and nature, thus formed a whole set of conceptual system and value system inside of Korean rational Confucianism. That's why the School of Wang Yang-ming was resisted in mid Joseon dynasty and failed in adopting by this country, which taking Confucianism as its moral support.

Even so, this paper indicates that not all of the scholars opposed the school at that time. There are some scholars did intensive study on school of Wang Yang-ming. Out of necessity, school of Toegea made private copies of 《Chuan Xi Lu (傳習錄)》 and 《Kun Zhi Ji (困知記)》 internally. Soae was the first Joseon scholar who read the works such as 《Chuan Xi Lu (傳習錄)》. Yulgok wrote a postscript for Chen Jian's 《Xue Fu Tong Bian (學蔀通辨)》. This shows that from the first half of 16th century, the school of Wang Yangming has been widely spread in Joseon academic circles and got an important effect. The establishment of School of Mind advocated by Soae was to correct the error of neo-Confucianism, which represents some viewpoints of Joseon academic circles. That means they had a certain cogitation on historical significance of Yangming Idealistic School.

[**Keywords**] School of Wang Yang-ming, Toegea Lee Hwang, Soae Ryu Sung-yong, Yulgok Yiyi, cultural psychology, Korean rational Confucianism

中国典故在越南喃籍中的接受与改变

吕明恒*

摘　要

接受中国用典传统，汉语典故多用在汉喃书籍；典故引用已成为评价儒学程度的标准之一。

为深刻了解越南古典诗文，前辈学者已编辑越南喃籍里所引用的典故手册和词典。但，此类典故的手册和词典不可答应学习与研究越南喃籍所记词汇的要求。

解读喃字书籍实际上可指出：为保留越南的传统诗律（七言八句诗，六八诗），维持诗赋的对联性，体现散文里直译、仿译法的醇厚性等问题，汉语典故已很灵活使用在越南喃籍。本论文自喃籍里具体的例句，指出它的汉语典源，仔细分析词语结构，从此提出在越南喃籍里造出汉语变体典的规律。

汉语变体典多用在越南喃籍。本论文第二部分提供中国典故在越南喃籍里的改变情况与综合数量。

研究中华典故可深刻了解中国古典文学、传统文化等问题。分析中国典故在越南喃籍中如何接受与改变，可明白中国与越南早就有多样性的文化交流。为了解中国与越南的文化交流想要从考察中国变体典出发。

关键词：中国典故，越南喃籍，接受与改变，变体典

---

* 吕明恒，越南社会科学院，汉喃研究所副教授，博士。

前 言

用典是中国文学，特别古文学中常用的艺术手法。典故是中华古籍解读的障碍之一。在中国，用典传统早已出现，形成了典故专攻的大量队伍。由此，典故词典已连续出版。按阮俊强博士"自 1949 年至 2009 年，中国已出版 90 多部典故词典。其中再三再版的典故词典也不少。可以认定：中国人解读典故的必要性是好多！"①

在越南，与中国文化接触已带来两个结果：（1）语言文字方面的结果体现在使用汉字并借用汉字和它首部造出"喃"字，（2）文学方面的结果体现在 a/用汉字写出的文学版本（即汉人和越人写出的汉字文学版本，叫**汉字文学**），b/汉字文学的译版（叫**汉译文学**）和 c/用喃字写出的文学版本（叫**喃字文学**）等三主流的形成。与中华文学接受，越南儒士同时也接受汉文学中典型的艺术手法，即用典法。但，越南的用典和中国的用典如何差别？本论文集中考察中华典故在越南的使用及改变。

一 中华典故在越南古籍中的接受与改变

1. 用典传统的接受

越南文学用典过程，可以说与越南人使用汉字过程并行。中国文学里，典故出自后期作品；但，越南典故出自初期汉字文学和喃字文学作品。原因为：写出汉字和喃字的作品时，中国文学典故已有成千上万的历史，越南文学作者只要单纯借用汉语典故。

喃字出现并广泛使用时（第 14 至 19 世纪）越南兼用两种文字②，导致汉字文学与喃字文学并存，从此形成两种典故：**汉越典**③和**纯越典**④。

---

① 阮俊强：《中国典故概述》（科学研究专题）所属《喃字文学中的典故》，越南社会科学院研究，吕明恒主编（高板）。
② 自从第 17 世纪，在越南出现"三行文字"：汉字，喃字和国语字。
③ 此典故的特点：文字：汉字，声音：汉越音。
④ 此典故的特点：文字：喃字，声音：越语声音。

此两种典故分别使用：汉越典出现在越南汉字文学与喃字文学作品，纯越典只限用在喃字文学作品。

自第 20 世纪起，形成用国语字①写出**国语字文学**。当时，汉越典和纯越典对一般人来说是难以解释的。要注视：用典传统仍旧保留在国语字文学作品中。但，典故类型有差：用在国语字文学的典故大部分为**越典**②。可认为：与中国用典传统接受已带来两个结果：（1）用典习惯；（2）借用中华典源并造出新典③。在越南，接受—使用并改变中华典故过程，参看表 1。

表 1　　　　　　　　　　依时间的越南用典情况

时间	汉越典	纯越典	越典
第 14 世纪以前④	+	0	0
第 14 世纪	+	-	0
第 15 世纪	+	-	0
第 16 世纪	+	+	0
第 17 世纪	+	+	-
第 18 世纪	+	++	-
第 19 世纪	+	++	-
第 20 世纪初	0	-	+
第 20 世纪后半至今	0	0	-

说明：以上第三表有概括性，还没指出具体的数量，所以不可提出仔细的统计表。其表之内，(+) 表示数量多，(++) 表示数量比较多，(0) 表示没有，(-) 表示数量少。

资料来源：参见吕明恒《喃籍里典故使用的初考》，《汉喃杂志》2012 年 6 号。

2. 中华典故的改变

以上介绍越南人接受中华用典传统的大概。与中华用典传统接受，给越南带来三种典故。为深刻了解在越南汉喃书籍里，中华典故如何改变，我认为要从越南**汉字文学**作品和**喃字文学**作品里所记的典故（即汉越典

---

①　国语字：意为"我国文字"。此文字由拉丁字母写出的文字。

②　越典的典源是越南的事迹，如：历史故事，民间事迹，民歌等。

③　从典源看起，越南文学典故造出可分别：①纯越典：出自中华典源，用喃字记。喃字书籍里的典故大部分属于此类 ② 越典：据中华用典法，典源出自越南故事，历史传和成语熟语；此类数量不多；皆用在喃字文学和现代文学作品（使用文字：喃字或国语字）

④　以前：有"汉典在越南接受并使用以前的意思"。

和纯越典）出发，仔细分析并指出它的典源，从此可指出它的造典规律。

（1）汉越典

a/概念

汉越典特点：用记的文字：汉字，声音：汉越音，词语：汉越词，语秩序：遵守汉语词法和语法。汉越典可分有两类：（1）借用中华典故词或典源；（2）选择中华典源（典故因素）组成新典。第一类由中国人造出，第二类由越南人接受中华典故再组织而成。此两类皆用在越南汉文书籍。

b/证据分析

（*）**汉越典第一类**：借用中华典故词或典源

《列子·汤问》载：伯牙善鼓琴，锺子期善听琴。伯牙琴音志在**高山**，子期说"峩峩兮若泰山"；琴音意在**流水**，子期说"洋洋兮若江河"。伯牙所念，锺子期必得之。后世遂以"知音"比喻知己、同志。

以下由越南诗人翻辉益和阮攸借用"高山"和"流水"两个典源（词语）连成新典"高山流水"：

……**高山流水**无人知

海角天崖何处寻……（越南诗人阮攸）

高山流水有知音

两地神交记意深……（越南诗人翻辉益）

（*）**汉越典第二类**：选择中华典故因素再组织而成新汉越典。比如《旧唐诗·狄仁杰传》写：其亲在河阳别业，仁杰赴并州，登太行山，南望见白云孤飞，谓左右曰"吾亲所居，在此云下。"瞻望伫立久之，云移乃行。故文学常用白云为典故。其典有以下造典因素："河阳""仁杰""并州""太行""南望""白云"，皆可造新典故。但，不找到"千理""瞻云"等词语。以下"千理瞻云"典故由越南诗人借用并合一两个典故因素而成（初改中华典故）：

………

班堂恰是欢愉会

千理瞻云动好城。（乙巳开春试笔，翻辉益）

（2）纯越典

a/概念

纯越典的词语构造和文字与汉越典多有差别。纯越典特点：用记的文字：喃字；声音：越音；词语：纯越词；词语秩序：遵守越语词法语法。纯越典只用于越南喃文书籍里：特别是越南诗赋。原因为：(1) 属于越南传统文学当然用民族文字（喃字）；(2) 遵守越语词法和语法所以可保存（即体现）越南韵律，诗律（即平仄，登对。此为越南传统六八诗，双七六八诗，对联的重要标准）。

b/证据分析

"海誓山盟"用于誓言和盟约如山和海一样永恒不变。多用以表示男女相爱之深，坚定不渝。此源典出自宋代辛弃疾《南乡子·赠妓》词："别泪没些些，海誓山盟总是赊。"后来，中国文学多用此词表示男女相爱之深，坚定不渝。越南文学中其典多有变化，造出 24 变体，具体：

㴜沛滝痾，波噲嫩願，波嫩，波岁，指嫩滝，指岁誓滝，噲波誓滝，海誓山盟，盟山，没哙貝渚嫩，願碌誓漊，願嫩誓波，願滝岁，嫩痾波沛，嫩願波哑，岁愿滝解，滝沛岁涞，凿岁滝，誓滝指岁，誓山海，誓撸渚嫩，誓海盟山，誓水，撸渚誓嫩，拍坦指丕。

以上所提变体典皆由典故词语次序倒转或典源因素再组织而成。以下试考典故词"海誓山盟"，看看它如何变化并使用在越南古文学（即喃字文学）：

典故词词语秩序倒转

典故词"海誓山盟"用在越南诗歌时，为保留韵律要转为"誓海盟山"

例 1：底哙誓海盟山

㗂混熺沛填恩生成《断肠新声》，24a3

例 2：底哙誓海盟山

㗂恩熺沛填恩朱未《雲仙传》，第 1859—1860 句以上两例："山"和"恩"可协韵。如果用源典词"海誓山盟"，"盟"和"恩"不可协韵→不可保留越南六八诗的韵律。越典"誓海盟山"特点：所记的文字：汉字；声音：汉越；词语：汉越词（与汉语典第一类同）。但要注视的是词语秩序：与汉语词秩序有差。

（-）用越语词可保留纯越语诗歌

以保留纯越诗歌的韵律，"海誓山盟"转为纯越典：

嗷嗔誓擼渃嬾，嘐群痕碍嘐群滚昂《大南国音》，93a9。誓擼渃嬾：有"向（即指）水和山说誓言"的意思。在这里以"嬾"（越语有"山"的意义）代替"山"。原因为："嬾"和"群"可协韵→可保留越南六八诗的韵律。

（-）用纯越典可保留诗歌平仄韵律

大众皆知：按唐诗律，在七言八句诗的结语句，韵律为：仄仄平平平仄仄、平平仄仄仄平平。遵守唐诗韵律，越南喃诗的结语句与韵律对比如下：

招榠把桃牢拯裞
Gieo mân trả đào sao chẳng đoái
平仄仄①平平仄仄
誓滝指岿女芾悁
Thề sông chỉ núi nõ nào quên
平平仄仄仄平平
《林泉奇遇，13b9》

此诗句如果用汉越典"海誓山盟"或"誓海盟山"甚至纯越典"誓擼渃嬾"皆不可协韵（不合六八诗的韵律）。

考察在越南喃字文学里，中华典故的接受与改造可得出认定：

写出（创造）越南汉喃诗文过程中，中华典故显示于以下三类：①单纯借用典故词或典源（**汉越典第一类**）；②典故因素再组织而成新典（**汉越典第二类**）；③改变典故词或典源（**纯越典**）。其中，第二和第三类只限用在喃字文学作品。表2辨别越南中古文学里，各典故的出自版本，

---

① 第一和三字可不论韵律。

典源现状和造典方式等方面的差异。

表2　　　　　　　　　　越南典故辨别

典故种类	记典文字	出自版本	典源现状	造典方式
汉越典（1）	汉字	越南汉字文学版本	汉典词或典源词语借用	单纯借用
汉越典（2）	汉字	越南汉喃文学版本	典故因素组织而成	再组织
纯越典	喃字	喃字版本	汉典原借用	借用与改变
越典	喃字	喃字版本	越南汉喃书籍	创造
	国语字	越语版本	越南新传	创造

中华典故在越南古籍中的接受与改变可带来两个结果：①用典传统和；②接受典语，典故因素再组织而成纯越典。具体见表3。

表3　　　　　　　　接受用典传统和造出新典情况

文学类型	典类				用典传统
	汉越典1	汉越典2	纯越典	越典	
汉字文学	x	x			x
汉译文学	x	x			x
喃字文学			x		x
国语字文学				x	x

二　变体典的造成各法

1. 概念

（1）典语：别称"典故词""典故词语"，"典面"为表达典故的词语；（2）典源：典故的来源，为典义和典语的联结语；（3）典义：中国称"典故义""典义"，为典故意义；（4）典故因素：造成典源的内容；（5）变体典：改变典故词，借用并再组织而成。

2. 数量

据汉典源和典故因素，越南汉喃文学已出现大量变体典。考察结果可指出很多再三引用的典故，引起出现多样变体，如：月老（53变体），誓海盟山（29变体），牛郎织女（24变体），丹书铁券（22变体），桃夭

(21 变体)、仓桑（19 变体）、春萱（15 变体）、定省晨昏（15 变体）、白兔（15 变体）、鲤鱼跳龙门（16 变体）、知仁（15 变体）、投桃报李（12 变体）、女娲（12 变体）、奉巾栉（10 变体）①……

表4　　　　　　　　喃字书籍不造出变体的大观

次序	韵	典故总数	不带变体的典故	
			数量	%
1	A	56	24	42, 8
2	B	269	100	37, 1
3	C	415	145	34, 9
4	D	302	103	34, 1
5	E	7	1	14, 28
6	G	133	48	36, 09
7	H	193	73	37, 8
8	I	1	1	100
9	K	184	78	42, 39
10	L	182	74	40, 6
11	M	132	52	39, 3
12	N	328	126	38, 4
13	O	26	6	23, 07
14	P	87	37	42, 5
15	Q	55	24	43, 6
16	R	52	25	48, 07
17	S	120	30	25
18	T	496	202	40, 7
19	U	8	6	75
20	V	89	30	33, 7
21	X	53	24	45, 28
22	Y	10	5	50

3. 造变体的可能

以下考察"牛郎织女"造变体典的可能：

---

① 吕明恒：《喃字文学典故词典》（高板）。

(1) 中华源典

牵牛星和织女星是银河对岸的两星。中国传说曰：织女是天帝的侄女，多年织锦，与天河牛郎结婚后，不用功织锦。天帝谴责她，离间他们。每年只能七月七日在天河见面，俗叫"七夕"。那天喜鹊为桥让他们过汗。中国后代（南朝，汉代，明朝）诗文皆用为典故，表示男女相爱但不可在一起。

(2) 此典传到越南

按内容，此典的造典因素，有：银河，天河，鹊桥，牵牛，牛郎，织女，那天喜鹊，天帝，七月七日，七夕，织锦，架桥，过江等词语。其为越南喃字文学的预料。为造典因素。寻找他在喃字文学的体现，可见：其变体典故多样，使用灵活：

a. 从源典内容出发：源典内容提及地点，人物，时间→造出喃字文学的新典。具体如下：

a1. 用记地点的造典因素

中华源典：银江，鹊桥→越南喃字文学：淩银，桥银，桥乌，桥乌鹊，汉江乌桥，银河，银汉，乌桥，滝银，滝银桥乌。

a2. 用记人物的造典因素

中华源典：牛郎，织女→越南喃字文学：婀织扒牛，婀织姊姮，扒牵牛，扒牛，扒牛婀织，牛郎，牛女和织女。

a3. 用记第二人物的造典因素：

中华源典：喜鹊（架桥让牛郎，织女见面）→越南喃字文学：鸪乌鹊，鸪鹊，乌鹊。

a4. 表示时间的造典因素：

中华源典：七月七日夜→越南喃字文学：梦氹眙秋，七夕。

a5. 其他造典因素：连关于给牛郎，织女架桥过江，喃字文学中出现两个新典：北棣戈滝和俳戯队桥。此类变体按故事内容简介而成。

b. 从典语词的造词法出发

此节从典语的造词法，考察喃字文学里中华源典"牛郎织女"造典的可能性

b1. 用记地点的造典因素：

(-) 正名与俗名结合：桥乌俗名桥乌鹊→新典：桥乌鹊。

(-) 两个造典因素（两个指地点的名词）合成新典，如江名和过江

的桥名是独立的造典因素。但，在喃字文学里此两个因素结合成新典，如

滝银（造典因素）+ 桥乌（造典因素）→新典：滝银桥乌；

汉江（造典因素）+乌桥（造典因素）→新典：汉江乌桥．

（-）以全体为部分：源典没有"浚银"和"桥银"，只有"滝银"地名。在这里"浚银"和"桥银"有银河津和在银江架桥的意思。此两点（浚银和桥银）使用在喃字文学。

（-）越化汉越典造成纯越典

中华造典因素"银河"（汉越词，汉越典第2类）越南诗人借用并越化此词语造成纯越典"滝银"。汉越典"银河"与纯越典"滝银"并用在喃字文学里。同类有汉越典"烏桥"和纯越典"栱（桥）烏"。

b2. 典源所记人物的造典因素

基本上，造典可能性与用记地点的造典因素多有同样。有以下差别（不出现于记地点的造典因素）：

（-）词语秩序倒转：

为喃诗的协韵，典故词语可倒转：有作品用"婀織扒牛"，也有作品用"婀織扒牛"。

（-）典故词语因素结合或省略

中华源典语"牛郎织女"（4音节）有时不可使用在越南喃字诗句，要省去并造成新典（两个音节）："牛女"。原因是在越南传统六八诗，如果用源典语"牛郎织女"不可遵守诗律字数或登对（对联）：

塘河北壤河東，工**牛女**竜冬埃苇計《國音賦，15b7》；

漓倘少貴𩛝𩜾，事**牛女**意仍喀典秋《天南語錄，22a1》.

以下参看"牛郎织女"的变体典：

婀織扒牛，婀織姊妲，北栱戈滝，俳戟隊桥，浚银，栱银，栱烏，栱烏鵲，扒牽牛，扒牛，扒牛婀織，鴣烏鵲，鴣鵲，織女，汉江烏桥，夢㐌晧秋，银河，银汉，牛郎，牛女，烏桥，烏鵲，滝银，滝银栱烏，七夕。

可以说：

考察典故"牛郎织女"在越南喃字文学的体现可了解在越南，中华典故如何接受和改变。改变过程，按源典内容，采取可以为纯越典的关键词（造典因素）。引用在越南喃字书籍时，据词语构造法和越南诗律，此类关键词多有改正，造成新典。

结语

本考察已全面反映中华典故在越南书籍中的接受和改变。从此可了解越南喃字文学里典故使用的大观。

论文篇幅有限，不可广泛分析其他典故。但，通过考察中华典故"牛郎织女"，可了解喃字书籍里造新典的方式。造新典规律有：（1）正名与俗名结合，（2）结合两个造典因素，（3）以全体为部分，（4）越化汉越典，（5）词语秩序倒转，（6）典故词语因素结合或省略。

为深刻了解造典方式，造典的层次要多考察其他典故，可以带来多兴趣。此为以后研究的问题。

主要参考资料

a. 越语资料

1. 《翻辉益诗文》，越南社会科学院，汉喃班，社会科学出版社（河内）1978 年版。

2. 《阮攸汉字诗文》，文学出版社（河内）1988 年版。

3. 吕明恒：《喃籍里典故特征初考》，《汉喃杂志》2012 年 2 号，第 40—50 页。

4. 吕明恒：《越南典故词典编辑的考察》，《词典学与百科书杂志》2013 年 1 号，第 67—75 页。

5. 吕明恒：《喃籍里典故使用的初考》，《汉喃杂志》2012 年 6 号，第 20—34 页。

6. 吕明恒：《汉语典故月下老人的变体》，《词典学与百科书杂志》2016 年 4 号，第 67—75 页。

7. 阮俊强：《中国典故略考》，《科学研究专题》（属于喃字文学典故研究，吕明恒主编）。

　　b. 汉喃资料

8.《斷腸新聲》，AB.12，汉喃研究所。

9.《雲仙傳》，AB.62，汉喃研究所。

10.《大南國音歌曲》，AB.146，汉喃研究所。

11.《林泉奇遇》，AB.78，汉喃研究所。

12.《國音賦》，AB.184，汉喃研究所。

13.《天南語錄》，AB.478/1—2，汉喃研究所。

Indian Civilizational Literature in East Asia and the India−China Cultural Synergy:

The Forgotten Perspectives in the Works of Probhat Kumar Mukherji and the Untold Facts in the Course of India−China Cross−Cultural Communications

Prof. Priyadarsi Mukherji[*]

Abstract

Probhat Kumar Mukherji (1892—1985) has been the most renowned biographer of Rabindranath Tagore (1861—1941). Probhat Kumar Mukherji was also a historian with a unique foresight to the unfolding of events in the global arena. He has been a close associate of Tagore in the construction of his dream university—Visvabharati. In 1931, when Tagore completed 70, Probhat Kumar dedicated his book titled *Indian Literature in China and the Far East* to Tagore. Probhat Kumar also authored a book on Chinese Buddhist Literature. And also put due emphasis on China and her history in his books titled *History of the World*.

The book *Indian Literature in China and the Far East* chronicles the history of the spread of Indian religions outside India. The author maintains that the earliest literature has been religious literature. The author sought to record the history of the vast Buddhist literature written in Sanskrit—as they are preserved in Chinese translation. The book covers almost all the significant aspects that emerge in the discourse of Chinese Buddhist literature. It includes many hitherto unknown monks who travelled between the two countries of India and China to

---

[*] Prof. Priyadarsi Mukherji, chair person of Centre for Chinese & South−East Asian Studies Jawaharlal Nehru University, New Delhi, India.

seek *nirvana*, their contributions and lasting legacies in the sphere of culture. The book encompasses a period beginning from the earliest contacts between the two most ancient civilizations, and ending the discourse with the Yuan-Manchu period.

The books on China and Chinese Buddhist literature authored by Probhat Kumar Mukherji left an indelible mark on the academics of Bengal, the seat of culture and intellectual discourse in colonial India. The book *Indian Literature in China and the Far East* offers a unique perspective of the Indian civilizational impact that remained obliterated due to the academic inaccessibility of scholars and also due to the intellectual racism of the West in the field of studies in histories and religions. The paper would seek to unravel the forgotten chapters that remain obscure in the eyes of the academics today.

Despite the fact that the word "Sinology" had originated in the West, the Chinese culture studies experts must not be oblivious of the fact that China has been the greatest recipient of Indian cultural concepts and that its culture has been aesthetically embellished with Indian art motives and music. One must partake a profound study of Ji Xianlin and Jin Kemu—pertaining to the Indian cultural influence on China. Their approach was devoid of Sinocentrism. Viewing the Chinese traditional culture through the Western kaleidoscope or certain recent Chinese attempts at refuting or obliterating the Indian influence on Chinese culture are absolutely preposterous. It is irrefutable that the stories originating in the fertile plains of India—enriched almost the entire corpus of Chinese folktales. One must not forget that the influence of Indian epics has enriched the folk literature of the non–Han minorities of China as well. Experts cannot afford to exclude them from the area of Sinological research or China studies. On the other hand, the scientific and technical innovations that the early Chinese had initiated, brought forth material affluence through means of production.

It would be a fallacy to consider Sinology as a monolithic academic discipline bereft of changes. China's foreign contacts began with the Sino-Indian cultural exchanges. That was China's first step in cross – cultural communications. That was the period of genuine globalization with people going abroad without a passport or a visa. The epics and mythological tales originating in the fertile plains of India naturally enriched not only the tales of the Han Chinese, but also enriched the folk literature of the ethnic minorities of China. The spiritual civilization of India has had an everlasting imprint in almost every part of the world through ethical tales. The material civilization of China equally enriched the life of not only Asia but also the world over. Thus, Sinology in itself is a cross-cultural composite academic discipline. The Sinologists and Indologists have no way to ignore that the Chinese and Indian cultures flourished through a long course of cross-cultural communication. Therefore, I propose to create a new discipline called "Sin-Indology" (汉印学). This would be a domain where the world views of China and India would equally converge and diverge. And this will be an interdisciplinary subject.

As early as in 1931, in the international university (Visva-Bharati) of the poet Rabindranath Tagore, a renowned Indian Sinologist, a historian and the most authentic biographer of Tagore— named Prabhat Kumar Mukherji (1892–1985) authored a book titled *"Indian Literature in China and the Far East"*. The spread of Buddhist literature in China in successive ages have been discussed in this book. Later, after the founding of new China, the renowned orientalist Ji Xianlin (1911–2009) wrote in his book titled *"Collected Essays on History of Sino-Indian Cultural Relations"* that— "Indians were the primary creators. Later religious missionaries, including Buddhist monks, went to borrow the works and use them in the Buddhist scriptures. And those entered China when the texts spread outside India. The literati in China took interest in the texts and further plagiarized them. They used them in their own works. Some used them to propagate the Buddhist concept of *Karma*, and thus exhorted the believers. Instances can be found of stories finding popularity in the Chinese folk realm."[①] There is another book named *"Essays on Indian Culture"* authored by Jin Kemu (1912–2000), which is a collection of papers on Indian culture. He

---

① Ji Xianlin, "Collected Essays on History of Sino-Indian Cultural Relations", Beijing: Sanlian Book Company, 1982, p. 125.

writes in his book— "Today's India can be understood by comprehending ancient India. We can also know about our motherland China by understanding India."①

早在 1931 年，在印度诗翁泰戈尔建立的国际大学，著名的印度汉学家、史学家及泰戈尔学泰斗墨晓光（1892—1985）曾著述名为《印度文学在中国与远东的传播》一书。书中谈到了佛教文学历代在中国传播的情景。此后，新中国成立后，中国著名东方学家季羡林（1911—2009）在其名为《中印文化关系史论文集》一书里写道："印度人民首先创造，然后宗教家，其中包括佛教和尚，就来借用，借到佛经里面去，随着佛经的传入而传入中国，中国的文人学士感到有趣，就来加以剽窃，写到自己的书中，有的也用来宣扬佛教的因果报应，劝人信佛；个别的故事甚至流行于中国民间。"② 另外一本书叫《印度文化论集》，是金克木（1912—2000）发表的关于印度文化的一些论文的结集。书中他提到过："由印度之古可以有助于了解印度之今，由了解印度也可以有助于了解我们的祖国。"③

In the preface of the *Indian Literature in China and the Far East*, the author has explained that the history of Indian literature abroad, is practically the history of the spread of Indian religions outside India. Earliest literature is religious literature. The term "Indian" in this context has been used in a more comprehensive sense unlike what has been used by western scholars, which covers Sanskrit, Pali and Prakrit. The author goes beyond these classical languages, and points out that the translations appearing outside India included old Bengali, Dardic languages, central Asian dialects and even Elu.

The author thereupon explains the term "Literature" in the title of the book. Pure literature does not seem to have gone to China, at least, there is no record of such works. The bulk of literature that went outside India with the monks, was Buddhist. The majority of these books are unknown in India because the originals are lost. It is well-known to the students of Buddhism that-

---

① Jin Kemu, "Essays on Indian Culture", Beijing: Chinese Social Sciences Publication, 1983, Preface, p. 3.
② 季羡林:《中印文化关系史论文集》，三联书店 1982 年版，第 125 页。
③ 金克木:《印度文化论集》，中国社会科学出版社 1983 年版，（自序）第 3 页。

Pali and Prakrit were not the only vehicles of expression. Sanskrit came to be used largely as the literary language by the Mahayanists; and even many sections of the Hinayanists used the same language. Several thousands of books were written in Sanskrit. The history of this vast Buddhist literature written in Sanskrit, is generally omitted from the orthodox history of Sanskrit literature and when dealt, only the extant books are described. The book *Indian Literature in China and the Far East* has been first attempt at compiling the entire history of Buddhist Sanskrit literature as they are preserved in Chinese translation, whether the original is extant or extinct.

The Chinese did not undertake the study of Sanskrit and Buddhism as an academic refinement, nor for an economic gain. They studied with the intense sincerity of a devotee. Thousands of pilgrims from different parts of Asia came to India and the channels of communication of those days were neither attractive nor pleasant for such undertaking.

The study of Buddhism changed the life of millions. They explained the old texts with new interpretation. Thus a vast rich indigenous literature grew in Chinese. It gave rise to new thought movements and several sects grew in the East. Buddhism has been a dynamic force in China and Japan, and the creative genius of the people is manifested by the rich literary production of the present age.

While expounding upon the Chinese translation, the author says that generally the translation was made with the help of interpreters, who had imperfect knowledge of the Buddhist terminology. The translator himself, for his want of good knowledge of Chinese, could hardly detect the imperfect expressions used by the interpreters. It took them several centuries to develop a Buddhist vocabulary. The literal Chinese translations of Sanskrit texts are readable. A good Chinese scholar would hardly read them. The Chinese love literature and their litterateur are very particular about the style. That is why, a book with several translations done at different periods can be found.

When the translation was undertaken at the instance of an emperor, several boards were formed to superintend the work. Some to see the correctness of the interpretation of the Sanskrit text, some to see the use of correct idioms and some to look to the literary finish of the whole. It must be admitted that this is the best method of rendering one language into another—when the two are so different as Sanskrit from Chinese.

The book has been segmented around the contents as given below:

1. Earliest Contact
2. China's Contact with Central Asia
3. Buddhism in Three Kingdoms
4. Buddhist Literature in Southern China
5. Beginning of Sino-Indian Contact
6. China's Direct Intercourse with India
7. Agama Literature in China
8. The Qin Dynasty
9. The Life and Works ofKumarajiva
10. Hindu Monks in South China
11. The Age ofParamartha
12. Hindu Culture under the Northern Tartar
13. Literary Activity in the United China
14. The Age of XuanZang
15. The Age of WuZetian
16. Bodhiruchi and the Amita Cult
17. Yi Jing and the Chinese monks in India
18. Tantrism in China
19. The Last Phase under the Tang
20. The Last Hindu Monks
21. The Closing Scene
22. Yuan-Manchu Period

Lastly an alphabetic list of Sanskrit Works translated into Chinese—with names of translators, has been provided along with a list of translators of the Chinese Tripitaka in different dynasties.

Some of the prominent historical features reflected in this book are as follows:

The name China (*Cīna*) in Sanskrit texts:

Sanskrit literature abounds with references to China (*Cīna*). Some Greek writers use *Tzinista* which seems to be a corrupt form of Sanskrit *Cīnasthāna*. The epic *Mahābhārata* mentions the name several times. There, the *Cīnas* are referred to as a people sprung from Vaśiṣṭha's cow. They are said to have brought presents at the *Rājasūya* sacrifice of Yudhiṣṭhira. On the way from Himalaya to king *Subāhu*, the Pandavas crossed the country of the *Cīnas*.

The works of poet *Kālidāsa* talks of *Cīnāngśuka* (Chinese silk) in the compositions named *Śakuntalā* and *Kumārasambhava*. The word *Cīna* also exists in *Raghuvangśam*. Kautilya also knew China. In *Arthaśāstra*, he talks of *Cīnasī*— some kind of apparel from China. However, on account of the uncertainty of Indian chronology, no particular date can be fixed in regards to the earliest references to China.

<u>Chinese names for India</u>:

However, the knowledge of the Chinese about India is more definite. The earliest use of *Shen-tu* was made by the Chinese envoy Zhang Qian (123 BC). We find the general terms used for India as *T'ien-chu*, *Hsien-tu*, *Shen-tu*, etc. The term *Shen-tu*, or *Shin-tu* emerges from the word *Sindhu*, the sea of Tethys that once separated the Indian landmass from the Sino-Tibetan landmass in the north. Archaeological discoveries reveal that an Indian colony with Buddhist population was in existence in the 2nd century BC in China. In the Annals of the Early Hans, India is mentioned by name for the first time as *Shen-tu*.

<u>First Cultural Contacts</u>:

The starting point of Sino-Indian cultural synergy is generally put at 64 AD. This was the time when two Indian monks—Kāśyapa Mātanga (迦葉摩騰) and Dharmaratna (竺法蘭) were brought to China by the returning party sent by Han Ming-ti. These two Indian monks were put up in the *Pai-ma-sse* (白馬寺) —the White Horse Monastery in Luoyang. The earliest Chinese work on Buddhism is the *Sūtra of the 42 Sections* (《四十二章經》), attributed to the first missionaries Kāśyapa Mātanga and Dharmaratna. This *Sūtra* throws light on the development of Buddhism in India from the passing of Gautama Sakyamuni till the 1st century AD.

Two Hindu monks from India—who spread Buddhist culture in China during the Han era—have been Mahabala and Dharmaphala. The total number of works translated during the Han period was about 434, of which 227 were by the workers in the spread of Buddhist culture. Out of these, 207 names of translators are lost. As chaos, confusion and contest continued up to the 6th century, the fate of the Buddhist missionaries was always influenced by the vicissitudes of the ruling dynasties. Centres of Hindu culture and Buddhist activities were always identical with the residences of the dynasties and the missionaries either worked under their patronage, or were expelled by the rulers, who preferred Taoism or Confucianism to Buddhism.

In 224 AD, an Indian monk named Vighna 維難 accompanied by another compatriot named Liu-yen, came to China. After traversing many countries, he reached China with a copy of the *Dhammapada* (《法句經》, 意為 "法之路"), which he probably secured in Ceylon, on his way to China.

The three kingdoms of Wei, Shu, Wu faded in course of time. And the dynasty of the Western Jin (西晋, 265-316 AD) in Chang'an kept up the fire of Hindu culture burning in its monasteries. The Buddhist monasteries attracted Indian monks from abroad and offered shelter to the Chinese Buddhists. During five decades they translated more than 500 works. Dharmaraksha's name tops the list of the translators of this age. It may be mentioned here that the practice of assuming Hindu names was very common among Central Asian, Chinese, Korean and Japanese Buddhists. Dharmaraksha worked at Chang'an from 284 AD till 313 AD. He also founded a school of translators. Later due to political troubles in the north, he was compelled to move to Shandong.

Here one must pay attention to the fact thatDharmaraksha had translated the great *Saddharmapundarika* (《妙法蓮華經》). The catechism of Amitabha, the Bodhisattva Avalokiteshvara, whose name translated into Chinese, became *Kuan-yin*, "the one who perceives sounds". This is a wrong translation of the Sanskrit word which has been arbitrarily taken as *avalokita* and *svara*.

Another important Sanskrit text which greatly changed the religious conceptions of the Chinese Buddhists— rendered into Chinese by Dharmaraksha— was the celebrated *Ullambana Sutra* (《佛說報恩奉盆經》). The Chinese are aware of the story of Maudgalyayana (目連). Since then, Dharmaraksha virtually popularized the idea of ancestor-worship. The 15th day of the 7th lunar month has remained in China the day of the festival in honour of the dead.

China's Direct Communication with India:

After the Tartars had overrun the steppes of north China, the EasternJin dynasty that rose to prominence in south China, took power at Chien-ye (建業), todays' Nanjing in 317 AD. Nanjing was already a centre of Hindu culture and Buddhist propaganda during the rule of the Wu dynasty (222-280 AD). Many translators travelled to China. A monk named Srimitra from Kucha (龟兹) had been to north China, 307-312 AD. Due to the political turmoil in the western Jin territory, Srimitra left north for Nanjing. He was a Tantric Buddhist (佛教密宗) and is considered the pioneer of Tantrism in China.

The Agama literature (阿含經文學) which was translated by Dharmaratna, was better rendered with comprehensive translations by Gautama Sanghadeva (瞿曇僧伽提婆) and Dharmanandi (達磨難提). Sanghadeva was a man of Kashmir and arrived at Chang'an by the Central Asian route in 383 AD during the reign of the later Jin dynasty (387-417). The next great and illustrious Indian was Buddhabhadra (佛陀跋陀羅) who translated the *Avatamsaka Sutras* (《大方廣佛華嚴經》).

The Life and Works of Kumārajiva:

In this chapter, the author deals in great detail the works of the great Indian monkKumārajiva (鳩摩羅什) who lived during the later Qin dynasty (384-417 AD). Kumārajiva lived between 332 AD and 413 AD. He lived in Kucha for 30 years. But later came to Chang'an in 401 AD. The emperor made him the 國師 or *Rājya-guru*. Kumārajiva lived in Chang'an till 413 AD. As the *Rājya-guru*, he wielded extensive power. In the land of his adoption, a special hall was built by the Emperor where he preached the teachings of the Buddha to 3000 disciples. Though his mother-tongue was neither Sanskrit nor Chinese, yet he was a master of both. He initially was a scholar of Hinayana literature. But while passing through 疏勒 Shu-le (Kashgar), he came in contact with Sūryasoma, a staunch Mahayanist.

Kumārajiva preached Mahayana in China and translated all the principal works of this school into a beautiful and lucid language. He translated the great commentaries of Nāgārjuna (龍樹). In 404 AD, he also translated Āryadeva's (提婆) principal works—*Śataśāstra* (Treatise in One Hundred Verses) or 百論. Another thinker of the age who was introduced into China by Kumārajiva was Harivarman (訶梨跋摩). *Satyasiddhi-śāstra* (成實論) of Harivarman was translated by Kumārajiva, and this became very popular among the Chinese.

The Hindu Monks in South China:

This chapter highlights how Liu-yu, a general of the Eastern Jin dynasty (317-420), founded a new regime at Nanjing in 420 AD, called the Liu-Sung (420-479). The new king Sung Wu-ti (宋武帝) was a patron of Confucianism, but not unfavorably disposed towards Buddhism. However, the Chinese officials agitated to prevent the multiplication of monasteries and superstitious ceremonies of the Buddhists. This was the beginning of the desire to curb Buddhism by restrictive legislation that was displayed persistently in subsequent centuries. But still, the six decades of the Sung rule were favorable to the propagation of Hindu culture and Buddhism in south China.

Since Fa Xian's return to south China in 414 AD, Chinese students felt almost a romantic passion for India, the home of Buddhism. In 420, a group of 25 monks started for India, to visit the holy places. The leader of this group was Fa-yong who took the Hindu name of Dharmakara (Tan-wu-qie). In 423 a Hindu mink named Buddhajiva arrived at Nanjing. Then Fa Xian was still alive. Buddhajiva (佛生) rendered *Pancavarga Vinaya* into Chinese in collaboration with Chu-Tao-Shang and Che-Chang in 423. He also translated the *Pratimoksha* and *Karmavacha*. There were two other monks—Gunavarman (求那跋摩) and Gunabhadra (求那跋陀羅), who came to China during the 4th-5th century AD. They translated a number of sutras into Chinese. More monks visited China in order to render the scriptures into Chinese.

This book in fact has recorded in detail all the significant features in the history of India-China cultural synergy that is unique as we arrive at the debate over the true sense and characteristics of globalization. It was between India and China that globalization assumed genuineness as the monks of the two countries did not require any passport or visa.

Here I must say that the renowned scholar Probhat Kumar Mukherji whose academic works we have just been discussing—was my paternal grandfather. The book *Indian Literature in China and the Far East* needs to be reprinted and translated into Chinese.

While talking about the shared heritage of China and India, we can firstly begin with the story of Pan Gu splitting the Heaven and the Earth apart. Popular in the southern China, Pan Gu emerged from a gigantic egg. This fabulous egg originated in India from the Brahmanda. In Indian myths, Purusha is the masculine, and Prakriti the feminine element in the Nature. In Sanskrit, the word Prakriti also means Nature. After the death of Pan Gu, his body parts turned into myriads of elements in the Nature.

It is well known that the ethnic minorities of China, especially those residing along the Sino-Vietnamese border, have the customs of worshipping the yoni of Nüwa. The Han tomb paintings depicting Fuxi and Nüwa have been two gigantic snakes intertwining each other.① In the pictures, they are human-headed, dragon-bodied creatures. There is an ancient Hindu temple in a small town called Halebid in the Indian state of Karnataka. The same depiction of a pair of intertwined human-headed, snake-bodied figures can be seen inside the temple. Here it should be pointed out that the giant snake from the Indian myths later transformed into a dragon in China, Japan, Korea and Vietnam. Similar to the tradition of worshipping the yoni in China, there has been the tradition of worshipping the phallus in India. The phallus of Lord Shiva becomes the object of worship. The Chinese character 祖 depicts this fact. 示 (to express) combined with 且 (the phallus) reflects this ancient customs. Here I would like to point out that the practice of worshipping snakes has been the most ancient customs in the world. The character 蛇 has such a connotation.

Talking about the import of Chinese sericulture into India, Ji Xianlin pointed out that the ancient book titled *"Arthashastra"* from India of the 4th cen-

---

① Li Li, "A Study of Paintings depicting Divinities on Han Tombs", Shanghai Classics Press, 2004, p. 13.

tury BC—had mentioned about the arrival of Chinese silk in India. Prof. Ji also said that the Indians came to know about silk in the post-Vedic period. He also said that the varied expressions meaning silk in Sanskrit reflected the fact that the ancient Indians were much more knowledgeable and emancipated about silk compared to the ancient Greeks and Romans. There are a number of words in Sanskrit that mean silk. All these words are compounds, composed of the words—Kita and Krimi. The meaning is insect or worm. And Kitaja and Krimija mean "Born out of worms". Besides, the word Kausheya is an inflexion of the word Kosha which means cocoon. The thing produced by the cocoon is called Kausheya. Ancient India knew that silk emerges out of the oral emission of silk-worms, and also knew that it is extracted from the cocoons. [1]

The Chinese monk Yi Jing travelled toIndia during 671-695 AD in search of Buddhist texts. Yi Jing's book "*The Thousand Words of Sanskrit*" shows that apart from the word 丝, there are varied words like 绢、绫、锦、绣 etc in the sense of silk. These sufficiently indicate that the Chinese silk had entered India and south-east Asian countries quite early. [2] Indians specially enjoyed the gorgeous look of the silk brocade from Sichuan—with multicolored floral designs. The south-western parts of China had flourishing border trade ties with the northern and north-eastern regions of India. There were figures of Maitreya Buddha and the Avalokiteshwara embroidered in silk. It is apparent that spreading of religion had a close bond with transportation of silk. In the Indian vocabulary, the word 锦 had the meaning of China. The Indians called China by the name 锦 (cina); and thus 锦 became popular throughout the world. The examples are—China, Chine etc.

The only exception had been in the case of Russian. In all probability, Russia began communicating with China during the Liao dynasty (907—1125). During that period, theKhitan tribe had been ruling over certain northern regions of China—under the reigning title of Liao. Thus, the Russians started

---

[1] Ji Xianlin, "Collected Essays on History of Sino-Indian Cultural Relations", Beijing: Sanlian Book Company, 1982, pp. 76-77.

[2] Chen Yan, "An Preliminary Study of the Southern Sea 'Silk Route'", cited in "Papers on Oriental Studies", Peking University Press, 1983, pp. 33-35.

calling China as "Kitay". The word "Khitan" became synonymous to China.

In the article titled— "*An Incomplete Dunhuang Manuscript concerning the Migration of Sugar from India to China*"①, Ji Xianlin wrote how the sugarcane juice from India had been made into jaggery and molasses. Such types of sweet items were called *sharkara* in Sanskrit. Therefrom originated the Chinese word 石蜜. During the Tang dynasty of China, the Indian techniques of making sugar entered China. Hence, the Chinese word 糖 carries the name of the Tang dynasty. The Chinese churned out the white sugar granules, and sent it back to India. And this time the Indians did not know that it was actually a product of their land. So, they started calling it "Chini", meaning— from China. Similarly, the Indian jaggery or molasses were made into sugar candy in Egypt and sent back to India. And the Indians called it "misari", meaning—from Egypt. However, the words for sugar—used in Europe or America, all originate in the Sanskrit word "Sharkara". For example, sugar in English, sucre in French, Zucker in German, sakhar in Russian, azúcar in Spanish, etc. The English word candy comes from the Sanskrit word *khanda*, which in Chinese is 石蜜.

The Indian "Panchatantra" has been popular in the whole world since long. People acquainted with the fables of La Fontaine, and the Grimm brothers' tales, can find in them the Indian tales. Ji Xianlin rightly pointed out that the orally-transmitted folktales in many countries of Asia, Africa and Europe— have been borrowed from "Panchatantra".② Not only do we see its influence on Chinese folk literature, but can also find its effect on Chinese character. For example, we know the story of the race between a hare and a tortoise. The finishing line of the race had a silk ribbon. The tortoise defeated the complacent hare in the race. The hare reached late and hence emerged the word 才 (纔) meaning "reaching late" in Chinese. While analyzing Chinese characters, we find the positions top and bottom—imply the meaning of winning and

---

① Ji Xianlin, "An Incomplete Dunhuang Manuscript concerning the Migration of Sugar from India to China", cited in "Papers on Oriental Studies", Peking University Press, 1983, pp. 1–17.

② Ji Xianlin, "Collected Essays on History of Sino-Indian Cultural Relations", Beijing: Sanlian Book Company, 1982, p. 417.

getting defeated respectively; showing which side is the victor. Here the tortoise is the winner and therefore the tortoise is placed above the hare. In between, the word 比 tells us about the race.

Speaking about the top and bottom placement of characters, we can also see how the ancient Chinese viewed the Human Body. The character 體 not only contains the spinal chord, but it also has 曲 symbolizing the spiritual culture, and 豆 symbolizing the material culture. This shows that the brain on the top needs music, and the belly below needs the beans for food. In the eyes of the human ancestors, the position of spiritual culture was evidently higher than the material culture. And hence, 曲 was placed above 豆.

The Chinese fables and myths contain a tale of a rabbit sitting inside the moon. Ji Xianlin again points out that starting from the ages of the *Rig-Veda* from more than a millennium before Christ, Indians believed that a rabbit resides in the moon. The Sanskrit vocabulary can divulge this information.① The Sanskrit words for moon all contain the derivatives of the word *Shasha*, meaning rabbit. For example, Shashadhara and Shashabhrit mean— "containing the rabbit". Shashalakshana means— "with the shadow of the rabbit". And Shashi, meaning "beholding a rabbit", is actually the moon.

Among the Hindu deities, there is one goddess named Durga. Her incarnation is Kali. There is a garland of human skulls around the neck of Kali. She represents the passage of time. The word Kal in Kali—means time. And Kali means the Mother of Time. The male companion of Kali is Mahakala—the Great Divine Keeper of Time. In the ancient Chinese text "*Shuyiji*", there is a story of Guimu, the Mother Ghost. It is said that Guimu gives birth to ten ghosts every morning, and by evening she devours all of her ten children. From the story we can gather that her children were the ten suns or the passage of time. While discussing this topic, we can recall the characters of ten suns and the three-legged ravens in the story of "Yi the Archer shooting down Nine Suns". It is worth noticing that 鬼 and 晷 are homonyms. 晷 has three interrelated senses: shadow

---

① Ji Xianlin, "Collected Essays on History of Sino-Indian Cultural Relations", Beijing: Sanlian Book Company, 1982, p. 121.

of the sun, time, and solar scale for watching time. The word 時 (time) originally contains 日 (the sun) and 寺 (temple). The words 日規 and 日晷 have the same meaning.

In the history of Sino-Indian cultural bond, we come across the historical event of Zheng He embarking on sea voyages across theIndian Ocean. However, there is hardly few people who would know about the linguistic kinship between the southern Indian languages and Chinese—having connection with the Sea Silk Route. Between 1405 and 1433 AD, Zheng He went seven times on sea voyages. On every voyage, he visited the southern Indian state of Kerala. The local Malayalam language contains a number of words that sound similar to the Chinese words. For example, both would say 你 (ni) for "you"; 您 (nin) stands for "ningal"; 姐姐 (chiechie = elder sister) becomes "chechi"; Kerala Muslims call "ittiri" for 一点儿 (a bit). 墨水 (moshui = ink) is masi in Sanskrit. 哥哥 (keke = elder brother) is ikka which comes from Arabic Kaka. Besides these instances, Bengali and Tamil also have many words with prefix Cheena or Cheeni, showing that these items had arrived from China. Like, Chinese nut, Chinese Kaolin, Chinese stringed – crackers, Chinese silk etc in Bengali. In Malayalam, we see Chinese fishing net, Chinese frying pan, Chinese sweet potato, Chinese porcelain jars for preserving pickles, etc. Such examples are not few in other languages as well. In rural Bengal, the colloquial word for River is *Gaang*. This word sounds very similar to the word *Kaang* (江) that means River in Shanghai or Zhejiang or even Cantonese dialects of China. It seems that the name of the longest river in India—Ganga, has the original meaning of river.

Besides all these, both India and China share the same cultural heritage of numbers, especially the odd numbers. Like, the Tripitaka of the Buddhists, the three human lives, three jewels, etc. The Confucian school has the three principles and five regular occurrences. The five metals, five natural elements, five inner organs, five sacred mountains, five poisons, five cereals, five external organs, etc; and then seven feelings, nine springs, etc. Both India and China share the mystical numbers: 72, 81, 108, etc. But always the sum total of the digits comes to nine. Viewing from the angle of Chinese culture, the word nine is homophonic with the word 久 meaning longevity. And from the view of Sanskrit, the sound *nava* for nine also means new. The concept ingrained in the newness implies optimism exactly as in the word 明 (bright) when used in the 明天、明年 that are embedded in hope, prosperity and optimism.

The famousChinese Indologist Jin Kemu said that the five-character and seven-character poems in China have come from the Indian poetics. The ancient Indian poetry rhythms have also been the mother of almost all the famous poems later in the history of Indian literature. In Chinese poetries, there are either five syllables or seven syllables; and in Indian poetries, there are words with five or seven syllables in each line. Jin Kemu said that while reciting the Sanskrit scriptures, the varied pitches used therein— had direct influence over the different tones in Chinese language. The Sanskrit *Udātta* is the Chinese high pitch; *Anudātta* is the low pitch; *Guru* is the heavy or the bass tone; *Laghu* is the neutral tone; and *Svarita* is the medium or the falling tone. ①

While talking about the mathematical formulas used in writing Chinese characters, and to delve deep into the Chinese psyche, we find in the word 靈 meaning soul, the picture of a witch uttering *mantras* to invoke a soul under a rainy sky. There are three mouths in the character, indicating the repetition of *mantras*. From antiquity till today, Indians recite *mantras* in different places to invoke god or the souls of dead, and the *mantras* end by saying ' *Shanti*' thrice in succession. It means peace, peace, and peace; let peace reside in all beings of the world. The three mouths in a row in 靈 indicate the monotonous reciting of the incantations. Hence no top-bottom alignment in it. But in 品 we find a triangular alignment, showing piling of things. Similarly, in 晶、森、焱、淼、毳, the triads reflect piling, density, intensity or extremity. Besides, we find a tetrad in 器, or a dyad in 骂 or 哭。Certain machines, utensils, containers or physical organs have different outlets, like exhausts for gas, pipes for letting out water, or air-ventilators. In Sanskrit similarly, the word *yantra* means all these which we see in Chinese.

---

① Jin Kemu, "Essays on Indian Culture", Beijing: Chinese Social Sciences Publication, 1983, pp. 313–318.

印度著名汉学家、史学家、泰戈尔学权威
墨晓光 [Probhat Kumar Mukherji] (1892—1985)

Before concluding my observation, I should clarify certain points raised by Ji Xianlin. He was in disagreement with those who advocated that "Sino-Indian cultural relations historically constituted a one-way traffic". He said, "I consider that the India-China relations going as far as two to three millennia have had a special characteristic. The most outstanding of all was the process of mutual learning. Both of them had been innovative. They illuminated and permeated each other. In every historical era, this has been the trend. I believe, it would further be like this in future. This is a commendable characteristic. The two brilliant cultures of the great peoples of China and India have lighted the path of progress of mankind. In the process of mutual contact and learning, it

1976 年，84 高龄的墨晓光

was also obvious that each of these two cultures had preserved and developed their uniqueness. And at the same time had absorbed and learnt the culture of the other side. In no stage of history had there been a "one-way traffic". Bias in favor of China, or in favor of India—run quite contrary to the historical facts."①

谈到中印两国分享的文化遗产，我们首先可以从盘古开天辟地的故事开始。在这个流行于中国华南的故事里，盘古是从一只巨卵里出现的。这个巨卵发源于印度的"梵卵"即 Brahmaṇḍa。印度神话中，Purusha 是阳性，而 Prakṛti 是阴性。梵语中，Prakṛti 一词也有大自然、自然界、天性的意思。盘古死了以后，他的身体各个部位曾变成世界自然万物。

众所周知，中国少数民族地区，尤其在中越边境地带，有女娲生殖器

---

① Ji Xianlin, "Collected Essays on History of Sino-Indian Cultural Relations", Beijing: Sanlian Book Company, 1982, pp. 3-4.

1940 年 9 月 7 日，中国画师徐悲鸿在印度国际大学给墨晓光画过肖像

崇拜的习俗。伏羲与女娲本来在汉墓神画中是两大巨蛇缠绕在一起的形象[①]。画面中他们两位均作人首龙身。印度的卡纳塔克邦的名为哈雷毗特的小镇有一座古老的印度教寺庙，庙里同样有人首蛇身的雕塑，是二龙尾各自后卷的形象。这里要指出印度巨蛇的神话人物后来在中国、日本、韩国、越南就变为龙。像中国的女阴崇拜习俗一样，印度也有男性崇拜的习俗，将湿婆神的生殖器当成崇拜对象。中国汉字中的"祖"字描述其事实。"示"+"且"便反映出这古老的习俗。这里我想顺便指出崇拜蛇是世界上最古老的习俗。"蛇"字中包含着这个意思。

谈到中国蚕丝输入印度的过程，季羡林指出按公元前 4 世纪时印度名为《治国安邦书》的古籍，中国丝绸早已输入印度。季老说，吠陀时代以后印度人民知道蚕丝。他还说，从梵文"丝"字里可以看出，古代印度人民对蚕丝的认识比古代希腊人和罗马人更早、更高明。梵文里有许多词都有"丝"的意思。这些词都是复合词，组成部分都有 kiṭa 或 kr̥mi 这个字，意思是"虫子"，kiṭaja 和 kr̥mija 意思就是"虫子生"。此外还有

[①] 李立：《汉墓神画研究》（神话与神话艺术精神的考察与分析），上海古籍出版社 2004 年版，第 13 页。

Indian Literature in China and the Far East by Prabhat Kumar Mukherji〔334 pages + 18 pages with an alphabetic list of Sanskrit Works translated into Chinese—with names of translators +4 pages containing a list of translators of the Chinese Tripitaka in different dynasties〕was published in 1931.

1931年，墨晓光用英文出版《印度文学在中国与远东的传播》一书。

kauśeya，是从 kośa 一词演变来的，kośa 的意思是"茧"，茧产生的东西就叫作 kauśeya。印度古代知道丝是虫子吐的，知道丝是茧抽成的。①

唐代义净于公元 671—695 年去印度求经。义净的名为《梵语千字文》书里，除了"丝"字外，还有绢、绫、锦、绣等字。足见中国的丝织

---

① 季羡林：《中印文化关系史论文集》，三联书店 1982 年版，第 76—77 页。

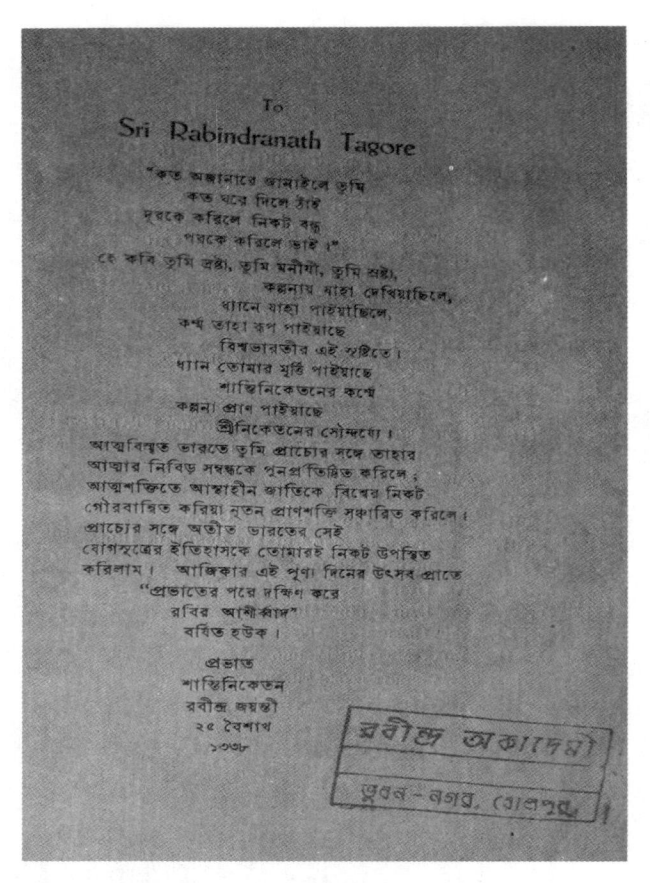

In 1931, when Tagore completed 70, Prabhat Kumar Mukherji dedicated his book titled *Indian Literature in China and the Far East* to Tagore. These were his words of dedication. The words of dedication were written in Bengali.

1931年5月7日,泰戈尔七十诞辰的那一天墨晓光把这本书亲自赠送给泰翁。

品早就传布到印度和东南亚各国了。① 印度人特别欣赏来自今之四川的蜀锦,是彩色花纹的丝织品。中国西南部与印度北部、东北部都有繁荣的边境贸易关系。丝织品中绣有弥勒佛像、观世音像等。可见传布宗教和传布丝绸就有了必然的联系。印度人的词汇中"锦"字就有"中国"之意。印度人把中国称为"锦";从此,"锦"字在世界各国得到推广,如 China,

---

① 陈炎:《南海"丝绸之路"初探》,见《东方研究论文集》,北京大学出版社1983年版,第33—35页。

```
                    CONTENTS
        LIST OF TRANSLATORS OF THE CHINESE TRIPITAKA
          I.   EARLIEST CONTACT
         II.   CHINA'S CONTACT WITH CENTRAL ASIA            12
        III.   BUDDHISM IN THREE KINGDOM                    21
         IV.   BUDDHIST LITERATURE IN SOUTHERN CHINA        29
          V.   BEGINNING OF SINO-INDIAN CONTACT             39
         VI.   CHINA'S DIRECT INTERCOURSE WITH INDIA        53
        VII.   AGAMA LITERATURE IN CHINA                    68
       VIII.   THE TS'IN DYNASTY                            91
         IX.   THE LIFE AND WORKS OF KUMARAJIVA             89
          X.   HINDU MONKS IN SOUTH CHINA                  135
         XI.   THE AGE OF PARAMARTHA                       155
        XII.   HINDU CULTURE UNDER THE NORTHERN TARTER     170
       XIII.   LITERARY ACTIVITY IN THE UNITED CHINA       188
        XIV.   THE AGE OF HIUEN-TSANG                      208
         XV.   THE AGE OF WUTSO-T'IEN                      240
        XVI.   BODHIRUCI AND THE AMITA CULT                251
       XVII.   YI-TSING AND THE CHINESE MONKS IN INDIA     262
      XVIII.   TANTRISM IN CHINA                           288
        XIX.   THE LAST PHASE UNDER THE T'ANG              295
         XX.   THE LAST HINDU MONKS                        305
        XXI.   THE CLOSING SCENCE                          313
       XXII.   YUAN-MANCHU PERIOD                          325
        LIST OF SANSKRIT BOOKS TRANSLATED
```

The book contains 22 chapters depicting in detail the history of the period that marked the flourishing of cultural communication between India and China.

分成二十二章的本书为印度与中国的跨文化交流及中印关系史的详细记载。

Chine 等词。

只有俄语是例外的，俄罗斯很可能在辽朝（907—1125）时与中国开始交往，那时契丹人以辽朝的名义统治中国北部一带。因此，俄罗斯人将中国称为 Китай（Kitay），是直接将"契丹"一词当成中国之意。

在题为"一张有关印度制糖法传入中国的《敦煌残卷》"一文中，季羡林[1]指出从印度的甘蔗汁如何制造 guṛh 即糖或赤砂糖，后制造赤砂糖。这种糖在梵语里被称为śarkarā，汉语中的石蜜是从此而来的。中国唐

---

[1] 季羡林：《一张有关印度制糖法传入中国的〈敦煌残卷〉》，见《东方研究论文集》，北京大学出版社 1983 年版，第 1—17 页。

代时，印度制糖法传入中国，因此"糖"字带有唐朝之名。中国人炼糖炼成白砂糖，又把它送到印度。印度人这一回不知道那是他们本土的食物，因此把它叫作"Chini"（意思是中国的）。同样，印度的赤砂糖到了埃及就变成糖果，又回到印度时，被叫作"Misari"（意思是埃及的）。不过欧美国家的"糖"字都来自梵语的śarkarā；比如英文的sugar，法语的sucre，德语的Zucker，俄语的caxap（发音：sakhar），西班牙语的azúcar等。英文的candy来自梵文的khaṇḍa，即"石蜜"。

印度的《五卷书》早已闻名于世。人们较熟悉的拉·封丹的《寓言》、格林兄弟的童话里可以找到印度故事。季羡林正确地指出：在亚洲、非洲和欧洲许多国家的口头流传的民间故事里，有从《五卷书》借来的故事。[①] 不仅在中国民间文学而且在中国的汉字中也会找到《五卷书》的影响。比如，我们都知道兔子和乌龟赛跑的故事。赛跑的终点线有丝带。比赛中乌龟战胜了自满的兔子。兔子来得晚，因此中文有了"纔"字。分析汉字时，我们会发现字中上下位置标志胜败之意，指出哪一方占优势。这里乌龟战败了兔子，因此龟在上，兔在下，中间的比就有"比赛"的意思。

谈到汉字中的上下位置，我们可看到中国古人如何认识"人体"。"體"字不仅有脊椎骨，而且有"曲"字——代表精神文明，其下有"豆"字——代表物质文明，表示上头的脑子需要音乐，下面的肚子需要食物。在古人的眼里，精神的位置比物质高，因此"曲"在上，"豆"在下。

中国寓言、神话中会找到月亮里面有一只兔子的说法。季羡林指出这种说法来自印度。从公元前一千多年的《梨俱吠陀》起，印度人就相信月亮里面有兔子，梵文的词汇就可以透露其中的消息。[②] 月亮的梵文词都有śaśa（兔子）这个词作为组成部分，譬如śaśadhara 和 śaśabhṛt，意思是"带着兔子的"；śaśalakṣana，意思是"有兔子的影像的"。

印度教所信奉的诸神当中有位女神叫难尽母，她的化身是Kālī。Kālī的脖子上挂着一串头颅，她代表时间的流逝。Kālī一词中的Kāl有时间的意思，而Kālī一词有时母的意思。Kālī的男配偶是Mahākāla即大时天。

---

① 季羡林：《中印文化关系史论文集》，三联书店1982年版，第417页。
② 同上书，第121页。

中国梁朝的《述异记》中可看到鬼母的故事。据说，鬼母每天早晨生出十只鬼，到了晚上她就吞下自己的孩子。从故事的情节来看，她的孩子好像是太阳或者是时间的流逝。谈到这一课题时，我们可以想起"羿射九日"的故事中十个太阳及三足乌鸦。值得注意的是：鬼和晷是同音词。"晷"字有相关的三种意思：日影、时间与日规。"時"字本来包括"日"与"寺"，意思是日规与日晷完全相同。

中印文化关系史上有郑和下西洋的历史事实。不过对"海上丝绸之路"和印度南方语言与汉语的亲属关系有知识的人实在不多。1405—1433 年郑和七次航海时，每次都到印度南方的喀啦啦地区。当地的马拉雅兰语有不少与汉语非常相似的词语，譬如，两种语言里有"你"；"您"是 ningal；姐姐是 chechi；喀啦啦邦回民把一点儿说成 ittiri。墨水是梵语中的 masi；哥哥很可能来自阿拉伯语的 kaka；转变为马拉雅兰语的 ikka。除了这些例子之外，孟加拉语、泰米尔语也有不少带有 cheena 的前缀，说明那些事物曾从中国引进印度各地。譬如，孟加拉语中有"中国花生""中国陶土""中国编连成串的爆竹""中国丝绸"等。马拉雅兰语中有"中国渔网""中国煎锅""中国白星芋属的植物""中国的红薯""放咸菜的中国瓷罐"等。这种的例子在其他语言也不少。孟加拉的乡村里对河、江有个通俗的词叫 gāng；这一词与中国南方的上海话、浙江方言、粤语对"江"词的发音（即 kāŋ）是非常相同的。看来印度北方最大河流 Gangā 或恒河本来有大江的意思。

除了这些之外，中印两国分享的文化遗产还包括不同数字，尤其是带奇数的词句，比如，佛教的三藏、三生、三宝；儒家的三纲五常；五金、五行、五脏、五岳、五毒、五谷、五官；七情；九泉等。两国还通过佛教分享些神秘数字，譬如，八十一、一百零八、七十二等。但每一个神秘数字的总数是九，从中国文化的角度去看，跟长久的"久"谐音，而从梵文的角度去考虑，有新颖的意思了。

中国著名印度学家金克木说：中国诗歌中的五言诗和七言诗，据说，来自印度古典诗律。印度古典诗律也是印度文学史后期著名诗歌作品的母亲。中文诗里每一行有五言或七言，即五个字或七个字；而印度梵文诗里每一行带有五个音节或七个音节的词句。金克木说：念梵文经典时的音调曾对汉语不同声调有一定的影响。梵文中的 udātta 高调、anudātta 低调、

guru 重调、laghu 轻调及 svarita 中调或降调。①

谈到把数字公式应用于汉字书写方式而来推断中国人的思维方式，我们在"靈"字会发现，下雨天一个巫婆吟咏招魂的镜头，字中有三个口，表明吟咏动作的重复。从古时候到现在，在印度不同场合上向上帝或某人的灵魂祈祷后，三次说"山低"（Shanti），意思是安宁、和平；其含义是"让世界万物得到安宁"。"靈"字中三个口呈一条直线，单调乏味地吟咏，没有上下位置的可能性。但是"品"字有三角形的结构，说明把某些产品堆积起来。同样的三角形结构出现在：晶、森、焱、淼、掱 等字中。这都是由三合一组的形式组成的，反映出积累、积聚、密度、极度等意义。除了三合一组之外，还可以找到四合一组（如 器）或二合一组（如 骂、哭）。某个机器、器具或器官都有不同出口：排气口、排水口或通风口等。梵文中 yantra 一词同样有机器、器具、器官的意思，把内脏各部也称为 yantra。

结束之前，还得讲季羡林所提出的几点，他不同意"中印文化关系在历史上是一边倒的买卖（one-way traffic）"。他说："我认为，长达二、三千年的中印友好关系有很多特点，其中最突出的就是互相学习、各有创新、交光互影、相互渗透。在任何一个历史时期，都是这样的，我相信，将来也还会是这样的。这是一个很可贵的特点。像中印这样两个伟大的民族，都有独自创造的光辉灿烂的文化，这些文化曾照亮了人类前进的道路。在相互接触和学习中，也必然会既保存发展了自己文化的特点，又吸取学习了对方的文化。在什么时候也不会是'一边倒买卖'，不管是倒向中国，或是倒向印度，都与历史事实不符。"②

---

① 金克木：《印度文化论集》，中国社会科学出版社 1983 年版，第 313—318 页。
② 季羡林：《中印文化关系史论文集》，三联书店 1982 年版，第 3—4 页。

你翻译什么?

——《诗经》《宋词选》翻译工作的反思(散记)

松冈荣志[*]

0. 很难翻译,或者不能翻译?

我们进行翻译(此限定"笔译"的意思)工作时,经常碰到不少难翻译的问题。比如说,日本家庭里吃饭的时候,首先大家要一起大声地叫"itadakimasu"(就是说,谢谢老天爷、阿弥陀佛等的意思)。但,中国社会或家庭里一般没有这样的习惯,所以这句话很难翻译,几乎不能翻译的。

1. 《诗经》《宋词选》的翻译工作

我去年翻译《诗经》,作为现代日文版而出版了,今年也刚做完了《宋词选》的翻译工作。在此,我想举个例子来介绍我最近翻译工作中碰到的几个代表性的问题,而进一步探讨两国语言和文化之间存在的难于了解的核心问题。

2. 雎鸠怎么叫? ——动物

《诗经》国风开篇的第一首"关关雎鸠,在河之洲",大家都知道的。那么,"关关"是什么呢?历代学者都说雎鸠的叫声。那,它叫什么呢?应该怎么样翻译呢?《诗经》当然有不少现代汉语的翻译,下面是程俊英和蒋见元两位教授翻译《诗经·周南·关雎》的一部分。程教授(1901—1993)是中国第一代女教授。她的译文在风格上似不跟其他男教授的译文一样。

---

[*] 松冈荣志,日本国立东京学艺大学名誉教授,日中翻译文化教育协会会长,北京师范大学客座教授。

```
关  雎        关  雎
关关雎鸠，    雎鸠关关相对唱，
在河之洲。    双栖河里小岛上。
窈窕淑女，    纯洁美丽好姑娘，
君子好逑。    真是我的好对象。

参差荇菜，    长长短短鲜荇菜，
左右流之。    左手右手顺流采。
窈窕淑女，    纯洁美丽好姑娘，
寤寐求之。    醒着相思梦里爱。
```

这是很有趣而值得注意的问题。现代汉语本来似无性别差异，但不能不说也有风格不同的。此有篇幅限制，不能详细地谈谈这个问题，只好提议而矣。

3. "雎鸠"是什么鸟？

它似是鱼鹰，也就是说"鹗è"，辞典的解释如下：

1）鹗科海雕属鸟类。体大，翅长。生活在海滨和面积更大的<u>内陆水域中</u>。体长约65厘米。上体褐色，下体白色，头上有白羽。（《不列颠百科全书》）

2）ミサゴ。タカ目ミサゴ科の猛鳥。全長60センチメートルほどで、翼が細長く、腹が白いのでカモメに似る。（『大辞林』）

4. 雎鸠怎么叫？

前辈学者对"关关"的解释如何？《传》曰："关关，<u>和声也</u>。"

余冠英《诗经选译》（人民文学出版社，1958年）："关关"，形声字，犹如呱呱，形容雎鸠的<u>鸣声</u>。（p.1，注1）"呱呱（guāguā）"就是"形容鸭子、青蛙等的响亮叫声。"（《新华字典》第11版，p.167，2011年）中国的当代读者看这个解释时，很可能把雎鸠看作鸭子之类。

那么，日本学者和作家的翻译如何？

（1）吉川幸次郎（1958年，岩波书店）译为：

<u>かあかあ</u>と鳴くみさごの鳥は、川の中州にいる。[そのように]も

のしずかなよい娘は、立派な方のよいつれあい。

　　日语里，象声词"かあかあ（Kaa-kaa）"表示乌鸦的叫声。日本读者看到这个解释时，应该把雎鸠看作乌鸦之类。

　　（2）加纳喜光（1983年，学习研究社）译为：

くっくっと鳴くみさご鳥/河のなかすで呼びかわす/はるかにゆかしい乙女ごは/殿方のよき妻となる人

　　日语象声词"くっくっ（kut-kut）"表示鸽子的叫声。日本读者看到这个解释，也应该把它看作鸽子之类。

　　（3）海音寺潮五郎（1984年，讲谈社）译为：

河の洲に/みさご二つゐて/鳴きかはすや/ほろほろと

　　象声词"ほろほろ（horo-horo）"表示雉（野鸡）的叫声。

　　他们的翻译不一样，大家不知道哪个翻译是正确的。但一听鱼鹰的叫声，就明白了。它的叫声是"Pi-pi-pi"，完全不跟乌鸦、鸽子、野鸡一样的。

5. 英文的翻译如何？

　　下面是汪榕培先生的英文翻译：

关雎	The cooing
关关雎鸠，	The waterfowl would coo,
在河之洲。	Upon an islet in the brook.
窈窕淑女，	A lad would like to woo,
君子好逑。	A lass with nice and pretty look.

　　这个"coo"也是鸽子的叫声。顺便要介绍另外一个很有趣的问题。看内容来说，英文的翻译的第三句和第四句颠倒了。就是说，英文诗歌也重视押韵，为了押韵（脚韵），译者主动地改它们的位置。从日文翻译的立场来说，这个不可能的。日文传统诗歌基本上没有押韵，只有"5-7-5（俳句）"和"5-7-5-7-7（短歌）"等节拍而已。日文当代诗歌更自由，没有押韵，没有节拍。

　　顺便介绍我的日文翻译：

ミサゴ鳥

つがいのミサゴ鳥が　二羽

河の中洲で　鳴き交わす
若くて　きれいな　あのむすめ
ほんとに　ぼくに　ぴったりだ

6. 兰草怎么香？——植物

古代的兰草是一种香草。大家都知道它很香，但不一定知道它怎么香。

古代的兰草是什么草？

《诗经·郑风·溱洧》：溱与洧，方涣涣兮。士与女，方秉<u>蕳</u>兮。

"蕳 jiān"就是泽兰，日语说"フジバカマ"。《楚辞》里用过不少"兰"字，例如"幽兰""秋兰"等。

7. 费了四年时间

我们家费了四年养它，终于知道了它怎么香的秘密。

第一年　　花开了，但花和叶子都没有什么香味儿。

第二年　　花开后，把花和叶子干燥了，但还是没有什么香味儿。

第三年　　花开了，我们不理它，花和叶子凋谢了。

第四年　　花开了，我们不理它，花和叶子立枯了。过了几个月，遇到梅雨时节，中午突然下起雨来。为了收拾衣服开窗了，就有了很香的味道。

8. 古代生活中的兰草

（1）把兰草缝进衣襟、衣领等里面，当人出汗或空气湿润时，香味儿渗出来。

（2）把它缝进枕头或被褥等里面。

（3）把它放在水里，渗出香味儿使用等。

兰草在地里枯后，再遇到雨水等湿气，才散发香气。

9. 愁与"愁い（urei）"有什么不同？

词里有不少"愁"字，日语说"愁い（urei）"。但，两者其实似是而非的。下面是北宋的词人柳永的作品。右边是我的日文翻译。

凤栖梧	柳　永
伫倚危楼风细细，	そよ吹く風に　高殿の上
望极春愁，	手すりに　身を寄せ　眺めれば
黯黯生天际。	どこまでつづくか　けだるい　春景色
草色烟光残照里，	草は緑　かすみは輝く　夕まぐれ
无言谁会凭栏意？	悲しくて　やりきれぬ　この気持ち
	おまえになんか　わかるものか

下面是英文翻译（许渊中译，高等教育出版社，2006 年）。

I lean alone on balcony in light, light breeze;
As far as the eye sees,
On the horizon dark parting grief grows unseen.
In fading sunlight rises smoke over grass green.
Who understands why mutely on the rails I lean?

从英文翻译来说，这里的"愁"是"别离的悲哀"的意思。那么，日语的"愁い（urei）"呢？

《日本国语大辞典》第五卷（小学馆，1974.P.1108）曰：

（1）春天的忧虑

例：春愁薄处吹芦管、午梦残时啜茗杯（《济北集》二）

（2）青春时期特有的感伤的情调

例：少年时期的"哀而乐"的情调

含义上来看，中文"愁"的含义是比较具体的，但日语"愁い（urei）"的含义却是模糊的、抽象的。我认为明治时代文明开化以后，日本学者吸收欧美哲学思想的过程中，误会了不少"哲学、思想"词汇是高度抽象的"玄学"词汇。

"愁い（urei）"不能直接使用它来翻译中文"愁"，翻译工作中经常有同样的问题。译者每次需要当场考虑而下决定译文，负担相当重的。

（2016 年 10 月初稿，12 月改稿）

"一带一路"推动形成文明秩序
——在"东亚文明交流国际研讨会"的演讲

王义桅*

中华民族伟大复兴有何标志？丝绸之路的复兴可以说是鲜明标志。丝绸之路是文明交流互鉴之路，中国也是文明型国家。"一带一路"通过复兴古代丝绸之路又超越近代全球化，正在推动沿线国家文明的共同复兴，推动形成21世纪文明秩序。

15世纪奥斯曼土耳其帝国的崛起切断了两千年的丝绸之路，欧洲人被迫走向海洋，导致欧亚大陆文明的衰落。重振丝绸之路成为丝绸之路沿线许多国家的共同梦想。20世纪90年代，联合国开发规划署（UNDP）画了一张大地图，图上有把中国和欧洲联系起来的三条欧亚大陆桥，然而这些都只是写在地图上，没有变成现实。现在我们就是想实现过去提出的"大陆桥"这样一个梦想。

"我们要实现亚欧的互联互通"，三年前，习近平主席在哈萨克斯坦提出了这样的畅想。哈萨克斯坦是全球最大的内陆国，它离任何一个海岸都非常远，没有高速公路也没有高速铁路。所以，我们不仅要修高速公路还要修高速铁路，帮助构建网络空间的联系，至少要连接65个国家。与此同时，中国国内至少有18个省份都可以被连接起来，特别是对中国中西部的省份将会大有益处，比如说新疆，面积占到了中国内地的六分之一，有8个陆上邻国，极具开发潜力。我们应该依靠未来发达的交通体系把新疆与海洋连接起来，与欧洲连接起来。如今，我们已经有了高速铁路、高速公路，可以直接联通内陆省份与欧洲，新疆、云南这些曾经位置偏远的内陆省份也逐渐开始迈向改革的前沿。如果大家看一下中国的地

---

* 王义桅，中国人民大学国际事务研究所所长、教授。

图,会发现在整个亚欧大陆当中有三条经济发展带,第一条始于重庆至新疆联通中亚、俄罗斯然后进入欧洲;第二条是往北走通过蒙古进入俄罗斯;第三条是从巴基斯坦走到印度洋。除此之外,还有很多其他包括道路、管线在内互联互通的项目,如果这些项目都能够完成,实现一个系统效应,或者说战略和路线图的协同增项,这就实现了亚欧大市场,甚至可以把非洲都包括进来,这就是我们未来的梦想——重振丝绸之路,重振亚欧文明。

到底什么是"一带一路"呢?

我用一二三四五六来概括:

一是一个概念——一带一路。

二是两只翅膀:一个是陆上,一个是海上,即丝绸之路经济带、21世纪海上丝绸之路。

三个原则:共商(集思广益——利益共同体)、共建(群策群力——责任共同体)、共享(人民受惠——命运共同体)。

四个关键词:互联互通(如果把"一带一路"比着亚洲腾飞的两只翅膀,互联互通就是其经络——习近平)、战略对接、产能合作、开发第三方市场(开放合作、和谐包容、市场运作、互利共赢)。

五个方向——五通:政策、设施、贸易、资金、民心。其中孔子学院为民心相通做出了突出贡献。

六大领域——六大经济走廊。中国经中亚、俄罗斯至欧洲(波罗的海);中国经中亚、西亚至波斯湾、地中海;中国至东南亚、南亚、印度洋。中巴、孟中印缅、新亚欧大陆桥以及中蒙俄等经济走廊。其中,中巴经济走廊注重石油运输,孟中印缅强调与东盟贸易往来,新亚欧大陆桥是中国直通欧洲的物流主通道,中蒙俄经济走廊偏重国家安全与能源开发。

那么,"一带一路"沿线国家为什么能够做到互联互通呢?以中国为起点,新丝绸之路经中东和中亚,一直通到欧洲,这样会有更多国家分享中国发展带来的红利,因此我们要特别强调所谓的"中国模式"。中国人经常说"要想富先修路""要快富修高速",中国有大量的外汇储备,将其投资到基础设施当中去,这就是中国高铁的效率。中国用十年不到的时间,就修了2万千米的高速铁路,但这样依然不够。即便中国有4万亿美元的外汇储备,但在亚洲投资设施方面仍然有8万亿美元的缺口,所以我们需要"PPP项目",通过公私合营项目来获得更多的钱。

当然这是一个大项目，它有很多的风险，首先第一是经济风险，因为这是长期大量的投资，有些国家可能还不是世贸组织的成员，有些国家可能还不是市场经济，所以有很大的挑战。还有政治风险，各国内部的不稳定、国际地缘政治的风险以及传统和非传统的安全威胁都涵盖其中。国家边界之间存在很多国际水域，比如说在东亚国家，如果你要在某个国家建大坝，还需要考虑其他国家的感受，从而进行协调；有些国家的法律体系非常复杂，比如说在波兰，欧盟法律、波兰的法律和地方法律同时存在；还有许多非政府组织扮演着非常重要的角色。同时也可能面临道德风险，存在宗教、文化、习俗的隔阂。如果没有很好的沟通联系，人们会否定中国制造、中国建造，使之无法落地生根。

说起来容易做起来难，我们该怎么去实现"一带一路"的构想呢？我想孔子的智慧可以运用于解决问题的过程中——己欲立而立人，己欲达而达人。每个国家都有各自的发展需求，中国的"一带一路"是服务于实现联合国2030年后可持续发展议程。在基础设施的建设方面："北斗"2018年覆盖"一带一路"沿线国家，2020年会实现全球覆盖，而且不依赖于因特网，这样对于道路建设和远程教育都十分有利，因为某些偏远地区可能还没有通电，这些举措使贫苦地区的人们也可从高科技中受益。此外，中国的发展经验，有些是成功的，有些不那么成功，我们要与"一带一路"国家分享中国发展的成功经验，规避其错误，特别是避免走"先污染后治理"老路。中国人有"中国梦"，其他国家人民也有自己的梦，所以"一带一路"就是为了帮助其他的国家来实现他们的梦想，实现沿线国家共同的繁荣和文明的共同复兴。

国际金融危机爆发后，中国对世界经济的贡献平均达三成，是排名第二位的美国的一倍。作为实体经济投资的一种方式，关注基础设施建设，推动实体经济的发展，"一带一路"将会成为世界经济复苏的引擎。通过这张图我们可以看到，"一带一路"国家的GDP只占到了世界经济的29%，人口占到了全世界的63%，所以还有很大的发展潜力。

总结起来，笔者认为"一带一路"主要是希望实现全球的繁荣。在"后危机时代"，在穷国和富国之间、东西方间存在巨大差距，甚至一个国家内部的差距都是显著的，这必然会导致很多风险，"一带一路"即是要实现全球再平衡。如果从这张地图上来看，今天有数十亿计的人在搞现代化，但是仍然使用数百年前欧洲所开发的航路和标准。如今电子商务发展迅速，所以在大西洋和太平洋之间的现存贸易航路就不够了，很多过去的设施都需要进行再建设，例如巴拿马都希望对老运河进行改造和升级，因为这个运河还是一百多年前美国人开凿的。

这是一个"夜晚的世界"，只有那些生活在日本、北美和欧洲这些国家的沿海地区灯火辉煌，证明实现了现代化，而在世界的其他地方卫星看不到灯光，依然生活在"贫困的黑暗"之中，所以"一带一路"就是要让所有人在晚上都有电，见到光，这就需要工业化。按照世界银行数据，当今世界产出的八成来自于沿海地区的 100 千米的地带，这种"全球化"是"部分全球化"，我们还需要更多的互联互通，助推人类文明的共同复兴，打造更包容的全球化。

"一带一路"倡议可谓"源于中国而属于世界"。"国际经济体系已经全球化，而世界政治结构还是以民族国家为基础。"这是全球治理的软肋。基辛格博士在《世界秩序》一书中写道："评判每一代人时，要看他们是否正视了人类社会最宏大和最重要的问题。""一带一路"能否成功，就看它能否解决人类社会最宏大和最重要的问题。"一带一路"就是在解决中国问题的同时解决世界问题，在解决世界问题时解决中国问题。

从人类文明史和全球化史视野看，"一带一路"倡议完全可成为国际秩序新理念的实验场。

当今世界，正在形成三种秩序：

一是文明秩序，以文明国为基本单元。"一带一路"将人类四大文明——埃及文明、巴比伦文明、印度文明、中华文明，串在一起，通过由铁路、公路、航空、航海、油气管道、输电线路和通信网络组成的综合性立体互联互通，推动内陆文明、大河文明的复兴，推动发展中国家脱贫致富，推动新兴国家持续成功崛起。一句话，以文明复兴的逻辑超越了现代化的竞争逻辑，为 21 世纪国际政治定调，为中国梦正名。"一带一路"所开创的文明共同复兴的秩序可称之为"文明秩序"。

二是国际秩序，以民族国家为基本单元。近代威斯特伐利亚体系开创以民族国家为基本单元、以主权平等为核心价值的国际体系，随着西方中心论的建立而演变为西方的国际秩序，全球化是其典型说法。直到战后建立名义上以联合国为核心、实质以美国领导的国际秩序，虽经苏联为首的社会主义阵营挑战而未解体，维系至今。经济基础决定上层建筑。今天，非西方的产出已超过西方，但非西方国家的国际话语权与政治权力仍然从属于西方，"一带一路"着眼于发达—发展中国家的共同现代化，实现南北、南南平衡发展，推动国际秩序朝向更加公正、合理、可持续的方向发展。

三是公民秩序，以公民而非国家为基本单元。《世界秩序》一书写道："任何一种世界秩序体系若要持久，必须被视为是正义的，不仅被各国领导人所接受，也被各国公民所接受。"（ⅩⅦ页）当今世界，权力不仅在东移也在下移，各国都面临着社会化公民运动的内部压力，推动建立全球层面的公民秩序。"一带一路"以政策沟通、设施联通、贸易畅通、资金融通、民心相通等"五通"消除贫富差距、以创新、协调、绿色、开放、共享等"五大发展理念"实现社会公平正义，打造包容性全球化。

文明秩序、国际秩序、公民秩序的三位一体，就是命运共同体，体现世界各种文明、国家、公民寓命于运及寓运于命的有机统一。文明的回归而非现代化，乃人类社会的归宿。唯如此，才体现世界多样性。

一句话，"一带一路"倡议着眼于沿线国家共同现代化、文明共同复兴及包容性全球化三大使命，着眼于打造文明秩序、国际秩序、公民秩序三位一体的命运共同体，使中国站在国际道义制高点。

汉字与东亚近代的启蒙思潮
——梁启超与潘佩珠的《越南亡国史》

王志松*

目　次

1. 问题所在
2. 《越南亡国史》的发表形态与政治主张
3. 文集中的互文性
4. 《越南亡国史》的反响及其改编作品
5. 《越南亡国史前录》与滇剧《苦越南》
6. 结语

1. 问题所在

《越南亡国史》是越南近代启蒙先驱潘佩珠于 1905 年发表的汉文著作，20 世纪初在东亚地区广为传播，影响巨大。然而，该著的作者却长期被误认为是梁启超，直至 1990 年初黄国安等学者经过考辨才认定是巢南子（潘佩珠）。① 毫无疑问，作者的重新认定无论对于客观理解《越南亡国史》的内容，还是重新评价潘佩珠的启蒙思想，均有极为重要的意义。但另一方面，从《越南亡国史》传播的角度看，作者名的误会作为一个文化现象仍然存在一些值得思考的问题。首先，为何会对该文的作者产生误解？其次，该文既然长期以梁启超之名传播，那么如此误讹在传播过程中有什么作用？最后也是最重要的，该文一般是和《记越南亡人之

---

* 王志松，北京师范大学外国语言文学学院日文系教授。
① 参见周佳荣《梁启超与〈越南亡国史〉的关系——〈中国大百科全书〉勘误一则》，《明报月刊》4（1991）；黄国安《〈越南亡国史〉是梁启超撰写吗?》《东南亚纵横》1（1992）；徐善福《关于〈越南亡国史〉的作者问题》《东南亚纵横》，3（1992）。

言》、《越南小志》一起传播，这几个文本之间是什么关系？它们对《越南亡国史》的理解到底起到什么作用？本文以在中国接受为视角就上述问题试作考察。

2.《越南亡国史》的发表形态与政治主张

在考辨《越南亡国史》的作者名时，黄国安作为一个重要论据曾指出，梁启超接到潘佩珠的文稿后即刻将其单独发表在《新民丛报》第 67 号上。① 但笔者查阅《新民丛报》该号却没有发现《越南亡国史》，只有梁启超的《记越南亡人之言》。黄国安大概混淆了这两者。其实问题的关键也正在于此：《越南亡国史》的作者名之所以长期被误会与该文的发表形态有很大关系。

据笔者调查，《越南亡国史》没有以"巢南子"之名单独发表过，一般与梁启超的《记越南亡人之言》一起发表，有时加上《越南小志》。目前所能见到的最早版本是发表于广智书局 1905 年出版的文集中。该文集封面书名"越南亡国史，附越南小志"，内容包括《叙》、"例言"、《越南亡国史前录（记越南亡人之言）》、《越南亡国史》和《越南小志》。署名情况如下：封面署"新民社员编"，《叙》署名"饮冰识"，"例言"和《越南亡国史前录（记越南亡人之言）》无署名，《越南亡国史》署名"广智编辑部纂，越南亡命客巢南子述"，《越南小志》署名"新民社员编"。

该文集有两点值得注意：其一，尽管每篇文章都有不同的署名，但封面书名是"越南亡国史，附越南小志"，即将《越南亡国史》和梁启超的《越南亡国史前录》当作一个整体，看成是正文。因此，文集内的《越南亡国史》一文尽管有"广智编辑部纂，越南亡命客巢南子述"的署名，但书名的表述方式已经造成误会，为后来的传播始终将这两篇文章绑定在一起埋下伏笔。其二，"新民社员"的署名一般是梁启超和《新民丛报》编辑部人员经常共同使用的笔名，但该文集中因包含梁启超所著《越南亡国史前录》和《越南小志》，极容易将封面的"新民社员"理解为"梁启超"。因此，《越南亡国史》一文在该文集中以如此方式发表，可以说是作者名被误会的最直接原因。

---

① 黄国安：《〈越南亡国史〉是梁启超撰写吗?》，《东南亚纵横》1（1992），第 37 页。

而更深层次的原因则在于，《越南亡国史》的内容与梁启超本人的政治主张基本相同。或许应该这样说，《越南亡国史》不仅是潘佩珠在梁启超的建议下撰写的，其内容本身也深受梁启超启蒙思想的影响。

清末，亡国史撰写是维新派的一个政治策略，希冀借此证明"维新变法"的正当性与迫切性。① 当时维新派撰写大量各衰亡国家历史，通过叙述"亡国后的悲惨境况"强调"不变法将道致亡国"的主张。1896年，梁启超在《波兰灭亡记》中叙述了波兰不图自强而托庇大国，终遭俄、普、奥瓜分而亡的史实。1898年，他又在《俄土战纪叙》中分析了土耳其衰败的主要原因在于"内治不修"和"外交不慎"，指出中国的情况与之相类，呼吁应把"俄土之事，悬诸国门，以为我四万万人告也"。② 康有为也于同年撰写《波兰分灭记》呈递光绪皇帝，促成戊戌变法。戊戌变法失败后，亡国史撰写则又变为改造国民的启蒙策略。1902年，《新民丛报》上的一则"绍介新书"广告写道："读亡国之史，使人痛，使人惧，使人怵然自戒。史也者，诚养国民精神之要务哉！虽然，处将亡之势，而不自知其所以亡者，则与其读建国史，不如读亡国史。"③

潘佩珠从小习汉学，擅长汉文，深受梁启超等清末启蒙思想家的影响，赴日之前已经研读过梁启超的《中国魂》、《戊戌政变记》和《新民丛报》等。梁启超这些著作所贯穿的基本思想是，面对西洋的进逼，必须通过变法自强才能生存下去。梁启超在《论近世国民竞争之大势及中国前途》中指出"今日世界之竞争国民竞争也"。《戊戌政变记》的主要内容也是"鳌革积弊，修明内政，取法泰西，实行改革"④。这样的基本立场也贯穿在《越南亡国史》之中："越南若及是时，大修兵政，大振民权，君臣上下，励精图治，深求外洋之智学，洗刷积腐之规模，迨天之未阴雨，彻彼桑土，绸缪牖户，国犹可为也。"⑤《越南亡国史》的政治主张与梁启超的思想基本上是相通的。

---

① 刘雅军：《"衰亡史鉴"与晚清社会变革》，《史学理论研究》4（2010），第59—68页。
② 梁启超：《俄土战纪叙》，《饮冰室合集1》文集之三，中华书局1989年版，第33—34页。
③ 《绍介新著》，《新民丛报》6（1902）。
④ 梁启超：《戊戌政变记》，《饮冰室合集6》专集之一，中华书局1989年版，第1页。
⑤ 潘佩珠：《越南亡国史》，新民社员编《越南亡国史》，广智书局1905年版，第4页。

《越南亡国史》的初版是作为"通俗时局鉴"丛书之一种于 1905 年刊行的。1904 年,为了扩大启蒙影响,梁启超主道的广智书局面向更广泛的读者开始发行"通俗时局鉴"丛书。其"通俗时局鉴发印缘起"曰:

> 时局之危急,人皆谓知之。虽然,真知之者能几人哉?盖今之时局由种种方面造成,其现象与其原因皆极复杂,非皮相其一二者所能解释也。夫知之尚未真,亦乌从而救治之抑?今之时局又断非一二人所能救治也。必全国大多数人咸怵然确信其危急,人人有剥肤之感,然后救治乃可得施。本局故博延通人以通俗之文撰成小册,使至忙之人可以读,至贫之人可以购,至浅学之人可以解,是亦本局对于国民尽涓埃之义务也夫。①

该丛书第一辑共六种,《越南亡国史》是第三种,其他五种是饮冰室主人著《中国国债史》、新民丛报社社员编《日俄战后满洲处分案》、饮冰室主人著《中国铁路史》、披发生著《势力范围解》和饮冰室主人著《朝鲜及西藏》。由此可见,梁启超有意识地将《越南亡国史》纳入其启蒙话语之中。

随着《越南亡国史》传播的扩大,在一些新的版本中"越南亡命客巢南子述"的署名被去掉,被径直当作梁启超的作品,如《世界亡国惨史》(醒社编辑出版,1915 年)、《外史鳞爪》(商务印书馆,1916 年)、《饮冰室专集:各国兴旺小史》(商务印书馆,1936 年)等。这其中不排除为扩大影响,一些出版社有意突出梁启超的名字,借其名声以达到宣传的效果,但重要原因还是如上所述在于其发表形态的特殊性和内容与梁启超的政治主张相通。

3. 文集中的互文性

既然《越南亡国史》一般是和其他几个文本一起传播,甚至被看作与《越南亡国史前录》是一个整体,那么该文与其他篇章之间的关系便值得考察。还是以广智书局的初版文集为例来思考该问题。

潘佩珠著《越南亡国史》无疑是该文集的核心。该文由五部分组成,

---

① 《通俗时局鉴发印缘起》,新民社员编《越南亡国史》,广智书局 1905 年版,扉页。

"发端"写著述的缘由;第一节"越南亡国原因及事实"分析越南由盛而衰的原因在于内部腐败、不求进步和抑制民权,认为亡国的直接原因是奸臣的卖国求荣;第二节"国亡时志士小传"记叙阮碧、何文美等抗法志士的简历;第三节"法人困弱愚瞽越南之情状"列举法国榨取越南的种种苛政酷律;第四节"越南之将来"则表达了越南人誓与法国殖民者抗争到底的气概。

置于该文之前的文章是《越南亡国史前录(记越南亡人之言)》,梁启超曾以"记越南亡人之言"之题发表于《新民丛报》第67号上,主要记录梁启超与潘佩珠见面的经过以及潘佩珠所述越南亡国的种种惨状。开篇如下:

> 年月日,主人兀坐丈室,正读日本有贺长雄氏之满洲委任统治论,忽有以中国式名刺来谒者。曰□□□。旦以一书自介绍,其发端自述云,吾侪亡人,南海遗族,日与豺狼鹰鸱为命,每磨眼望天,拔剑砍地,辄郁郁格格不欲生,噫,吾且死矣,吾不知有生人之趣矣。次乃述其愿见之诚,曰:吾必一见此人而后死,吾必一见此人而后死无憾。①

开首第一句出现的书名《满洲委任统治论》并非偶然。该书作者有贺长雄氏是明治时期著名国际法专家,作为法律顾问曾参加甲午战争和日俄战争。该书是他在日俄战后出版的一本关于如何处理满洲问题的政论著作。他是民间人士,但又是国家制定政策的主要法律顾问,因此他的言论在相当大的程度上会左右政府的政策。在处理日俄战后的满洲问题上,依据有贺的观点,首先要国际社会承认满洲是清国的一部分,主权在清国。之所以要国际社会承认此点,并不是真心维护清国的国土统一,而是防备一旦否认其主权,其他列强将参与其中争夺利益。其次,强调日本在满洲的经济利益,而且为了保护日本的经济利益,清国有必要将部分统治权委任给日本。② 这其实是为下一步侵吞中国埋下伏笔。这样一种满洲问题的处理办法可以说与法国侵吞越南的过程极为相似。

---

① 梁启超:《越南亡国史前录》,新民社员编《越南亡国史》,广智书局 1905 年版,第 1 页。

② [日]有贺长雄:『満州委任統治論』,早稻田大学出版部 1905 年版。

实际上，"通俗时局鉴"丛书的第二种便是《日俄战后满洲处分案》。关于该书，广智书局在新书介绍中说："今日最大最急最危险之问题，度无有逾于满洲之处分者。庞然数省之地存亡系于俄顷，而影响且将及于本部所谓牵一发而全身动也。吾国人于日本之所以待满洲者究如何，及我国所以保满洲者当如何，莫或知之，莫或研究之，殊可浩然叹。此编由本社社员编辑，先取日本朝野上下有名人物之论满洲处分者，集其论说而译之，以著彼都隐志，以饮冰室主人之宏著作结论焉。全书凡六万余言，诚今日举国人士所当急读也。"① 因此，梁启超在文章的第一句中特别叙说主人正读《满洲委任统治论》，显然是他对中国遭列强侵吞的现实抱有强烈的危机感。

开头部分的叙述方法也颇具特色，采用小说手法不断设置悬疑。某日，梁启超正在读书，突然有素不相识的人来求见，求见信中称因亡国痛不欲生，非见梁不可："吾必一见此人而后死，吾必一见此人而后死无憾。"这种近乎极端的求见言行，让读者产生好奇想了解此人。梁启超即刻邀客入见。一见之下，"客容憔悴，而中含俊伟之态，望而知为异人也"。这样的外表描写让读者更加提高了对此人的兴趣。但梁启超并不急于解密，而是以家中嘈杂无法尽兴畅谈为由，"订密会后期行，越二日复见于所约地"②。这样一波三折拖延解密的手法，无疑进一步刺激了读者的好奇心。这段文字与《越南亡国史》的前言部分相吻合，形成内容上的呼应。

紧接着记录潘佩珠越境赴日的经历。法国为了维持殖民统治，极力断绝越南民众与外界的交往，"严海禁，私越境者罪且死"。潘佩珠冒充华佣才得以蒙混出国。出国之事如果泄露，不仅个人有性命之忧，家人也会遭受牵连。因此，潘佩珠"奉母以终其天年"，遣妻寄子于偏僻乡里后才冒死出国。③《越南亡国史》列举诸多法国殖民当局对越南人实施的种种严刑苛政，作者的亲身经历无疑更是对这些严刑苛政的生动注释。

置于文后的《越南小志》则对越南的地理和历史作了一个概述性介

---

① 新民社员编：《越南亡国史》，广智书局1905年版，封底。
② 梁启超：《越南亡国史前录》，新民社员编《越南亡国史》，广智书局1905年版，第1页。
③ 同上书，第2页。

绍。在地理部分，强调"与我两粤云南三省毗邻"，① 便于中国读者对越南的地理方位有一个基本认识。在历史叙述部分则侧重近二百年的历史，与《越南亡国史》叙述法国殖民越南的过程有重合之处，但两者的叙述方法不同。《越南亡国史》叙述侵占的过程简略，而《越南小志》则按西历具体列举与法国交涉的大事件和条款内容，充实了《越南亡国史》的记述内容，同时也使历史记述更加客观化。比如关于1874年的西贡条约，举出以下条款：

（第二款）法国大皇帝嗣后以越南国王系操自主之权并不尊服何国。越南若有内患外寇，国王一有请援之举，法国立即随机相助。

（第三款）越南已约法国为之保护，如此后越南与各外国交通，则须合法国之意，事乃可行。（中略）今后越南与他国立盟互市，则须预行照会法国。

（第五款）越南国王现在所割畀于法国者，其所辖治之地（中略）均归法国管理，独操自有之权（下略）。②

从这些条款可以清楚看出，法国吞并越南的心机和手段。第二款表面承认越南的独立，其实是要让越南摆脱附属于清国的地位，转而接受法国的保护。第三款明确规定越南接受法国保护，要越南今后与外国建交和通商均需获得法国的允许，不承认其国家主权。第五款，强行要求越南承认法国对所割之地的自主权。这种侵占越南的步骤和手段与《越南亡国史前录》中出现的《满洲委任统治论》内容有惊人的相似之处。

需要留意的是，《越南小志》与《越南亡国史》的出发点并不相同。《越南亡国史》的主题是记叙越南亡国的过程，悲叹丧国之痛，呼吁恢复越南的国家主权。在"越南之将来"中反复强调："这一般人是与法人有身仇家仇的，断断不肯与法人共生活，若说他肯与法人共生，便是他非人种，我不敢说"③。《越南小志》虽然也同情越南人亡国痛楚，但基本立场却是以此警示中国人，并认为法国侵占越南的根本目的是为了吞并中国，

---

① 新民社员编：《越南小志》，新民社员编《越南亡国史》，广智书局1905年版，第51页。
② 同上书，第59页。
③ ［越］潘佩珠：《越南亡国史》，新民社员编《越南亡国史》，广智书局1905年版，第42—43页。

文章的落脚点在中国。《越南小志》最后说，法国入侵中国之铁路已预定测量，"其规模之远大，计画之精密，真令人羡煞，令人吓煞"。"老开云南铁路既成，云南已为法之俎上肉，盖长已矣。此后进取以图中原，封豕长蛇之势，且未有艾。我国及今不图，数年之后，羽翼已就，横绝四海，则我舍束手待毙之外，更何翼哉，更何翼哉。"① 这样的警示内容，使中国读者能够切身感受到越南的亡国绝非与己无关，而是日益逼近的灭顶之灾。

《越南亡国史前录》和《越南小志》虽然在内容上与《越南亡国史》有所不同，各有侧重，但又相互联系，互为呼应。如果说《越南亡国史前录》的小说手法有利于提高一般读者的阅读兴趣，那么《越南小志》的"中国立场"对于该文集在中国的传播则具有直接的刺激作用。

4.《越南亡国史》的反响及其改编作品

《越南亡国史》出版后在中国引起广泛反响。这之前中国媒体也关注越南的讯息，但1905年之后以"越南亡国"为关键字的作品标题骤然增加：1905年10月2日《京话日报》（403号）刊载《请看越南亡国的苦楚》、1906年《第一晋话报》发表痴庵的《越南亡国惨话》、1907年《云南》第5期刊载照片"大越南国大皇帝陛下御尊影（亡国君之愁容）"、《丽江白话报》发表滇剧《苦越南》、1908年《竞业旬报》第16期发表《时闻：越南亡国如此乎》、《新朔望报》发表新剧《越南亡国惨》、1911年《南风报》发表南国恨人述《越南亡国始末谈》、1913年《庸言》第1卷第22期发表冷泉亭长的《劫灰馀尽（第二回）：经越南目睹亡国惨》，等等。上述文章和戏剧有些是受《越南亡国史》的影响关注越南现状有感而发的，有些则是参考《越南亡国史》的内容写的，大多数是两者兼而有之。

痴庵的《越南亡国惨话》目前只见第一回。就所见内容而言，明显受《越南亡国史》文集的影响。该文从地理位置开始介绍，称越南是美丽富饶的国土："却说这个越南国土是法人最艳羡的，法人不但艳羡越南，还想占了越南，得了根据地方，然后漫漫的谋算那花天锦地的中国。

---

① 新民社员编：《越南小志》，新民社员编《越南亡国史》，广智书局1905年版，第72页。

这是法人的深心毒计，积蓄了二百余年，务要达其目的的。"① 在此表明该文主题，是要通过叙述越南亡国的史实警示中国读者，这与《越南小志》的立场相通。在探讨有关灭亡的原因时，认为主要是奸臣卖国，而这样的把握又显然来自《越南亡国史》：

> 无知如嗣德母子昏愚，信用那两个奸臣，任其颠倒播弄。那阮文祥比践诚更为狡猾。既有法难，他就借这外交手段胁制朝廷，又以重金贿法，约为奥援，意想乘机篡夺。凡有机密事件均泄露于法。这时候越南王想联英德两国拒法。终以文祥泄漏败坏也。②

《越南亡国史》的相关文字如下：

> 文祥比践诚更甚，善于奉迎掩饰，深得主上心。尝蓄篡夺之志，因国政内腐，法房外窥，知法势强盛，遂借外交手段，胁制朝廷，以阴行己志，多以重贿结法人，约为法人奥援。彼为机密院大臣，每有机密，辄先泄于法。法人亦以重贿饵之。③

两相对照可以看出，《越南亡国惨话》的上述文字基本上是从《越南亡国史》的叙述化用而来的。但历史上的阮文祥与《越南亡国史》所述内容并不同。嗣德帝1883年驾崩后，遗命阮文祥、陈践诚、尊室说三位辅政大臣共掌朝政。一年之内，三位辅政大臣连续废掉协和帝建福帝。法国趁越南朝廷争夺皇位之际进攻顺化，逼迫越南于1883年和1884年两次签订条约，承认法国对越南的保护权。第二次签订条约的大臣就是阮文祥。毫无疑问，在丧失主权的过程中辅政阮文祥负有重要责任。但他为了保住自身的权位，与法国也有对立的一面。协和帝登基后感受到三位辅政大臣的威胁，曾试图通过联合法国势力对抗他们。阮文祥等人便杀死协和帝，另立建福帝，后又立咸宜帝对抗法国势力。最后尊室说挟持咸宜帝逃

---

① 痴庵：《越南亡国惨话》，《第一晋话报》6 (1906)，第18页。
② 同上书，第20页。
③ [越]潘佩珠：《越南亡国史》，新民社员编《越南亡国史》，广智书局1905年版，第7页。

亡，阮文祥则留下继续担任辅政大臣。① 由此可见，阮文祥与法国的关系，有妥协投降的一面，但也有矛盾冲突的一面，并非一意里通外国的卖国者。

阮文祥里通外国的情节在新剧《越南亡国惨》中得到进一步强化。② 在该剧"头本"中，阮文祥以丞相的身份登场，自白道：

> （净白脸　扮丞相　便衣上）（引）黄金宰相　管什么国破家亡（诗）自幼飞黄入庙廊　贪泉饮罢坏心肠　总然卖去安南国　且赚金银满万箱　（白）老夫　越南国大丞相阮文祥是也　扶保幼主嗣德登基以来　国中大权在老夫一人之手　且喜嗣德年幼无知　诸事听老夫作主　更有范太后既昏且贪　使老夫得以上下其手　现在法国势力甚大　自从割去我国六府地方　太后母子非常害怕　昨有兴安巡抚上了一本　言道　我国可以结联英美　抵制法国　是老夫常受法国厚礼　故此诳哄太后　不从与兴安巡抚之计　亦免得法国吃亏　并且老夫的官位　仗著同法国相好的势力　就越发坐的安稳了③

这段自白基本上是将《越南亡国史》中的相关文字以第一人称道出，活脱脱地刻画了一个卖国贼的形象。

关于越南首都失守时阮文祥的所作所为及其可耻下场，《越南亡国史》记载如下：

> 顺京失守时，文祥实引法兵入城。阮福说出兵迎敌，使人向祥乞济师，祥却向法营通信，绝弹药弗给，城遂陷，法得国。祥自以为功，谋求封王，法人恶其反侧，恐留之为后患，徒之海，溺其尸，以空铁棺回，令祥子孙出十万金以赎。④

---

① 参见刘祚昌等主编《世界史　近代史下》（高等教育出版社1984年版，第338页）、李云泉《〈清史稿〉补正》（《暨南史学》第八集，广西师范大学出版社2013年版，第315页）。
② 该剧发表于1908年（柚生道人，《新朔望报》1908），后再刊于《春柳》8（1919）。因未见《新朔望报》发表的全本，本文引用自《春柳》版本。
③ 柚生道人：《越南亡国惨》，《春柳》8（1919），第839页。
④ ［越］潘佩珠：《越南亡国史》，新民社员编《越南亡国史》，广智书局1905年版，第7页。

历史上的阮文祥确实死于法人的迫害。阮文祥被法国人流放到太平洋上的塔希提岛，并于 1886 年 2 月死在那里。同年 7 月，阮文祥的遗体被尊室订带回顺化安葬。① 即阮文祥虽然死于法人的迫害，但既不是被人投海而死，也没有"令祥子孙出十万金以赎"。所谓"徙之海，溺其尸，以空铁棺回，令祥子孙出十万金以赎"，不过是民众出于对卖国贼的痛恨编造的故事。阮文祥回乡安葬之事发生于 1886 年，距潘佩珠写《越南亡国史》有十年，照理作者应该知道真实情况，但他还是选取了更具民间传奇色彩的版本。

这样的情节安排显然更能满足一般读者的善恶报应的伦理观。由此可见，潘佩珠尽管接受启蒙思想，对亡国的原因有政治军事层面上的分析，但还没有完全摆脱传统的伦理道德观，依然用善恶报应的思维来解释历史现象。这样的伦理道德观也为新剧《越南亡国惨》所接受，几乎原封不动地将这个情节搬进来。

（多白）丞相前者有信　不发军火接济阮福说　并引本帅入城使本帅得破顺京　丞相真是莫大之功　（阮白）老夫当得效力　从前将军也曾言道　破了顺京　废去嗣德王位　所有越南一国权利　全归法国掌管　但是要封老夫一个王位　富贵终身　想如今将军当践言了　（多白）你待怎讲　（阮白）将军践言才是　（多三笑介）（唱）好一个　卖国奴　良心丧尽　他不想　苦坏了　越南万民　叫人来　用绳锁　将贼绑定　（阮白）哎呀　将军　难道不念老夫屡次帮助贵国的大功麽　（多唱）讲什么　帮本帅　屡建大功　似你这　贪富贵　残害同种　对我国　那里有　恳切忠诚　将此贼　沉大海　溺杀奸佞　用铁棺　诈他家　十万黄金②

新剧在善恶报应的基础之上，还增加传统的"忠诚"的观念。在剧中法人杀阮文祥的主要理由是认为他缺少"忠诚"。

---

① Oscar Chapuis, *The Last Emperors of Vietnam: from Tu Duc to Bao Dai*, Greenwood Press, 2000, p. 22.

② 柚生道人：《越南亡国惨》，《春柳》8（1919），第 847 页。李伯屏《波兰埃及越南朝鲜亡国史》[《新学海》1（1920，第 8 页）也采用了这个情节："法人又恶其反覆，竟投之于海，又令其子孙以十万金赎空棺而回。"]。

与此同时，新剧在改编过程中还借鉴了中国的古典文学。比如，何文美抗法故事，在《越南亡国史》中仅有短短数语："何文美河静人，以书生应召，深沉有智，能易服混入法营屯，为义曾疆间，时偷取法屯军械火器，装载入山。"① 在新剧中借用《水浒传》智取生辰纲的情节对这个内容作了扩充。原文本来是何文美混入军营盗窃军械火器运送到起义队伍，但在新剧中改写成，何文美和阮仕假意投降法人诳引炮队入山，使计用酒将法军士兵灌醉夺取火炮。经过这样的改编，增加了戏剧情节发展的曲折性和观赏性。

该剧发表后畅销一时。据当时《顺天时报》报道："田际云新编的《越南亡国惨》新戏，早已印成单行本，在爱国报馆寄卖，三千本听说现已销去两千五百多本，存者不多。田际云因此又要重行排印一万本，在前门外六大茶楼及东安市场内广为销售，使人知道这新戏的内容宗旨。"此次重印是为了配合该剧的公演，以便公演时"将来人各一本，那么看戏时便可一目了然"。②

5.《越南亡国史前录》与滇剧《苦越南》

滇剧《苦越南》（1907年）则是赵式铭根据梁启超的《越南亡国史前录》改编的一部戏剧。全剧共三幕，主要内容如下：第一幕"亡命"，写越南爱国志士巢南子不满法国的殖民统治，乔装华佣出国，东渡日本欲见梁启超，"求他大笔淋漓，写出我亡国惨状，以打动邻邦人民伤类之意，博得其同情之心，将来或能助我收回故土，光复祖国"③。第二幕"登瀛"写梁启超在家里与巢南子第一次见面，但因家中人多嘈杂，约定再次见面。第三幕"望洋"写梁潘二人在酒楼第二次见面，潘佩珠痛陈亡国后之种种惨状，梁启超听后深为感动，许诺编写一本《越南亡国史》。该剧先在《丽江白话报》连载，随后排练上演。当时戏评说："有

---

① ［越］潘佩珠：《越南亡国史》，新民社员编《越南亡国史》，广智书局1905年版，第14页。
② 《戏本畅销》，《顺天时报》（1910-3-19），第7版。
③ 马学良主编：《中国近代文学大系第10集·第25卷·少数民族文学集》，上海书店1992年版，第307页。

范伶者,扮演剧中人巢南子,其演《亡命》一出,声泪俱下,座客掩袂。"①

从上述剧情可以看出,该剧将剧情主线放在潘佩珠请求梁启超写《越南亡国史》上,显然是因作者名误会造成的。这样的剧情展开也使该剧在主题和内容上与原作相比产生一些变化。最主要的一点是增加了启蒙式的劝诫内容。《越南亡国史前录》主要记录潘佩珠所痛陈的种种亡国惨状,《苦越南》则在此基础之上增加了避免做亡国奴的劝诫内容。剧中梁启超听了潘佩珠的一席话,思绪翻腾,悲愤交加,有如下一段唱腔:

> 听了这悲伤语我心如捣,禁不住泪珠儿红透鲛绡。
> 看起来这世界无有公道,优的胜劣的败此理昭昭,
> 文明围野蛮律出人意料,纵有那写生手也难画描。
> 这现象是我国天然对照,切莫作釜中鱼快乐逍遥!
> 为军人要知道当兵荣耀,做官的要知道为国勤劳。
> 为工艺要专心改良制造,营农林要审识干湿肥饶。
> 为教师要莫学冬烘头脑,为富翁要莫学钱癖和骄,
> 为女子要莫学身材婀娜,为学生要莫学奴隶根苗。
> 劝大家猛回头真心学好,把邻邦作鉴戒亡羊补牢!②

尽管《越南亡国史前录》记录亡国种种惨状也有警示国人的启蒙意味,但一般民众只看到黑暗,并不知道应该如何去做,因此《苦越南》作为面向一般观众的戏剧,具体明了地指出了前进的方向。

并且为了突出这一主题,该剧还增加了两个人物,即酒保和他的妻子。梁潘第二次聚会地点是一个华侨开的酒馆。梁潘上场之前,作者花了一些笔墨介绍酒保的身世。酒保祖上因得罪朝廷,流亡海外,酒保也因此在海外走南闯北增加很多见识。眼见西方列强吞食中国,民族意识尤为强烈:"复我炎炎主权,回我茫茫禹域,张我赫赫声名,雪我重重耻辱。"其妻也受西方近代文明的熏陶,具有妇女平等意识,要为妇女"争得平

---

① 转引自中国戏曲志编辑委员会《中国戏曲志·云南卷》,中国 ISBN 中心,2000 年,第 139 页。

② 马学良主编:《中国近代文学大系第 10 集·第 25 卷·少数民族文学集》,上海书店 1992 年版,第 315—316 页。

权，（略）买丝线绣成自由旗，插向胭脂坡！"① 他们夫妻俩经营着小酒馆，没有从事启蒙运动，但显然已经具备初步的现代意识，是梁启超力图塑造的"新国民"的潜在对象。他们甚至打算"日后若有积蓄，或做些慈善事业，或认购铁路股本，也算尽我夫妻一分子义务"②。这两个人物的增加对于理解该剧具有重要的意义。梁启超著述启蒙，是单方向地传播知识，但在《苦越南》中通过新增加这两个新派人物便形成与梁的启蒙思想之间互动的呼应关系，是改造中国社会的希望所在。

  需要指出的是，这两个人物的增加应该与作者本人的经历有关。作者赵式铭是云南剑川州高等学校校长。虽然身处中国的边陲，但时刻关心中国的命运。1895 年，在北京签名参加康有为等人发动的"公车上书"的青年陈思诚、杨继元等落第归滇，把"公车上书"的抄本拿到丽江府的知识分子中间传布。当时在家乡当小学堂校长的赵式铭，看到后思想产生极大震动，和老师们举办读书会、讲演会、放足会、运动会等活动。1907 年，赵式铭在丽江中学任教，创办《丽江白话报》，发表很多文章，对国民的因循懒惰、愚昧保守、迷信落后等封建社会的恶习痛加针砭，宣传科学文化知识。《苦越南》就发表在《丽江白话报》上。③ 在此意义上，赵式铭本人也可以算是与那个受启蒙思想影响而觉悟的"酒保"一样的人物。

  还有一个值得关注的问题是，关于日本在启蒙话语中的位置。该剧中日本作为改革维新成功的亚洲国家，被塑造为一个文明国度，由此使该剧的启蒙话语获得连贯的逻辑性。以下唱词是对日本文明景象的赞颂：

  （巢南子上）（白）小生自从那日离了故土，晓行夜宿，来到横滨，你看扶桑三岛，佳气葱葱，真好一个海国也！
  才离了我祖国来到日本，河山改风景异气象一新。
  这壁厢劝工厂宽敞齐整，那壁厢博物院罗列纵横，
  这壁厢戴白帽警兵站定，那壁厢设浴池冷暖随人。

---

① 马学良主编：《中国近代文学大系第 10 集·第 25 卷·少数民族文学集》，上海书店 1992 年版，第 311，312 页。
② 同上书，第 312 页。
③ 吴重阳：《中国少数民族现当代文学研究》，中央民族大学出版社 2013 年版，第 367—368 页。

> 有的是存古式和服圆领，有的是仿西装袖窄短襟，
> 有的是作高髻风流秀韵，有的是著丝裙异样鲜明。
> 论用具木察里装贮食品，论房屋多种树围绕四邻，
> 论饮食用盐蔬非常节省，论居处常拂拭不染纤尘。
> 那街上未听见争吵任性，那国中并未曾见个游民。
> 各监狱设讲堂普通读本，各町区有规则学校如林。
> 看罢了不由我长叹几声，叹只叹我越南腐败得很，
> 却难怪受宰割民不聊生。
> 心头事急欲吐正如喉鲠，纵有那万班景不暇留神。①

但是在原作《越南亡国史前录》中，梁启超对文明的思考呈现出复杂矛盾的态度。一方面他认为进化是优胜劣汰，残酷无情，但又并不完全认同欧洲那种野蛮掠夺的殖民方式。梁启超发现自美国摆脱英国殖民之后，欧洲的殖民政策发生了一些变化，即宗主国承认殖民地国家的"人民权利义务"。当然这种变化，在他看来当时还仅限于白种人之间，而对其他种族还是采取歧视的立场。在此梁启超特别提到日本人由于同属黄种人，对台湾采取的殖民政策与欧洲不同，主要是同化政策。这种同化看似温柔，但包藏着灭绝种族的野心。梁告诫说，日本近来对朝鲜也表现出同样的野心："第二越南之现象，已将见矣。同一日本，而待台湾与待朝鲜，何以异焉。"② 由此可见，与《越南亡国史前录》相比较，《苦越南》的作者只看到日本近代化成功的一面，没有看到其对亚洲邻国的殖民野心，在戏剧改编过程中过于强调启蒙而将原作的思想复杂性简单化了。

6. 结语

潘佩珠的著作《越南亡国史》没有单独发表过，一般与《越南亡国史前录》、《越南小志》一同出版传播，其独特的发表形式造成作者名极易误会。但这种特殊的发表形式在结果上有利于扩大传播。该著是在梁启超的影响下写就的，在取法西洋实施社会改造的政治主张上与梁的观点有

---

① 马学良主编：《中国近代文学大系第10集·第25卷·少数民族文学集》，上海书店1992年版，第309—311页。

② 梁启超：《越南亡国史前录》，新民社员编《越南亡国史》，广智书局1905年版，第11页。

相通之处，但是在解释亡国原因时则保留了传统的伦理道德观，如不顾史实强调奸臣卖国的品德问题等。这种传统伦理道德观尽管不符合新史学的科学立场，但却是容易被当时一般读者所接受的重要因素。同时代的作品《越南亡国惨话》和《越南亡国惨》不仅接受了这种传统伦理道德观式的历史解释，还有意扩大发挥之，形成启蒙话语中的一个重要声部。与此同时，一起传播的《越南亡国史前录》在内容和写法上不仅对于理解正文有明显的引道作用，还为滇剧《苦越南》提供了创作素材，而《越南小志》的中国立场对于《越南亡国史》在中国的接受发挥了重要作用。即是说，这三个文本以《越南亡国史》为核心，共同构成一个大文本，在内容上有交叉之处，也有不同，文本之间互相参照，形成张力，在中国近代的启蒙活动中发挥了独特的作用。

References

［1］Xinmin Agency member（新民社员），eds. *Fall of Vietnam*（《越南亡国史》），Guangzhi Book Company，1905.

［2］Liang Qichao（梁启超）. *Collected Works of Yinbingshi*（《饮冰室合集》），Zhonghua Book Company，1989.

［3］Ma Xueliang（马学良），editor. *A treasury of modern Chinese literature*（《中国近代文学大系》），Shanghai Bookstore，1992.

［4］Oscar Chapuis，*The Last Emperors of Vietnam：from Tu Duc to Bao Dai*，Greenwood Press，2000.

［5］Liu Yajun（刘雅军）. "*Learning from the Declined Nation 's History and the Social Reform in the Late Qing Dynasty*（《"衰亡史鉴"与晚清社会变革》），Historiography Quarterly，2010（4）.

Chinese Characters and the Morden Enlightenment Thoughts in East Asia
——Liang Qichao and *Fall of Vietnam* by Phan Bôi Châu

Wang Zhisong

Abstract

Fall of Vietnam is a Chinese work published in 1905 by Phan Bôi Châu, the pioneer of morden enlightenment in Vietnam, which has been widely spread and has great impact in East Asia n the early twentieth century. However, the author has been considered Liang Qichao for a long time. The real author, Phan Bôi Châu, has been confirmed till 1990s. This paper is to discuss why the author would be mistaken from the perspective of communication, and its meaning while being spread in China and so on. This paper suggests that this work has not ever been published separately, but always with *The history of national subjugation in Vietnam Prequel* and *Brief Introduction of Vietnam* by Liang Qichao. This unique publishing form is an important reason why the author has been mistaken for Liang Qichao, but as a result, also beneficial to spread. This work was written under the influence of Liang Qichao, which has in common with the political view of following the western example of social reconstruction, but retains the traditional moral principles when explaining the reason of the country's destruction. There are overlap and difference in these three texts, which constitute a large text with *Fall of Vietnam* as core, played a unique role in the enlightenment in modern China.

Keywords: *Fall of Vietnam*; Phan Bôi Châu; Liang Qichao; enlightenment; acceptance

高等教育与东亚文明的未来

吴清辉　伍鸿宇[*]

内容提要

高等教育与东亚文明的发展有着密切的联系。儒学是东亚文明的重要思想根基，特别在教育方面，更是中华诸子百家中最有贡献的。展望东亚文明的未来，我们不能忽视高等教育与儒学之间的相互促进。在高校的博雅教育之中，应充分吸纳儒学在人格塑造方面的深厚思想，并在育人理念、教育途径、授课方式等方面积极汲取儒学的智慧。同时，高校也应以历史性的反思，国际化的视野，前瞻性的思维，审视儒学的现代意义与文化地位，在教学与研究两方面切实推动儒学的发展，为东亚文明的未来贡献力量。

关键词：高等教育；东亚文明；东亚儒学

Higher Education and the Future of East Asian Civilization

Abstract

Higher education and the development of East Asian civilization are closely linked. Confucianism is the important ideological foundation of East Asian civilization, especially in the area of education, her contribution is of unparalleled importance amongst all flourishing schools of philosophy of China. Looking into the future of East Asian Civilization, we cannot ignore the mutual benefit between higher education and Confucianism. In the liberal arts education of colleges and universities, we should fully absorb the deep thought of Confucian-

---

[*] 吴清辉：北京师范大学—香港浸会大学联合国际学院校长；伍鸿宇：联合国际学院中国语言文化中心主任。

ism in the shaping of personality, and actively learn the wisdom of Confucianism in the aspects of educational philosophy, approaches, and teaching methods. At the same time, universities should also reconsider the modern meanings and cultural status of Confucianism in East Asia with a historical reflection, an international perspective and forward-looking thinking. Universities should promote the development of Confucianism in both teaching and research, so as tomake contribution tothe future of East Asian civilization.

Key words: Higher Education; East Asian civilization; Confucianism in East Asia

在全球化的今天，东亚文明的发展前景如何？这是一个宏大的命题，需要多维度的思考与探讨。儒学是东亚文明的重要思想根基，特别在教育方面，更是中华诸子百家中最有贡献的。本文的讨论着眼于高等教育与儒学之间的互动关系。我们看到，随着东亚经济的持续发展，儒学对促进东西方文化交流与人类社会发展具有越来越重要的意义。儒家文化的核心是人，孔子一生"学而不厌，诲人不倦"（《论语·述而》），为了实现理想，"发愤忘食，乐以忘忧，不知老之将至"（《论语·述而》）；他提出"有教无类"（《论语·卫灵公》）的主张，广聚学子，相互切磋，教学相长，为我们留下了丰富的思想资源。正如有学者指出，儒学的"首要目的不在于以知识的眼光审视我们所面对的这个世界，而是立足于'教化'以成就人，并由此建立人安身立命的超越基础"[①]。

培养什么样的人，是当今教育界思考的重要问题。事实上，儒学自身的发展与其思想核心都与教育有着紧密的联系。回顾儒学在东亚发展的历史，展望东亚文明的未来，我们不能忽视教育与儒学之间的互相促进。今天的高等教育应在育人理念、教育途径、授课方式等方面积极汲取儒学思想资源，并以历史性的反思，国际化的视野，前瞻性的思维，审视儒学的现代意义与文化地位，在教学与研究两方面切实推动东亚儒学的发展，为东亚文明的未来贡献力量。

---

① 李景林：《教养的本原：哲学突破期的儒家心性论》，辽宁人民出版社1998年版，第3页。

一 历史与现代：东亚教育与儒学的互动

东亚现代性所呈现的教育图景，有着长久以来的儒学历史渊源。历史上东亚国家教育机构的建立与教学模式多受儒学影响；学校教育同时又是主要的儒学传播途径，并由此促进了东亚共同精神价值的熔铸。

从历史的角度看，以日本为例，政治家小山松吉（1869—1948）观察到，儒教早在上古时期就传入了日本，来自中土的阿直岐学者来日宣讲儒教，博士王仁带去了《论语》与《千字文》，于是汉学的研究在当时兴盛起来。小山松吉写道："儒教提倡的忠孝、仁义之教，从太古开始就成为我国民行为的指导方针。我国民与儒教共鸣并巩固了祖先崇拜的信念，于是酝酿形成了忠孝一本的淳风美俗为本。"① 在学校建构方面，日本全面学习和模仿中国唐代的教育制度，自大化革新至 12 世纪末期，形成了国家设辖的大学寮、地方管理的国学和民间自发创立的私学这样一套比较完整的学校系统。这些学校不仅是培养官僚的教育机构，而且因为其教学的主要内容是儒家经典，它们同时也构成了中国儒学的传播体系。② 到德川时代，朱子学在日本广泛传播，被定为官学。各地兴建的私塾也多参照《白鹿洞书院揭示》治学。日本著名的儒学家、教育家广濑淡窗创立了"日本近世最大规模的汉学私塾"咸宜园，传扬朱子学的理论，重视道德修养。众多学校的建立极大地促进了日本儒教的发展。

再看越南的例子。阮朝绍治帝宣称："朕为天下主，教孝作忠，以教风化。"李朝、陈朝兴科举，学校教育经过长时期的发展，形成了较为完备的儒学教育体制。越南儒学教育的目的，是要将学生培养成既有专门的知识，如文、史、地、兵、算等，又具有封建社会所需要的道德规范的各种人才。在儒学教育最盛行的时候，即使是普通越南民众，都会或多或少地选择接受儒学教育，因此，儒学教育时代总体上提高了越南人的文化

---

① ［日］小山松吉：《日本精神读本》，共同印刷株式会社 1936 年版，第 25 页。
② 关松林：《儒学东进及其对日本古代教育的影响》，《华东师范大学学报》2004 年第 2 期。

程度。①

在今天，不少东亚国家都非常重视儒学在育人方面的文化滋养作用。韩国成均馆大学在开设基本教养科目儒学课的说明中写道："儒学教育是为了解东方人的人生观及思维结构而设置的。在此设置儒学科目是为了能动地涵养圣贤的生活态度，宣扬成均人的意识，进而能够找到民族主体性的契机。"② 新加坡总理李光耀说："从治理新加坡的经验来看，特别是1959年到1969年那段艰辛的日子，使我深深地相信，要不是新加坡大部分人民受过儒家价值观的熏陶，我们是无法克服那些困难和挫折的。"③ 所以新加坡教育部早在1980年就确定"儒家伦理"为选读课程之一。相关部门还成立了"儒家伦理委员会"，邀请国际著名新儒学学者去新加坡讲学，并提供编写方案，完成了世界上第一部中英文对照的《儒家伦理》教材，供华语学校使用。④ 更不用说，在中国，习近平主席明确提出，教育要善于继承和弘扬中华优秀传统文化精华。许多高校都设置了儒学研究机构，儒家思想也是文化素质选修课的重要内容。

显然，在东亚各国的教育史中，我们能够看到一条儒学传播的脉络，教育与儒学的相互促进所体现的意义与价值是不容忽视的。杜维明先生指出，在儒学传统的影响下，东亚现代性呈现出一幅连贯的图景，教育是其中最重要的特征："教育应该成为社会的全民信仰。教育的首要目的是性格的锻造。教育致力于培养完整的人，应该既重视知识也重视伦理。……除了提供知识和技能的教学之外，学校还必须为文化能力和精神价值的鉴赏力的发展提供适合的环境。"⑤ 展望高等教育与东亚文明的未来，我们应该加强教育与儒学之间的互动关系。"在儒家看来，学就是学做人"⑥，充分彰显儒学修身、育人的思想核心，既是儒学发展的重要议题，也是高等教育未来要开拓的方向。

---

① 税贞建：《法国殖民统治下越南儒学教育的嬗变与终结》，《长江大学学报》2015年第7期。

② 钱丽艳：《浅析中国儒学对韩国教育的影响》，《才智》2013年第4期。

③ 转引自曾长秋、胡佳《儒学文化滋润核心价值观教育——对新加坡儒学教育的观察》，《中国德育》2012年第12期。

④ 同上。

⑤ 郭齐勇、郑文龙编：《杜维明文集》（第四卷），武汉出版社2002年版，第595页。

⑥ 杜维明：《儒家思想新论——创造性转换的自我》，曹幼华、单丁译，江苏人民出版社1991年版，第49页。

二 反思与探索：儒学促进当代高等教育改革

历经百年风雨，中国高等教育既取得了巨大的进步，也走了不少弯路。在近代西风东渐的影响之下，教育体系完成了从旧学到新学的巨大转变，但在新学发展的过程中屡经波折，对儒学的批判偏离了继承扬弃的方向，由于特定的历史原因，我们现有的教育体系全盘引入西方模式，是在完全推翻旧学的基础上建立起来的，虽然由此更换了新鲜血液，使中国教育焕发了生机，但却也切断了传统文化的根脉，我们几千年儒家教育文化中的思想精粹未能得到很好的继承与发展。正如有学者所言，"很明显，儒家的教育理念，可以为现代乃至后现代的知识分子提供丰富的社会资本、文化能力和精神价值。不过，要想使这一理念成为事实，工作是艰巨的，道路也是漫长的"[①]。

教育滋育人的生命，人的生命发展是关系到民族、国家的未来，然而在工具理性极端膨胀的当今社会中，人往往沦为现实功利的奴隶，难以处理好人与自然、与社会的关系，难以达成内心世界的圆满。心灵问题、社会问题、生态危机，诸多阴云遮蔽了生命的华彩，这不能不令我们对当下教育进行深刻反思。有学者指出："未来社会的发展仍需要价值指导。面对人与自然、社群、天道诸种复杂关系的调治问题，面对东亚社会的现代化问题，儒家的核心价值有重大意义。在人生的安立、精神的归属方面，在社群伦理乃至全球伦理、环境伦理的建设方面，仁义礼智信等核心价值观仍然是我们重要的精神资源。"[②] 在经济全球化、教育国际化的今天，无论是缺乏世界性的眼界，还是缺乏民族文化的熏陶，都难于培养符合时代需求的人才。因此，我们需要充分汲取儒家的精神资源，探索高等教育的改革之路。

（一）儒学与博雅育人理念

博雅教育（Liberal Arts Education）在西方有悠久的历史，总体特点

[①] 郭齐勇、郑文龙编：《杜维明文集》（第五卷），武汉出版社2002年版，第589页。
[②] 郭齐勇：《东亚儒学核心价值观及其现代意义》，《孔子研究》2000年第4期。

是旨在培养具备理性、智慧、审美情操的全人,这样的人对不同学科有广泛的认知和融会贯通的能力,能以批判性思维独立思考与创新。20 世纪二三十年代,中国学界就对博雅教育有所认知,如吴宓在《大学之起源与理想》一文中,指出大学应该培养"博而能约""圆通智慧"的"通才"①。但我们后来的教育发展受各种因素的影响,走上了与之相反的路向。近年来,随着中外合作办学的发展,博雅教育的理念再度受到重视。Liberal Arts Education 有不同的几种译法,而"博雅"较好地传达了其内涵的价值取向。博雅教育之"博"与专才相对,强调博通;"雅"强调内在心灵修养的境界。孔子讲"君子不器",学校教育讲"六艺",可见儒家传统教育理念的博雅之义。所以,今天我们发展博雅教育,不仅是引进西方理念,也是对儒学传统的回归。

儒家向来重视修身,其思想成果构筑了东亚儒学价值理念的共性特征,"仁、义、礼、智、信,或者说仁爱、敬诚、忠恕、孝悌、信义等基本观念的某些主要内涵是普遍的,稳定的,是东亚各儒学大师的精神追求和信念、信仰,在不同时空环境中对社会文化具有价值导向的功能"②。我们的博雅教育应该体现这样的价值理念导向,凸显儒学生命教育的人文关怀。事实上历史上的大儒办学,这样的精神指归是其突出特色。

白鹿洞书院是中国历史上最具影响力的书院之一,由宋代大儒朱熹主持。朱熹制定的《白鹿洞书院揭示》表述了其办学的基本理念,提出了为学、修身、处事和接物的重要原则,包括:

(1)五教之目:父子有亲,君臣有义,夫妇有别,长幼有序,朋友有信。

(2)为学之序:博学之,审问之,慎思之,明辨之,笃行之。

(3)修身之要:言忠信,行笃敬,惩忿窒欲,迁善改过。

(4)处事之要:正其谊(义)不谋其利,明其道不计其功。

(5)接物之要:己所不欲,勿施于人;行有不得,反求诸己。

从中可见"明人伦"是教育的基本目标,要求学生按学、问、思、辨的实践去"穷理""笃行",并且进一步指明了修身、处事、接物之要,作为实际生活与教育的原则。

---

① 吴宓:《大学之起源与理想》,《建国日报》1948 年第 4 期。
② 郭齐勇:《东亚儒学核心价值观及其现代意义》,《孔子研究》2000 年第 4 期。

我校（UIC）于 2005 年奠基，创建之初即面临着办一所什么样的大学来回应中国高教改革和社会发展的问题。众所周知，今天的大学必须承担社会责任，同时应该具有自身的精神品格，不应在社会世俗价值观的冲击下迷失，它应该用非常高的理念来提升这个社会。儒家办学的价值取向为我们树立新的博雅育人理念提供了借鉴。在 UIC，我们倡导"博"而能"雅"，强调人文素质的养成，努力培育具有创新能力的国际精英人才。所谓精英，不是仅仅具备卓越的专业技能，而是有文化、有情怀、有创造力的"全人"。这里所讲的"文化"是指文化传承，是对学生传统文化本根的培植，儒学是主要的根系；"情怀"是指人格品质、生命境界、家国情感，以及由此而建立的与国家民族未来发展紧密相关的人生理想，儒学修身为学的方式是培养情怀的重要途径；"创造力"是对学生批判性思维与创意能力的培养，儒家和而不同、博学笃行的精神品质是开拓创新的原动力。这样的"全人"，情系家国，心怀天下，才能是创造未来的英才。

（二）儒学与教育途径拓展

王国维先生在《孔子之美育主义》中说："且孔子之教人，于诗乐外，尤使人玩天然之美。故习礼于树下，言志于农山，游于舞雩，叹于川上，使门弟子言志，独与曾点。……由此观之，则平日所以涵养其审美之情者可知矣。之人也，之境也，固将磅礴万物以为一，我即宇宙，宇宙即我也。"[①] 他的话道出了儒家"游"的为学境界。儒家游学从书斋走入大千世界，在追随名师、壮游天下的过程中，达成"胸次悠然，直与天地万物，上下同流"的完满人格精神境界。正如有学者所言，游学之旅，也是求道之旅。"若游而从师，所谓'从师学道鱼千里'从游于一位有德君子身边，夫子步亦步、夫子趋亦趋，甚且从之绝粮，助之守城，也是道义的追求。这即是游的精神之另一面向，新的开展：远游以求道，乃是意义的追寻"[②]。

现代大学教育往往局限于课堂讲授，对于人文素质课程来说，难以深入情感、触及灵魂。今天发展高等教育，我们有必要丰富教育途径、打破

---

① 佛雏编：《王国维哲学美学论文辑佚》，华东师范大学出版社 1993 年版，第 256—257 页。

② 龚鹏程：《游的精神文化史论》，河北教育出版社 2001 年版，第 63 页。

单一教学局面。而儒家的游学精神内核，恰恰与博雅理念是相合的。我校在这方面也做出一些尝试和探索，虽然经验有限，但我们乐于与大家分享和讨论。作为我校国情国学教育的一个部分，我校设计开展了暑期游学活动，每年暑期由专家教授带队，以游学的形式，走入到自然山水与人文胜地之中，观天地造化，察人文风情，亲身感受中华文化魅力。如2007年"庐山游学营"，从南昌出发，赴白鹿洞、庐山、上饶、景德镇、鹅湖书院等地，一路上游览风景名胜，凭吊历史文化名人，进行传统书院文化考察。2008年"山东游学营"，师生们走访了济南、章丘、聊城、泰安、曲阜、邹城以及枣庄，先后游历了大明湖、千佛山、趵突泉、泰山、三孔（孔府、孔林、孔庙）、周公庙、孟庙、荀子墓、微子墓、张良墓、微山湖、灵岩寺等众多名胜。师生一起观景、闻道、瞻仰先贤，一路行来，儒家文化的浸润深入人心。2009年的"中原文化游学营"，访龙门石窟和佛教祖庭白马寺，观少林寺"机锋辩禅"，抵中国文字博物馆和殷墟博物馆研读安阳甲骨，到黄河岸边感怀远眺。还有历年举办的台湾游学营，游历台北、宜兰、新竹、日月潭、阿里山等地，不仅汲取了深厚的文化滋养、开阔了社会文化视野，还与我国台湾地区的高校进行了广泛的校际交流。

有参与游学的学生感言："对我们而言，平日多被某些'现实'的目标局限于一个狭隘的环境之中，琐碎而庸碌。看多了功利的人，想多了世俗的事，很需要有那么几天，跳脱出这拥堵的环境，在一个漫长而辽阔的时空中来重新审视自我，观察世界。寻往圣之足迹，发思古之幽情，与天地精神相往来。"其实学生有此"感"，才能有所"兴"，课本中的清词丽句、审美情怀才能在他们的心中生动起来，融入他们自身的精神建构中去。

在教育国际化的今天，游学还应该走出国门，开阔更宽广的文化视野，这已经成为许多高校的共识。联合国际学院（UIC）成立十余年，已与海外19个高校机构合作，让学生有机会分别到德国、法国、美国、加拿大、日本、韩国等国家进行交换学习。其中有日本山梨学院大学国际博雅学院、立命馆亚太大学；韩国庆熙大学、首尔国立大学、忠北大学这样的东亚儒学文化圈高校，学生在这些大学游学，可以感受、比较儒学文化在东亚各国的发展与变化，拓宽对于儒学传播的认知、增强文化自信、培育人文情怀。

（三）儒学与教学方式创新

儒家讲"君子和而不同，小人同而不和"，不论是在孔门教育，还是在后来的书院教育，都是倡导学术思辨与批判性思维的。书院教育特别强调教学与学术研究的融合，建立"讲会"制，不同学派的学者可以自由讲学，体现出学术争鸣的风气；学习方式以自学研究为主，问难论辩为辅；总体上是一种无门户之见，培养学生学习主动性的开放式教学。"直到明清时期，书院讲会制度仍然流行。从讲会制度的组织、仪式、规模及规约来看，讲会制度已超出了书院教学的范围，成为一个地区性的学术讨论会及学术交流会。这样既扩大了书院的影响，提高了书院的社会地位，又丰富了书院的教学内容，提高了书院的教学水平和学术研究的水平。"[①]这样的教学法其实今天看来仍具有先进性，与当下国际教育的思想导向恰恰是一致的。

新时代的大学生作为社会先进的文化群体，特别是在信息传播开放的环境下，他们的视野更为开阔，自我意识和民主意识不断增强，在接受心理特征方面具有较为明显的独立思考和独立判断的取向，在行为方式上具有理性、自信、自主、自觉的特征。因此，大学生的学习有很强的主体性、探索性、怀疑性、自我选择性。单向"灌输"的教学方式并不适合他们，反而容易降低学习的热情和期待，令学生产生抵触情绪，影响课程的教学效果。

为此，我校也进行了一些有益的探索。为提升学生对传统文化的热情和对当代国情的关注度，我校借鉴书院教学方法，每学年组织两次"国情国学教学研讨会"，邀请海内外相关领域的专家学者前来参会，发表各家学术见解。在论题的选择上，我们以传统与现代、中国与世界的视角来开阔视野、激发思考。我们举办过"传统与现代：当代中国社会的反思"、"传承与传播：全球化时代的中华文化"、"中国参与世界：中西文化交流"为主题的研讨会、"钓鱼岛问题的多维透视"、"多视角看两岸关系"、"辛亥革命百年回眸与反思"、"百年中国教育历程：回顾与展望"、"中国传统生活方式的现代观照"、"文学经典与现代生活"等主题的研讨

---

① 郭齐家：《文明薪火赖传承——儒家文化与中国古代教育》，山东教育出版社2011年版，第141页。

会。通过当代杰出学者的讲学论道,以开阔的视野、多元的视角,分析国情,诠释国学,从而增进学生对当代社会生活的认知,培养他们批判思辨的能力。

三 传承与传播:高等教育助推东亚儒学发展

展望东亚文明未来,经济全球化会带给我们更多的挑战,也赋予我们更多的责任。我们认为,一所大学的国际化教育发展策略,不仅是将先进的教育理念和模式引进来,更应该将本国本民族的优秀文化介绍给世界。传承与传播儒学,推动东亚儒学的发展是高等教育工作的重要内容。

(一) 高等教育与东亚儒学的传承

正如学者所言:"科学技术可以是国际的,思想言论也可以是自由的,而文化特征却是(也必然是)民族的。没有民族特征的文化是没有生命力的,任何一种有价值的文化必然是植根于本民族文化之中,吸收历史文化营养而创建起来的。"① 孔子建立的儒学历经了二千多年发展,他倡导的价值观诸如"仁者爱人""尊师重道""自强不息,厚德载物""行有不得,反求诸己""己欲立而立人,己欲达而达人"等,都是当代青年人需要汲取的精神养分。② 高校是社会和文化发展新趋势的引领者,如果高等教育不能够珍视和尊重文化的传统,构建民族的精神生活空间,就无法延续历史文脉,形成生生不息的文化的生命力和创造力。

实际上,传承儒学也恰恰是与中国人文学科的近期走向相呼应。2013年11月26日,习近平主席到山东曲阜考察;2014年9月24日,习近平主席在国际儒联发表了关于儒学和传统文化的长篇讲话,全面谈到了他对儒学的认识。从这两个事件中,有学者敏锐地发现,"我们的精神气候、文化气候、学术气候正在发生深刻的变迁,正在发生方向性的转折"③。

---

① 舒大刚:《孔子儒学与中国现代高等教育》,《中国文化报》2006年11月23日。
② 同上。
③ 王学典:《中国向何处去:人文社会科学的近期走向》,《清华大学学报》(哲学社会科学版)2016年第2期。

这位学者所言的方向性的转折,指的是儒学研究、传统文化研究、国学研究的复兴,传统文化研究正在从边缘重返主流。近年来清华大学、北京大学、中国人民大学、武汉大学等高校都纷纷成立了国学研究机构就是表现形式之一。

我校虽然推行国际化教育,以英文作为教学语言,但同时也一直十分重视对学生的民族精神和文化传统的教育。例如,一年一度的"中国文化创意大赛"就是这样的一种努力。我们举办文化创意大赛的初衷,就是希望学生以新锐的批判思维、深刻的文化体验与巧妙的艺术构思,探求传统文化生生不息的源泉和路径,使同学们确立"传统为根,文化为本"的理念,思考如何面对传统与现代、中国与世界等诸多问题。至今大赛已成功举办了11届,前后有超过70个同学自创的舞台表演作品和超过70部DV作品参加比赛。参赛同学以艺术的形式呈现出他们如何理解中国传统文化,如何解读当代文化现象,学生们在文化创意的实践中表现出对中国文化的热情和执着。

此外,我校正在着手创办中华文化传播研究院,作为传播中华文化的重要基地。我们的计划是在研究院筹建具有传统文化特色的书院,书院将借鉴传统书院管理模式,吸引对中国传统文化感兴趣的UIC学生。学生可以在书院中研读传统文化经典、体验传统文化生活、参与文化交流活动。我们拟在书院中建"中华文化体验馆",集衣食住行之展示,琴棋书画之体验和传统文学经典之研习为一体,成为传统文化体验式教育的重要场所,推动中华文化在当代社会的传承创新。

(二) 高校与东亚儒学的传播

日本学者池田大作指出:"当21世纪宣告黎明时,东亚不仅在经济层面,甚至深入到精神领域,定会为世人瞩目,成为导引人类历史的动力,被寄予极大的期待。"[①] 东亚要完成这样的历史使命,就必须进一步推进儒学传播。

大学作为科研重镇,应该采用多种形式加强东亚儒学学术界的交流,不仅在校园里,而且在社会上增强儒学传播的影响力。召开高水准的学术研讨会是重要的途径。联合国际学院(UIC)曾于2009年成功组办了第

---

① [日] 池田大作:《二十一世纪与东亚文明》,《中国社会科学》1993年第1期。

五届儒学国际学术研讨会,"以儒家思想与生态文明"为主题征集会议论文,得到了学界积极回应。来自中国内地及港澳台地区以及美国、东南亚等地,包括美国夏威夷大学、中国人民大学孔子研究院、澳门大学社会科学及人文学院、香港孔教学院、马来西亚孔学研究会、台湾师范大学等八十多家高校和机构的一百二十多位学者参加了本届大会,并向会议提交了近百篇总计约七十万字的论文。

与会学者围绕"儒家思想与生态文明"这一主题开展了卓有成效的学术交流,其中"如何深入发掘儒家生态思想资源并有效实现现代转换"是与会学者发言热议的重要理论问题。正如有学者谈到,儒学作为一个价值观念、一个思想体系不应该成为博物馆藏品,而应该经常拿出来看看、议议,通过理论创新,使它在现实生活中发挥更为积极的影响力。进入21世纪后,由于人类偏离了"正德厚生利用"的正道,利己主义、享乐主义、消费主义泛滥,导致了严重生态危机。而儒学"天人合一"的生态文明观,早就为人类的未来指明了科学发展的方向。与会学者联署发表了《第五届儒学国际学术研讨会生态宣言》,呼吁全球儒学界深度开掘和创造转化儒学中蕴藏的生态智慧,广泛借鉴和吸取其他文化和理论的营养,融合创新,构建生态儒学,推进儒学的现代发展,强化儒学的时代效用。今年12月8—9日,我校将有幸与中华炎黄文化研究会、北京外国语大学联合举办"21世纪中华文化世界论坛第九届国际学术研讨会",主题确定为"生态文明视野下多元文化对话与社会发展"。这是继2009年第五届国际儒学大会之后,在我校举办的大型儒学国际学术研讨会。这次研讨会同样以生态文明为主题,展开更高层次的学术交流,为东亚儒学的交流和传播发挥新的作用。

在2009年第四届东亚峰会上,时任中国总理温家宝先生倡议加强东亚高等教育合作,这是东亚区域合作的重要内容。东亚各国地域相邻、文化相似、诉求相通,通过高等教育合作可以更好地加强和平共处、共同发展的联系纽带,可以有力地促进东亚国家的可持续发展。[①] 东亚儒学正是构筑这种相似、相近的重要精神联系,它在高校教学改革和教育合作方面的意义不容忽视,值得我们更多的研究与挖掘。事实上,要不断扩大东亚

---

① 何天淳、刘宝利主编:《东亚峰会框架下的高等教育合作》,云南大学出版社2011年版,第107页。

儒学的影响圈，我们还有许多工作要做。如何拓展多种途径，增进东亚文化圈高校在儒学研究上的联系？如何广泛传播东亚儒学，为新时代人类文化发展贡献力量？诸多问题，还有待我们不断探索与实践，从而为东亚文明的未来做出应有的贡献。

Tarok hnit Japan: The Personal Collections of Professor Ashin U Ottama about China and Japan

Zaw Lynn Aung[*]

Abstract

Although there are manyancient historical sources about the relations between ancient China (especially with Yunnan) and Myanmar are available, very little is known about the early 20th century modern China in the colonial period of Myanmar (1885 – 1948). Likewise, relations between Japan and Myanmar on economic, cultural, and political matters have been started since the early 20th century. Though very few articles about China and Japan were written in the newspapers of Myanmar in the first decade of the 20th century, no major works about China and Japan have been emerged. After the Russo–Japanese War in 1904–1905, a Buddhist monk from Myanmar, U Ottama, who later became the pioneer and leader in the early nationalist movement in Myanmar, went to Japan while he was touring in Europe. While he was staying in Japan, he met Chinese students and Chinese nationalist leader Dr Sun Yet-sen. He travelled to China accompanied by Dr Sun Yet-sen in 1909. He again visited China in December 1928 and attended the funeral of Dr Sun Yet-sen as a delegate of India National Congress in June 1929. With an aim to disseminate about contemporary China and Japan at that time of the days, a book named *Tarok hint Japan* (*Tarok hnit Japan*): *China & Japan*, was published by U Ottama in 1938. In this book, U Ottama's perceptions on China and Japan can be seen. However, this book is now a rare one to obtain. As an attempt to elucidate Myanmar nationalist leader U

---

[*] Zaw Lynn Aung, PhD, Department of History, University of Yangon, Myanmar.

Ottama's perceptions on China and Japan, this research paper is written.

Key words: U Ottama, China and Japan

Introduction

Relations between China and Myanmar, especially Yunnan, has been existed for many years. The Chinese began migrating to Myanmar in larger numbers in the late eighteenth and early nineteenth century. By 1891, a total of 37,000 Chinese were counted in Burma, more than half of whom had come in by sea routes[1]. According to the population census, the Chinese population grew to 122,000 by 1911. In 1931, there was an estimated 194,000 Chinese, comprising 1.3% of the total population[2]. Yet, despite their long sojourn and large numbers, very little is known about them and their homeland, China in the early 20th century. Likewise, relations between Japan and Myanmar on economic, cultural, and political matters have been started since the early 20th century. Japan's victory over Russia in the 1904–1905 was impressed many Myanmar, as it did other Asians. Although it has been written very few articles about China and Japan in the newspapers in the first decade of the 20th century, no major works about China and Japan have been emerged. However, due to the endeavors of a monk named U Ottama who had travelled Japan and China, a book named *Tarok Hnit Japan*; *China & Japan* was published in 1938. As an attempt to examine *Sayadaw* U Ottama's perceptions about China and Japan and how *Sayadaw*[3] wanted to learn lessons to Myanmar people from Chinese and Japanese people, this paper is written.

I. I: *Sayadaw* U Ottama

After fifty years under colonial rule since 20th century, some of educated

---

[1] V. Purcell, ., *The Chinese in Southeast Asia*, London: Oxford University Press, 1965, p. 67.

[2] Mya Than (1997) The Ethnic Chinese in Myanmar and their Identity. In L. Suryadinata (ed.), *Ethnic Chinese as Southeast Asians*, Singapore: Institute of Southeast Asian Studies, 1997. p. 118.

[3] Sayadaw is the Myanmar term use for senior monk or abbot of the monastery for respect.

young Myanmar began to have political awakening. Since young Myanmar had proficiency in English language and well educated, they had political knowledge. World political events and upheavals led Myanmar people to political awakening. Japan's victory over Russia in 1905 motivated national spirits in Asian countries including Myanmar. Meanwhile, taking the example of Young Men Christian Association (YMCA), in Myanmar Era 1568 (1906 AD) Young Men Buddhist Association (YMBA) was established for the purpose of Myanmar national interests.

In doing national struggle after forming political organisations based on religion, apart fromnon-professionals, members of *Sangha* also took part in. They were *Sayadaw*s U Ottama,[①] U Naginda, U Visuddha, U Candobhasa, U Sobhana, U Wimala, U Wepulla, U Asabha, U Vimalabuddhi, U Adicca and U Vicara. Among them, the most heroic monk was U Ottama who had been the pioneer and pathfinder in the freedom movement in Myanmar. On the *Sayadaw*'s political activities and undertakings, the following writings are well-known.

"The martyr who sacrificed his life for Myanmar's independence was national leader U Ottama. In the past years, Myanmar's independence was lost, people were colonized, and Myanmar people felt frightened and wanted to surrender in their mind. Unfortunately Myanmar' nationalist spirit was fainted just as embers were covered with ashes. The *Sayadaw* was the first who threw ashes away, and made embers brighter."

"Myanmar people must bear in mind the good deeds of *Sayadaw*."

"With the aim to make the nation free from bondage, the *Sayadaw* U Ottama guided and led the people just as clearing weeds, and changing into cultivated land. He did not care being imprisoned again and again."[②]

UKhant (Pantanaw) praised the *Sayadaw* like that.

[①] (a) See Photo (1) (b) See Photo (2).

[②] U Khant (Pantanaw), "*Rakhine Pyitha Amyotha Gaungsaung Gyi*" ("The Great Rakhine Nationalist Leader"), *Myawady Magazine*, Vol. 8, No. 9, July, 1960, 189 (Hereafter cited as U Khant, *Rakhine Nationalist Leader*).

> "The *Sayadaw* was a Rakhine national who was also a great leader of Myanmar people. The *Sayadaw* was born to U Mya and Daw Aung Kyaw Thu at Yupa Quarter, Sittway on 1st Waning day of *Pyartho*, 1241 (27 December 1879). *Sayadaw*'s younger name was Paw Tun Aung. He had one younger brother – Kyaw Tun Aung and one younger sister – Ma Ain Soe. ①"

U Maung Maung, the author of *From Sangha and Laity: Nationalist Movemonts of Burma* 1920–40 noted *Sayadaw* U Ottama that

> "The real politically-violent and forceful agitation courting police action was to come later under the tutelage of U Ottama, a *rahan* who could well be termed the Gandhi of Burma, in the sense that he brought about a change in the aims and methods of all political activities in Burma from 1920 onwards. ②"

U Ottama was born in 1879 in Sittway (Akyab) in Rakhine State (a state in the western part of Myanmar) from Rakhine parents. While in school he and his younger brother distinguished themselves in studies. They were selected to be taken by an Anglican missionary to England to be educated. As the parents could not bear to part with them they were taken out of school to prevent them from running away for better education or enter government service when they grow old. However, as a Buddhist novice (a customary rite for young men) he educated himself in the sacred texts and eventually at the age of 17 arrived at Calcutta and matriculated. Coming back to Myanmar, he entered monastery again as *Upazin* (an ordained monk) and studied all that could be learnt of scriptures and Pali grammar in Pokokku, one of the distinguished centres of Buddhist studies in Myanmar. Again he went to Calcutta at the age of 20 in 1899 and he

---

① Bama Khit U Ba Yin, *Sayadaw U Ottama* (Ven. U Ottama), Yangon, International Department of Book Distribution, no date, p. 10 (Hereafter cited as Ba Yin, *Sayadaw U Ottama*).

② U Maung Maung, *From Sangha and Laity: Nationalist Movement of Burma* 1920–40, New Delhi, Manohar, 1980, p. 14 (Hereafter cited as Maung Maung, *From Sangha and Laity*).

served in the Bengal National College founded by Rabindranath Tagore and C. R. Das, as teacher in Pali and Buddhistic studies and became well versed in Bengali, Nagari and Sanskrit. In 1902, he became Professor. During that period, he was deeply inspired by the great Indian leaders Tagore, Tilak and Gandhi. ①

When *Sayadaw* was teaching Pali and Buddhism, nationalism rose in his soul. Hearing Sir C. P. Rhine's words, "We are not absolutely slaves," *Sayadaw*'s nationalism grew stronger and stronger. ②

To study international economic and social affairs in wide scale, he travelled to France from Calcutta in 1903. From there, he continued to travel to England and Germany. ③

I. II: U Ottama and Japan

While *Sayadaw* was in Europe, there was a war between Japan and Russia. Because Japan defeated Russia, East Asian countries especially Myanmar emulated Japan, and their nationalism rose that they were able to fight against the big powers in Europe. ④

Therefore, *Sayadaw* felt that the reason why Japan won a war over Russia was technical skill. Having decided to go to Japan instead of living in western countries, *Sayadaw* came back to Yangon from France in 1907. After that *Sayadaw* left for Japan on 4 February 1907 and he arrived at Yokohama Port on 7 March 1907. ⑤

His travelling events and experienceswere written in the book "About Ja-

---

① Maung Maung, *From Sangha and Laity*. pp. 14–15.

② Ba Yin, *Sayadaw U Ottama*, p. 26.

③ Thakhin, Ba Maung, *Wanthanu Ayedawpon Thamine* (1906–1936) (History of Vamsānu Ayedawpon (1906–1936)), Yangon, Sarlokngan Press, 1975, p. 16.

④ Albert D. Moseotti, *British Policy and the Nationalist Movement in Burma*, Xeror University, Microfilms Ann Arbor Michigan List, 1917, p. 16.

⑤ Michael Mendelson, E., *Sangha and State in Burma*, London, Cornell University Press, 1975, p. 202.

pan" compiled by *Sayadaw* himself. ①

Sayadaw said

"... Our Buddha *Sasana* is greatest religion in Majjima Region, India in ancient time. But at that time Buddhism is not flourished in India, Why? Our Buddhism is flourished since two thousand years ago. ②"

Therefore, to spread Buddhism, *Sayadaw* went to India and taught and learn their religious faiths, customs, disciplines, and ways and means. At that time, *Sayadaw* heard that a *Rahanta* who preaches the Buddha Dhamma in Tibet. With the wishes to go there, he went of Dajilin, near the foot of Himalayan and informed that if he could go to Tibet or not. He became to know that if he can speak Tibet language, he could go there. Therefore, he learned Tibet language in May. But in November, he returned to Calcutta because of cold in winter. *Sayadaw* continued to learn Tibet language in April. When he can speak Tibet language a little, he went to Tibet. ③When he arrived at the border, he was rejected to enter. So he went to Karimaya (Kashmir State). From there he went to Ladat (Lhabap), where lies fifteen days long journey from Karimaya. He was again rejected to enter. So he disappointed and travelled to India, Egypt and France. ④

During Russo-Japanese War, he travelled around Europe. From the beginning to end of the war, Japan won a victory over Russia. When *Sayadaw* had read this news, he wondered that:

"... Japanese, like as oil lamp in the east, could not influentially in politics in Asia in ancient time, won over Russia. In compare with Russia, Japanese were short and small. They had never been going with war against Europeans. But Russia had fought against European frequently. The East- Asian

---

① Prof: U Ottama, *Japan Pyi Akyaung Ahtupatti (Biography about Japan)*, Yangon, *Thuriya Newspaper* L. td, 1914, p. 1 (Here after cited as U Ottama, *About Japan*).

② U Ottama, *About Japan*, p. 2.

③ Ibid., p. 2.

④ Ibid., p. 3.

people eat rice, and Europeans eat wheat. A small island like Japan fought against a big power like Russia, and won a victory. Why? "①

Then *Sayadaw* said:

"... As we are left behind in all sides, our religion will not be in progress. If our country and our people are in the state of development and prosperity, Buddha teachings and Buddhism will gain fame and strength as well as spread over the globe. As I had thoughts and opinion like this, I decided to go to Japan to learn Japanese's diligence, disciplines, behaviour, customs, religion, and thoughts. ②"

Sayadaw returned to Myanmar in 1907 and he left Yangon for Singapore by ship in 4 February. After that, he continued his journey to Japan in 18 February and arrived at Yokohama Port in 7 March.

On finding out how to live in Japan, he understood that as a Buddhist-monk, he couldn't go round for alms, and there was no society to provide him just as a European preacher. But he was able to live in India for two years without help and support, depending on knowledge and education. Thus, *Sayadaw* tried to live in Japan in any way, and attempted to work in Buddhist Institute in Japan.

He wrote to the Minister Otani, Chairman of Buddhist Institute in Japan. It read:

"... I have gained nine years of monkhood, and have proficiency in eight subjects such as English, Sanskrit, Pali, Bengali and Nagari and so on. Thus, the minister might apply my knowledge in your institute. If you would like to do so, reply to me. ③"

Two days later, *Sayadaw* received a reply. In the reply, the minister ad-

---

① U Ottama, *About Japan*, p. 3.
② Ibid., p. 4.
③ Ibid..

vised him to study Japanese culture, customs, behaviour and manner. During that time, he fulfilled the needs. He was made *Sayadaw* to study under a Japanese who can speak English.

Within one year, *Sayadaw* passed the examination in Japanese Language. Thus, the minister appointed *Sayadaw* as a Professor of *Pali* and *Sanskrit*. When being told to pay salary as other professors, *Sayadaw* replied:

> "... So grateful you are that I have no desire to accept salary, but I would like your looking after as before. ①

After over two years *Sayadaw* taught at that school, he told the minister that he wanted to go back home. The minister asked how much he wanted for the journey. The *Sayadaw* said:

> "... On my way home, I would like to visit to Korea, Manchuria Port Arthur, Annan in China, Thailand and Sri Lanka and India." ②

Then the Minister calculated and gave him all the expenses. In the book, he himself wrote that in 1910, he left Japan and arrived back in Myanmar in 1911. ③

Sayadaw went back to Japan in the year 1912, and brought younger sister Ma Ein Soe, and thirty-one young men together with him. ④Because everyone interested in Japan, on the request of U Tun Aung, a Physician of Yangon Hospital and the Headmaster U San Shwe, State High School of Pyay, he collected the data, facts and information of Japan, and then he compiled and wrote a book about Japan in 1912 after he arrived in Japan. This book described Japanese people's diligence, hardworking, intelligence and good behaviour and

---

① U Ottama, *About Japan*, p. 4.
② Ibid., pp. 4-5.
③ Ibid., p. 5.
④ (a) Mg Mg Pye, *Burma in the Crucible*, Rangoon, Khittaya Publishing House, 1951, p. 14
(b) See Photo (3).

manner. The letters from Japan sent by U Ottama could shown clearly situations of Japan at that time. In his letters, *Sayadaw* stated that the reformations were made in Japan from 1868 to 1912, since the reign of King Meiji. As a result, Japan caught up with western countries. ①

Between 1921 and 1927, *Sayadaw* spent more times in prisons than outside for preaching patriotism and sedition. ②After *Sayadaw* Ottama was released from jail on 27 February 1928 and then left for Japan again. ③*Sayadaw* wrote many letters to Myanmar from Japan. In these letters, *Sayadaw* wrote about his experiences and knowledge he received in Japan. His letters delivered his knowledge and experience for Myanmar people to emulate and practice. He wrote about various kinds of political parties and Japanese peoples' desire to have royal system. The king had authority to turn down the current *Hluttaw* "Diet", also possessed vote power to reject bills presented and approved by *Hluttaw* representatives, but he could approve the bills. They were quite different from representatives of Myanmar *Hluttaw*. In Japan, infiltration of Russian Communists was blocked in many ways. Moreover, royal coronations held in Tokyo, and entertainment and festivities which were prohibited more tightly than before were written in *Sayadaw*'s letters. ④

I. III: U Ottama and China

While U Ottama was residing in Japan in March 1907, there were over 30,000,000 Chinese students studying in Japan. Most of the Chinese students frequently visited to *Sayadaw* U Ottama. *Sayadaw* said to the Chinese students that:

> " Your country is the largest in the world with the population of over 500 million people. It is the largest country in the world in population. Have you ever noticed the foreigners came and exploited the resources of your

---

① See Appendix (1).
② Maung Maung, *From Sangha and Laity*, p. 15.
③ *Wuntharnu Myanmar Newspaper*, 28 February 1928, p. 10.
④ *Deedok Newspaper*, Vol. 4, No. 39, 29-12-1928, 7.

country in various ways? You, Chinese people, do not need to wage war to these foreigners. If you, over 500 million Chinese people, were united, you can drive out these foreigners from China by just blowing with your mouth. You should take the example of Japan which has only 40 millions in population but no one dare to insult this country because the people of Japan are united and educated and clever. Have you ever witnessed the development of Japan in 45 years? If you imitate the Japanese ways, your country, China, will be better than Japan. You should love your country and nationals. You should dare to sacrifice for your parents and country. You should not spend so much money, but try hard and should not quarrel with others. ①"

As *Sayadaw* U Ottama said so, the Chinese students called him as Ottama The Rebel. During the stay in Japan, Dr Sun Yet Sin, the nationalist leader of China, met with him for advice. *Sayadaw* said:

"... Since China is partially colonized, it needs to make some efforts and emulate the western countries' discipline, ways and means. Myanmar and India was completely under the colonization of the British, and so they must try to do more as much as they can. "②

Moreover, *Sayadaw* said that ancient customs and culture of China such as braids and having foot binding were hindrance of improvement of civilization. Therefore, these customs were to be given up, and western policy, methods and ways were emulated for progress of Chinese people. ③Dr Sun Yet-sen invited *Sayadaw* U Ottama to visit China. *Sayadaw* Ottama took three months leave from the university where he was lecturing and he visited to Korea, Beijing, Nanking, Shanghai, and Amoy with Dr Sun Yet-sen. During his tour to China, Dr. Sun Yet-sen explained *Sayadaw* Ottama about traditions, customs

---

① U Ottama, *China & Japan*, pp. 77-78.
② Ba Yin, *Sayadaw U Ottama*, p. 32.
③ Ibid., p. 32.

and culture of China. *Sayadaw* U Ottama noted that Sun Yet-sen was committed to the overthrow of the Manchus and the establishment of a republican government and he had desire to form 'Asia Federation' with Japan, Thailand and India.

On 30 December 1928, *Sayadaw* U Ottama again left Japan for China. He arrived in China on 1 February 1929. According to his diary or records, he stayed at a Chinese monk's house on 2 January 1929, instead of staying at a Chinese hotel. And he moved to the house of manager of Mitsui Department Store. Then he paid a visit to a Chinese Monastery, the largest in Amoy Town. On 5 January 1929, he went to Kulon Su Island of Amoy Island. On 6 January 1929, while he was reading and studying Chinese newspaper and histories, Chinese monks came to visit him. On 7 January 1929, he went sightseeing to Amoy *Kyun* (island). In his diary, *Sayadaw* wrote: on 21 January 1929, he met with an old Chinese man who was imprisoned like him because of engaging in politics, on 22 January 1929 he saw a Korean, and he was invited to visit his town by an old Chinese on 23 January 1929. ①*Sayadaw* journey around China to have experience and knowledge and *Sayadaw*'s diary of his visits to China was beneficial to Myanmar people. *Sayadaw* arrived back from China to Myanmar on 1 February 1929. *Sayadaw* again back to China to attend the funeral of Dr Sun Yet-sen as a delegate of India National Congress in June 1929 and proceed to Japan again.

His book, *Tarok hint Japan: China and Japan*, which was published in 1938, was the first book about the 20th Century China in Myanmar literature. In his book, *Sayadaw* mentioned about the connection of culture and civilization between China and India. It was said that

> "... China was an old and ancient country apart from India. The population of China was fifty millions while India was thirty millions. The religion, Buddhism, literature and culture of China was connected with India. It has been near 2,600 years that the relations between China and Japan

---

① *Deedok Newspaper*, 23-2-1929, 14-6.

has been existed. The civilization of China was over 5000 to 6000 years old. ①"

Sayadaw also mentioned the relations between China and Japan in culture and literature. He stated that

"... Over 1,000 to 2,000 years ago, the Japanese wore the clothing as the same as Chinese people. All the literary treatises in Japan were come from China. The writing alphabets used in Japan were derived from China. However, Chinese and Japanese could not communicate although their writing alphabets were the same but they could understand and communicate if they wrote down the letters. ②"

He then briefed about the history of China and about the Great Wall that

"... In the ancient time, like in Myanmar, China had twenty-five provinces and each province had over ten millions people. A governor or a warlord ruled each province. These governor or warlords were the absolute ruler of the provinces. These governors collected taxes from the provinces and they had to present these taxes to Beijing as yearly tributes. There were three ethnic groups in China as Chinese, Manchu, and Mongolia, in which Chinese were largest in population. ③

"... In the ancient time, the king of China asked their astrologers that who would come and invade his kingdom. The astrologers said that the people from northern part of China would come and invade the kingdom. Thus, the king made a great wall, which was in length of 300 to 400 miles long and 37 *taung* (55.5 feet) height. In its widest part, four horses can gallop in the same time. This wall was built 10,000 people in a

---

① U Ottama, *China & Japan*, p. 1.
② Ibid., pp. 1-2.
③ Ibid..

day and the construction period took over ten years. It is one of the Seven Wonders of the World. ①"

Moreover, being an internationalized Buddhist monk, Sayadew had travelled to the European countries. *Sayadaw* criticized the ancient customs and culture of China such as braids and having foot binding were hindrance of improvement of civilization. *Sayadaw* U Ottama stated that Chinese and Manchus were not the same races. In the ancient time, the Chinese coil their hair in knots like the way of *Sakya* races in India. He stated the hairstyle with its shaved front and braid down the back the head was the hairstyle of Manchus. *Sayadaw* U Ottama also discouraged foot binding which was the custom of applying painfully tight binding to the feet of young girls to prevent further growth. *Sayadaw* U Ottama heard that this custom was practiced to prevent the young girl from eloping with the man who was disagreed by the parents. This practice was correspondingly adopted as a symbol of beauty in Chinese culture and the men like these sort of feet as lotus feet. Therefore, these customs were to be given up, and western policy, methods, and ways were emulated for progress of Chinese people. ②

In his book, he also wrote about the Chinese students in Japan. He mentioned that although there waged the war between China and Japan, over ten thousands of Chinese youths were sent to Japan for the study after Sino-Japanese War in 1894. After the Russo-Japanese War in 1904, over 100,000 Chinese youths from China were sent to Japan to study. Because of the increase of sending Chinese youths to Japan, there were less scholars from China in Europe and America[③].

Sayadaw also wanted to see the unity of China and Japan for the propagation and flourishing of Buddhism in the world. He stated that

"... Although the literature of Japan derived from China, Japan has

---

① U Ottama, *China & Japan*, p. 3.
② Ibid., pp. 3-4.
③ Ibid., p. 7.

been a modernized country because of its westernized education. I hoped that the whole Asia continent would gain independence if China and Japan were united. Especially if these two Buddhist countries were joined together, the glory of Buddhism would be shone in the world. ①"

Conclusion

Sayadaw Ottama encouraged and urged entire Myanmar people as well as members of *Sangha* to take part in politics for freedom of the nation. *Sayadaw* U Ottama was the first Myanmar to teach in the Japanese University where he earned a name as an educationist and respect from the Japanese people. Moreover, being a citizen from the British colonized country, he had sympathy for the Chinese people therefore he encouraged the Chinese students who studied in Japan to have unity among them and to strive for the independence of their country from the Manchu rule. He was also a friend of Chinese nationalist leader Dr Sun Yet-sen and they had due respect each other. Due to his books, *Biography about Japan* (1912), *The People of Japan* (1921) *Tarok and Japan*: *China & Japan* (1938), Myanmar people became aware of their East Asia countries and people. A lot of lay persons and members of *Sangha* gradually grew in patriotism through political knowledge and awareness because of *Sayadaw* U Ottama. Thus, it is said that the beginning of Myanmar politic was *Sayadaw* U Ottama. ②

References

AyeKyaw; Maung, "U Ottama's letters from Japan", *Ngwetaryi Magazine*, No, 55; 3rd January, 1965. P. 30-45.

---

① U Ottama, *China & Japan*, p. 31.
② Thakhin, Lwin, *Arzani Ashin U Wisara (Martyr Ashin U Visāra)*, Yangon, Looklatye Yaungsone Press, 1971, p. 41.

BaMaung, Thakhin, *Wanthanu Ayedawpon Thamine* (1906 - 1936) (History of Vamsānu Ayedawpon (1906 - 1936)), Yangon, Sarlokngan Press, 1975.

Bama Khit U Ba Yin, *Sayadaw U Ottama* (Ven. U Ottama), Yangon, International Department of Book Distribution, no date Khant, U (Pantanaw), "Rakhine Pyitha Amyotha Gaungsaung Gyi" ("The Great Rakhine Nationalist Leader"), *Myawady Magazine*, Vol. 8, No. 9, July, 1960, pp. 170-190.

Lwin, Thakhin, *Arrzani Ashin U Visāra* (*Martyr Ashin U Visāra*), Yangon, Looklatye Yaungsone Press, 1971.

Maung Maung, U, *From Sangha and Laity: Nationalist Movement of Burma 1920-40*, New Delhi, Manohar, 1980, p. 14.

Mendelson, Michael E., *Sangha and State in Burma*, London, Cornell University Press, 1975.

Moseotti, Albert D. *British Policy and the Nationalist Movement in Burma*, Xeror University, Microfilms Ann Arbor Michigan List, 1917.

Mya Than, "The Ethnic Chinese in Myanmar and their Identity". In L. Suryadinata (ed.), *EthnicChinese as Southeast Asians*, Singapore: Institute of Southeast Asian Studies, 1997. pp. 145-190.

Ottama, U, Prof. *Japan Pyi Akyaung Ahtupati* (*Biography about Japan*), Yangon, *Thuriya Newspaper* L. td, 1914.

Purcell, V., *The Chinese in Southeast Asia*, London: Oxford University Press, 1965.

MgPye, Mg, *Burma in the Crucible*, Rangoon, Khittaya Publishing House, 1951, p. 14.

Newspapers

Wuntharnu Myanmar Newspaper, 28 February 1928, p. 10.
Deedok Newspaper, Vol. 4, No. 39, 29-12-1928, 7.
Deedok Newspaper, 23-2-1929, 14-6.

Appendix (I)

Of the *Sayadaw*'s letters, the ones written on 17th and 21st of May, 1921

Photo (1) *Sayadaw* U Ottama (1879–1939)

Source: Ba Yin, *Sayadaw U Ottama*.

Photo (2) *Sayadaw* U Ottama (1879–1939)

Source: U Ottama_ . html.

were sent from Hongangi in Tokyo, Japan.

In observing the history of the development of Japan, Meiji Reforms,

Photo (3) *Sayadaw* U Ottama and Myanmar Scholars in Japan

Source: *Leading Pioneer of Independence Sayadaw U Ottama* (1879-1939) arranged by Maung Zeya, Yangon, Pyisagan Press, 2013.

which took place during the year 1868 to 1912, were full of essences. These reforms led out-of-date Japan to up-to- date one. Japan, which was unable to rival Western countries, was made to compete against the West. Japan had become a model country for far eastern countries.

In 1867, the emperor named Matsuhiato ascended to the throne in Japan after collapse of Shigon government. He made himself as the title of Meiji in 1868, and began Meiji reforms, which were important in the course of Japanese history. The word Meiji means the ruling of emperor who has wisdom and knowledge.

King Meiji passed Royal Charter known as Charter Oak in 1868. In accordance with thisCharter he made reformations of politics, economy, social and education. In 1889, a Constitution was drawn up systematically to elect authentic people representatives. The parliament was modeled on the Prussia system.

In 1872, take the figure of the structure of German forces, Japanese armed forceswere formed. Those who came of age 20 were conscripted into army. Likewise, Duke of Sarhumar province was appointed as Admiral, and navy was established as the English navy style. Modern warships were built. Japanese knew well the might of western military forces. With this knowledge, they made efforts to modernize Japan and its armed forces. As a result, in 1894–1895, Japan conquered war over China. They exploited through Trealy of Shimoniseke. Then, they defeated powerful Russian in 1904 – 1905. They made peace with Porthsmouth agreement. After that, they occupied Korea in 1910.

Of thewars which Japan won the Russian, Russo-Japanese War in 1904–1905 was very significant. The dwarf Japan could defeat the giant Russia, and thus, a number of banks in Japan rose to 151. In 1882, Central Bank of Japan for Japanese government was opened. Industrialization was encouraged and supported. Railways and motor roads were built. Mining was successful. In 1912, when U Ottama reached Japan, Japan was particularly developed. Economy is the main blood of development of a nation. For the success of Mega economic projects, white collar workers as well as blue color workers are critically required.

In 1871, the ministry of education was established, and thenlots of schools were opened. In 1872, compulsory primary education was proclaimed. The aims of educations were that students, who led the nation in future, were to be in high morality, to be loyal to the king and to obey and practice the tasks given with fail.

Japanese's traditional belief was that Japanese islands were born to combination of Sun God and Earth God. Thus, Japan is more holy than other countries. Likewise, Japanese king war also more scared than others. The confluence of these beliefs and reformation of education led Japanese to energetic mind and patriotism.

In the letter dated on 17th May, 1912, it reads, "Japanese houses are, indeed, paper ones, and so there are various colors. These places can't be written in chalk or charcoal. Myanmar people are in habit of writing like this. In Myanmar, evil characters and impolite words are written on doors, walls, surface of tables, schools, monasteries, carriages, toilets, and resting halls in chalk or charcoal. They are in bad characters and morality".

In the letter dated on 21st May, he wrote about the cleaning work undertaken by Municipal in Tokyo.

"On May 7, every year, due to the instruction by Tokyo government, houses are to be cleaned and tidied. In May every year, one road or one word is to be cleaned and tidied every day. At that time, objects, boxes, mats, household goods not in use, are to be piled up on roads. After that, police officers, policemen checked the houses. If pleased, houses are classified as clean ones, and a piece of paper is fixed on the door. The reason is for the public to be healthy and to prevent plague break-out."

In the letter dated on 21st May, he wrote about students in Japan.

"Japanese school girls and schoolboys are to attend schools at six, and they have to go to bed at 10 and get up at 5. We, Myanmar people are not disciplined in living, eating, and so on. Thus, Myanmar people are in ruins"

The *Sayadaw* wrote about Japan in is three letters, explaining Japanese people's habit, sanitation, education and discipline.

Sources: Maung Aye Kyaw; "U Ottama's letters from Japan", *Ngwetaryi Magazine*, No, 55; 3rd January, 1965. P. 43.

人权儒学与文明的对话

辛正根[*]

论文摘要

"儒学是谁的?"知道其起源的人们会理所当然地给出"儒学是中国的"这样的答案。儒学虽不及基督教或足球的广泛传播,却也正在缓缓地冲出东亚走向整个世界。在这样的现实之下,我们不妨将问题的时态稍做变化,当我们去询问"儒学将是谁的?"的时候,当事人又会给出怎样的答案?想要干脆利落地说出"儒学是全世界人民的"这样的答案并不是一件简单的事情。因为当我们想如同自然地说出基督教和足球是属于全世界一样说出儒学是全世界人民的学问的时候,总有什么在阻拦着我们。

19—20世纪的儒学被指控是妨碍包括中国在内的东亚国家近代化转变进程的重要因素,即,儒学被认为是落后、需要废除的无用之物。儒学尚且连自主寻求自我转变动力的机会都没有就被列入了无用之物的名单。到了21世纪,儒学被再评价为促进东亚经济成长与民主主义扩张的推动力,对于儒学的评价从一个极端走到了另一个极端。与19—21世纪剧变的现实不同,儒学平稳而真挚地把自己定位在必须要摸索出自我转变方向的位置上。19—20世纪时儒学的转变是被迫无奈的时代要求,而21世纪的转变则是儒学自发性的努力,在这点上我们可以看出二者的差异。就此,本文将对以下观点进行论证:未来21世纪体制的新儒学将首先从去中国化出发,进而必须向着人权儒学的方向

---

[*] 辛正根,成均馆大学校儒学大学教授。

发展。

关键字：儒教文化圈，去中国化，人性儒学，人权儒学，补儒论

I．论题提出

"儒学是谁的？"知道其起源的人们会理所当然地给出"儒学是中国的"这样的答案。儒学虽不及基督教或足球的传播广泛，却也正在缓缓地冲出东亚走向整个世界。在这样的现实之下，我们不妨将问题的时态稍作变化，当我们去询问"儒学将是谁的？"的时候，当事人又会给出怎样的答案？想要干脆俐落地说出"儒学是全世界人民的"这样的答案并不是一件简单的事。因为当我们想如同自然地说出基督教和足球是属于全世界的一样说出儒学是全世界人民的学问的时候，总有什么在阻拦着我们。

儒学在近代前期已然倏地从中国的范畴中脱离，获得了东亚共有财产和普遍文明（文法）的地位。正是因为这样的特征，东亚在按地域划分的世界文化中被称为"儒教文化圈"①。诚然，儒教在现代社会中作为东亚地区的共同分母，在作为某种凝聚力或是共同价值的角色运作时会招来一些异议，但是不能否认儒学是区别东亚与其他地域共同体的一个重要因素。如果以这样的思想前提来研究儒学的话，那么儒学的前面无须附加某种起修饰作用的限定语，儒学不是理所应当是中国的，某种意义上，可以是韩国儒学、日本儒学、越南儒学等，当然实际上也正是如此。

最近美国波士顿大学的学者内维尔主张儒学可以成功地在西方的思维中运转，并且没有必须将其限定在中国文化与传统中的必要，从而借此高高举起了"Boston Confucians"和"Boston Confucianism"的旗帜。在这样思维的基础上，内维尔还列举出了前例，即柏拉图与基督教超越其作希腊与犹太人文化的"根"的角色，在扩展到外部世界之后逐渐成为一种生

---

① 亨廷顿在其成名作《文明的冲突》中提出，日本不属于儒教文明圈，而是被划分为其他的文明。参见 Lee Hui-Jae 译，《文明的冲突》，GIMM-YOUNG PUBLISHERS，INC，1997。

活制度。①

从这样的思路来看,我们可以说今天的儒学可以在不否认中国起源说与文化圈划分的价值的同时,即超越民族性与地域性,向着可以保持其世界性的方向展开。② 对于现代儒学的研究是否要从"中国性"和"东亚性"中脱离这一命题,笔者认为现实已经到达了不可再做推延的警戒线上,本文将从这一点出发,进而展开对儒学去中国化的必要性论述,以及其应当遵循是从人性儒学到人权儒学的发展方向。"人性"是儒学以及宋理学唯一一个立足于整体性的立场,本文从这一点上出发的论议可能会带来异议和困惑。但是因为在朝鲜时代研究儒学与在 21 世纪研究儒学是不可能完全一致的,所以必须有对于这个观点的论证。在不同的时代用同样的方式去阅读同样的内容只能说成是对于过去的扩充,不能算是现代的应对。

19—20 世纪的儒学被指控为阻止和妨碍包括中国在内的东亚文明近代化转化的重要因素,即儒学被认为是应当废弃的无用之物。儒学尚且连自主寻求自我转变动力的机会都没有就登上了无用之物的名单。到了 21 世纪儒学被再评价为促进东亚经济成长与民主主义扩张的推动力,对于儒学的评价从一个极端走到了另一个极端。与 19—21 世纪剧变的现实不同,儒学平稳而真挚地把自己定位在必须要摸索出自我转变方向的位置上。19—20 世纪时儒学的转变是被迫无奈的时代要求,而 21 世纪的转变则是儒学自发性的努力,在这点上我们可以看出二者的差异。就此,本文将对以下观点进行论证:未来 21 世纪体制的新儒学将首先从去中国化出发,进而必须向着人权儒学的方向发展。

---

① Robert Neville, *Boston Confucianism*, Albany, NY: State University of New York Press, 2000. 参见此书的书评 Bryan W. Van Norden, Reviews of *Boston Confucianism*, *Philosophy East & West*, 53: 3 (July 2003): 413—417 内维尔"超越性"概念的研究的部分参考 Kim Sung-Won,《关于波士顿儒教(Boston Confucianism)的超越性概念的研究》,《宗教研究》47, 2007。对于波士顿儒学的研究倾向这一命题,提出脱离人生脉络的儒学到底是不是真正的儒学、超越历史阶段的儒学的特征是否具有普遍性以及与其相关的反驳。

② 2013 年 7 月 27 日在成均馆大学校举办的《国际儒学研究 Consortium 筹备会议》上,Roger Ames 在会议宗旨文中提出儒学是世界性的文化财产并作为世界的文化在不断发展,以及儒学必须进行转变,"贝多芬不仅仅是'德国人民喜欢听的音乐',更是全世界的音乐。与此相同,儒家不仅仅归中国和东亚所有,更是在作为可以回应我们所处时代的迫切问题的世界性的文化财产。儒学正在被刻画为世界的文化"(资料集,第 2, 4, 6 页)。

Ⅱ."波基尼（burqini）"之争和《兴夫传》

　　现在的法国与印度都在各自进行着一场关于服饰的争论。今年 10 月 30 日印度文化观光部长官在记者会上声称，为了可以在印度境内安全地出入，外国女性游客不可穿着较短的衣服和裙子。这一声明反映着将女性穿着特定服饰归为引发性犯罪原因的视角。在穆斯林文化圈中，夏天的时候女性前往海水浴场的话，不可身穿比基尼，而是必须穿着"波基尼"（一种将穿着者从头到脚踝全都包裹起来的女性泳衣）。

　　2009 年 8 月 12 日的法国，穆斯林女性试图身着波基尼进入游泳场的时候，被以卫生标准为理由拒绝入内。从那之后，波基尼之争就开始了。现在以法国东南部沿海为中心的 30 多个地方自治团体以限制个人自由为由禁止穿着波基尼，但是在今年 8 月 26 日，法国最高行政法院做出判决指出，禁止穿着波基尼是对个人基本自由权严重而明显的侵害，禁止的初衷是不正当的。与此同时，9 月 1 日法国尼斯地方行政法院命令里维埃拉市撤销对穿着穆斯林女性泳衣——波基尼的禁令，尼斯地方行政法院指出，对于恐怖袭击的担心不足以成为里维埃拉市禁止穿着波基尼的正当化理由，同时，波基尼也并不存在卫生、服装与安全上的问题。

　　波基尼之争并不仅仅单纯是关于女性在海水浴场和海边应当穿着什么样衣服的问题，而是带有复杂而多样化的文化间冲突的特征，是自由主义与干涉主义、世俗主义与严肃主义、个人的选择与共同体的秩序、女性与男性的性别角色之间的论争。将这一论争简而言之，可以整理为以下两个问题：其一，以预防犯罪的理由要求女性穿着波基尼的行为是可以进行正当化的吗？其二，穿着波基尼从根本上来看就是压制女性的自由吗？

　　儒学曾论议过服饰（制服）穿着与社会秩序的关联性的问题，对于波基尼之争可以说也具有一定的话语权。这样说来，那么儒学对于波基尼之争可以给出什么样的对应呢？在礼制的基准之上，儒教会主张波基尼与女性的角色相符合吗？还是会主张波基尼是为了达到使女性作为个体无法表露个人的性情所进行的压制吗？或是会因为波基尼在儒学的层面中是不包含任何意义的小问题就这样被忽略吗？

　　为了与世界文明对话以及提出未来社会的展望，儒学需要怎么去做？

需要带着儒学内在意义的体系,对在现代社会中提出的论争和现象进行诊断与处方,进而提出方向与规范。如果不这样做的话,尽管儒学仍可以出现在世界文明对话的篇章中,但是不能提出有意义的主张,"以前是这样的"或是"圣贤的话中有问题的答案"这样的观点仅仅只是对权威的强调。

《兴夫传》可以以板索里的形式进行清唱,也可作为经典小说来阅读。《兴夫传》讲述了这样一个故事:父母离世之后,哥哥孬夫没有将财产分给弟弟兴夫,而是选择了独占,最后因为恶行败家亡身。与此相反,弟弟兴夫因为救治了一只腿受了伤的燕子成了富人,最终饶恕了哥哥孬夫幸福地生活。孬夫独吞了父母离世后应当与弟弟分享的财产,因而兴夫不得不经受自己本不用体验的饥饿的痛苦。饱受饥饿之苦的兴夫不仅替别人受了杖刑,为了讨口饭吃去找哥哥的时候,还被兄嫂用饭勺打了耳光。

这时候,儒学认为,孬夫因为陷入了想要独占父母财产的私欲之中,所以给兴夫带来了巨大的苦难。那么兴夫为了不经受苦痛需要怎么做呢?答案是只要孬夫没有产生独吞父母财产的想法就可以。在这里儒学探讨了一个问题,即"人是怎么陷入私欲的"以及"怎样才能对私欲进行悔改,从而改过返善"。对于这两个问题,儒学通过公与私、人心与道心、人欲和天理、本然之性和气质之性等进行了论议,结果最终儒学将目光的焦点放在了行为(事件)发生的危害产生之前的未发(未然)本性之上,即,如果可以探究与统制人性的话,像孬夫这样的人就不会出现。

脱离《兴夫传》的故事背景而将焦点放在人性上的儒学,即人性儒学,可以说是带着不阻止人为恶、使人行善的体系与倾向。因为比起在行为发生后去处罚不良的行为,如果在行为进行之前,彻底地管制内心的世界,那么现实世界就不会因为恶产生苦痛,造成苦痛的孬夫与经受痛苦的兴夫也不会出现。

III. 儒学发展的时期划分与体制划分

儒学的发展可以以中国内部为中心来说明,也可以结合中国内外来共同说明。迄今为止,儒学的展开因为立足于起源论,所以理所当然地以中国内部为中心来说明。从 21 世纪儒学的展开方向必须要重新设定的层面而言，可以说以中国为中心的时代划分不再恰当。包含中国在内的周边国家与世界因为与儒学相联系而建立了关联性，为了说明其受到的某种约束性，必然要引入体制论来说明。①

1. 时期划分论

我们将春秋时代的历史人物孔子创造的学术性成果称为儒学或是儒教，然而事实上孔子从未将自己的学术成果规定成"儒学"。通过《论语·雍也》篇"子谓子夏曰：'女为君子儒，无为小人儒！'"的内容我们可以得到两个结论：其一，孔子认知到了自己与"儒"的关联性；其二，我们可以知道孔子在追求向着"儒"这一方向的转化。②

除此之外，与儒学的价值同步，研究儒学的人拥有儒家、儒林、儒者、儒学者等名称，并且这些用语没有在东亚引起什么特殊的问题。诚然，朝鲜时代的儒学者们因为在地理上位于中国的东部，所以就有将自己称为"东儒"的自我认知。③ 重视这样的自我认知，就像前文所言及的"Boston Confucianism"一样，之前不存在的新的"〇儒"（例如：西儒，新儒等）或是"〇Confucianism"（例如：Paris Confucianism 等）的造语与分化在某种意义上可以说是可能的。

战国时代，"儒学"或是"儒术"作为指向孔子学术性成果以及与其步调一致的活动的术语开始走向一般化，这是墨子与荀子的功劳。④ 在之后的《汉书》与《后汉书》中，有一批学者与活动被收录在《儒林列

---

① 本文是以《人文（人权）儒学：与儒学·圣学．道学．中华学．国学的轨迹一起》（《大同文化研究》第 81 辑，2013，459—510 页）以及成均馆大学校 BK21 东亚融复合事业团编《作为人权儒学对 21 世纪东亚学成立可能性的摸索》（《学问场与东亚》，成均馆大学校出版部，2013，第 70—128 页）的论旨为基础，补充了新的论议形式。

② 《论语·雍也篇》。

③ 这样的自我认识是通过朴世采（1631—1695）《东儒师友录》与宋秉璿（1836—1905）的《浿东渊源录》，并在河谦镇（1870—1946）的《东儒学案》中达到了巅峰。最后在林玉均外译，《增补东儒学案》，Nanam 出版，2008 书中得到翻译。十分有趣的是，在中国东儒被作为地名在使用。与此相关的网页作为参考 http：//jsnews.zjol.com.cn/jsxww/system/2011/01/28/013203862.shtml。

④ 墨子与荀子在不同的脉络之中使用了同样的话：墨子从批判孔子与儒术的价值的角度，荀子从继承孔子与儒术价值的角度。参照与此相关的资料：辛正根：《人文（人权）儒学：与儒学．圣学·道学．中华学．国学的轨迹一起》，《大同文化研究》第 81 辑，2013，第 465—469 页。

传》之中，与"儒学"相关的辞汇被正式确定作为创始者的孔子及其追随者的关系的存在。①

这样一来，儒学不仅仅是孔子个人的学术性成就。尽管儒学也是对孔子继承者们创造的一揽子学问的指代，在不同的时代，必然会显露出不同的特性。这是因为孔子的继承者们是依照自己所处的时代和问题意识来展开自己个人的活动的。②

例如，统一了春秋战国时期的秦帝国判定自由的学术活动会对国家的政治安全以及对政策的权威造成负面影响，所以秦帝国对学术活动进行了相当严厉的制约。焚书坑儒与挟书律等事件就可以看作是对这种制约实质的象征性体现。与此同时，在秦帝国崩坏的进程之中，保存在阿房宫内的皇室图书大部分都被烧毁。

汉帝国时的儒家，面对原典因法律、战争、纵火而消失的状况，积极进行了原典的复原工作。在原典的复原过程中，今文经学与古文经学虽然相互对立，但是就如同"春秋决狱"这句话一样，他们试图将所有的六经和孔子的话在对于现实管制的基准上进行适用。汉代的儒学与其说是对于原典的生产，不如说是对原典积极地进行了解释与适用。

到了唐王朝，儒学如同以前一样没有处于主道地位之上，一方面表现为与道教、佛教三教并存的状况，另一方面呈现出三教合一的局面。因为参与社会性实践与社会性理想的实现，学者之中也产生了一定的分化，虽然也存在经过长时间科举应试准备，以官员身份登上政治舞台一展身手的人，但是因为个人的、社会的原因没有得到官职，或是得到任用也只是辗转在一些微官末职上的人也同样存在。前者关注于如何将现实政治成功运行在系统之上，后者将自己怀才不遇的情绪表现在文学与艺术作品之中。

宋明时期，对于文化的认同感因为汉族与非汉族之间的较量而受到了严重的威胁，为了治愈和克服这样的状况，人们开始追问人类心性这样的

---

① 汉帝国的登场的造成了无法与春秋战国时代的环境相比较的巨大的变化。春秋战国时期的诸子百家，在从政治领道者开始就享有相对自由的局势之中，享受着富有个性的学术活动。而汉以后的学者，哪怕是作为继承古代文化和孔子学问的热忱的探究者这样的身份，也同时拥有着政府所属官员的二重身份。

② 与此相关的内容参考《中国哲学史新展望：他者与移民社群被驱赶的文化正体性不断的再构筑旅程（中国哲学史새롭게 바라보기：他者와 Diaspora 에 내몰린 文化正体性의 끊임없는 再构筑旅程）》，辛正根，《哲学史的转变》，文瓮，2012，第14—49页。

命题。宋明时期的儒学者们希望通过内在的省察与修养，建立一种可以抑制人不道德的戾气与欲望并从根源上让会使人生变得危险的事不去发生的道德体系。

清代与宋明的主观主义倾向不同，清代学者将焦点放在了确立不会被质疑的、最确切的依据之上。因此学者试图恢复的不仅仅是在以前没有被关注的音韵、声音的语言，而是宋明以前的学问的精神。

我们将孔子的"儒学"及自孔子以来展开的儒学的现象分为原始儒学、汉代训诂学、唐代词章学、宋明性理学、清代考证学等。这样的区分是说明中国儒学形成与展开的最普遍模式，并且广泛地被人们所接受。如果用分期来讨论的话，可以说成是儒学的五个时期。诚然，现代的研究者们也有将儒学的展开分为三期或是四期的情况。例如，杜维明等学者将儒学的展开分为原始（孔孟）儒学、宋明性理学、现代新儒学三个时期。学者李泽厚将汉唐儒学补充进这三个时期之中，将儒学的展开划分为四个时期。[①] 三期说的特征是试图以心性为主，对儒学的认同性进行把握。四期说则是将儒学作为文化心理读出来，从而再次发掘在以心理为主的读法中被掩盖的荀子和汉唐时代儒学者的价值。

总的来说，如果用几个时期来区分儒学形成与展开过程的话，虽然可以很好地展示出儒学随着时代的变化而发展的特征，但是最终无法说明儒学如何在除了中国以外的地区进行的运转和发展。这样一来，为了说明儒学的展开超出中国向着东亚和世界，就必须要抛弃主张起源特权的中国一国中心论。

2. 体制区分论

"儒家"与"儒学"用英文来表示的话是 Confucian，Confucianism。在含义上"儒学"与 Confucianism 虽然是同一个单词，但是各自的侧重点不一样。前者不可还原为孔子本人，而是被刻画成历史上以集团形式呈现的"儒"的学问。相反后者其实就是用 Confucius 来表示的孔夫子的惯用方法，并且可以说达到"孔子教"程度的对于孔子个人的刻画。并且，前者的儒学表现出了孔子继承发展自己以前的儒文化传统的历史性，而比

[①] 儒学三期说参照：成均馆大学校学而会《关于儒学第三期发展的展望》，亚细亚文化社 2007 年版。儒学四期说参照：李泽厚、卢承贤译《学说（原题：己卯五说）》，DULNYUOK Publishing co，2005。

起以前的儒文化传统，后者表露的是从孔子开始的个人性。这样而来用英文表示儒学的时候采用 Confucianism 这样的翻译，还是应当采用"儒学"中文发音的直接音译，这是将成为一个值得思考的问题。（在韩国儒学的读音是 Yuhak，日文中的发音是 Jugaku）

我们要如何去理解同一个学问对象却出现不同名称这样的现象。儒学如果只存在于中国国内的话，就不会出现儒学与 Confucianis 这样的异名同实、异义同实的现象。儒学不是在中国而是向其他空间世界进入的话，就会通过新的命名（起名）过程进行转换。与儒学是在中国内还是外的起源不同，而是进入时间世界的话，就会转变为了新的名字。儒学在从前近代到近代，从近代到 21 世纪知识情报化与世界化的转换时代，迫切的需求一个新的名字。

我们现在不是以中国的一国中心而是从整个世界的视角来分析儒学形成与展开的过程，从而来探求儒学的新的名字。

表 1　　　　　　　　　东亚儒学的五个体制以及特征

体制特性	地域（A）	课题（T）	名字（N）	备注（C）
西元前 6 世纪体制	黄河	尊王攘夷	儒术	地域学
960 年体制	海内（天下）	天下一统	圣学·道学	绝对的普遍学
1644 年体制	清、朝鲜、江户	普遍的竞争	中华学	相对的普遍学
1894—1895 年体制	国民国家	压迫性的大东亚共荣	国学	国权谈论
21 世纪体制	东亚/世界	人权的深化	人权儒学	共同体性

孔子批判继承了西元前 6 世纪的传统"儒"集团的学问，始创了君子儒，即儒学。当时孔子为了守护在与外族和野心家的斗争中大势渐去的周王室，揭出了尊王攘夷的旗帜，强调了作为维护社会秩序中心的君子的道德性素养。这样的儒学虽然是孔子的努力与希望，但是也并没有摆脱处在黄河下游地区的鲁国地域学上的地位。

西元前 6 世纪的体制儒学虽然因为汉帝国的登场而产生了变化，但是从根源上说并没有什么不同。即尽管儒学有从地域学到全国学的大的变化，以及研究与扩散的环境有所好转，但是从社会秩序确立的主干这一点来看并没有呈现出什么特别的差异。

经过魏晋南北朝、隋唐、五代十国，长时间地离开了中原地区的汉民族，需要恢复宋王朝丢失的故土以及自身受到挫败的文化自尊心。在这样的状况之中，儒家摆脱了西元前6世纪体制侧重于"治术"的倾向，试图通过学问和修养来实现内圣外王的道德理想。儒学不再仅仅是对超越性的圣人的效仿，而是希望实现未歪曲的自我本心，使自己成为圣人。因此与之前不同，儒学被称为"圣学"和"道学"。与此同时，儒学自汉帝国以来，以获得全国学地位为踏脚板，超越了中国向着东亚扩散。因而，960年的体制带有普遍学的位相。①

"道学"的用语是因为元代托克托编纂的《宋史·道学传》而被人们广泛使用。在"二十五史"中虽然有17处有《儒林传》和《儒学传》，但是在《三国志》《宋书》《齐书》《魏书》《旧五代史》《新五代史》《辽史》《金史》中都没有出现《儒林传》。② 只有《宋史》中录有《道学传》和《儒林传》，并将周敦颐、二程、张载、邵雍、二程门人、朱熹、朱熹门人的学问称为"道学"，并以此区别同时代的其他儒学者。依据《道学传》记载，"道学"这一名称原本并不存在，是为了指代二程（程颢和程颐）与朱熹学问的整体性而创造出来的用语。③

1644年，处在历史与文化边缘的清王朝，不仅仅在中原地区，更是让欧洲也臣服的大帝国使960年体制中的人们感受到了恐怖和希望。虽然清王朝强大的军事力量给个别国家带来了国家安全的威胁，但是被他们所践踏的中原文化的主权也在寻找着新的主人。清王朝、朝鲜、江户幕府通过主张所有文化的主权都超越空间与种族，各自声称自己是唯一继承了明的文化王国。

17世纪以来随着"西势东渐"的开始，以东亚为首的国际局势与之前的体制相比发生了变化。19世纪之后，东亚在与强大的外部势力

---

① 宋的新儒学从地域性展开为全国学，最终变化为世界的普遍学的相关内容，参见《元朝的儒学政策与元末的儒学》，《人文学研究》18，1991；权重达：《元代的儒学与传播》，《人文学研究》24，1996；权重达：《参与朱元璋政权的儒学者的思想背景》，《人文学研究》14，1987；李基东，《东洋三国的朱子学》，成均馆大学校出版部，2003。

② 权重达：《元朝的儒学政策与元末的儒学》，《人文学研究》18，1991，156页。

③ 《宋史·道学传》：道学之名，古无是也。三代盛时，天子以是道为政教，大臣百官有司以是道为职业，党庠述序师弟子以是道为讲习，四方百姓日用是道而不知。是故盈覆载之间，无一民一物不被是道之泽，以遂其性。于斯时也，道学之名，何自而立哉?

展开艰难斗争的同时，东亚的内部也进行着炽热的竞争。日本以明治维新作为起点，为了掌握东亚的主道权，以共同应对"西势"的名目举起了"大东亚共荣"的旗帜。1894—1895 年间清日战争（甲午战争）在朝鲜展开，揭开了新体制的序幕。这时候的儒学发展为维护个别国家的生存与自尊的意识形态的角色。也就是"儒学"试向着"国学"这一名称进行了转变。

直至今日，1894—1895 年的国学体制依旧展示着它的力量。东亚各国在振兴国学的名目下进行着儒学的研究。并且，尽管孔子强调"好学"，学者们还是以成为"国学大师"为荣。[①] 作为国学，儒学与民族主义相融合担起了国粹主义，即以文化保守主义身份展开的先锋的角色。到了 21 世纪，随着世界化、知识情报化的展开，作为国学的儒学产生了进行新的变化的需求。

21 世纪的体制之中，儒学脱离了挑唆冲突与对立的国学的视野，将以实现共存与连带的方式的角色介入到了现实世界之中。这时的介入不是不正当的干涉，而是表现为正当的权利的形态。在这样的脉络之中，21 世纪体制的儒学必然要具备人权儒学的特征。接下来笔者将对于 21 世纪体制儒学为什么必须要以人权儒学的形式重生进行阐述。

从整体上来看，儒学的生成与展开应当在以一国中心的潮流中，从包含整个东亚在内的世界的观点中进行再叙述。也就是说对于儒学进行的原始儒学、汉代训诂学、唐代词章学、宋明性理学、清代考证学的时代划分论需要被体制论代替，即西元前 6 世纪体制的儒学、960 年体制的道学和圣学、1644 年体制的中华学、1894—1895 年体制的国学。因为这样的话，就可以使儒学从中国史的范畴中脱离出来，在世界史的观点中将其提升到共同财产的位相和角色上。

---

① 在中国的搜索网站百度（www.baidu.com）上搜索"国学"话，会列举出"国学大师名录"这样的名单（http://baike.baidu.com/view/2592.htm）。依据《论语》，一个"好学"的大师是可能的，但是"国学"大师是不可能的。尽管如此，很令人可惜的存在被称赞为国学大师这样让人觉得脸上火辣辣的事情。《论语》中孔子虽然谢绝了对于自己的称赞和好意评价，唯有"好学"没有被孔子推辞。《公冶长》："子曰：十室之邑，必有忠信如丘者焉，不如丘之好学也。"

Ⅳ. 从人性儒学到人权儒学

儒学，特别是在960年的体制之后，试图在人心性的基础上创造出道德性的个人与道德性的社会。儒学得到了支配性的信徒的地位，虽然人们集中在心性上可能出现道德性的个人，但是无法确信道德性的社会一定会登场。并且在肯定世俗价值的现代社会中，纯粹化的心性只能产生道德上的失败者。在这样的层面之中，21世纪体制只能从下文所示的儒学的变化中寻找出路。

1. 人性儒学的运转体系

与孔子将人性看做社会属性不同，孟子将性善设定为道德的前提。孔孟之后，作为道学与圣学的儒学忽视了荀子提出的性恶的主张，将孟子的性善作为最根本的出发点。这样对于人的理解必然要拥有自我约束性。尽管主张性善是道德的前提，现实中人们不仅仅会做出与性善不相符的行为，更有甚者会做出与性善完全相反的行为，即人类存在性善的同时，却也陷入了无法依照性善来生活的不安的状况。

实际上孔子虽然没有直接说出性善的观点，但是在通过君子和小人构图中，对进行相反行为的人的类型进行了区分。孟子虽然也主张性善，但是为了解人无法依照性善活着的心理上的倾向，提出了大体与小体的区分。虽然依据人的大体的性向人可以实现性善，但是依据小体性向的话就无法表现出性善。在此之后的960年体制的圣学和道学之中，通过对于"本然之性"和"气质之性"、"天理"和"人欲"的区分，指出了哪怕是性善也无法按照性善活着的人的局限。

如果说性善的发觉是可能的话，我们应当如何去做？最终除了制定抑制没有集中在性善上的要素的运作这样的战略之外，没有其他切实可行的做法。这样的战略通过行为主体以自己本身作为对象、注视自己内面的动向，并通过用天理压倒人欲的"修养"来达成。这样的修养是最终归结于使天理一直显现、无化和最小化人欲运作的"存天理灭人欲"的口号。

为什么在960年体制的圣学中天理与人欲没有温和的共存，而是设立了稍显过激的最大化天理和消灭人欲的目标？这是因为人欲具有一定意义上对抗天理的力量，并且如果人欲达成现实化之后会带来相当危险的后果。在这个落脚点上进行的以下分析，可以看作是在人权儒学中对于人欲的地位和本质的区分。

到底人欲的正体是什么，圣学和道学对此表述的态度看似是攻势，实际上却是守势吗？人欲是感官上的快乐，指向物质上欲望，它们全具有排斥所有的特征。快乐是不希望与他人共有的彻底的"我"的感觉，物质则是完全拒绝与他人分享"我"所拥有的东西。

快乐与欲望不仅仅有排斥所有的特征，也带有不懂得满足的贪欲的特征。这样的特征在从用心理学来剖析人性开始所认知的东西一直没有变化地被坚持着。那么为什么对于快乐和欲望没能进行颠覆性的思考？因为在再生产的社会中卸下一个人贪欲的话，就无法避开新资源无法增长的掠夺性。掠夺性不是作为单纯的个人性向的表现结束，而是与依照阶级特权决定各自比重的社会秩序的冲突。①

我们可以通过《孟子》第一章的内容对快乐、欲望的排斥性和掠夺性进行确认。孟子为了说明自己的理想，去拜见了之前可以与秦国相抗衡，如今却国力有所削弱的梁国的惠王。惠王在第一次见到孟子之后就提问"亦将有以利吾国乎？"② 孟子与惠王恳切的期望不同，谈及了追求利益之后会带来的危机状况。"上下交争利"的话最终会造成连父母与子女之间的最根本的人伦都被背弃的危局。③

在这里孟子并不是在过度强调利益的危险性，而是在展示当时的时代已经无法再吸收这种追求利益招致的结果了。如何敏锐的反应快乐和欲望，特别是在物质所有的危险中，代表着儒家对于君主一样的领道者言及"利"的话语禁忌程度。④

在这样的状况之中，960年体制的圣学和道学中，人们要抑制因为社

---

① 参考：辛正根《儒教知识分子改善"社会"的意义》，《东洋哲学研究》第 26 辑，2001；辛正根《追求私利的正当性：从怨望的对象到主体的一员》，《东洋哲学》第 32 卷，2009。

② 《梁惠王上》："孟子见梁惠王。王曰：叟！不远千里而来，亦将有以利吾国乎？"

③ 《梁惠王上》："子对曰：王！何必曰利？亦有仁义而已矣。王曰何以利吾国，大夫曰何以利吾家，士庶人曰何以利吾身。上下交征利，而国危矣。万乘之国，弒其君者，必千乘之家。千乘之国，弒其君者，必百乘之家。万取千焉，千取百焉，不为不多矣。苟为后义而先利，不夺不厌。未有仁，而遗其亲者也。未有义，而后其君者也。王亦曰仁义而已矣，何必曰利？"

④ 辛正根：《董仲舒：中华主义的开幕》，太学社 2004 年版。

会秩序的破坏而延续的快乐和欲望,并从此中得到解放的人,即对于成为圣人的要求。这种需求的意义在《击蒙要诀》中有很好的展示。

> 人之容貌,不可变丑为妍,譬力不可变弱为强,身体不可变短为长,此则已定之分,不可改也。惟有心志,则可以变愚为智,变不肖为贤。此则心之虚灵,不拘于禀受故也。莫美于智,莫贵于贤,何苦而不为贤智,以亏损天所赋之本性乎?[①]

李珥并没有积极地考虑到使"已定之分"发生变化的某种祈祷和努力,与此相反,而是积极地追求对于"天所赋之本性"的保护和开发。对于人的欲望和快乐的人性论的应对是属于事前预防性和根本性的,但是在大量生产和过度消费的社会中,对于人性论的应当可以说是不具备适当性的。

2. 人权儒学的正位

今天的韩国社会整容上瘾的现象非常严重。整容是想要拥有自己现在不曾拥有的美丽的一种欲望,这种欲望可能会导致威胁,但是不能说是不正当或者是错误的。以及如果言及内面的美丽所具有的价值,我们无法去阻拦想要整容的人。但是想要整形的人为了自身"缺乏"的美丽经历苦痛,如果要抗辩剥夺这样机会的话,我们无法去反对这样的欲望。

李珥生活在没有整容医疗技术的年代,因此,他将整容认定为是对"已定之分"的违背。不仅仅是李珥,对于那个时代的人来说,整容是一个无稽的梦,是只有在幻想中才有可能的事态。如果李珥生活在拥有整容医疗技术的时代的话,他会如何看待整容呢?如果将整容的美彻底地限定在个人状况的范畴中,李珥对于整容的态度也不会是反对的,但是如果整容的美对社会秩序造成影响的话,最终李珥还是会提出反对的立场。

如今,我们活在对960年体制的道学和圣学中压制的"欲"提供保障的时代。因而无法用李珥的"已定之分"作为禁止整容欲望的理由,也不能将其认为是传达价值的愚蠢的行为。以"已定之分"作为妥当理由的罢工、生存权的保障、对于政府政策的批判等都是单纯的作为利益纠

---

① 《击蒙要诀·立志》。

纷来批判或是无法规定为破坏社会秩序的行为。而且人类在不损害他人的利益范围内对自身私利的追求也被保障为人的权利，即从将欲望认定（错觉）为道理的"认欲为性"的论法出发，我们无法去否定欲望的价值。

最终21世纪体制的儒学与之前体制的儒学不同，不得不在承认欲望和快乐的基础之上重新出发。这就是说人性儒学之中规定心、性、欲三者关系的"心统性情"需要被重新正位。当然之前体制的儒学中对于"欲"的地位的评价也不仅仅是只有否定。① 戴震在《孟子字义疏证》中误读的孟子为了捞取赏而进行分析性的工作。其中将"欲"的积极性认为是重要的作业。

> 人之患，有私有蔽。私出于情欲，蔽出于心知。无私，仁也。不蔽，智也。非绝情欲以为仁，去心知以为智也。是故圣贤之道，无私而非无欲。老庄释氏，无欲而非无私。彼以无欲成其自私者也，此以无私通天下之情，遂天下之欲者也。②

戴震试图再定义960年道学和圣学体制中一直被认为是威胁道德性的个人因素的"私欲"。依据他的主张，"私欲"不是一个单词，而是使不同的要素相结合的不当的新造词。通过这样的区分，戴震认为"私"如果不是排斥所有的话，那么就没有可以否定"欲"只是和"性"大差不离的存在的证据。如果接受他的主张，那么与我们今天作为"性爱"的意思而使用的词的意思不同，"性欲"这样的新造词也拥有了存在的可能性。

当然从戴震用"无欲而非无私"来批判老庄和佛教这一点，出现了21世纪体制与其他不同的人生的水平线。戴震所苦恼的问题设定本身可以说仍旧有效，即"在承认欲望的时候，不仅仅将其与私相连接，而是与公相联系的'公欲'，即如何设计可以产生'通情'和'遂欲'的欲望的构造？"但是也并没有超出只有"欲"和"公"相结合的时候才勉

---

① 21世纪体制之前的对于欲望的论议，在从《论语·颜渊篇》中"克己复礼为仁"的解释中展开了十分明确的责难，参见赵纪彬《反论语（原题：论语新探）》，辛正根等译，艺文书院1996年版，554—571页。

② 《孟子字义疏证·权》。

强被承认的局限性。虽然戴震将以前的哲学家批判为野心家，其实只能算是自顾自地无化与徒劳批判的哲学的差异。但是他对于"欲"肯定的看法可以说是打开了一条日后连同"私欲"一并承认的新道路。

这样看的话，如今我们将戴震所批判的老庄和佛教的"无欲而非无私"放在一个不会成为问题的自由的状况之中。即我们无论是对于"欲"还是"私"都站在与戴震不同的水平线上。而这一切是因为权利。权利是不被抑制而是可以被主张的存在。这样的脉络之中，在960年体制的延长线上，儒学不能被看作是压抑和控制私欲的驯服对象。21世纪的儒学为了成为人权儒学，"心统性情"之中对欲望进行再正位的话，有两条可以遵循的路：其一，儒学进行肯定私欲的脱胎换骨的转化。其二，如果儒学很难全面肯定私欲的话，那么可以进行有条件的肯定。①

这样的权利再次维持私欲和公欲的紧张关系的话，我们一直不停地在寻找私欲可以连接"通情"和"遂欲"的路。当这个权利不是限定在一个国家而是超越国家界限的时候，人权儒学就变得可能。这时的儒学可以在李珥所说的本性的中心的"天所赋之本性"和权利的中心的"天赋人权"（natural rights）可以相结合的水平线上找到自己的角色。这样的转化也绝不是遥遥无期的事。性善本身原本就不仅仅是道德上的平等，而是蕴含了政治上、社会上的平等。只是性善是与身份制社会相结合，肯定道德上的平等的，进而发展为政治社会上的不平等。而如今因为不再是身份制社会，用政治社会上的平等来解释性善的话，在性善之中分明蕴含着可以向人权发展的根据。②

Ⅳ. 结束语

至此，笔者论证了儒学和中国封闭性的结合不是21世纪体制的儒学可以前进发展的去路。如今的儒学站在去中国化的进程之中，并且有进行去中国化的需求，而它的方向便是"人权儒学"。现有体制如果带有接收

---

① 此内容需要复杂的追加论议，详细的内容笔者将另为文讨论。
② 黄裕生：《我们是否需要一种权利形而上学-论权利的基础与界限》，《科学文化评论》第3卷第6期，2006，第105—112页；参见陈来《儒家思想与人权话语》，《孔夫子与现代世界》，北京大学出版社2011年版，第21—34页。

君权、夫权、男权、皇权作为普遍性的自然秩序的人性儒学的特征的话，21世纪新体制的儒学就必须要向着拥护和扩张人权普遍性的方向发展。

在韩国，遭受生存危机的劳动者们最终爬上铁塔，进行了孤独的静坐示威。日本福冈核电站爆炸之后，核的安全性与未来性成为社会的一大悬案。这样的个案因为与人类基本的权利密切相关，使我们应当跨越国界，不是作为"国民"而是"世界公民"，发出自己的声音。①

在21世纪的体制中，儒学新方向成立的同时，儒家与各自的事态相契合地发出肯定或否定声音的话，人权与儒学相结合的人权儒学就得以成立。这样跨越国境的介入可以培养东亚人甚至是世界公民的共同体意识。正是在这一点上，笔者主张如果想要建立21世纪的新的体制儒学的话就必须要从人权儒学出发。

按时代划分的儒学因为容纳了不同的要素，所以克服了自身的缺点。可以说是一种的补儒论。例如近代的儒学容纳了自身没有的西学的科学和民主的要素，并将其作为踏脚石重生为了新儒学。这是儒学为了不忘记作为中国儒学的中心性的尝试。21世纪体制中不仅仅是为了儒学本身生存的补儒论，而是与补世论的观点站在了一起。因为世界性是比儒学更上一层的范畴。

在这样的视角中，为了现实化而研究儒学的人们，不应该困在政府的战略、排他性的民族主义的观点之中，而是应当去创造公有的世界。寻找抛开专案和政府的支援、可以自由讨论和商议的去路，这样的人的联网正在被需求。也就是所说的前近代儒学的不是中心与周边、传播和相容的单方面的关联，而是建立讨论与商议的双向关系的去路。

参考文献

《论语》，《孟子》。

戴震：《孟子字义疏证》。

李珥：《击蒙要诀》。

权重达：《参与朱元璋政权的儒学者的思想背景》，《人文学研究》1987年第14期。

---

① 参见辛正根《作为人权儒学21世纪东亚学成立可能性的摸索》，成均馆大学校BK21东亚学融合事业团编，《学问场与东亚》，成均馆大学校出版部2013年版，第123—124页。

权重达：《元朝的儒学政策与元末儒学》，《人文学研究》1991 年第 18 期。

权重达：《元代的儒学与传播》，《人文学研究》1996 年第 24 期。

Kim Sung-Won：《关于波士顿儒教（Boston Confucianism）的超越性概念的研究》，《宗教研究》2007 年第 47 期。

李泽厚、卢承贤译：《学说（原题：己卯五说）》，DULNYUOK Publishing co，2005。

成均馆大学校学而会：《关于儒学第 3 期发展的展望》，亚细亚文化社 2007 年版。

辛正根：《儒教知识分子改善"社会"的意义》，《东洋哲学研究》2001 年第 26 辑。

辛正根：《董仲舒：中华主义的开幕》，太学社 2004 年版。

辛正根：《追求私利的正当性：从怨望的对象到主体的一员》，《东洋哲学》2009 年第 32 卷。

辛正根：《哲学史的转变》，文瓮 2012 年版。

辛正根：《人文（人权）儒学：与儒学·圣学·道学·中华学·国学的轨迹一起》，《大同文化研究》2013 年第 81 辑。

辛正根：《作为人权儒学对 21 世纪东亚学成立可能性的摸索》，成均馆大学校 BK21 东亚融复合事业团编，《学问场与东亚》，成均馆大学校出版部 2013 年版。

李基东：《东洋三国的朱子学》，成均馆大学校出版部 2003 年版。

林玉均外译：《增补东儒学案》，NANAM2008 年版。

赵纪彬：《反论语（原题：论语新探）》，辛正根译，艺文书院，1996 年。

亨廷顿：《文明的冲突》，Lee Hui-Jae 译，GIMM-YOUNG PUBLISHERS，INC，1997。

黄缕诗：《对于江陵端午祭传承的探讨》，《人文学研究》2012 年第 17 期。

Robert Neville, *Boston Confucianism*, Albany, NY: State University of New York Press, 2000.

Bryan W. VanNorden, Reviews of *Boston Confucianism*, *Philosophy East & West*, 53: 3 (July 2003): 413-417.

http：//baike. baidu. com/view/2592. htm.

http：//jsnews. zjol. com. cn/jsxww/system/2011/01/28/013203862. shtml.

http：//www. cha. go. kr/cha/idx/SubMain. do？ mn = NS_ 04.

预言还是教学？——胡适的儒教解释学

绪形康[*]

1. 胡适提出了有关儒教的新理论

胡适在他晚年被采访而成的《口述自传》第十二章里，就 1934 年发表的《说儒》对儒教的起源提出怎样崭新的观点这一问题概括如下：

> 在三千年前（公元前一千一百二十年至一十年之间），殷人为周人所征服。但是这些殷遗民之中的教士，则仍保持着他们固有的宗教典礼；继续穿戴殷人的衣冠。他们底职业仍然是治丧、相礼、教学；教导他们自己的人民。这些被征服的"殷人"，可能还是新兴的周王国内人民的绝大多数，亦未可知。在西周东周统治的六七百年中，他们的礼教已逐渐渗透到统治阶级里去了。[①]

> 我并没有引用一条新证据。可是我却认为那篇《说儒》却提出一个新的理论。根据这个新理论可将公元前一千年中的中国文化史从头改写。我的理论便是在武王伐纣以后那几百年中，原来的胜负两方却继续着一场未完的"文化"斗争。在这场斗争中，那战败的殷商遗民，却能通过他们的教士阶级，保存一个宗教和文化的整体；这正和犹太人通过他们的祭师，在罗马帝国之内，保存了他们的犹太教一样。由于他们在文化上的优越性，这些殷商遗民反而逐渐征服了——至少是感化了一部分，他们原来的征服者。[②]

---

[*] 绪形康，日本神户大学大学院人文学研究科教授，国际连携推进机构亚洲学术研究中心主任。

[①] 欧阳哲生编：《胡适文集》1，北京大学出版社 1998 年版，第 419 页。

[②] 同上书，第 422 页。

《说儒》的新理论就归纳到如下三项：

其一，儒家源于被周民族征服下的殷遗民之文化复兴运动。

其二，这些文化复兴运动体现于正如罗马帝国内的犹太人通过他们的教士阶级保存其预言一样的"五百年必有王者兴"之悬记。

其三，孔子把原来的殷民族的宗教典礼改变为更普遍的教学体制而却感化了他们的征服者之周民族。

胡适承认他在《说儒》所使用的材料都不一定新鲜的，不但如此，在自述中胡适夸奖说的"新理论"也是他跟学术界同人之间的讨论中获得的诸见解而已。在这些讨论中发挥最重要作用的则是傅斯年的启发：透过胡适日记的记载，我们可以推演他写作《说儒》过程的同时，得知傅斯年对《说儒》所做的巨大贡献：

> 1934 年 3 月 14 日："拟作《原儒》一文，未动手。"①
> 15 日："动手做一文——《说儒》。"②
> 17 日："下午续作《说儒》一文，未完。"③
> 20 日："孟真来谈。他昨晚送来他的旧稿《周东封与殷遗民》诸文，于我作《说儒》之文甚有意。已充分采用。今天我们仍谈此题。"④

傅斯年在《周东封与殷遗民》里梳理周把殷殖民化之过程而指出，周需要几代人的时间才能巩固其在中国东部和中部的权力。⑤《说儒》之新理论的关键就在于借用傅斯年的这些看法来证明古代中国是多元民族构成的社会，就是说，东方的殷民族与西方的周民族所冲击、摩擦、融合的复杂过程中古代中国的宗教和文化的整体便是成立的：

> 在周初几百年之间，东部中国的社会形势是一个周民族成了统治

---

① 曹伯言整理：《胡适日记全编》6，安徽教育出版社 2001 年版，第 347 页。
② 同上书，第 348 页。
③ 同上书，第 349 页。
④ 同上书，第 349 页。
⑤ 王汎森：《傅斯年：中国近代历史与政治中的个体生命》，生活·读书·新知三联书店 2012 年版，第 123 页。

阶级，镇压着一个下层被征服被统治的殷民族。傅斯年先生说"鲁之统治者是周人，而鲁之国民是殷人"（引见上文）。这个论断可以适用于东土全部。这形势颇像后世东胡民族征服了中国，也颇像北欧的民族征服了罗马帝国。以文化论，那新起的周民族自然比不上那东方文化久远的殷民族，所以周室的领袖在那开国的时候也不能不尊重那殷商文化。①

其实，这些观点的兴起是从丁文江1923年在胡适所编辑的《努力周报》上发表的《历史人物与地理的关系》（第43、第44期，1923年3月11日）开始的："无论我们对于种族，环境同偶然产生的首领，这三种势力，偏重在那一种，总应该承认地理同历史有密切的关系，因为广义的地理，包括生在地上的人种。"②

1926年胡适在巴黎的时候，傅斯年曾经跟胡适说过：中国一切文学都从民间来的，同时每一种文学都经过一种生、老、病、死的状态。从民间起来的时候是"生"，然后像人的一生一样，由壮年而老年而死亡。胡适甚至认为"这个观念，影响我个人很大"。③

应用丁文江提倡的地理学与种族学及傅斯年开展的生物进化论来改造旧历史学以及推动新历史学步伐中，1926年《古史辨》第一册的问世则堪称深为震撼中国历史学界的大事件。

在《古史辨》的强烈引导下，傅斯年于1927年12月发表《论孔子学说所以适应于秦汉以来的社会的缘故》，正式拉开了中国历史研究之多元化趋势。当然那时傅斯年之观点还没达到后来他提出的夷夏东西说那样明晰的梳理，但他已经意识到殷周变革中西周封建制的奠定、其贵族与民间的互动关系及鲁国的儒化等现象都体现了对后来中国文化之深刻的意义。④

安阳发掘之后，历史学家逐渐放弃了其疑古的立场，胡适和顾颉刚原

---

① 胡适：《说儒》，《胡适文集》5，第10—11页。
② 丁文江：《历史人物与地理的关系》，《努力周报》1923年第43期。
③ 施爱东：《顾颉刚、傅斯年与民俗学》，中国社会科学院历史研究所·中山大学历史系合编：《纪念顾颉刚先生诞辰110周年论文集》，中华书局2004年版，第235—236页。
④ 傅斯年：《论孔子学说所以适应于秦汉以来的社会的缘故》，欧阳哲生主编：《傅斯年全集》第1卷，第481—483页。

来认为商朝属于石器时代,然而,见证青铜器的发现以后,胡适转变了他的立场,并在 1929 年告诉顾颉刚:"现在我的思想变化了,我不疑古了,要信古了!"①

傅斯年直到 1927 年才熟读王国维的《殷周制度论》而很赞同他所主张的古代文化多元论:殷和周的制度不仅是后者继承前者之关系,殷周变革时期却有了大规模的种族冲突,因此,儒教教义中"周沿殷礼"之核心观念便不能成立了。这年傅斯年又读到了王国维的学生徐中舒的文章,确信了殷和周是两种不同的族群。正在同一的 1927 年,四川的蒙文通也对古代中国族群问题开始思考,他的《古史甄微》则表达了太古民族显有三系的想法。②

1930 年山东龙山城子崖的大发掘,第一次发现了大量的黑陶器,这出土文物就证明了以山东为主的东部地区是与西部地区的彩陶文化完全不一样的文化系统。1930 年 12 月 6 日,胡适在中央历史语言研究所的茶会上说:"在整理国故的方面,我看见近年研究所的成绩,我真十分高兴。如我在六七年前根据渑池发掘的报告,认商代为在铜器之前,今安阳发掘的成绩足以纠正我的错误。"③

1931 年 2 月 17 日,胡适跟傅斯年进行谈话。谈话的主要内容则依据傅斯年的《新获卜辞写本后记跋》论二事:一因卜辞"伐芈"而论"楚之先世",一因卜辞"命周侯"而论"殷周的关系"。"两题皆极大贡献,我读了极高兴"。④

2. 胡适怎样发现儒教的"悬记"?

同儒家的原型是殷遗民的文化复兴这一观点相配,《说儒》的另外一个关键的新理论则是儒教原典是与犹太人的旧圣经可相比的"悬记"之记载。然而,要证明儒教之悬记内容的论证似乎碰到了严重的困难。1934 年 3 月 18 日,傅斯年《周东封与殷遗民》的启示下,写好儒教起源于殷遗民的文化复兴斗争以后,胡适的思考里究竟发生什么事情呢?他怎样摆脱这种写作中的困扰呢?

---

① 王汎森:《傅斯年:中国近代历史与政治中的个体生命》,第 100 页。
② 同上书,第 122—127 页。
③ 曹伯言整理:《胡适日记全编》5,安徽教育出版社 2001 年版,第 887 页。
④ 曹伯言整理:《胡适日记全篇》6,安徽教育出版社 2001 年版,第 61 页。

直到 1934 年 4 月 12—14 日的一天，胡适才能动手做《说儒》：

> 续写《说儒》。因引《左传》昭七年"孟僖子病不能相礼"一段，检《史记·孔子世家》对看，偶得一解，既可证《史记》引《左传》，又可证《左传》古本已分年编制，略与今本〔相同〕。
>
> 《左传》记此事在昭公七年，其时孔子十七岁，但"终言"其事，故下文续记"及其将死也"一大段。孟僖子死在昭公廿四年，在十七年之后；其时孔子三十四岁，《史记·孔子世家》记云：
>
> 孔子年十七，鲁大夫孟釐子病且死，诫其嗣懿子曰
>
> 《索隐》指出僖子死在昭公廿四年，并引贾逵云"仲尼时年三十五矣"。杜预注也说"僖子卒时孔子年三十五"。孔颖达云："当言三十四，而云五，盖相传误耳。"
>
> 《史记》所以误记此事在孔子年十七时，正是因为《左传》里此事系在昭公七年。此可证《史记》引的确是《左传》，又可证司马迁所见的《左传》本子已是分年编制的了。①

胡适在此发现的解决悬案之钥匙，则《史记·孔子世家》与《左传》昭公七年的记载是可以互相参照的着想。现在要探讨的是这种着想的发明权是否在于胡适这一问题。我认为，使胡适写成《说儒》的最迫切的内在动机就在于他对《中国哲学史大纲》中表达的疑古观点进行修正的愿望。

早在 1930 年 12 月 20 日给钱玄同写了一封信而讨论《春秋》的性质之时，胡适告知了"我从前（《哲学史》一〇三）曾疑《春秋》有'后来被权门干涉，方才改了的'。现在看来，在那种时代，私家记载不能不有所忌讳，也是很平常的事"这样的感观。② 胡适则公开宣传从疑古的立

---

① 曹伯言整理：《胡适日记全篇》6，安徽教育出版社 2001 年版，第 365—366 页。又参见陈勇、朱恺《现代学术史上的《说儒》之争述评》，陈勇、谢维扬主编《中国传统学术的近代转型》，上海人民出版社 2011 年版。

② 《胡适致钱玄同》（1930 年 12 月 20 日），杜春和、韩荣芳、耿来金编：《胡适论学往来书信选》（下册），河北人民出版社 1998 年版，第 1135 页。

场转变到信古的立场,并且论及孔子所看到的《春秋》绝对不是"断烂朝报"的状态,故而,当解释孔子的《春秋》之时,学者们就用不着微言大义的读法,乃至写出了毛子水的有关《春秋》之解释三条意见:

(1)《春秋》的底子可以是孔子以前史官所记录的。
(2) 孔子可以得到这样的记录,并且利用他。
(3) 孔子也许公布古代史官的记录,并接续记载当时的事。①

胡适从这样角度来继续梳理《春秋》以外史料的性质问题,进而认清非但《春秋》,《史记》以及《左传》也不如今文家指斥过那样不一定是被随意伪造的文本。1934年4月他开发的对《史记》与《左传》之间文本进行互相对照的着想,正是胡适这几年一直关心的学术思考之一。然而,第一次提出将《史记·孔子世家》与《左传》昭公七年的记载相比的说法,便不是胡适的,而是《古史辨》第三册中的学术见解。在1932年1月21日胡适写过:"夜读顾刚的《古史辨》第三册。此册仅论《周易》与《诗》两组问题,似较第一二册更有精彩。"②

那么,胡适从《古史辨》第三册里哪个文章中获得了他的着想?应当说是,俞平伯的《论商颂的年代》是使胡适摆脱理论方面的困扰之关键文章。

俞平伯在其中考证了商颂为商人作还是周人作的问题。这一问题便是今古文家之间长期争论但却没法解决的学术界之大悬案。古文家们透过《毛诗》与《国语》的分析认为商颂是虽然曾经散失但被正考父所补订的商代作品。与此相反,今文家们依据《史记·宋世家》《鲁诗》以及《韩诗》断言商颂是宋襄公时成立的周诗。

俞平伯的见解则较倾向于今文家的立场。他说:

> 若把这事归在宋襄公身上,却是很像。宋襄公本是夸大狂,他想做盟主,想去伐楚国,都是事实,不容得怀疑。把这事来说商颂正相符合。你们看他说"在从前,我们的成汤老祖的时代,哪一个鬼子

---

① 《胡适致钱玄同》(1930年12月20日),杜春和、韩荣芳、耿来金编:《胡适论学往来书信选》(下册),河北人民出版社1998年版,第1135—1136页。
② 曹伯言整理:《胡适日记全篇》6,安徽教育出版社2001年版,第172页。

敢不来朝觐！这是我们商人的老排场、老规矩"。这话说得何等夸大而滑稽，使人想得出宋襄公的神气来。但不幸得很，泓之战大败亏输，大话竟不中用。在此更有人疑心，以为既经大败，歌颂何为？不知作此颂时，或者正在筹划开战，或者战而未败，都说不定。说这诗为颂宋襄公总比较近似。/归到本传，我以为说商颂是周诗较为得体。①

将胡适对商颂的解释同俞平伯的见解相比，具见于胡适尽管采用这诗为宋襄公歌颂这一观点沿袭俞平伯的说法，但将商颂的年代放到殷民族的时代而却谈及这诗便是殷民族灭亡之后他们希望自己民族复兴的预言诗。还要关注的是，在其论文的后记中的顾颉刚对俞平伯之提问。顾颉刚则劝俞平伯用《史记·十二诸侯年表》将宋国及鲁国的事情联系起来，这一观点岂非给予胡适有关《说儒》资料的梳理中最有强力的解决钥匙？获得这些钥匙以后，胡适便再动手继续做《说儒》：

> 柔逊为殷人在亡国状态下养成的一种遗风，与基督教不抵抗的训条出于亡国的犹太民族的哲人耶稣，似有同样的历史原因。《左传》昭公七年所记孔子的远祖正考父的鼎铭，虽然是宋国的三朝佐命大臣的话，已是很可惊异的柔道的人生观了。正考父曾"佐戴、武、宣三朝；据《史记·十二诸侯年表》，宋戴公元年当周宣王二十九年（前799），武公元年当平王六年（前765），宣公元年当平王二十四年（前747）。他是西历前八世纪前半的人，离周初已有三百多年了。他的鼎铭说：

> 一命而偻，再命而伛，三命而俯，循墙而走，亦莫余敢侮。馆于是，鬻于是，以糊余口。

> 这是殷民族的一个伟大领袖的教训，儒之古训为柔，岂是偶然的吗？②

---

① 俞平伯：《论商颂的年代》，《古史辨》第三册下编，《民国丛书》第四编66，上海书店1992年版，第509页。

② 胡适：《说儒》，《胡适文集》5，第15—16页。

宋国所以能久存，也许是靠这种祖传的柔道。周室东迁以后，东方多事，宋国渐渐抬头。到了前七世纪的中叶，齐桓公死后，齐国大乱，宋襄公邀诸侯的兵伐齐，纳齐孝公。这一件事成功（前642）之后，宋襄公就有了政治的大欲望，他想继承齐桓公之后作中国的盟主。①

那时东方无霸国，无人与宋争长；他所虑者只有南方的楚国。果然，在盂之会，楚人捉了宋襄公去，后来又放了他。他还不觉悟，还想立武功，定霸业。泓之战（前638），楚人大败宋兵，宋襄公伤股，几乎做了第二次的俘虏。②

三百年后，宋君偃自立为宋王，东败齐，南败楚，西败魏，也是这点亡国遗憾的死灰复燃，也是一个民族复兴运动。但不久也失败了。殷商民族的政治的复兴，终于无望了。③

胡适瞩目这种民族复兴运动中酝酿的"救世圣人"的预言之兴起，同时关注这种预言就在犹太民族的"弥赛亚（Messiah）降生救世之悬记中最典型地表达的史实，进而试图发掘从民族复兴运动灭亡之后隐藏的殷商民族记忆中之悬记。

胡适把孔子的故事看作同犹太民族亡国后保持的预言一类的"悬记"："不做周公而仅仅做一个'素王'，是孔子自己不能认为满意的，但'五百年必有王者兴'的悬记终于这样不满意的应在他的身上了"。④ 胡适进而在《诗·商颂·玄鸟》这首诗中想要推演殷商遗民中流传的"悬记"。

胡适认为《商颂》的《玄鸟》篇里被歌颂的武王形象便是后来变成殷民族想念的圣人复兴的预言。为何胡适这样解释？因为只有《玄鸟》的民族英雄之诗歌，《左传》昭公七年所记载的孟僖子之悬记才能导致如此。不仅如此，如果将《左传》昭公七年的记载同《史记·孔子世家》

---

① 胡适：《说儒》，《胡适文集》5，第31页。
② 同上书，第31页。
③ 同上书，第32页。
④ 同上书，第41页。

的叙事结合起来,我们便能够了解这诗歌的更深层的意涵。毫无疑问,这孟僖子的预言就等同于孟子所指的"五百年必有王者兴"的悬记:

> 孔子生于鲁襄公二十二年(前551),上距殷武庚的灭亡,已有五百多年。大概这个"五百年必有王者兴"的预言由来已久,所以宋襄公(泓之战在前638)正当殷亡后的第五世纪,他那复兴殷商的野心也正是那个预言之下的产儿。到了孔子出世的时代,那预言的五百年之期已过了几十年,殷民族的渴望正在最高度。这时期,忽然殷宋公孙的一个嫡系里出来了一个聪明睿知的少年。①

> 《左传》昭公七年记孟僖子自恨不能相礼,"乃讲学之。苟能礼者,从之"。《左传》又说,孟僖子将死时,遗命要他的两个儿子何忌与说去跟着孔子"学礼焉以定其位"。②

但要强调的是,纵观俞与胡两位对《商颂》的分析之后,我们便发现胡适在他的论述中故意忽略了《国语》文本的探讨。而这一问题,后来江绍原抓起来集中控告的:"胡先生全作,无一处利用《国语》里的材料。然此书至少有一条确与胡先生所论及之点有关。"③江绍原同俞平伯交往较密切,他肯定知道胡适的论述之由来:"廿三日下午,友人俞平伯先生来谈。他觉得'大司马固谏'固是大司马之名,然此固像是公孙固而非子鱼。他又说'大司马'与'司马'是否一官,应予考定。我赞成这话;宋国于'司寇';外尚有'大司马',见《左传》;故'司马'上置'大司马',似可能"。④

在江绍原来看,胡适对儒教起源的探求方法是相当片面的、十分值得怀疑的,因而,他无情地嘲讽了胡适的学术作风:"形容宋人呆傻的故事,屡见古书。"现在胡先生新找路两条:一为创造"龙旂十乘(便能)大艰是承"的傻龙预言;一为自鱼后来转变态度,用苗语"谏"襄公"不这般敌人可以放过"。胡先生一身而兼"胡衣斯文陶日阴"(HISTO-

---

① 胡适:《说儒》,《胡适文集》5,第35—36页。
② 同上书,第23页。
③ 江绍原:《力劝宋襄公复兴殷民族者谁耶?》,《华北日报》1934年12月22—24日。
④ 江绍原:《"天之弃商久"是谁说的?》,《华北日报》1934年12月25日。

RIAN）与"胡由莫日斯脱"（HUMORIST）二胡矣，一笑"。①

3. 知识阶级的教学使命

儒教传统里对"三代"的理想时代有截然不同的看法；就是"复古三代之治"与"继周损益"之两种说法。前者以古文学派为代表，后者以今文学派为代表。如上所述，胡适在儒教的传统里发掘了作为殷商民族的文化复兴愿望的悬记，然而，假使儒教原典归纳为悬记的话，这一观点却非但冲突了"复古三代之治"之精神而且越轨"继周损益"的圈子，几乎成为同儒教传统的背离之位置。

的确，悬记指的不仅是像犹太人的教义那样面临危机时机的救亡意识，并且将会发动儒教传统里长期隐藏的革命意识。胡适在他的晚年写给杨联陞的一封信里，强烈意识到"悬记"所包含之革命色彩的意蕴：

> 谢 4 月 12 日信。关于王莽"定有天下之号曰新"的问题，我很赞成你的"并存"说，既是"正好有新都之封，而新又有维新之意"。"正好"者，在我看来，等于"偶然"而已。而当日的"新皇帝"的本意似即是西汉一百多年来学者悬想或"悬记"的"新王"。而"肇命于新都"，则是偶然巧合的一件事实，可以引作一个"预兆"。故我的说法是："新是维新之意，而莽恰巧从从新都侯起，故当时符命有'肇命于新都'之说。"
>
> 指出三点：（1）元、明、清三代用"美号"作国号，并非创作，实是推行一个原来很有力量的古代思想；（2）元明清以前，如魏，如晋，似是"地名"，其实是特别挑选地名以应符谶里的"美名"；（3）王莽的时代，其时代思想，其生平抱负及设施，皆足以使我倾向于承认元后怒骂的"新皇帝"的"新"是本意。②

胡适在这里将王莽的本意概括为"悬记"，充分意识到王莽所挖掘的、所追求的儒家原典里之革命精神。冯友兰之所以贬斥胡适的新理论，是因为他敏锐地看破了胡适《说儒》之观点对中国传统文化的破坏作用。

---

① 江绍原：《古宋君臣们的民族复兴运动》，《华北日报》1934 年 12 月 21 日。
② 参见胡适纪念馆所藏"胡适档案目录"。

他这样指控胡适：

> 儒之起是起于贵族政治崩坏以后，所谓"官失其守"之时。胡先生的对儒及孔子的看法，是有点与今文经学家相同。我们的看法，是有点与古文经学家相同。所谓儒是一种有知识、有学问之专家；他们散在民间，以为人教书相礼为生。关于这一点，胡先生的见解，与我们完全相同。我们与胡先生之不同者，即是胡先生以为这些专家，乃因殷商亡国之后，"沦为奴虏，散在民间"（《集刊》页二四二）。我们则以为这些专家，乃因贵族政治崩坏以后，以前在官的专家，失其世职，散在民间，或有知识的贵族，因落魄而亦靠知识为生。①

冯友兰所诽谤的"有点今文经学家相同"的说法便是非常准确的。毫无疑问，从胡适的发言（孔子所谓"从周"，我在上文说过，其实是接受那个因袭夏殷文化而演变出来的现代文化。所以孔子的"从周"不是绝对的，只是选择的，只是"选其善者而从之，其不善者而改之"）② 来看，他把儒教搞革命化的程度，就同那时代的今文学家、公羊学家们相比得更激进的。

虽然如此，最清楚意识到这一理论的危险性乃是胡适本人。为了淡化将儒家原典精神搞革命化的极端倾向，胡适在《说儒》的后半部分则采用将孔子描述为保持"有教无类"之理想的教育家之战略。然而，呐喊着悬记的预言、为了殷商民族的文化复兴而奋斗的孔夫子究竟是怎样会变成为拥护人文主义价值观的教育家呢？

> 这种柔道本来也是一种"强"，正如《周易·象传》说的"谦尊而光，卑而不可逾"。一个人自信甚坚强，自然可以不计较外来的侮辱；或者他有很强的宗教信心，深信"鬼神害盈而福谦"，他也可以不计较偶然的横暴。谦尊柔逊之中含有一种坚忍的信心，所以可说是一种君子之强。但他也有流弊。过度的柔逊恭顺，就成了懦弱者的百依百顺，没有独立的是非好恶之心了。这种人就成了孔子最痛恨的

---

① 冯友兰：《原儒墨》，《三松堂全集》（第十一卷）/哲学文集（上），河南人民出版社2001年版，302页。

② 胡适：《说儒》，《胡适文集》5，第44页。

"乡原";"原"是谨愿,乡愿是一乡都称为谨愿好人的人。①

胡适想要发现"谦尊柔逊"之儒的背后,便是潜藏着保持"坚忍的信心"之君子。胡适之所以这样进行梳理,是因为《周易·象传》里所运作的辩证法会导致跟"谦尊"与"柔逊"的取向截然相反的"坚忍"与"信心"。儒是透过《周易·象传》的辩证法可以获得包含"谦尊"及"坚忍"这样两种价值取向的统一人格。

其实,胡适从《周易》的卦爻辞的概念操作中抓住摆脱儒教革命化的启示,不是同《说儒》写作时期较远。恰恰相反,动手《说儒》之前的1934年3月5日,他仍然对《周易》中《象传》与《象传》之间矛盾的问题无法提交任何解决方案:

> 读《周易》一遍,颇失望。六十四卦之《象传》似是一人所作,毫无问题。其人似曾把全书想过一遍,其所作《象传》自成一个系统,亦不全与《彖传》相照应。②

但是,1934年4月14日弄清儒教的悬记性质以后,胡适则紧接着找到了调整《象传》与《彖传》之间矛盾的想法:

> 《易》卦爻辞已有"箕子之明夷"(《明夷》五爻),"王用享于岐山"(《升》四爻)的话,似乎不会是"文王与纣"的时代的作品。"文王囚居羑里而作《易》"的说法,也是更后起之说。《系辞》还是猜度的口气,可见得《系辞》以前尚没有文王作《易》的说法。《系辞》的推测作《易》年代,完全是根据于《易》的内容的一种很明显的人生观,就是"其辞危","惧以终始,其要无咎"。
>
> 《系辞》的作者认清了这一点,所以推测"作《易》者其有忧患乎?"这个观察是很有见地的。我们从这一点上也可以推测《易》的卦爻辞的制作大概在殷亡之后,殷民族受周民族的压迫最甚的一二百

---

① 胡适:《说儒》,《胡适文集》5,第51页。
② 曹伯言整理:《胡适日记全编》6,安徽教育出版社2001年版,第339页。

年中。①

通过将《易经》的成书年代放在殷民族被征服以后一二百年的漫长过程，胡适才能够描述将儒家原典精神的革命因素是随着时代的变迁而慢慢走上"中庸"的路上去。他说：

> 这个五百年应运而兴的中国"弥赛亚"的使命是要做中国的"文士"阶级的领导者，而不能直接做那多数民众的宗教领袖。他的宗教只是"文士"的宗教一样。他不是一般民众所能了解的宗教家。②

孔子集团便被称为"文士"阶级。胡适把儒教徒的历史使命奠定为"知识阶级"发动的思想运动。可见，《说儒》的写作中他碰到的种种困扰便是近代思想史上儒家命运的两难状态及悖论情况的直接反映。

4. 结语

1933年7月，胡适被邀到了美国，在芝加哥大学演讲"中国文化的趋势"（Cultural Trends in Present day China），共讲六次。芝加哥大学又召开 Haskell Foundation 主办的学术演讲会，邀请著名学者主讲世界六大宗教：印度教、儒教、佛教、犹太教、伊回教和基督教。胡适主讲儒教部分，做了三次的演讲：(1) "Confucianism and Modern Scientific Thinking"（《儒教与现代科学思想》）、(2) "Confucianism and Social Economic Problems"（《儒教与社会经济问题》）、(3) "The Task of Confucianism."（《儒教的使命》）。

在此，我想介绍一下其演讲的第三部分《儒家的使命》。胡适在开幕时，听到何铎斯（Dr. Hodous）博士的发言："儒教已经死了，儒教万岁！"才清晰地意识到儒教死了以后他本人才能够成为儒教徒的事实。胡适说：

---

① 胡适：《说儒》，《胡适文集》5，第21页。
② 同上书，第65页。

儒教，正如何铎斯博士所说，已经死了。它是自杀死了，可不是由于错误的冲动，而是由于一种努力，想要抛弃它自己一切逾分和特权，想要抛弃后人加到那些开创者们的经典上去的一切伪说和改窜。

我在大学演讲，有一次说过，儒教的最后一个拥护者，最后一个改造者，在他自己的一辈子里，看到儒教经典的一个主要部分，一个最通行，最容易读，因此在统制中国人的思想上最有势力的部分，已经被打倒了。这样说来，儒教真可算是死了。

孟子是儒教最伟大的哲学家，他的影响仅次于孔子，曾说过："人之患在好为人师"。儒教的典籍里又常说："礼闻来学，不闻往教。"儒教从来不教它的门徒跑出去站在屋顶上对人民宣讲，把佳音带给大地四方不归信的异教徒。由此可以看出来，儒教从来不想做一个世界的宗教，儒教也从来不是一个用传教士的宗教。

然而，这也不是说，孔子、孟子和儒家的学者们要把他们的灯放在斗底下，不把它放在高处，让人人可以看见。这只是说，这些人都有那种知识上的谦虚，所以他们厌恶独断的传教士态度，宁愿站在真理追求者的谦虚立场。这只是说，这些思想家不肯相信有一个人，无论他是多么有智慧有远识，能够说完全懂得一切民族，一切时代的生活与道德的一切错综复杂的性质。孔子就说过："丘也幸，苟有过，人必知之。"正是因为有这样可能有错误的意识，所以儒教的开创者们不赞成人的为人师的欲望。我们想要用来照亮世界的光，也许其实只是一把微弱的火，很快就要消失在黑暗里。我们想要用来影响全人类的真理，也许绝不能完全没有错；谁要把这个真理不如一点批评变成教条，也许只能毁坏它的生命，使它不能靠后来的新世代的智慧不断获得新活力，不断重新被证实。①

此后，胡适把现代宗教的使命概括为如下三项：第一，彻底而严格的自己考察；第二，宗教内部的改造；第三，把宗教的意义和范围扩大、伸长。从这个角度来看，宗教不过是"差一等的哲学"，并且"差一等的科学"而已。所以，现代世界的宗教必须是"一种道德生活，用我们所能

---

① 《胡适文集》12，第296—297页。

掌握的一切教育力量来教导的道德生活"。①

《说儒》所开展的儒教的新面貌及新理论，无论它是复兴衰落文化的悬记还是以人文精神为主的普世价值，都包含着胡适在《儒教的使命》所说的"哲学""科学"以及"道德生活"之三个因素，故而正好对应儒教死亡时代之儒家命运的两难状态及悖论情况。

在这种意义来讲，《儒教的使命》的主旨便是探究《说儒》思想内容之际的最好注脚。

---

① 《胡适文集》12，第297—300页。

近二十年来台湾的"东亚儒学"研究取向与发展特色

张崑将[*]

一 前言

  本论文所谓的"东亚儒学"乃特指近二十年以来台湾学者对跨国、跨文化的韩国儒学、日本儒学、越南儒学的相关研究,并不涉及对"中国儒学"的研究回顾,因这方面的研究远超出韩日越的儒学研究。1987年"解严"以前,台湾学术界有关儒学的研究,主要还是关注中国的儒学研究,对于东亚儒学的韩国、日本、越南的研究,可说是凤毛麟角,高明士教授早在 1984 年即撰有《唐代东亚教育圈的形成:东亚世界形成史的一个侧面》,此书是作者累积十年,从 1973 年以来分别在日本、韩国潜心研究的博士论文成果。此书从教育史的角度论述"东亚文化圈",认为东亚传统教育史的要素,不外礼与法,礼指学礼,包含礼仪、思想甚至宗教等要素;法指法制,即律令制,学制及含括在学令。高明士在此书中更区分东亚文化圈的五项要素:汉字、儒教、律令、中国的科技、中国化的佛教,以此展开作者的东亚文化圈的形成论述。[①] 其中涉及"儒学"一项,可谓着其先鞭。
  "东亚儒学"在台湾作为学术会议议题,滥觞于 1992 年 9 月由台湾清华大学与日本大阪大学合作举办了的"东亚儒学与近代国际研讨会",此后有关跨文化视野的儒学研究计画在中央研究院文哲研究所(当时为

---

  [*] 张崑将,台湾师范大学东亚学系教授。
  [①] 高明士:《唐代东亚教育圈的形成:东亚世界形成史的一个侧面》,台北:"国立"编译馆,1984 年。

筹备处）及台湾大学的研究计画或合作或分别推动。1998 年更是时机成熟，以"东亚儒学"为课题，而且提出大型研究计画，开启此一领域的研究风潮者，当属台湾大学黄俊杰教授领道的学术团队及中研院文哲所的多项研究计画，将近二十年来成果斐然。自从 1998 年起由台湾大学所推动的《中国文化的经典诠释传统研究计画》（1998—2000）、《东亚近世儒学中的经典诠释传统研究计画》（2000—2004），《东亚文明研究中心计画》（2002—2005），并在 2006 年开始由台湾大学人文社会高等研究院推行《东亚经典与文化研究计画》（2006—2010）以及《东亚儒学研究计画》（2011—2016），结合校内外、国内外许多学者专家进行研究，迄今已超过 17 年，终得累积丰硕之成果，陆续由台湾大学出版中心印行，共出版专书近两百部，依性质分为《东亚文明研究丛书》、《东亚儒学研究资料丛书》、《东亚儒学研究丛书》等书系。这项有关"东亚儒学"的研究计画，主要系以东亚为研究之视野，以经典为研究之核心，以文化为研究之脉络，既宏观东西文化交流，又聚焦东亚各地文化之互动。显然以"东亚区域""儒家经典""东亚文化"三大主轴作为研究核心，聚焦"东亚儒学"的研究。有关以上研究计画，黄俊杰教授曾在 2007 年发表的《东亚儒家经典诠释传统研究的现况及其展望》一文中，特针对"经典诠释传统"的重点进行过研究回顾与整理①，本文在不重复其研究成果下，介绍在此之后相关重要的研究成果，同时在"经典诠释"以外，也看到诸多研究趋势及特色。

"东亚儒学"的研究计画迄今所出版近 200 本专著中，中国儒学亦占不少比例，即便书名有关"东亚儒学"或"朝鲜儒学""日本儒学"等等，由于儒学的母体根源及大量的诠释作品还是来自中国儒者，故仍不能逃于中国儒学之领域，与之进行互为比较，始能见其特色。揆诸近二十年来有关台湾的东亚儒学研究专书不下五十册，论文更是不计其数，本研究不可能全部回顾，仅针对几项研究重要趋势，择其代表性作品及相关研究者进行简略归纳与分析。

---

① 参见黄俊杰《东亚儒家经典诠释传统研究的现况及其展望》，收入氏著《东亚儒学：经典与诠释的辩证》（台北：台大出版中心，2007）之第三章，第 57—129 页。

二 东亚儒学的研究趋势

《东亚文明研究丛书》从 2004 年第 1 本《东亚儒学的新视野》问世以来，迄今也超过 100 本，其中有关本文东亚儒学课题有以下 32 本，其他大部分专书多以中国儒学或思想研究，此处仅就日、韩相关的儒学研究成果进行归类与分析。

表 1　　《东亚文明研究丛书》有关"东亚儒学"专书表

序号	出版年代	作者与书名	序号	出版年代	作者与书名
1.	2004	黄俊杰：《东亚儒学的新视野》	17.	2006	黄俊杰：《德川日本《论语》诠释史论》
2.	2004	高明士：《东亚古代的政治与教育》	18.	2005	黄俊杰编：《东亚儒者的四书诠释》
3.	2004	张昆将《德川日本"忠""孝"概念的形成与发展——以兵学与阳明学为中心》	19.	2005	辻本雅史：《日本德川时代的教育思想和媒体》
4.	2004	子安宣邦著、陈玮芬译：《东亚儒学：批判与方法》	20.	2006	黄俊杰编：《东亚视域中的茶山学与朝鲜儒学》
5.	2004	黄俊杰编：《中日四书诠释传统初探》（上、下）	21.	2006	《东亚历史上的天下与中国概念》
6.	2004	张宝三、徐兴庆合编：《德川时代日本儒学史论集》	22.	2006	黄俊杰、林维杰编：《东亚朱子学的同调与异趣》
7.	2004	张昆将：《日本德川时代古学派的王道政治论：以伊藤仁斋、荻生徂徕为中心》	23.	2007	黄俊杰：《东亚儒学：经典与诠释的辩证》
8.	2005	高明士编：《东亚文化圈的形成与发展——儒家思想篇》	24.	2007	张昆将《德川日本儒学思想的特质：神道、徂徕学与阳明学》
9.	2005	李明辉：《四端与七情：关于道德情感的比较哲学探讨》	25.	2007	高明士：《东亚传统教育与法文化》
10.	2005	黄俊杰编：《东亚儒学研究的回顾与展望》	26.	2008	徐兴庆编：《朱舜水与东亚文化传播的世界》
11.	2005	陈玮芬：《近代日本汉学的"关键词"研究：儒学及相关概念的嬗变》	27.	2008	徐兴庆编：《东亚文化交流与经典诠释》

续表

序号	出版年代	作者与书名	序号	出版年代	作者与书名
12.	2005	高明士：《东亚传统教育与学礼学规》	28.	2009	叶国良、徐兴庆编：《江户时代日本汉学研究诸面向：思想文化篇》
13.	2005	杨祖汉：《从当代儒学观点看韩国儒学的重要论争》	29.	2008	韩东育：《从"脱儒"到"脱亚"——日本近世以来"去中心化"之思想过程》
14.	2005	张宝三、杨儒宾合编：《日本汉学研究续探：思想文化篇》	30.	2009	林鸿信：《基督宗教与东亚儒学的对话：以信仰与道德的分际为中心》
15.	2005	高明士编：《东亚传统家礼、教育与国法（一）：家礼、家族与教育》	31.	2011	林鸿信编：《跨文化视野中的人文精神：儒、佛、耶、犹的观点与对话刍议》
16.	2005	郑仁在、黄俊杰合编：《韩国江华阳明学研究论集》	32.	2015	蔡振丰、林永强、张政远编：《东亚视野下的日本哲学——传统、现代与转化》

说明：2004年之所以有如此多的专书出现，事实上从2001年开始即分别出版于喜马拉雅基金会，之后有关东亚儒学研究计画丛书，在台大出版中心成立后，全数移转到台大出版中心。

另外，台大高研院《东亚儒学研究丛书》自2009年出版第一本《东亚论语学》以来，迄今为止已有22本，兹罗列如下：

表2　　　　　　　　《东亚儒学研究丛书》专书表

序号	出版年代	作者与书名	序号	出版年代	作者与书名
1.	2009	黄俊杰编：《东亚论语学：中国篇》	12.	2012	黄丽生编：边缘儒学与非汉儒学：《东亚儒学的比较视野（17—20世纪）》
2.	2009	张昆将编：《东亚论语学：韩日篇》	13.	2012	田世民：《近世日本儒礼实践的研究：以儒家知识人对〈朱子家礼〉的思想实践为中心》
3.	2009	蔡振丰编：《东亚朱子学的诠释与发展》	14.	2012	黄丽生编：《东亚客家文化圈中的儒学与教育》
4.	2009	黄俊杰编：《东亚儒学视域中的徐复观及其思想》	15.	2012	黄俊杰编：《朝鲜儒者对儒家传统的解释》

续表

序号	出版年代	作者与书名	序号	出版年代	作者与书名
5.	2010	蔡振丰：《朝鲜儒者丁若镛的四书学——以东亚为视野的讨论》	16.	2012	徐兴庆编：《朱舜水与近世日本儒学的发展》
6.	2010	黄丽生：《边缘与非汉——儒学及其非主流传播》	17.	2013	任剑涛：《复调儒学——从古典解释到现代性探究》
7.	2010	林月惠：《异曲同调—朱子学与朝鲜性理学》	18.	2013	高明士编：《中华法系与儒家思想》
8.	2010	黄俊傑：《东亚文化交流中的儒家经典与理念：互动转化与融合》	19.	2014	金泳植：《科学与东亚儒家传统》
9.	2011	藤井伦明：《朱熹思想结构探索——以"理"为考察中心》	20.	2014	黄俊傑：《儒家思想与中国历史思维》
10.	2011	张昆将：《阳明学在东亚：诠释、交流与行动》	21.	2015	林月惠、李明辉编：《高桥亨与韩国儒学研究》
11.	2011	崔在穆著、钱明译：《东亚阳明学的展开》	22.	2015	黄俊傑编：《东亚视域中孔子的形象与思想》

从以上诸书的研究，约略可归类七项研究趋势：

（1）东亚四书学与经典诠释

《四书》之名，成于宋代二程，阐述义蕴，发挥精微，朱熹为之集注而集其大成。元明以来，科举取士，先《四书》而后《五经》，奉朱子理学及朱注《四书》为圭臬，四书学乃成为一股思想潮流，更影响近邻的朝鲜、日本，使东亚汉字文化圈笼罩在朱子理学与四书学的典范中，迄于19世纪末，长达六百年之久。因此，四书学向来为东亚研究关心的核心课题之一，以往的研究大都扣紧中国学者对四书的解释研究，不太了解韩国、日本名儒对于四书的独特解释。黄俊傑教授于2005所集编的《东亚儒者的四书诠释》及2006年的专著《德川日本〈论语〉诠释史论》二书可谓开风气之先，接着2009年又编有《东亚论语学：中国篇》及张昆将编《东亚论语学：韩日篇》。此外，蔡振丰2010年更有专著《朝鲜儒者丁若镛的四书学——以东亚为视野的讨论》。以下简述以上各书的重点研究。

黄俊傑教授所集编的《东亚儒者的四书诠释》，汇编了中国台湾及韩国、日本等学者的四书学研究。在日本方面，有从德川出版媒体的观点讨论德川时代儒者对四书学的吸收与对抗（作者辻本雅史）；关注的学派对象有德川时代古学派伊藤仁斋（作者平石直昭）、荻生徂徕（作者泽井启一）、山崎暗斋学派（作者田世民）、自然思想家安藤昌益（作者张昆将）；韩国方面，则扣紧朝鲜朱子学派以外的阳明学派（作者杨祖汉）以及实学派之集大成者丁若镛（作者蔡振丰）。

综而言之，本次会议关于四书学之议题，在中国四书学的研究方面比较偏重清代学者以及与当代学者的对话；日本四书学研究方面则比较偏重于日本古学派伊藤仁斋与荻生徂徕的儒学研究与解释；朝鲜儒学方面，则关注到平常台湾学界忽视的两位儒者，一是阳明学者郑霞谷，一是实学派的丁若镛，二者都不是在朝鲜朱子学正统之内的两位学者。本书局限在于对于朝鲜朱子学派大家（如李退溪、李栗谷等）的四书学解释之特色，乃至日本古学派以外（如朱子学派、阳明学派、怀德堂朱子学派等）等等，显然讨论与研究不足，都有待从微观的角度，个别地从单方面入手。除此之外，也应从宏观的视野，注意四书学作为中日韩彼此的同异或传承关系，如本书中辻本雅史教授即以出版媒体的观点关注从中国晚明的四书学著作传到日本后，分析日本四书学的兴盛与衰弱之过程；再如蔡振丰教授比较韩国丁若镛与日本古学派伊藤仁斋的《中庸》思想的解释。凡此种种，都是从自国的四书学，关注到与东亚其他国家四书学之关系，以思想比较或出版著作的传承方式，来探索自国与他国四书学之关系。以上微观与宏观之视野应同时并进。此外，本书开创了一个"东亚四书学"的概念，是相当值得开发的新概念，以证成东亚过去在儒学的世界中有自成一格的文化系统。

其次，黄俊傑教授专著《德川日本〈论语〉诠释史论》，全书分"导论""分论""个论"与"结论""附论"，共计十章，皆是环绕日本儒者的经典解释学与《论语》的解释。"导论"即破题引出中日儒家从"社会政治的内涵""形上学的内涵"与"心性论的内涵"三个面向与其互相依存的关系来界定"经典性"。接着，第二章分析中日经典解释中的"脉络性转换"的特殊性问题；"分论"提出日本古学派鸿儒伊藤仁斋之"作为护教学"与荻生徂徕"作为政治论述"的经典诠释两类型；"个论"分析日本儒者对《论语》的"学而时习之"、"吾道一以贯之"、"五十知天命"等三章的解释特色；"结论"从"实学"角度，提出日本脉络下的儒家经典诠释在东亚儒学的特质。"附论"分析被称为"日本近代化之父"的涩泽荣一对《论语》的解释特色。本书至少有以下两大特色与学术贡献,其一是华人学术界中第一本最有深度地探讨日本儒者有关《论语》这部经典的诠释史论。长期以来,华人学术界对于日本儒学的研究,侧重介绍日本儒学研究的发展(如王家骅的《日中儒学的比较》、朱谦之的《日本的古学及阳明学》等),或单一学派之研究(如朱谦之的《日本的朱子学》),较无法综观全局及深入地探讨日本儒学之特殊性。作者这部书则从中日韩最重视的《论语》这部儒家经典,以诠释史的观点,并且扩及朝鲜儒学,不仅补足了中日儒学比较研究的不足,更打开了东亚儒学研究方法论的先河。

该书第二个特点是对于中日韩儒学的比较研究,开拓了更广度与深度的研究视野。我们都知道日本人做了许多相关《论语》的研究,从早期的武内义雄《论语之研究》(1939)、宇野哲人的《论语》(1963)及四书的研究、竹添光鸿的《论语会笺》(1934)、金谷治译注《论语》及孔子的研究等,均不乏有中国的《论语》解释研究,也有一些日本国内学者对德川时代做过个别的《论语》经学上之研究。但作者该书不仅是涉足日本《论语》的解释研究而已,尚且更广泛地涉足中国、韩国的《论语》学研究,深入经学与史学之比较。作者分析缜密,不仅娴熟地运用中日韩之儒家经典文献,同时也提出许多比较思想方法论之特色,打破了经典研究只重视本国文献与资料之单面向研究,为东亚儒学研究开发了新视野。

再者,蔡振丰专著《朝鲜儒者丁若镛的四书学——以东亚为视野的讨论》,以第一手的文本研究为主,深入进行朝实学大家丁若镛(茶山,1762—1836)四书学的细部诠释,及其整体理论架构的讨论。此书的研究成果有以下几项特色:就方法论的特色而言,该书第二章以"意义取向"及"义理取向"分别代表丁茶山与朱熹的四书诠释系统,深有见解,并以此方法论贯穿整部书,除在比较"方法"中亦能窥见其"方法论",使全书理路通畅,自成一格。此书亦甚具有宏观的比较视野之特色,作者对朝鲜儒学的发展及论争有相当深刻的掌握,在第一章尤见作者之学术功力,不仅清楚掌握朝鲜儒学之脉络及问题意识,还广泛涉及丁茶山与日本古学派思想之关系与比较,呈现宏观的东亚比较视野。这与向来学者只注意在韩国本身看茶山学,或是只作日、韩或关注中、韩的茶山学之研究比较起来,有其相当的突破性,换言之,此书许多篇幅处理了丁茶山与日本古学派之关系与比较,同时作者本人对中国儒家经典亦相当娴熟,故四书学在其中日韩的宏观比较视野下，不仅相当深刻地呈现出茶山对照于中国朱子学的诠释取向，也对比了日本古学派反朱子学的诠释取向，从而开展独特诠释取向的"茶山学"，凸显"茶山学"在东亚儒学思想史发展的特殊地位。此外，该书亦兼及丁若镛对西学的受容情形、丁若镛思想中的近代意识及其所形成的朝鲜中华主义等问题。

最后，张昆将所汇编《东亚论语学：韩日篇》是《东亚论语学：中国篇》的姊妹作品。此书所收论文共计十五篇，朝鲜《论语》学中分别有朱子学派（如李退溪、崔象龙）、实学派（如丁茶山）、阳明学派（如郑齐斗）等七篇论文，虽无法涵盖整个朝鲜的《论语》学，但所研究的对象均是各学派重要代表人物的《论语》思想，颇可一窥朝鲜《论语》学之特色。至于日本《论语》学，亦有阳明学派（如中江藤树）、古学派（如伊藤仁斋、伊藤东涯）、古文辞学派（荻生徂徕、龟井南冥）、折衷学派（如片山兼山），乃至有国学派的铃木朖（1764—1837）等共八篇论文，涉及学派颇多，但所研究人物亦皆一时之选，故亦可呈现江户时代《论语》学发展的多元面貌。该书以韩日为主的论文中，聚焦于五项主题：（1）比较《论语》的重要篇章或价值理念在东亚各国儒者解释的同调与异趣。如本书收入《丁茶山〈论语〉诠释中的"仁""心""性""天"及其理论意义》及《〈论语〉诠释的两种类型——以朱子与丁若镛的诠释为例》二文属之。（2）将"东亚论语学"作为东亚思想发展的过程，而不是仅作为思想发展的结果。依黄俊傑教授的说法，所谓"作为思想发展过程的东亚《论语》学"的研究兼摄以下二义：其一是分析《论语》学的发展过程中，所呈现的东亚各地域与时代之思想特质与思想倾向；其二是运用新资料，探讨重要儒者如朱子（1130—1200）、李退溪（1502—1571）、荻生徂徕（1666—1728）、伊藤仁斋等的《论语》学在东亚扩散发展之过程。该书所收韩日各篇论文，都触及这个主题。（3）挖掘东亚各国儒者未被广泛刊行或出版的孔子（551—479B.C.）或《论语》之解释作品，加以分析并解释其特色，如该书收录《铃木朖的〈论语〉解释》及《片山兼山遗教〈论语一贯〉的解释特色》、《金仁存之〈论语新义〉考—北宋"新学"对高丽中期儒学的影响》三文属之。（4）孔子的形象、祭典、神话在东亚各国历代的转变与涵义，如收入在本书的《江户日本儒礼实践的〈论语〉》即属此类。（5）注意将《论语》视为宗教的解释特色，这类主题在《中国篇》多有触及，《韩日篇》则比较缺乏，未来韩日的《论语》学，可多朝这项主题加以开发。

（2）朝鲜朱子学

朝鲜朱子学应该是作为"东亚朱子学"研究的一环，2009年蔡振丰即编有《东亚朱子学的诠释与发展》一书，八篇中就有三篇朝鲜儒学的论文，比例最高。同时，相较于以下所要回顾的朝鲜儒学出版的三本专书而言，朝鲜儒学有自成一项研究趋势的特色，故以下以此三本回顾为主。

朝鲜王朝（1392—1910）时代，朱子学蔚为主流，流衍甚广。台湾最早研究朝鲜儒学的是蔡茂松[①]，2000年后近年来在朝鲜朱子学发表论著较多的是李明辉、杨祖汉与林月惠，对于朝鲜儒学的研究取得突破性的发展，分别出版了《四端与七情：关于道德情感的比较哲学探讨》《从当代儒学观点看韩国儒学的重要论争》《异曲与同调：朱子学与朝鲜性理学》，可以这样说，公元2000年以后台湾的韩国儒学研究迈向一个成果丰硕时期，摆脱过去只限于语言或文学研究者片面地认识朝鲜儒学的研究局限，直从哲学的或思想的高度与深度探索朝鲜儒学，更赢得韩国思想与哲学界的重视。以下针对三位学者的代表作，进行简略回顾与评论。

首先，李明辉《四端与七情：关于道德情感的比较哲学探讨》一书，一如书名一样，针对朝儒最重要的"四端七情"哲学论争，从一个比较哲学的视角，既有中西哲学比较，又有中韩哲学比较。全书分八章，可以区分四部分，第一部份"道论"引出"四端七情"问题与德国伦理学的发展，第二部分梳理德国伦理学论争，釐清德国现象学伦理学对康德伦理学之批判与修正，以此连结到四端七情论辨议题的相关意义。第三部分处理中国朱子学及刘蕺山理气论异同的问题。有了前面中西哲学的基础，第四部分才直探朝鲜的四七论辨，涉及李退溪、奇高峰、李栗谷、成牛溪的四七论与理气论的哲学比较问题。李明辉这部书至少指出以下学界难以突破的观点：其一是李退溪对"四端之心"的诠释较合乎孟子的文本，但他为了迁就朱子的义理间架而摇摆不定。奇高峰则是根据朱子的义理间架来质疑李退溪的诠释，但也沿袭了朱子对孟子文本的曲解。其二是认为退

[①] 蔡茂松：《韩儒丁茶山及反朱学内容之研究》，《成功大学历史学系历史学报》，第4号，1977—6，第131—172页。作者指出茶山的学问，强调实学，他的道德伦理学，是中性心体而加以求善行事以成德。主张仁义外在，不在心内。也不是一个由体而用、体用俱全的哲学间架，作者指出这些都是茶山反朱学的主要原因。这篇文章中，作者很详尽地分析茶山反朱学的思想内涵，使我们看到李氏朝鲜还有旗帜鲜明的反朱子学之印象。

溪的理气论对于阳明学有所误解，但他对朱子思想的创造性的解释，却与阳明学思想暗合，如他主张四端（仁义礼智）与七情（喜怒哀乐爱恶欲）为异质，承认理具有活动性，而四端即是理本身的活动，这都与朱子思想脱逸，与阳明学不谋而合，因为阳明的"心即理"说同时包含"理具有活动性"与"四端与七情异质"这两点。从此观点视之，退溪与阳明二者到底是思想的对手或是同道，相当清楚。作者由此间接论议阳明学在韩国始终不发达的原因，与李退溪对朱子学的"创造性诠释"有很大的关联。显然，要得出退溪学与朱子学的关键差异，若不能从哲学思想的比较视野，根本不可能看出二者的关键差别，可见退溪学不能仅就朝鲜儒学本身观之。就笔者所知，退溪著作亦传到德川日本，已见儒者如山崎暗斋（1618—1682）及其弟子论之，并鲜明地引退溪之论排斥阳明学，而阳明学在德川日本的17世纪末与18世纪中期，也是衰弱不振的年代，与退溪排斥阳明学著作的思想传入是否有关，尚待进一步观察。因此，退溪学若能就东亚学术思想史的视野观之，则更能证成李明辉之观点。

其次，杨祖汉《从当代儒学观点看韩国儒学的重要论争》一书，累积作者多年研究成果，扣紧朝鲜儒学三大论争，即"无极太极之辨""四端七情之辨"及"湖洛论争"。"无极太极之辨"是朝鲜的第一次有关儒家哲学的重要辩论。杨祖汉对相当文献进行深入疏释，认为李晦斋对朱子思想的理解颇为正确，表现了朱子思想的某些特色，而与李晦斋辩论之曹汉辅，则有陆王哲学的思想倾向。同时，关于四七之辨，杨祖汉更能从李退溪晚年提出的"理到"说，确认李退溪主张"理"这个概念具有活动性。从金沙溪与郑愚伏对"理到说"的论辩之中，杨祖汉认为李退溪、郑愚伏一系与李栗谷、金沙溪一系之思想型态确有不同，而这种不同之关键就在于"理"是否具有活动性之上。杨祖汉认为，如果肯定孟子所说的"四端"是纯粹至善的，则"理"便必有其活动性；而如果"理"有其活动性，则必可肯定逆觉本心之工夫；而由于有这种工夫，儒家内圣之学与成德之教乃有真实之根据。作者此点分析可以说更能证成李明辉的四七论中所言退溪何以理气论何以与朱子歧出，却又能包容阳明学之理由。该书在四七论基础下，又衍生出曹南冥有关"下学而上达"论的诠释。作者指出曹南冥对李退溪与奇高峰关于"四端七情"之辩论，表示不以为然，更斥奇高峰为欺世盗名。曹南冥认为谈论天理，必须以能孝弟、尽伦常之道为前提。曹南冥一生重视进退出处，不肯曲学阿世，很能表现儒家重践履、重视人之行为品格之特色。曹南冥之论亦显示了当时韩儒对四、七之辩的另类评论。杨祖汉在本文中亦比较曹南冥、顾炎武及朱子对"下学而上达"的诠释,并且探讨孔子言下学上达的原义。同时,此书涉及的第三论争是"湖洛论争",主要聚焦于"人性物性异同论"的论争,起于18世纪两位代表人物,一是主张人性物性相异,及未发时心体有善恶的韩元震(1682—1751),另一是主张人性物性相同,及未发时心体纯善的李柬(1677—1727),二人各有支持者,迄今学术界仍争议不已。此一论争涉及朱子学的宇宙论及心性论之问题,在中国虽偶有学者触及,但未如朝儒详细并引起学派论争,并能激起相当哲学意味的讨论。

再次,林月惠《异曲与同调:朱子学与朝鲜性理学》一书,针对朝鲜性理学的发展、诠释特色、论争议题等做出比较完整性的分析。本书至少有两大特色,其一,对于朝鲜性理学思想争议的源流,往往能探其源流,并加以比较,以窥其同异,特别对于罗整庵思想对朝儒李退溪思想的异同比较。其二,对于朝鲜性理学有关朱子关键概念的诠释,如"理气论"、"四端七情"、"格物、物格、理到"、"人心道心"等思想议题,亦有详尽的分析,特别在"人心道心"思想议题上就有四章的分析,作者追溯明儒罗整庵的人心道心之说,及罗整庵著作引起朝儒的"人心道心"论争,并专章处理李退溪与李栗谷的"人心道心",堪称将"人心道心"论争之源流、比较、辨析与发展,处理得最为详尽,分析得最有体系。本书最后有附录整理中国台湾、内地有关韩国儒学的研究书目,以及韩国近五年的韩国儒学研究书目,对于学界掌握最近的韩国儒学研究动态,相当有帮助。

(3)东亚阳明学

21世纪的阳明学研究,除了探索各自阳明学的特色以外,更应寻求一跨国界、跨文化的彼此交流与合作,由散发而汇流,积单一为会通,从东亚出发以开发阳明学在21世纪的新意义。目前以"东亚"的比较视野来看待阳明学的发展,仍江山有待,但也有某些学者已开始从事这样的研究尝试,在韩国有崔在穆的《东アジア阳明学の展开》(2006年)一书,在日本则有荻生茂博的《近代・アジア・阳明学》(2008年)出版,在中国台湾则有张昆将的《阳明学在东亚:诠释、交流与行动》(2011年)。以下以简述三书之重点。

2006年崔在穆的《东アジア阳明学の展开》一书,着眼于阳明学在

东亚三地域的继承与发展，选择三地域的代表性阳明学者，比较其内在论理的构成关系及其展开。这些内在理论包括以下五部分：（1）"良知体用论与良知现成论的屈折与展开"，作者比较了中国的王畿与王艮、韩国的崔鸣吉与郑齐斗、日本的中江藤树与大塩中斋之良知体用论。（2）是"万物一体论的展开"，崔在穆比较了王阳明、韩国的崔鸣吉、日本的中江藤树与大塩中斋之万物一体论。（3）是"人欲论的展开"，作者选择了中国的梁汝元与李贽、韩国的许筠与郑齐斗、日本的中江藤树与大塩中斋之人欲论。（4）是"权道论的展开"则选择比较了中国王畿与李贽，韩国的崔鸣吉、张维与郑齐斗，日本的中江藤树与熊泽蕃山等人的权道论。（5）是"三教一致论"，作者选择了王畿、与李贽、韩国的许筠与郑齐斗、日本的中江藤树。由上述五内容约可窥知，作者集中在王学左派如王畿、王艮、李贽，韩国集中在崔鸣吉与郑齐斗，日本则集中在中江藤树与大塩中斋等阳明学的内在理路思想。①

2008年荻生茂博专著《近代・アジア・阳明学》（东京：ぺりかん社，2008年）一书，系由生前好友汇集成书，内容多涉及日本阳明学及中日阳明学的比较研究，亦有一篇韩国阳明学的研究。这里着重介绍其中日或日韩阳明学的比较研究之文章，集中在第三部分"アジアの近代と阳明学"之四篇文章：有《幕末・明治の阳明学と明清思想史》、《近代における阳明学研究と石崎东国の大阪阳明学会》、《日本における〈近代阳明学〉の成立：东アジアの〈近代阳明学〉（Ⅰ）》及《崔南善の日本体验と〈少年〉の出发：东アジアの〈近代阳明学〉（Ⅲ）》，前三章涉及中日阳明学的比较交流之关系研究，从幕末阳明学者与明清儒者的交流关系，大量着墨于大塩中斋的著作与明清思想家的交流关系，从而反省近代日本与中国维新与革命分子借阳明学与明治维新的原动力之意识型态，从事推动国民或国家精神道德之近代文化性格之问题，这些观点可与该书第六章《近代中日阳明学的发展关系及其形象比较》合观。最后一章则考察一位短期留日的韩国近代知识分子崔南善（1890—1956）受到当时日本阳明学风潮与亡日的梁启超办报之影响，回国后办《少年》杂志（1908年11月），鼓吹西学，该杂志成为韩国近代杂志的滥觞，荻生

---

① 崔在穆的《东アジア阳明学の展开》（东京：ぺりかん社，2006年）一书，此书后来经钱明教授翻译，在台湾台大出版中心出版，收入《东亚儒学研究丛书》，2011年出版。

氏主要考察崔南善此一短期留学的日本体验对其思想的冲击与影响。① 综而言之，荻生氏的研究相较于上述崔在穆的研究，相当重视东亚三国家的"近代阳明学"之发展关系与性格之比较，荻生氏本有一系列有关韩国与中国近代阳明学之研究计画，惜于2006年2月英年早逝，殊为学界所痛惜。

接着，2011年张昆将出版《阳明学在东亚：诠释、交流与行动》，区分"诠释篇""交流篇"与"行动篇"三个主题。首先在"诠释"方面，第二章"东亚阳明学者对《知言养气》章的解释之比较"是透过比较王门后学对《知言养气》章的解释，选择中国的王龙溪（1498—1583）、朝鲜的郑霞谷（1649—1736）及日本的山田方谷（1805—1877）等三位阳明学者，探讨阳明学在东亚的多元性与特殊性。另外，第三章"吉田松阴对孟子学的诠释特质与其批判"涉及《讲孟馀话》与《孟子》经典的解释比较问题，所以事实上也是中日经典文化比较的论文。其次在该书第四、五章的"交流篇"中，或透过中韩阳明学之比较，或将中日阳明学加以对勘，希冀呈现阳明学在中日韩交流的鲜明特色。本书第三个主题是有关阳明学的"行动篇"，在第六章"近代中日阳明学的发展及其形象比较"中比较了近代以来阳明学在中日知识份子之间，往往与国家主义或爱国主义纠缠不清，在利用阳明学的不同手段下，存有颇不相同的阳明学形象，也造成阳明学在中日之间的不同发展。第七章"东亚阳明学与维新革命"，则特别扣紧日本与韩国中具有革命行动精神的阳明学代表人物，阐释阳明学在东亚的维新与革命之特色。张昆将此书各章之论述，并不局限于一国、一文化或一思想家之分析，而以阳明学为共同公分母，或作中韩之比较，或以中日之对比，乃至将中日韩阳明学置于同一平台加以比较，透过跨文化的视野，呈显东亚阳明学互动与交流的文化轮廓。此书有心于使阳明学超越一国的平面视野，透过彼此文化、思想与脉络的比较，呈现阳明学在异国间成为立体的角度与视野，抉发值得深入探索的新议题与新意义。

（4）东亚教育史

1987年解严以前，台湾学术界有关儒学的研究，主要还是关注中国的儒学研究，对于东亚儒学的韩国、日本、越南研究，可说是凤毛麟角，

---

① 荻生茂博的《近代・アジア・阳明学》（东京：ぺりかん社，2008年）。

高明士教授专从"东亚文化圈"的角度，其中涉及"儒学"一项，可谓著其先鞭。

台湾最早将"东亚"作为一个研究整体，且能窥其同异者，当属高明士教授。高明士早在 1984 年即撰有《唐代东亚教育圈的形成：东亚世界形成史的一个侧面》①，此书是作者累积十年，从 1973 年以来分别在日本、韩国潜心研究的博士论文成果。此书特从"教育史"的角度论述"东亚文化圈"，认为东亚传统教育史的要素，不外礼与法，礼指学礼，包含礼仪、思想甚至宗教等要素；法指法制，即律令制，学制及含括在学令。高明士在此书中更区分东亚文化圈的五项要素：汉字、儒教、律令、中国的科技、中国化的佛教，以此展开作者的东亚文化圈的形成论述。高明士在此书特别着重教育史的"变"与"常"，批判一些西方学者因过份着重强调历史之"常"，而认为东方传统社会是"停滞"的。因此，高明士在《序言》即重新检讨以往学者对中国文化的传播，都以"影响"的角度来说明者，因为所谓"影响"是常侧重于优势文化单方向的输入，对于对方"自主采择"的情况多所忽略，由此高明士的"东亚文化圈"的形成，既关注中国文化普遍性所特强调维持"天下秩序"的"常"，也注意诸国主动摄取的"变"，特别在诸国主动摄取中国文化这一点，强调东亚世界在近代以前不但是一个整体，而且是一个有机体，彼此息息相关，牵一发而动全身。高明士在上述的"由变中求常"的方法论研究基础上，我们举他对东亚儒学的孔庙祭祀而言，高明士指出韩国从高丽到李朝时代，先后以本国十八贤入祀圣庙，越南到陈朝有三贤入祀圣庙，日本诸藩校也有本国圣哲入祀圣庙，这种共同以本国圣哲入祀圣庙，可说是庙学制成圣教育之进一步的发扬，东亚传统教育共同诸特质中，令人注目者，莫过于此。② 高明士的研究既能注意日韩越三国在吸收中国儒学之"同"，亦颇能关注到其"异"的特殊现象。

近几年来，透过台湾大学《东亚文明研究丛书》的出版，高明士将多年研究的成果，一一整理出版《东亚传统教育与法制研究（一）：教育与政治社会》及《东亚传统教育与法制研究（二）：唐律诸问题》，两册共收十七篇论文，就其内容而言，包括讨论法律教育、华文教育、儒家教

---

① 高明士：《唐代东亚教育圈的形成：东亚世界形成史的一个侧面》，台北：国立编译馆，1984 年。

② 高明士：《唐代东亚教育圈的形成》，第三章"越南古代的学校教育"，第 407—444 页。

育思想、法律与政治社会，以及唐律诸问题，可谓具有多角度探讨传统教育与法制诸问题，在中国大陆知识界引起广大的回响。高明士并在2003年主编了《东亚文化圈的形成与发展：儒学篇》及《东亚文化圈的形成与发展：政治法制篇》两书①，从东亚视野出发，颇与黄俊傑教授所推动的"东亚儒学"的相关研究计画互相辉映。

揆诸越南儒学的研究，台湾学界自20世纪60年代除有少数学者关心以外，可谓后继无人，除高明士比较有体系化的深入研究以外，余者尚停留于早期的介绍阶段，较少注意韩、日、越南各自儒学的特色。因而对越南儒学的理解仍处于草昧朦胧的阶段。比起今日韩、日儒学的研究，越南儒学有极待耕耘的空间。此外，战后初期的东亚儒学研究，比较少关注内在义理的比较，这方面乃在20世纪90年代兴起，至今方兴未艾。

（5）东亚儒学人物思想与形象交流

东亚儒学交流人物何其多，但要成为跨国文化交流且有思想专著并具有影响力的思想人物者，并有学者进行专门比较研究者并不多见。本节从丛书中挑选出孔子形象、影响日本的朱舜水（1600—1682），以及影响韩国儒学近代解释的高桥亨（1878—1967）作为代表人物，进行以下回顾与分析。

首先，黄俊傑在2015年新编《东亚视域中孔子的形象与思想》一书，收有11篇论文、外加2篇附录，在正文收录的分别有"中国篇"5篇，"日本篇"4篇，"韩越篇"2篇，中国篇分别涉及战国至汉初的孔子形象、乐道者的孔子形象、觉浪道盛与方以智的孔子观以及西藏文化中的孔子形象等等；"日本篇"则有德川各派儒者的孔子形象、朱舜水的孔子形象、日本圣人观的孔子地位问题、服部宇之吉的孔教论等。"韩越篇"则有朝鲜君臣对话中的孔子与《论语》以及越儒范阮攸解释《论语》的孔子形象之分析。以上所收11篇，涉及佛教人物思想中的孔子，以及日本神道学中的孔子形象，甚至西藏文化中的孔子形象，显然孔子在其他宗教上有其固定被吸纳的地位与形象。其次，该书偏重近代以前的孔子形象，至于近代乃至当代的孔子形象的研究，显然还有待耕耘，该书的汇整只是个起始工作，其中朝鲜与越南丰富的孔子形象还值得进一步开发，尤

---

① 高明士主编：《东亚文化圈的形成与发展：儒学篇》、《东亚文化圈的形成与发展：政治法制篇》两书均由台湾大学历史学系出版，2003年，后亦收入台大出版中心的《东亚文明研究丛书》。

其是当代韩国。

　　其次,谈到东亚儒学中的交流思想家,必然提起漂洋渡日且影响日本儒学深远的朱舜水。2008 年徐兴庆将其累积多年的朱舜水研究成果,出版专著《朱舜水与东亚文化传播的世界》。作者指出在东亚内部的交流史过程中,明末清初文化讯息的异质流动是个极值得注意的现象,朱舜水则是促成此异质流动潮流中极值得注意的核心人物。朱舜水的思想,影响日本德川初期的产、官、学界极深,本书聚焦在朱舜水思想体系的整合研究,从其"经世致用"的理论主张、对佛教思想的批判作深入的探讨。本书同时以上述朱舜水的思想主张为主轴,从比较的观点,提出新的问题意识,检讨朱舜水与德川光国、安东省庵、隐元禅师、独立禅师、心越禅师、木下顺庵、雨森芳洲等人的思想异同,并指出朱舜水的儒教传播,对德川社会"前期水户学"的尊王关系与后期水户学的攘夷、倒幕及其与明治维新的关系作定位,拓展中日学界未曾探讨的新视野。

　　再者,有关近代日本高桥亨在韩国儒学界的影响与批判的研究。2015年由林月惠、李明辉主编的《高桥亨与韩国儒学研究》一书出版。该书出版缘由是高桥亨对朝鲜儒学的研究与解释框架存有不同的解读,经过台湾学者林月惠、李明辉的努力与召集,特在 2012 年邀集中国台湾地区、日本、韩国三方关心高桥亨的研究者,于台湾人文社会高等研究院召开"高桥亨与韩国儒学研究",会后并在 2015 年将会议论文集修正后汇整成书,于台大出版中心出版。

　　高桥亨这位日本跨越战前与战后、活跃于朝鲜思想研究领域的第一人,他以"主理派/主气派"之框架诠释朝鲜儒学史,影响甚大。本书即以高桥亨为焦点,对韩国儒学研究展开多元的对话与展望。该书以 2012 年"东亚视域中的韩国儒学研究"国际学术研讨会中所发表的论文为主,兼及此一议题的期刊论文,汇聚长期关注高桥亨与韩国儒学研究的韩国、日本及中国台湾等地学者之研究成果,以东亚儒学的视域,展开学术对话的宴飨。全书共收入韩国、日本及中国台湾等地学者的 11 篇论文,可说是此一议题的最新研究成果。该书在道论中提到,大多学者对于高桥亨以"主理派/主气派"来诠释韩国儒学史的解释框架,进行客观的评价与深入的批判。从后殖民的角度来看,唯有彻底清理并客观评价高桥亨的韩国儒学研究,才能摆脱其韩国儒学史的解释框架,凸显韩国儒学研究的主体性。犹有进者,更有学者或从朝鲜儒学的资源,或从比较哲学的视域,超越高桥亨的解释框架，展开新的思想冒险与哲学尝试，以活化韩国儒学研究。同时，本书着眼于韩国儒学研究的第二序反思，涉及对殖民地史观下的韩国儒学研究、其方法论与解释框架之批判，进而对韩国儒学研究提出新展望。总之，该书的出版，对于东亚学术界的贡献至少有以下三点：其一标示中国台湾对于韩国儒学研究的新进程，提升了中文学界的韩国儒学研究水准；其二是回应了韩国与日本学界的研究成果，显示中国台湾在韩国儒学研究上的开创性与开放性；其三是将日韩学界彼此之间少有交集的学者，透过会议交流及该书的完成出版，展现一个东亚学界平等对话、相互激荡的典范。

(6) 东西宗教对话

"东亚儒学"强调跨领域、跨学科、跨语言的人文精神，企图寻求自成一格的共同性核心价值，因此与西方宗教对话，也是必然发展的一项趋势，这套丛书著墨在东西宗教对话者，当属林鸿信。

林鸿信在 2009 年出版《基督宗教与东亚儒学的对话：以信仰与道德的分际为中心》，可以说是丛书中第一本有关东西宗教对话的专书。2011 年林鸿信又编《跨文化视野中的人文精神：儒、佛、耶、犹的观点与对话刍议》，区分东亚儒学篇、佛教篇、基督宗教篇、犹太教篇以及对话刍议篇五个部分，共收录九篇论文，由四大传统针对人文精神的主题提出论述，并且在发表中推动对话精神，以呈现跨文化视野的思维与丰富的人文精神内涵。此书与上一本的专著，堪称这套丛书有关东西或东亚宗教对话之双璧。本回顾以 2009 年的专著为主。

《基督宗教与东亚儒学的对话：以信仰与道德的分际为中心》一书主要采用 19 世纪基督宗教思想家齐克果强调宗教信仰之优先性的观点，作为东亚儒学传统之参照，以厘清信仰与道德之间的关系。此书共有正文七章及附录两篇，如黄俊杰在序中所说，此书通贯性的问题意识在于探讨"宗教信仰"与"伦理道德"两者之间既不可分离又互为紧张的关系。作者从孔学中的"天""天道""天命"等概念，指出儒学宗师孔子在伦理道德"有限性"的践履中体证了"无限性"的生命意义，而这无限性的生命意义又道引规范了有限者的存在，在此可见一种"从信仰到道德又从道德到信仰的循环"——从宗教性向道德性出发而又从道德性向宗教性回转。当有限之人面对无限之道时，弘道之人必自居于所弘之道下而不陷入"人大道小"的诱惑，由此而觉醒到尚有先行于人的存在者之宗教情操。因此，该书关怀"宗教信仰"应优先于"伦理道德"之观点出发，颇印证了龙树菩萨在《大智度论》中所说"信为能入，智为能度"，亦可作为东西宗教在信仰与伦理之间优先顺序的取舍态度。该书由此态度重新看待儒学的诸多重要概念，故多能对儒家宗教体验的"终极关怀"提出具有宗教性的新解，展现基于伦理道德实践之于已知与宗教信仰执著于未知，深入探讨与比较人文学与神学之间的相因相成关系。

(7) 东亚儒学中的关键概念史研究

许多儒学单位关键词，在同文化下本已有些诠释上的争议，但在异文化上的理解更加显题化与特殊化。近二十年来被研究者关注的儒学单位观念词语有"公"与"私"、"忠"与"孝"、"王道"与"皇道"、"天下"、"中华"……关注这项课题的研究者不少，黄俊杰、甘怀真、陈玮芬、童长义、张崑将的研究均有所触及，特别的是陈玮芬的关键词研究。

陈玮芬继其硕博士阶段对日本近代汉学有关的"斯文会"及"孔子教"的研究，近年来的研究，专在这些攸关时代转变的词语之诠释研究，于2005年将其多年来研究的论文汇集成《近代日本汉学的"关键词"研究：儒学及相关概念的嬗变》一书。诚如子安宣邦对这本书的序言提到："我发现如果着眼于近代日本汉学者对传统儒学语词的理解和阐释，以及该阐释与汉学者所处的历史语境之相关，更可以凸显儒学概念在近代日本思想界发生的作用，以及国粹主义、天皇体制、民族主义、与殖民主义之间复杂的辩证关系。"子安这里所提到的"历史语境"实牵涉到经典或古代学者的立说与当代学者的解释之间的内在交互作用之诠释问题，陈玮芬此书处理"东洋""东亚""西洋""支那""道""王道""皇道""天道""天命""国体""儒学""儒教""汉学""孔子教""支那学""忠孝""革命"等关键词语进行考察，将儒学经典当作东亚的思想基轴，进行儒学语词、概念的溯源；进而探讨"近世"与"近代"、"中国"与"日本"甚至"东洋"与"西洋"的思想联系，分析近代日本汉学者如何以儒家思想为基础，发展出独特的诠释；而后又如何投射到东亚其他地域，甚至反过头来影响中国。陈玮芬希望透过这样的过程，彰显近代汉学者在进行儒家概念的解释时呈现的"普遍性"与"特殊性"之间的张力，以及它们在"文化认同"与"政治认同"间取舍的张力。以下笔者针对台湾学者对儒学关键词这项课题的研究，稍介绍其研究成果。

1. "诚"与"实学"之关键词

童长义是长年研究日本江户儒学的先锋学者,他的硕士论文《江户儒学史的"诚"(まこと):以神儒交涉为中心》(1990年),以及博士论文《伊藤仁斋研究:以"实"概念为中心》(1999年),可以说是国内研究德川儒学具有厚实研究基础的开始者。童长义在《神儒交涉——江户儒学中"诚"的思想研究》指出在日本语言脉络中"まこと"的汉字,有"诚"、"实"、"真"、"纯"、"信"、"忠"、"谅"等字,并认为最实际可行而与"诚"字义训相近的字眼,莫如最重要的"忠信"德目,而"まこと"一词又往往与传统神道所特重的关键德行语,童长义由此一窥江户的神儒交涉的复杂关系。① 此外童长义在博士论文《伊藤仁斋研究:以"实"概念为中心》中指出,仁斋在面对程朱的"实学"、"实理"的意涵时,对于程朱对"实证"与"实感"之侧面视而不见,而放大了其中形上本体侧面的讨论比重,相当不满。因此仁斋在自己的议论中,把"实"字限定在最平实、最浅白的层次,广泛地制造词汇,几乎到了泛滥的地步,"实德""实心""实语""实说""实材""实智""实知""实见""实务""事实""实行"纷然杂出,几乎搜罗了宋元明以来诸儒文献当中出现过的实字头词,给予最平浅、最字面意义的意涵而使用着。②

2. "公""私"之关键词

"公"与"私"是近三十年来东西方政治哲学界及思想史学界对"公私领域"问题兴起一股研究的热潮。2005年《东亚文明研究丛书》出版江宜桦与黄俊杰共编之《公私领域新探:东亚与西方观点之比较》,此书是在2003年底与日本公共哲学会共动研究所携手合作举行国际学术研讨会,会后编辑成专书。该书分"东亚公共哲学的开展""东亚思想传统中的公与私"及"西方政治思想中的公与私"三部分,分别收录金来自中国内地、港台以及日本等东亚地区的十四篇文章。在此书的道言中,江宜桦如是简单摘要各篇论旨:第一个部分与"东亚公共哲学的开展"有关,计有金泰昌、山脇直司、顾肃、江宜桦等人所著之四篇论文。其中,金泰昌的论文力主以东亚文化资源中的"活私开公"取代"灭私奉公"的概

---

① 童长义:《江户儒学史的"诚"(まこと):以神儒交涉为中心》,硕士学位论文,台湾大学,1990年。
② 童长义:《伊藤仁斋研究:以"实"概念为中心》,博士学位论文,台湾大学,1999年。

念。他认为"活私开公"的概念可以用中国哲学的"理"（穷理）、韩国哲学的"气"（养气）与日本哲学的"场"（整场）来建立，由之形成一个"世界—国家—地域"三位一体的共动结构。山胁直司的论文延续金泰昌的观点，认为公共哲学必须超越鄂兰与哈伯玛斯的理论格局，建立"政府的公共""人民的公共""私人的领域"的"三元论"架构。除了上述二篇主张汲取东亚文化资源的论述外，该部分也有顾肃的论文，反对回归、汲取传统的论述及主张，而主张以多元主义式的对话方式建立新的公共哲学，相近的论点亦可见于江宜桦的论文。

第二个部分探讨"东亚思想传统中的公与私"，计有蓝弘岳、黄俊傑、义江彰夫、黑住真、金凤珍、黄克武等人分析中日韩思想资产的六篇文章。其中，蓝弘岳及黄克武的论文，皆指出东亚传统道德语言所产生的"公共"概念与西方理念中的"群己权界"存有误差，因而呼吁学者注意在跨文化与语言翻译过程中的落差，并努力从中抽取更为开放、丰富的公共概念。黄俊傑、义江彰夫、黑住真、金凤珍等四人的论文分别就中国、日本及韩国近代的思想发展，论传统学者在公共概念上的创新、发展及局限，他们的论文可以做为"东亚公共哲学"承古开新的参照论点。

第三个部分为"西方政治思想中的公与私"，计有童世骏、蔡英文、贝淡宁（Daniel A. Bell）、陈祖为等人所撰之四篇文章。他们基本上从西方的观点谈"公共"或公私领域的理论发展及其局限，但部分也涉及中国或东方思想的问题。童世骏关切者乃公私领域的画界问题；蔡英文则分析公共领域中民主共识如何可能的问题；贝淡宁的文章再次以孟子与桃应的对话彰显家庭亲情与公共义务之间的紧张关系，并检讨自由主义对此困局回应之不足；陈祖为则聚焦于自由主义中立性论旨的批判，并主张良善生活应成为公共哲学讨论的标的。

此书聚集中国内地与台湾地区及日、韩等地学者，为东亚的"公私领域"问题提出一个全面性的思想探讨，有心为公共哲学的讨论创造了一个有别于过去论述方式的新局面，发展出一个具有东亚特色的公共哲学。

3. "王道"之关键词

"王道"一词是儒学研究的关键课题，2004 年张昆将出版《日本德川时代古学派之王道政治论》，扣紧"王道"的关键词及其思想内涵，分析古学派伊藤仁斋倡"王道",荻生徂徕倡"先王之道",二者有鲜明不同的立场。① 相较于张昆将专注日本前近代儒者的"王道"关键词分析,陈玮芬所撰《"道"、"王道"、"皇道"概念在近代日本的诠释》一文,则拉到了近代日本汉学研究者利用"王道"一词的特殊解释。陈玮芬指出自日本中世以降,不论是古学派、儒家神道,或者国学、水户学的学者,都试图透过各种论述,结合王道论与血统论,弱化其间的矛盾,他们的王道观力求摆脱天命之纠缠,直指历代假借天命之在我而行篡夺之事实,也抹去了对君主的积德作用,淡化了人君的"德治思想"。陈玮芬指出日本汉学家的"王道"论述充分表现出欲对现实政治环境予以改造的实用性格,这一点为近代汉学者所继承,但是其理论所造成天皇与幕府政权间的紧张,这是后儒所亟欲迴避的。陈文亦指出儒家与神道道统论之间的冲突,以及"王道"与"皇道"论述中的矛盾,在1932年,中国东北的土地上出现由日本政权扶植的"满洲国"(伪满)之后,更明显地表露在这个新的政治舞台之上,却又随着1945年日本的战败、溥仪的退位宣言而迅速地烟消云散。②

4. "忠""孝"之关键词

台湾学者对儒学的"忠""孝"关键词在日本的质变有深入研究者,有张昆将所著《德川日本"忠""孝"概念的形成与发展》(2004)一书中,集中讨论德川日本"忠""孝"这两个概念的发展。张昆将这本新书旨在分析日本近世"忠""孝"两种思维的典型,而以阳明学者从中江藤树(1608—1648)到大盐中斋(1793—1837)所强调的"孝",与兵学者从山鹿素行(1622—1685)到吉田松阴(1830—1859)所著重的"忠"作为分析的主轴。张昆将指出德川日本的阳明学者与兵学者都具有本土性的神道意识,所以他这本书也追溯日本传统思维方式的特色,探讨近世日本思想家"忠""孝"的两种纯粹思维之典型。这种植根于传统的神道宗教意识,就是提供"忠"与"孝"的超越原理之根据,因此,在理论上与实践上,恰可作为幕末水户学者与勤皇学者倡道"忠孝一体"的最佳思想资源,并成为近代日本"祭教政"三位一体的理论基础。这与中国

---

① 张昆将:《日本德川时代古学派之王道政治论》,台北:台大出版中心,2004年。
② 陈玮芬:《道、王道、皇道概念在近代日本的诠释》,收入高明士主编《东亚文化圈的形成与发展》,台北:台大出版中心,2005年。

以"仁本论"作为超越原理相当不同。① 张昆将企图从这个角度观察中日两民族对于道德单位观念的重要歧异,进一步掌握日本思想家的特殊思维。

相较于张昆将关注近世的"忠""孝"思维,陈玮芬所著《井上哲次郎的〈敕语衍义〉:关于"忠孝"的义理新诠》一文,则关注日本近代的"忠"、"孝"特殊思维,该文借著井上哲次郎的《敕语衍义》对于"忠孝"道德的新解释,并将之比较中国古代的忠孝观,分析日本在天皇体制下的"忠孝一本"的解释特质。② 目前日本学界对于《教育敕语》的研究已经相当多,但专对于井上哲次郎的《敕语衍义》之研究则非常有限,作者能扣紧《教育敕语》的忠孝一体思想,实抓住《敕语》的真精神,进行考察与研究。其次,作者对影响日后日本教育政策甚大的井上哲次郎之《敕语衍义》,进行详尽分析,可补学界对于只知《敕语》而不知《衍义》之不足。

5. "中国""天下""天皇"之关键词

在东亚思想史上,"中国"或"中华"这个极具指标性的概念,虽然形成于古代中国,但其内涵在近世韩国、日本与越南、琉球乃至现代中国台湾地区却经历转变。"中国"或"中华"概念在朝鲜时代(1392—1910)常以"小中华"概念注入了"箕氏朝鲜",之后甚至有"檀君朝鲜"的主体情感;在德川时代(1600—1868年)的日本,被挪移来指称日本而非中国本土,与近世日本思想史上日本主体性之发展桴鼓相应;在越南近世的前后黎氏王朝(1460—1789)与阮氏王朝(1802—1945),渐次展现其文化主体性,也多强调越南是古代中国圣人炎帝神农氏之后;"中国"概念在现代台湾,则显示了"文化中国"与"政治中国"的撕裂及其辨证关系。"中国"或"中华"概念在东亚区域的转折变化,特别在现今东亚崛起的时代里,极具探讨其价值与现代意义。黄俊杰教授是国内最早注意日本儒者有关"中国"一词的特殊用法,自2013年起迄今,已经举办四届的"东亚视域中的'中华'意识国际学术研讨会",时间从

---

① 张昆将:《德川日本"忠""孝"概念的形成与发展》(台北:台大出版社,2004),该书原系作者台湾大学历史研究所博士学位论文(2002年),原题《日本德川时代"至孝"与"纯忠"思维的典型》,经修订后出版。

② 陈玮芬:《井上哲次郎的〈敕语衍义〉:关于"忠孝"的义理新诠》,《清华学报》新33卷第2期(2003年12月),第399—437页。

古代到近现代，空间从中国、日本、韩国，也涉及琉球与越南的中华意识课题，堪称讨论中华意识区域最广、专题最多，源源不绝，展现中华意识的多元丰富及其错综复杂的历史过程与转变，会议论文集的专书亦将于2017年初出版，以飨学界。

有关"天下"、"天皇"的关键概念，甘怀真近年来关注东亚儒学有关"天下"、"天皇"一词的政治与思想性的研究，其中有《从日本律令制度看王权与儒教："天下"观念与律令的成立》、《日本古代的儒学与王权：以"天下"观念为例》、《"天下"观念的再检讨》及《日本江户时代儒者的"天下"观念：以会泽安〈新论〉为例》等几篇的研究，这几篇论文均收入《东亚文明研究丛书》之中。

甘怀真《日本江户时代儒者的"天下"观念：以会泽安〈新论〉为例》一文考察了幕末水户学者会泽安《新论》中的论述如何理解与诠释儒学的"天下"观念，进而创造一套新的政治论述，以应付世变。作者指出，对于会泽安而言，其使命是如何借由儒教的论述，即运用儒教的语言与概念，重新理解与诠释所面对的诸日本的事实，包括过去的历史与现状，在重新建构新的政体时，一方面解决日本当前的危机，另一方面赋与这个新国家以儒家理想。在此同时，如何将儒教诠释为普世性的文化，一种高尚的文明标准；而同时也可以用来建构日本的民族国家。此文借由后期水户学代表人物会泽安《新论》一书中的儒教论述，以"天下"概念的分析为主，探讨儒家学说作为政治论述或政治诠释学，如何在19世纪中期，作为日本迈入"现代性"的知识凭据。①

甘怀真也在《中国古代皇帝号与日本天皇号》一文中借由皇帝号的研究，讨论秦至唐间，政治人物、学者如何利用皇帝号的诠释，以创造其自以为合理的政治制度，同时也借由日本天皇号的比较研究，试图了解源于中国的某些语言、概念，如何传播于"东亚世界"，中国域外政权如何利用这些源于中国如语言、概念，以进行其本国的政治斗争。这篇文章讨论日本的天皇号时，指出其主要目的也在说明中国的政治语言符号及其概念如何在不同的历史脉络中被使用。这篇文章在最后指出，中国所创的帝王尊号，如"天子""皇帝"，在东亚的古代成为一普遍的概念，日本也

---

① 甘怀真：《日本江户时代儒者的"天下"观念：以会泽安〈新论〉为例》，收入张宝三、杨儒宾共编《日本汉学研究续探：思想文化篇》，台北：台大出版中心，2005年。

采用了此概念的形式，但至于其实质内涵，则不是中国方面所能决定的。亦即日本采用了此类语言的形式，并不必然道入此语言在中国方面的意义，更何况中国方面的意义也在不同的诠释者间有不同的意义。①

另外，甘怀真在 2007 年主编《东亚历史上的天下与中国概念》一书，搜罗了中日及美国知名学者有关"天下"与"中国"共八篇文章，编者区分以下八个部分：

1. 从天下到中国（平势隆郎）

作者讨论涉及先秦时代的"中国""天下""夏"的名称与概念，论证先秦时代的政治是"多元中心"，如周王朝是一种松散的政治组织，并非一元中心的帝国政治组织。进入到春秋战国时代，诸大国发展出"己身为中国"，也就是中国只是作为中原王权自称的说法，尚未确立"中国"的政治论述。

2. 天下作为一种政体（甘怀贞）

作者论证"天下"作为一种皇帝制度的政体，是依照"天—天下—天子—民"之理论模式，即是皇帝制度国家是一种"政治/哲学"的伦理型，与现代的国家型态是基于近代主权、领土、认同等"政治/法律"之理论，不可等同而论。

3. 帝国的想象（王健文）

作者分析新的"秦汉帝国"是如何创造新的华夏意识，借着安德森《想象的共同体：民族主义的起源与散布》一书中所谓的"被束缚的朝圣之旅"的学说，探讨汉代各地菁英阶层的一体感如何产生，从而如何产生新的华夏意识。

4. 作为天文政治学的天下观（曾蓝莹）

作者从新疆出土"五星出东方利中国"诸文字的织锦，分析天文学中的"天下"与"中国"的概念，议题新颖，但能否形成一个所谓"天文政治学"之概念，尚待厘清。

5. 作为地理政治学的天下观（葛兆光）

作者从地图探讨古人的世界像，传达文字所无法直接表达的知识内容，在传统历史地理学之外，加入思想史的方法与理论，解读出图像的诸

---

① 甘怀真：《中国古代皇帝号与日本天皇号》，收入氏著《皇权、礼仪与经典诠释：中国古代政治史研究》，台北：台大出版中心，2004 年。

多文字之外的密码，并看出地图各层的天下与天下之外的异域世界观。

6. 天下观到国际公法（张隆志）

作者透过牡丹社事件看到"近代日本帝国"与"传统的中华帝国"的前哨事件，透过中日双方彼此谈判过程之解析，厘清日方开始引用欧洲国际法的理论，挑战中国天下理论的司法与行政权。

7. 东亚考古学成立的纠葛（吉开将人）

作者从中国考古学兴起的学术考察，直探中国民族主义形成的历程。作者在结论中指出东亚考古学重视东亚（中国及其周边）作为一个整体，故探究这个区域内的诸地域间的文化互动。相对之下，中国考古学关注中国文明的自律性发展，以及中国国家的一脉相传。此文令我们省思，作为"天下"的东亚与作为"一国"的东亚，在近现代考古学的意识型态之争。

8. 中国概念在近世日本与台湾的展开（黄俊杰）

作者从"文化中国"与"政治中国"两个认同课题的概念，分析近世日本对"中国"概念的理解纷争，从而再将之放到近代受殖民以及民族主义风潮下的台湾统治菁英对"文化中国"与"政治中国"两概念之间的紧张性关系。

本节仅是选择一些有代表性的专书及作者分析台湾近二十年来有关"东亚儒学"的研究取向与趋势，不可能面面俱到，必有遗珠。同时，台湾亦有一些东亚儒学研究是在此丛书之外，亦非本文所能范围。但从以上的分析，略可知悉台湾近年来在"东亚儒学"的研究成果，已然形成一股研究风气，以此为基础，接引后续的研究者，投入这方面的研究，开发出具有"理一分殊"而自成一格的东亚儒学之领域与特色。

三　东亚儒学研究的潜力与展望

揆诸上述有关东亚儒学的研究，虽成果可观，但颇多集中于特定几位学者，期待年轻学者投入东亚儒学研究。因此，未来东亚儒学的课题，应积极培养人才，继续此一领域的延续与开发，方不致得来不易的研究新领域产生断层。另外，东亚儒学目前比较缺乏越南儒学的研究人才，主要是越南方面的材料尚多属于未公开或难以取得，将来如何突破这方面的限制，以及训练这方面的年轻学者投入研究，相当有其必要性。

其次，从上述的趋势回顾，约略可嗅出研究者企图提炼出一种具有"东亚共通学"的方法论特色。除了黄俊杰教授多年来提炼的"中国诠释学"或"东亚经典诠释学"的方法论以外，我们从上面的回顾趋势中亦可看到有"东亚四书学""东亚公共哲学""东亚教育学""东亚朱子学""东亚阳明学""东西宗教学的对话"等共通性质的文化与思想。换言之，未来因集中思考"东亚共通性"这样的主题思维，必能寻出一个或找回本属于自成一格的东亚文化共同系统，而不再是处处以西方文化系统来框限东亚文化的发展，这也就是东亚儒学将来发展的潜力，值得期待。

如果我们认真回顾的话，"东亚儒学"这个提法与概念，正式出现在台湾学者的论述及著作中，并逐渐扩及中国内地及日本、韩国等地的学术界，似乎变得言之成理的一件事情。从历史背景来看，台湾社会没有经历过文化大破坏，反而保留了儒学文化传统，加上台湾社会属汉语语言体系，没有日本、韩国、越南学者学中文的第一层障碍，对古代典籍的掌握程度甚佳，甚至可说是保留中华文化元气之最佳场所。站在各国主体文化立场而言，韩国学者显然不太强调"东亚儒学"，而且先不说不从事研究儒学者出现的排斥情况，一些资深的韩国儒学研究者也不轻易论"东亚儒学"这样的课题，反而凸显强烈的"韩国儒学"之特色，而且以独立而具特色的韩国儒学为傲。至于日本，因为走过战前对"东亚"一词的敏感，多数学者几乎也不谈"东亚儒学"，即便谈到"儒学"，也多持"批判儒学"的立场。由此可知，"东亚儒学"只能由作为边陲的台湾同时又具有强烈的"中国性""东亚性"的台湾学者提出，既可消退"中心一元"论述的质疑，也可包容各国独特的儒学。

那么中国内地学界对"东亚儒学"的态度又如何呢？现阶段的中国儒学研究者眼中多仍是中国儒学，特别近二十年来国学热、儒学热之发展，此时此刻仍处于找回"文化自信"的阶段，可能比强调一个"东亚儒学"还来得迫切。但这不意味中国内地思想界将来不会发展出一个"东亚儒学"的研究视野与开放的态度。也正由于中国内地现今正处于重视并推动文化复兴与文化自信，若与周边国家的儒学正处于萎缩不振的阶段相比较而言，对东亚儒学的研究而言，反而是一个契机。因为依此恢复传统文化的趋势，将来势必也会发展到注意儒学的"东亚性"或"世界性"，故未来"东亚儒学"的研究与方法透过中国的重视与研究，仍具有相当的研究潜力。

由此看来，现阶段"东亚儒学"在台湾的推动与发展，似乎是最包容且多元的，同时也最具有客观性的"东亚性质"。在日本，因近代"大东亚共荣圈"对东亚各国的伤害，曾经出现过殖民帝国目的的"太过东亚"之现象，"东亚"的思考课题曾经因为忌讳或敏感的关系而在战后消失一段很长的时间，直到 1990 年因"东亚共同体"的经济议题，"亚细亚"或"东亚"才又成为热门讨论的话题。至于韩国，历史上并没有在军事或经济上主道过"东亚"，但自从东南亚国协（ASEAN）成立以后，历任大统领从经济、国防、韩美同盟的基础上，积极讨论"东北亚统合"、"东北亚多边主义"乃至"东亚共同体"之课题。而在中国内地，过去因"文化大革命"的破坏，并从 20 世纪 90 年代国学热的文化自觉，到今日建立文化自信的阶段过程中，关注"东亚儒学"尚不是目前急迫之事。不过，儒学本来就具有跨国、跨文化的特色，乃至具有普世性的核心价值理念，一旦中国文化界、思想界发展成熟后，东亚儒学亦可能成为一个积极发展的学术领域。

因此，我们如果将台湾目前所发展的"东亚儒学"研究现象，放置在中日韩从过去到当代的"东亚论"之历史轨迹上，也许就会看出他们之间的不平衡现象，以及"东亚儒学"出现在当今台湾学术界的重大历史意义。首先，在地理边陲的台湾谈"东亚儒学"，比较不会有"自我中心论"的疑虑；其次，"东亚儒学"的提法既重普遍的课题，也强调特殊的面向，在"存异求同"的方法论上，追求多元共存、共享、共同欣赏的依存关系；再次，"东亚儒学"着重儒学在长远文化上的彼此共通交流、经典思想沟通、民间友朋之心灵交流，而不是基于现实短期利益的经济、军事、政治、民族的东亚利益结盟关系。最后，"东亚儒学"所采取的是承认有一个"文化核心价值"，但既不是"中华中心论"，也不是"去中心论"，而是承认并尊重每个文化核心价值彼此涵摄，正如朱子（晦庵，1130—1200）所说的"不即不离"之关系。就此而言，"东亚儒学"的提法实有其深远的意义及其必要性。

Will China Sinicize and Confucianize the World? Case Study: Malaysia

Peter T. C. Chang*

Introduction

President Xi Jinping's "Belt and Road" initiative represents the People's Republic of China's (PRC) bold aspiration to establish a sphere of common prosperity. Covering a large swarth of continental and maritime Asia, with radically diverse cultural terrains, Beijing is acutely mindful that aside from geopolitical and economic challenges, this grand vision posits a complex set of ethnic and religious intricacies. To that end, China has embarked upon a concerted soft power campaign, deploying a range of institutions and resources to facilitate and enhance inter-civilizational engagement and understanding.

This paper examines the PRC's ongoing effort to promote the harmonious co-existence between diverse peoples and traditions. And we will do this by looking at Malaysia, which is an intriguing case study on two accounts. At the outset, Malaysia provides critical insights from the perspective of race, namely, the Chinese and Malay relationship. Host to a sizable Chinese diaspora, the Malaysian government is all too conscious of the imperative to maintain racial harmony; a goal that at times seem elusive. Furthermore, as a country with a Muslim majority, Malaysia is an apt constituent to study the com-

---

* Peter T. C. Chang, 张添财, 马来亚大学中国研究所高级讲师, Sonior Leeturer of Institute of China Studies, Clniversity of Malaya.

plicated interactions between the Confucian and Islamic worlds. This project will analyze the impact of China's soft power upon these delicate issues. I plan to argue that as the Sino-Malaysia bond become tightened through the "Belt and Road" initiative, Beijing is likely to assume a more proactive and constructive role in mitigating the tenuous Chinese and Malay race relations, and the awkward cohabitation between Confucianism and Islam.

More broadly, the overarching concern of this article is to examine whether China, as a resurgent global power, will seek to Sinicize and Confucianize the world. Modern China, as Lucian Pye has argued, is in fact a civilization pretending to be a state. This means that among others, the Chinese principality is founded upon a distinct ethnic cultural identity, imbued with a corresponding sense of civilizational pride. Indeed, as the Middle Kingdom, Imperial China asserted its tributary power, coopting the lesser periphery states into its sphere of political, economical and ethical influence. However I plan to explain that the Chinese dominance has distinct features that set it apart from, for instance, Imperial West. While the latter has sought to Christianize their colonies, the former is less inclined to convert the world wholly into its own image. And this is because the Chinese practices a form of inclusive superiority. Guided by the principle of meritocracy, the Confucians recognize the moral efficacy of and are open to collaboration with other religious traditions. These form the underpinning of the Chinese pluralistic vision enabling Confucian China to advocate a unified yet diverse dominion, sustaining the harmonious co-existence of different races, religiosity, and civilizations, under the Heaven.

A) Pax Sinica

At the closing of the 20th century, analysts were forecasting a reconfiguration of world order, from the prevailing pax Americana to an emerging pax Sinica. And as with all transitions, this rebalancing of global dominance from West to East is generating some trepidations. How will China exert its power and and what are the probable impacts upon the world?

To be sure, China is not yet a full pledged superpower and its dominance is chiefly in the economic realm. Even so the Chinese imprints are already felt across the globe. And the recently launched Belt and Road initiative is one apt example: a blueprint that encompasses both continental and maritime corridors, with the aim is to engineer a Pan Asia sphere of common prosperity. When actualized, this will undoubtedly bring about an increase in China's sway over the rest of Asia.

Now China is no ordinary superpower. As mentioned, China a civilization state, calling to attention the distinct ethnic and cultural underpinning of the Chinese world. Among others, this contention underscores the Middle Kingdom's conception of a dominion where diverse philosophical and religious traditions co-exist harmoniously under the Heaven. Indeed rulers of modern China has invoked this ancient aspiration of the peaceful co-existence of all people. Will Beijing, through its ambitious Belt and Road initiative, bring about the actualization of an inclusive and pluralistic world order? A small yet vital part of the BR scheme, Malaysia present itself as an intriguing case for study.

B) China and Malaysia

In 1974, then Malaysia Prime Minister Tun Abdul Razak took the bold step to reestablish diplomatic ties with China, the first Asian country to do so. This became the bedrock of a largely cordial relationship between the two countries. Since the 1980s the economic bond between China and Malaysia grew, with Chinese exports increasing tenfold, becoming Malaysia largest trade partners. A growth that is expected to continue with Beijing launch of the BR initiative.

That said Sino-Malaysia alliance is not without difficulties. Though a relatively reticent claimant pertaining to the South China Seas disputes, the risk of tension remains. More broadly Malaysia is caught in the cold war vortex, trying to balance the competing demands of China on the one hand, and US on the other hand. Indeed there is concern that China's increasing sway may unduly impact Malaysia national security and sovereignty.

This trepidations extends into the cultural domain, will a resurgent China, like the West, seek to impose its values and norms upon the world? A former colony of Western powers, Malaysia is acutely sensitive of such cultural domination. Will China sinicize and Confucianize the world? Will this bring about a threat to the Malay and Islamic characteristics of Malaysia? This concern is made complicated by a sizable overseas Chinese community in Malaysia, who relationship with the Malay majority has been edgy at time. This domestic ethnic tension is fueling the Malay concerns with regard to China cultural dominance.

B1) The Chinese Diaspora in Malaysia

While the history of Chinese settlement in Malaya dates back to the Zheng He era, it was the late 19th to early 20th century outflow from Southern China that form the bulk of Chinese immigration to Malaysia today. Pushed by internal turmoil broiling within, these primarily economic refugees sailed towards the southern seas, seeking better fortunes and life. Many landed in the British ruled Malaya, became absorbed into the tin mining industry, rubber plantations and various cottages industries.

In 1957, upon independence from the British, most of the Chinese chose to remain and were accorded Malaysian citizenship. They assumed dominance in the economic sector, while political control is largely ceded to the Malays. This uneasy division of power and labor was sustained for over a decade. In 1969 a racial riot rocked the young nation bringing to surface the underlying tension, fracturing the country along ethnic lines. While diverse and complex, economic disparity is one of the root causes. Unequal distribution of wealth along racial lines was the underlying factor. As a correction the Malaysia government implemented the 1970 National Economic Plan (NEP) to elevate the Malay economic status through affirmation actions.

Four decades on, the NEP did not meet its overarching goal, namely, to narrow the economic gap between the races. Wealth was redistributed but did not trickle down sufficiently to provide uplift to the majority of the Malays. In fact, the Malays remain a mere passengers rather than driver of the main economic locomotives of the country.

In recent decades, the ethnic tension in Malaysia has taken on a religious dimension, the result of the embrace by the Malays of a more conservative form of Islam. Since the 1980s, influence from the Middle Eastern has infused into Malaysia a stricter and fundamentalist interpretation and practice of the Islamic faith. This turn towards religious conservatism is creating strains in a multiracial and multireligious Malaysia. The Chinese and Indians have expressed concerns their fundamental rights to religious freedom are being challenged and in some cases, curtailed.

The communal affairs in Malaysia is complicated at best. Undoubtedly the crux of the problem is the Malay unease and mistrust towards the Chinese, the latter perceived as a threat to the former wellbeing. The question at hand, how will the PRC's increasing presence in Malaysia affect this tense relationship? Will it compound or alleviate the Malay trepidation?

B2) China and the Chinese Diaspora

We begin with a look at the PRC treatment of the Chinese diaspora in general. In 2016, Beijing started issuing the equivalent of China's Green Card (call "Chinese Card") to overseas Chinese when they visit, study, work, or live in China, conferring them some basic rights, treatments, and perks similar to local residents. In the first instance, this is Beijing attempt to minimize the lost of talents due to migrating Chinese, mostly to the West. With this problem that could evolved into a form of dual citizenship Beijing hopes to retain some of these skills. Indeed, the Chinese diaspora represents a pool of human resource vital to China's development. And this pool includes the overseas Chinese in Malaysia, who are playing crucial roles as intermediaries in China's investment abroad.

Beijing's active cultivation of the Chinese diaspora underscores one key feature of the aforementioned China as a "civilizational state", namely, "citizens" of the Chinese civilization state could well transcend modern state boundary. Herein lies a potential problem pertaining to the PRC and Chinese diaspora linkage, it could raise the sensitive issue of sovereignty and patriotism.

Beijing's overreach with regard to the Chinese in Malaysia could be construed as undue interference in domestic affairs, straining the two countries bilateral ties. And if seen as putting China's interest ahead of Malaysia, the patriotic credentials of the Malaysian Chinese could be put to questions, compounding the prevailing Malay suspicions and perception of the Chinese as "foreigners" not fully committed to their adopted home.

B3) Cultural and Economic Diplomacy

As correctives, Beijing has to recalibrate its approach towards Malaysia. For a start, China has to step up direct engagement with the Malay majority, to supplement the present linkage with the Chinese minority. This must happen across the board, between governmental agencies, NGO, civil societies, and most importantly, at the people to people level.

One arena where existing interaction can be improved upon is the education sector. The Confucius Institute, for example, is currently providing contact through language course. The recent opening of Xiamen University international campus in Malaysia is an important development towards building more robust educational exchanges between the two countries and peoples. While these are positive progress, these programs need to be more strategic in recruiting Malay participations, to increase the contact between the Chinese and Malay communities. Furthermore, mainland Chinese should be encouraged with study the Malay language and culture.

The religious domain is another critical sphere of engagement. The PRC interaction with Malaysia, and its Muslim Malay majority, can be enhanced through the agency of the Hui Muslim. By faith Muslim yet culturally Chinese, the Hui represents a unique constituents who could play the vital role of civilizational emissary bridging the Chinese, Malay, and Islamic worlds.

More broadly, in the realm of pop culture, there are indictors pointing to the creation of Chinese entertainment products with a pan Asia appeal, in the mold of the hugely successful and popular Korean Pop and Japanese Pop. Such a development along a pan Asia trajectory could render the Chinese culture less Han-centric, thus more appealing to the non-Chinese world in general, and the Malays community in particular.

Last but not least is the economic factor. In large part, the fragile communal fabric in Malaysia is symptomatic of weak economic fundamentals. More specifically, failure to achieve fair distribution of economic opportunities and wealth has fueled the rising ethnic sentiment. On this account, the current inflow of China's capital could be a mitigating factor. If administered judiciously, these investment can generate economic uplifts that could ameliorate the fragile communal fabric in Malaysia. Needless to say, the converse is also true. China's mercantilism, if ruthlessly pursued, could aggravate the already intricate Chinese Malay race relations.

In summing up, the social cohesion in Malaysia remains fragmented, as the Malay majority continues to harbor reservation towards the Chinese minority in particular, and China in general. For this reason Beijing needs to take proactive steps to allay the Malay trepidation, to dispatch greater cultural and economic resources in order to strengthen bonds between the peoples and the two countries.

C) China: A Cultural Hegemon?

Even as cultural and economic diplomacy is deployed to stabilize the ethnic situation in Malaysia, the broader question remains, what is the endgame of China's projection of soft power? Will China, like erstwhile Imperial West, set out to transform the world into its own image? A familiar retort against this concern is the historical argument that Imperial China never colonized in the manner of Western Imperialism, and the fate of the Malacca sultanate is often upheld as an apt illustration. As is well accounted, in his numerous visits, Zheng He established a tributary ties between China and Malacca, allowing the latter to retain political and cultural autonomy. It was about 50 years later, with the arrival of the Portugese that resulted in the subjugation and demise of the Malay sultanate. Base on these contrasting precedences, apologists argue that like its ancient forebears, modern China is unlikely to embark on a campaign of conquest. But could it be that the Malacca episode, and more generally Ming China non aggressive maritime exploration be mere happenstance? Various theories sought to explain these East West differences. In what follows I argue that Imperial China behavior is not a historical accident, rather it stems from an underlying worldview that affirms pluralism and inclusiveness.

C1) Inclusive Superiority: Many Ways versus One Way

To be sure, like the Christian West, Confucian East also regard themselves as custodians of moral precepts that is efficaciousfor all humanity. But unlike the former, the latter did not seek to evangelize or Confucianize the entire world. If espouses a universalistic vision, why did not Confucian East exude similar Christian West zeal to transform the world? This dissimilitude can be attributed to these two Axial Age religions different strategies, namely, the Christian 'one way' versus the Confucian 'many ways' approach to actualize their respective conception of the ultimate good. I shall elaborate.

At the core of the Christian belief is the affirmation that all human can attain salvation in the afterlife. But to achieve this, a person must conduct his or her present life in accord with two sets of norms. The first are behavioral codes embedded within General Revelations. These are commonly known as the natural law, which is accessible to all human being. The second are the Special Revelations. These represent decrees uniquely manifested by God to a specific group of people, at a particular time in history, namely, the descendants of Abraham. This 'chosen tribe' subsequently evolved into the wider faith communities customarily referred to as Religions of the Book, namely, Judaism, Christianity and Islam.

In Christianity, the Bible is extolled as the final depository of these specially revealed sacred pronouncements. Accordingly, Christians believe they alone procured the complete prerequisite knowledge for human salvation. And the only 'one way' to secure eternal life is to live our temporal existence in conformity with the Holy Scripture.

It is on this account that Christianity conceived itself as a 'chosen tradition', the divinely elected recipients of Special Revelations, and entrusted evangelists of the Good News to a humanity mired in iniquity. These are the key motifs that drive the Western missionary enterprise to Christianize the world, as so to save the world. More recently, it inspired the modern American sense of 'manifest destiny', as the predestined Western civilization to provide moral and political leadership to the rest of the world.

The ultimate good, for Confucianism, is to live the sagely life of a *Chun Zhi*. And to consummate this idealized selfhood, a person must order his or her conduct in alignment with *Tien Li*. And for the Confucians these Heavenly Principles are naturally discernible by all humankind, without the necessity for extraneous supernatural revelation.

Thus, unlike Christianity, ancient China has no equivalent notion of *Tien* communicating only to a specific race. Rather, according to the early Chinese thinkers, every proclamations of Heaven are universally accessible to the entire human race Correspondingly, each persons and by extension traditions, posses the essential knowledge to bring into fruition a sagely existence.

Now, while the Confucians believe all has the potential, not everyone actualizes it. Mo Tzu and Mohism, for example, was refuted by the Confucians for espousing teachings that contravene the Way. But for those who fulfill this innate capability, Lao Tzu and Daoism, for instance, the Confucianists would accord them due recognition and welcome their collaboration. This pluralistic affirmation is encapsulated by the Chinese practice of multiple-religiosity. It is not uncommon to meet a Chinese person pledging allegiance to Confucianism, Daoism, and Buddhism, all at the same time.

What these underscore is the Confucian universal concept of moral efficacy. Unlike the Christian doctrine of the 'chosen tradition', for the Confucian, moral superiority is not predestined. Instead, it is egalitarian, open to all, and bestowed on the basis of meritocracy. That is to say, each person and traditions have to develop their potential, prove their competency, and hence worthiness to assume leadership role.

What this means is that as oppose to the Christian 'exclusive' 'one way' scheme to attain salvation, the Confucian moral enterprise affirms an 'inclusive' 'many ways' approach to realizing the *Dao*. Put differently, the ancient Chinese do not regard Confucianism as the sole custodian and transmitter of the *Dao*. There are other worthy intermediaries who can effectuate the actualization of harmony on Earth.

Herein lies the main theological and philosophical explanation for the Chinese apparent lack of zeal to Confucianize the world. Surely, as with the Christians, the ancient Chinese sages were critical of the moral condition of their times and worked to transform the world-at-large. But unlike Christianity, they do not see the remedy as residing in Confucianism alone, some other traditions are as capable of dispensing corrective measures. It is for this reason that historically the Confucian East was never as encumbered by nor transfixed with the sacred burden of the Christian West, as God's elected tradition to venture forth and evangelize the world.

C2) Will China Confucianize the World?

Returning to the present age, as part of a wider soft power campaign to soothe the PRC's image abroad, Beijing has installed an extensive network of Confucius Institutes across the globe. This has become a controversial project not least because some have questioned if these institutes in their present form are legitimate conduits of the Confucian precepts. Other critics, especially those in the West, warn of an ideological Trojan Horse implanted in universities to propagate the PRC's illiberal worldview. Be that as it may, the question at hand is that if and when the Confucian tradition is fully rejuvenated, will modern China seek to 'Confucianize' the world?

Given the preceded analysis, and if history is received as a reliable indicator, the answer could be no. Certainly, as an Apex Civilization the Confucians may attempt to 'civilize' what they perceived are the lesser civilizations. However unlike Christianity, the Confucians would not seek to remodel the world wholly in its own image. The universal order envisioned by the ancient Chinese sages, as explained, is a pluralistic one, where multiple philosophical and religious traditions existed side by side and even synthesized with one another. Therefore if the Confucian ideals are affirmed, then a China led new world order will be one where diverse civilizations, when proven meritorious, could co-exist harmoniously to provide humanity with collective moral leadership.

D) Conclusion

As an emerging global power, concerns are growing over the manner China will asserts its sways. While no different from others, there are key differences in how the Chinese may seek to reshape the world. It is probable that the Chinese would strive for a pluralistic rather than a homogeneous world order. This however is contingent upon modern China staying faithful to their forebears principles of universalism and pluralism. And it is by upholding these ideals that Beijing's vision of a harmonious world is more likely to be realized.

ENDNOTES

1. Armstrong, Karen. (1999). *A History of God*. London, UK: Vintage, Random House.

2. Merk, Frederick. 1963. *Manifest Destiny and Mission in American History. A Reinterpretation.* Cambridge, Mass. Harvard University Press.

3. Ching, Julia (1977). *Confucianism and Christianity: A Comparative Study*, Tokyo: Kodansha International, 1977.

4. The Confucian inclusiveness is not unconditional. Historically, Mohism and various Buddhist sects, among others, were excluded from the Confucian order on grounds of incompatibility in values. In modern times, religious movement with extremists or militant tendencies, for example, could face similar censure. In some ways, the contemporary conservative Confucianists' reservations towards aspects of Christianity may have some validity. This is true with regard to the Christian's view of other belief system, especially the fundamentalists' position which forbid any form of interreligious cooperation. A Christian exclusivity that would lead the Confucians to judge them as unqualified for partnership.

5. By contrast, in Christianity, a believer rarely lay claim to a multiplicity of faiths. This attests to the Christian sense of superiority, a trait in common with the Confucians. However unlike the latter, the former's supremacy is non-inclusive. This is due to the Christian dogma that as the sole recipient of God's special revelation, the Christian church alone posses what is indispensable for human salvation. For this reason, notwithstanding some liberal exceptions, mainstream Christianity especially the fundamentalists disregard the efficacy of the other world religions. In point of fact they consider any form of religious syncretism like those practiced by the Chinese as sacrilegious. See Paul F. Knitter, *No other name?: A critical survey of Christian attitudes toward the world religion.* (N.Y. Orbis Books, 1985).

6. Indeed, the early Chinese sages did not espouse any equivalent Old

Testament notion of the chosen race or tradition, wherewithal the Confucian mastery could be ratified as irrefutable. Nor is there a parallel American's sense of manifest destiny whereby Confucian China would be enthroned as predestined supremo. Rather, the Confucian's reign may be said to be founded on meritocracy. It is conferred by virtue of the tradition's astute discernment and ardent pursuit of the Heavenly Ways. The implication henceforth is that the Confucian leadership is not a given. It is contingent on their abiding sustainment of a way of life that conforms with the *Dao*. If the movement strays from the Way then the legitimacy to govern is forfeited. To some extent the history of modern China is demonstrative of one such said period. When internal decay reduced this venerable tradition into irrelevance, it was accordingly banished from the mainland. Thus the Chinese moral philosophers who invoke the *Tian* to exact accountability upon the Emperor are evenly subjected to the litmus test of the Mandate of Heaven.

7. An additional explanation for this parochialism is the Confucian doctrine of concentric circle. Its basic premise is to recognize the stages of engagements, with local obligations generally taking precedence over global matters. The admonition is to resolve family matters ahead of acting on challenges at the village, provincial and national level. Putting this colloquially, until one's household is in order, it is inappropriate and premature to meddle with affairs at the outer circles. The Confucian 'mind your business first' priority has unintended effects. It molded into the Chinese psyche a preoccupation with domestic issues and a corresponding reluctance to engage others. This partly explains why the Sino civilization, despite exhorting a universal vision, rarely venture beyond its immediate boundaries to interact with the world-at-large.

8. As is the situation right now, most of the established Confucius Institutes operate as defacto 'cultural centers' with the Chinese language classes as its core and most popular offering. Other activities include promotion of arts and crafts, with some branches even providing trade and business related services. At this early stage of its inception, programs aim at elucidating Confucianism as a moral-political philosophy remains underdeveloped. Though this could change

as the Confucius Institute project mature into a more scholastic venture. See James F. Paradise, China International Harmony: The Role of Confucius Institutes in Bolstering Beijing's Soft Power. *Asian Survey*, vol. xlix, no. 4. (2009), pp. 647-665.

中国的国学（孟子学）能热到马来西亚来吗

郑文泉*

摘 要：本文是针对继孔子学院、荀子学院之后于 2016 年马来西亚设立的孟子学院分院一举，分析中国的国学热、儒学热是否因而能被移植或复制到马来西亚来的条件之事。现实马来西亚或不缺乏孟子的资源，但学术意义的孟子学较为零星，社会意义的孟子文化则甚为丰沃，可举出的至少就有（一）孟子的"良知"观念对现实社会运动领袖如陈嘉庚（1874—1961）、沈慕羽（1913—2009）的影响、（二）孟子的"穷则独善其身，达则兼济天下"处世观对"三园"到南洲诗社等古典诗人的亦吏（侨领或公务人员）亦隐（隐逸诗人）之处世生涯极有作用这两点。然而，现实的情形是马来西亚或不缺乏民间的陈嘉庚热、沈慕羽热，但这些都没有被视为孟子文化意义的范畴来理解，而有赖于孟子学院的马、中合作，进一步通过学术研究和社会传播的两个渠道来加以促进与提升。

关键词：国学热、孟子学院、孟子学、孟子文化、马来西亚

Can the Mencius Institute of China be Popularizein Malaysia?

Tee Boon Chuan

Department of Chinese Studies

University ofTunku Abdul Rahman (Malaysia)

teebc@ utar. edu. my

Paper presented at *The International Conference on East Asian Civilizational Exchange* in Beijing, 10 – 11 November 2016, held by Institute for Advanced

---

* 郑文泉，马来西亚拉曼大学中文系副教授，中华研究院副院长。

Study of the Humanities and Religion, Beijing Normal University, China.

Abstract

The Mencius Institute founded in 2016 was the third Confucian institute in Malaysia following the first Kongzi Institute in 2009, and the second Xunzi Institutute in 2014. The paper aims to expose the potential of Malaysia in popularizing the Mencius Institute as well as its counterpart in China. In the reality, Malaysia is no less the Mencius heritage consists of Mencius studies and more richly the Mencius culture in which two traditions can be traced out: 1) the impact of Mencius conception of Conscience ("liangzhi") on major socio-educational activism led by Tan Kah Kee (1874–1961) and Sim Mow Yu (1913–2009), and 2) the influence of Mencius ideal of self and altruistic life on early "Three-Yuan" Poets (from Khoo Seok Wan, 1873–1941 to Lee Choon Seng, 1888–1966) to recent Nam Chou Poetry Society (founded in 1960). However, the said "Mencius culture" especially is no longer understood as Mencius heritage in the society, and should be re-enhanced by several academic and social programmes initiated from the Mencius Institute of Malaysia.

Key words: Chinese Classical popularity, Mencius Institute, Mencius Studies, Mencius Culture, Malaysia

中国国学热的移植：孟子学院马来西亚拉曼大学分院

2016年8月4日，中国江苏师范大学孟子学院首家海外分院，正式在马来西亚拉曼大学设立。按照孟子学院的成立宗旨，是"弘扬孟子精神，传播孟子文化，深化儒学研究，推动国学复兴"，具体办法则包括"积极搜集整理孟学史料，深化孟子思想研究，开展了一系列富有成效的学术活动"等。① 随着孟子学院的设立，再加上2014年挂牌的马来西亚

---

① 参见江苏师范大学《孟子学院马来西亚拉曼大学分院正式成立题辞》，http://www.xznu.edu.cn/35/01/c9675a210177/page.htm，2016年10月20日阅。此事也获得中国孟子文化网以《马来西亚拉曼大学孟子学院揭牌，传播中华文化》为题报导，http://www.mzchina.org/show.aspx?id=163，同上日期阅。

中华荀子学院（设在民办的马来西亚中华国学书院，与河北邯郸学院合作）、2009 年的马来亚大学孔子学院（与北京外国语大学合作），先秦儒家三大家，孔子、孟子、荀子的马来西亚分院可说都齐了。中国自 20 世纪 90 年代兴起的国学热、儒学热，现在可说是热到国外来了。

问题在于，中国的国学热、儒学热是一个由下而上的文化趋向，有其民间底气与需求，故能维持至今。① 仔细来说，孔子学院的孔子由于是个传统标志与象征，是国家对外的形象宣示与代表，故能远逾民间基础而为国家汉办的作业，暂可不表②；但是，孟子学院靠的是中国孟氏宗亲联谊会的支援，荀子学院则是地方的（燕）赵文化的依据，有其民间或地方的支撑与成因。然而，马来亚大学孔子学院的设立过程牵扯上孔子是否一宗教人物而一波三折，最后迟至 2009 年才准予挂牌③；孟、荀二院则一来马来西亚没有孟姓人氏，二来马来西亚也没有诸如（燕）赵文化的地域历史与文化，殊难唤起民间的"热"情与"热"力支持。换句话说，孔、孟、荀三家分院是可以在马来西亚设立，但其中国的民间热情度是否能够移植甚至复制到马来西亚来，则不无疑问。

和孔子学院有汉办背景的支援不同，孟、荀二院是个彻底的民办（民资）学院，其营运条件与空间很值得观察。以 2014 年挂牌的马来西亚中华荀子学院来说，迄今似仍未有投入运作的征象，其母体马来西亚中华国学书院于是年起活动亦告中辍，原因或非外人可解。④ 孟子学院才刚挂牌，既没有自己专属的办公人员，目前也是由拉曼大学中华研究院兼顾，整体营运方式还不明朗，有待厘定。和荀子学院不同的是，孟子学院的支援单位是拉曼大学中华研究院，隶下中文系现有十位左右可从事儒学研究的学术人员，且校方亦有"儒学与现代社会"（英语媒介）的校定选修课，可说是解决了它的人力问题，剩下来的只是经费和项目的细节安

---

① 关于这点，参见韩星《民间儒学普及 30 年》，王殿卿、张践主编：《儒学教育传播与应用 30 年》，吉林人民出版社 2015 年版，第 68—133 页。

② 孔子学院也不是儒学学院，而是一如英国文化协会（The British Council）功能般的中国语言文化学院。

③ 在印度尼西亚，孔子学院则以"汉语文学习中心"（Pusat Bahsa Cina、Pusat Bahasa Mandarin）之名成立，孔子一名专属印度尼西亚孔教，以免混淆。

④ 当时颇有将拉曼大学视为合办单位之一者，实误，例见马新民《荀子文化当为邯郸文化发展战略之首》，中国荀子网，2016 年 10 月 20 日阅。马来西亚中华国学书院的活动，https://zh-tw.facebook.com/mysinology/，同上日期阅。

排。作为上述十位成员中的一员，本文对孟子学院在马来西亚的挂牌之未来意义，聊表一己之见如下，以收集思广益之效。

孟子学院的诱发：马来西亚孟子资源的挖掘

很显然的，孟子学院马来西亚拉曼大学分院的设立，使"孟子"两字开始进入人们（至少是学人们）的眼帘，估计也将陆续成为人们（包括媒体）的话题。从学术研究和社会传播的角度来说，在马来西亚谈论孟子的首发问题，就是它的起点或切入点为何，也就是孟子与马来西亚现实的相干性问题。对这个问题的自然回答之一，就是诱发人们去找寻与挖掘现实中的马来西亚孟子的资源，以为谈论孟子话题的衔接点与其合理性之证明。所以，随着孟子学院在马来西亚的设立，人们直接的反应可想是：马来西亚有"孟子"吗？

这里的"孟子"打上一个引号，是因为人们口中的"孟子"，很可能是指孟子学，也可能指孟子文化，不一而足。当它是前者时，人们指的是马来西亚有没有孟子学著作或学人；若是后者，则是问马来西亚（华人）社会的哪一些观念、体制与行为与孟子有关。作为学术意义的孟子学观念或不难理解，至于文化意义的孟子文化或须一释于此：它是指社会上一些可被关联到孟子或《孟子》的观念、体制与行为，如"良知"在日常语言或判断上的运用、"孟母三迁"在子女教育上的启迪、孟子后裔在宗亲会上的组织、孟子"穷则独善其身，达则兼济天下"在世人处事态度上的依傍，如此不等，均是孟子或《孟子》生活化的表征与现象。言下之意，现实的马来西亚有学术意义的孟子学，或文化意义的孟子文化吗？

从 20 世纪以来的学术史证据来看，马来西亚应该没有孟子学[①]，而孟子文化存在的可能性也没有现成的文献可证明。在过去的一百多年，马来西亚并不是没有孟子或《孟子》研究，但成果极其零星，构不成学术史意义的孟子学传统。从辜鸿铭（1857—1928）到邬拜德拉（Obaidellah Mohamad，1945 年生，前马来亚大学中文系教师）的著作史来看，我们

---

① 这是以本文所知的情形而言，参见郑文泉《马来西亚近二百年儒家学术史》，中国儒学联合会"儒学与东方文化"项目报告（约 16 万字），2015。

找不到任何的《孟子》注经之作（外人如傅佩荣《傅佩荣解读孟子》2006年重印于马来西亚者不计），译经的话也只有后者唯一的马来语译本《孟子》（*Meng Zi*，1995），是孤立的现象；孟子或《孟子》的专家、专书研究，社会上亦罕见［民间学人有专治《易经》如石诗元（Cheok Si Guan，1928—2014）者，《孟子》则无］，主要集中为研究生的学位论文写作（多是马来西亚学生至国外大学中文系深造者），如黄文斌《孔孟的天道性命思想》（1996年硕士论文）、林良娥《先秦政治思想研究：孔子、孟子与荀子》（2000年硕士论文）、叶秀清《〈孟子〉的叙事及其哲学意义》（2002年硕士论文）等①，但未能持之以恒，在今天也未能以孟子学人之闻名于世；即使是普及类的孟子或《孟子》著作，有的也是外人作品的重印，如傅佩荣的《呣！孟子》（台湾原版《与青少年谈孟子》）等，本地作者如不是偏重于孔子（如张弓《孔子说》《孔子智慧》等六书）就是泛论儒学者（如许文荣《儒家思想问答》等），孟子学的传播极其有限。凡此种种，足示马来西亚的孟子或《孟子》的学术研究很是零星、单薄，远不足以支撑孟子学的学术骨架与材料。

相较之下，我们对孟子文化的要求就简单得多，因为这时候的取舍不是有没有人研究，而是现实上有没有跟孟子相关的文化现象可说。按本文过去的观察与分析，现实马来西亚至少有两处源自孟子而来的社会现象如下：

1. 孟子的"良知"观念对现实社会运动领袖的启发，其代表人物分别为"前半生兴学，后半生纾难"的陈嘉庚（Tan Kah Kee，1874—1961）和"华教的救亡运动"典范之沈慕羽（Sim Mow Yu，1913—2009）。

2. 孟子的"穷则独善其身，达则兼济天下"的处世观对现实亦吏（侨领或公务人员的济世之心）亦隐（诗人隐情）的处世态度极有影响，这点从"三园"到南洲诗社的诗人群体皆是。

首先，让我们看看孟子的"良知"观念在陈嘉庚和沈慕羽身上的作用。按陈嘉庚一生事迹与为人，新加坡华社在其1961年逝世时的挽联"前半生兴学，后半生纾难；是一代正气，亦一代完人"，堪称实评。陈嘉庚一生作为与孟子的联系，按他自叙少时所学为"《三字经》及《四

----

① 按以上三位均已入聘拉曼大学中文系者。完整学位论文目录，见郑文泉《表一：新、马1967—2007年思想类儒学学位论文（中文）一览》，载氏著《东南亚儒学：与东亚、北美鼎足而三的新兴区域儒学论》（吉隆坡：马来西亚孔学研究会，2010），第131—135页。

书》等",及"至十三四岁读《四书注》,始有解说,十六岁略有一知半解"看来①,语甚谦敛,实收效甚大。从一方面来说,陈嘉庚的"兴学"与"纾难",都出自他个人强烈的"天职"观念,前者如:

> 民国光复后余热诚内向,思欲尽国民一份子之天职,愧无其他才能参加政务或公共事业,只有自量绵力,回到家乡集美社创办小学校,及经营海产罐头蚝产。
> 每念竭力兴学,期尽国民天职,不图经济竭蹶,为善不终,贻累政府,抱歉无似。②

后者之"纾难"(救亡)如:

> 余经济有限为诸君所知,然为尽国民一份子之天职,愿购一十万元。
> 海外华侨安居乐业,略尽业务,何敢言劳?出钱出力实国民人人天职,在此救亡时代,中外同胞当然一体。③

而上述"天职"的观念源泉,则出自孟子的"四端之心"。其不忍之心与"兴学"之天职联言者,如《陈嘉庚教育文集》所见有:

> 国家兴亡匹夫有责,自当急起直追以尽天职,何忍袖手旁观。④

而与"纾难"之天职联言者,亦如《南侨回忆录》所示同为不忍之心:

> 不忍坐视闽民凄惨于不救,故不计利害,唯有以积极进行为

---

① 参见陈嘉庚《南侨回忆录·个人企业追记》,岳麓书社1998年版,第457页。
② 同上书,第4、21页。
③ 同上书,第54、134页。
④ 参见陈嘉庚《本报开幕之宣言(实业与教育之关系)》,《陈嘉庚教育文集》,福建教育出版社1989年版,第186页。

天职。①

按不忍之心为恻隐之心，陈嘉庚《南侨回忆录》一书多处另有是非之心、羞恶之心、辞让之心的展露②，足示其为孟子"良知"之统绪，此皆可按下不表者。按《南侨回忆录》一书有直言"良知"为"良心"或相关概念者，然不若"余非木石，敢置度外"一说最为透彻与传神③，陈嘉庚的"前半生兴学，后半生纾难；是一代正气，亦一代完人"可归之于孟子良知学的文化展现，应无疑义。

至于晚陈嘉庚约40年出生的沈慕羽，前者的"后半生纾难"正好构成了后者的"前半生纾难"及从政的生涯，即彼此都是当年抗日援华运动中的领导和地方干部的合作关系。仔细说来，沈慕羽一生的主轴可说是"兴学"即维护华文教育事业（1933年起至2009年卒），副业才有前半生政治（至1966年被撤销党籍乃止）与后半生孔教（1974年起领导马六甲孔教会至卒）的区分。④ 沈慕羽一生之所以无畏无惧、义无反顾地"为了争取华文的地位，我被开除党籍；为了华人的大团结，吃两年官司；前年为了华小高职的事，而被坐牢"等"华教的救亡运动"之事⑤，背后来自于"不忍眼看着本族的语文教育日趋衰微"的天赋情感⑥，原因是"人是有自尊心的，每个人都爱护自己的文化，是良知良能""爱护本族文化，是良知良能，不能看作是沙文主义或种族主义，如我是沙文主义，则马来人及印度人色彩更浓，岂能例外"等天赋的文化情感。⑦ 沈慕羽的"良知良能"显然和孟子的天赋道德义的"良知良能"说法有异，但也足见孟子的"良知良能"对他"兴学"一生的影响之大，已难以让人不将之与

---

① 参见陈嘉庚《南侨回忆录·个人企业追记》，岳麓书社1998年版，第353页。
② 同上书，第353、432、458等页。
③ 见陈嘉庚《南侨回忆录·战后补辑：我之华侨团结观》，第437页。
④ 沈慕羽的生平事迹，可见"永远的沈慕羽"网站：http://smy.jiaozong.org.my/index.php。
⑤ 参见沈慕羽《全马华校校友总会必须成立（二）》，《沈慕羽言论集》（吉隆坡：马来西亚华校教师会总会，1988），上册，第174页。
⑥ 参见沈慕羽《华教危机重重》、《教总第16届会员大会》及《全马华校校友总会必须成立（二）》，《沈慕羽言论集》，上册，第197页。
⑦ 参见沈慕羽《教总第20届会员大会》、《校友会的功用与使命（一）》，《沈慕羽言论集》（上册），第31、168页。

孟子挂钩了。①

如果说上述陈嘉庚、沈慕羽还只是观念式的孟子文化，那么以下"三园"及南洲诗社的古典诗坛例子，就是立体的孟子"穷则独善其身，达则兼济天下"之文化现象。众所周知，孟子对古典诗歌的影响之一是透过白居易的"吏隐"诗来达成的，即前者的"穷则独善其身，达则兼济天下"的处世态度，被实践为后者如下《与元九书》所阐释的诗歌模式：

> 仆志在兼济，行在独善，奉而始终之则为道，言而发明之则为诗。谓之讽喻诗，兼济之志也；谓之闲适诗，独善之义也。故览仆诗，知仆之道焉！②

按白居易以为孟子的"达则兼济天下"可发为诗歌上的"讽喻诗"，"穷则独善其身"则为"闲适诗"，"兼济"的现实基础是居为"吏"（小官），"独善"则为"隐"。和孟子说法稍异的是，白居易的"吏隐"诗不是居吏时为"讽喻诗"，不居吏时才为"闲适诗"，而是吏亦隐、隐亦吏的同时俱在的并存模式。

上述同时俱在的"吏隐"诗模式，就是我们在"三园"的诗集首先可以感受到的诗歌题材与氛围。按"三园"指邱炜萲（菽园，Khoo Seok Wan，1873—1941，有诗《菽园诗集》等）、陈延谦（止园，Tan Ean Kiam，1881—1943，有诗《止园集》）和李俊承（觉园，Lee Choon Seng，1888—1966，有诗《觉园集》等）三人，同为频密唱和诗友，背后也还有其他诗社的广大交往圈子。三园其实都不是吏，彼此的"兼济之志"是通过"侨领"的身份来达成的，具体说来就是（如）丘菽园投入康、梁的维新运动，陈延谦支持孙中山（1866—1925）的革命事业分任新加坡同盟会会长等职，最晚成的李俊承（民国成立时才23岁）则先后为新加坡筹赈会、南侨总会的重要领导，对民国政府的捐输救济更是不在话下。由于这样的缘故，三园的诗歌有"兼济之志"的吟咏和表现，

---

① 沈慕羽一生事迹的儒家渊源，参见郑文泉《天下乎？华社乎？沈慕羽与二十世纪马来西亚儒家的定型》，吉隆坡：林连玉基金"沈慕羽国际学术会议"论文，2009年12月12—13日。
② 参见《白居易集》卷二十八，喻岳衡点校，岳麓书社1992年版，第427页。

是很自然的事，所异是多发为白居易的"（时事）感伤诗"，而不是"讽喻诗"。至于同一时间的"独善之义"的诗歌，三园和白居易都是佛教居士，也与禅门人物多有唱和及往来，不但陈延谦的《赠厦鼓耆英会》一诗指出"香山韵事古今传"（此香山或香山居士，白居易之法号），李俊承以下的诗也直法白居易（白乐天）的禅悦之趣：

《酬丕唐居士》
潇洒襟怀白乐天，半谈诗酒半谈禅。吟成句媲梅花瘦，悟到心如朗月圆。
落笔烟云还绚烂，经霜松柏更鲜妍。知君已识浮生理，早向东林种白莲。①

上诗和作者同一时期的如下"兼济之志"诗，似意有未合：

《丙子献金购机寿蒋委员长》（1936年）
中原胡马竟忘归，到此方知事已非。秦苑秋风嘶铁骑，燕山明月照戎衣。
枕戈难夺三军气，舞羽曾扬上国威。今日祝公千万寿，献机端望复邦畿。

《乙酉内战》（1945年）
汉帜飘南岛，烟尘净九州。三军方解甲，内战忽临头。
无术销兵劫，含悲写国忧。可怜民疾苦，谁与挽横流。②

然而，对白居易式的"吏隐"诗人来说，同一时间发为"知君已识浮生理，早向东林种白莲"和"无术销兵劫，含悲写国忧"实在不是什么矛盾的事，毋宁是兼顾孟子"穷则独善其身，达则兼济天下"的处世态度的持衡表现。不唯如此，三园还有不少比附白居易的诗歌或行为的事迹，如丘菽园将自己的《菽园诗集》寄托到禅寺，以为：

---

① 参见李俊承《觉园集》（新加坡：作者自印，1950），第23页。
② 以上分见李俊承，《觉园集》，第16、54页。

《余诗稿因避蚁蛀,爱抄副本奉托痴公,幸许代为保存,如香山寺珍藏〈长庆集〉故事,他日佳话流传,好添海外禅门公案,书怀述感,寄视痴公,聊当息壤》

知归兜率白香山,身后名心未肯删。幸许骚笺依梵藏,待寻铁塔向禅关。

编袪脉望休招蠹,句杂娵隅自解蛮。一集偶然留副本,乐天故事且追扳。①

按上三园的白居易渊源,是断不可否的,而白居易的"吏隐"诗又祖述孟子的"穷则独善其身,达则兼济天下"的处世观,那么彼此又间接受影响于后者,是孟子文化的诗歌展示,也是不可否认的。

三园之后的马来西亚古典诗坛,特别是和李俊承有唱和关系的李冰人(1903—1996)、林蕴光(1893—1977)等在1973年筹立的麻坡南洲诗社(其前身为1960年的"丹绒吟苑")②,白居易的"吏隐"诗也得到若干程度的维持与弘扬。按南洲诗社成员(今仍有50位之多)除农、工、商人士外,还有不少居领导地位的成员具国立中、小学公务人员的身份,是名副其实的"吏",而"吏"或"兼济之志"诗的吟咏也远非个别诗人现象,而是整体诗社的群体行为。关于这点,我们从南洲诗社的社课,足多民生、时事类的"米贵""怡保昆仑朱罗石山崩坠惨剧""能源危机""咏青皮书"等题目,即可想知(诗例容略)。

表1　南洲诗社(1973—1976)社课题目(依《南洲诗词汇刊》期次)③

期次	题目	期次	题目	期次	题目
第一期	米贵	第十一期	能源危机	第二十期	踏青、乙卯清明
第二期	癸丑七夕	第十二期	甲寅上巳感赋	第廿一期	三三修契庆南洲
第三期	秋色	第十二期乙	裸奔	第廿二期	咏青皮书

---

① 参见丘菽园著,王盛治、丘鸣权编《菽园诗集》(出版地、出版社不详,1949),中册,卷六,第26—27页。

② 按李冰人此处生年,依马仑编著《当代马新文人事迹》,书辉出版社2016年版,第304页。

③ 转引自符爱萍《南洲诗社山水诗的生命美学(1973—1990)》(沙登:马来西亚博特拉大学博士学位论文,2015),第62—63页。

续表

期次	题目	期次	题目	期次	题目
第四期	癸丑中秋感赋	第十三期	悍妇行	第廿三期	艾醴香粽过端阳
第五期	秋声	第十三期乙	每逢佳节倍思亲	第？期	迎月
第六期甲	癸丑重阳	第十四期	核武	第？期	恒产
第六期乙	岭上梅	第十五期	甲寅诗人节诗祭拜屈平	第廿四期	选美有感
第七期	怡保昆仑朱罗石山崩坠惨剧	第十六期	九日感怀	第？期	女权咏
第八期	举世荒声似乱流	第十六期乙	榴梿	第廿五期	悼敦拉萨总理
第九期	癸丑岁暮述怀	第十七期	悼黄则健老先生	第廿五期乙	龙年感赋
第十期	怡保昆仑喇叭矿湖泥崩惨剧	第十八期	腊鼓		
第？期	甲寅挥春	第十九期	乙卯人日		

至于南洲诗社成员的"隐",本文此前曾以其前三任社长李冰人(任期1973—1976)、周清渠(任期1979—1982)、周庆芳(周庆芳教师,1983—1986)为对象,发现其"独善之义"之"闲适诗"不再与禅挂钩,无复"禅悦"之趣,而是共同表现为白居易也景仰、效仿的隐逸人物陶渊明(约365—427)之甘于"守拙"、安于闲适的诗境。① 关于这点,且让我们管窥第二任社长周清渠(1906—1984?,公立学校校长)的"隐"诗史,即可得知:

《守拙》(1940年南渡前诗)
耕读守我拙,名利让人贤,浮云看世态,尼父亦喟然。
我生古人后,无缘为执鞭,怡然从所好,忽忽年复年。
不做趋炎客,有愧酒中仙,淡泊以明志,狂狷谁与肩。
佛说有净土,翘首望长天,悠悠任所之,寒暑随播迁。②

---

① 参见郑文泉《白居易与二十世纪马来西亚"吏隐"诗》,"传统、递进与发展:2016马来西亚中国古典诗歌"国际学术研讨会论文,金宝:拉曼大学中华研究中心、孟子学院,2016年11月5—6日。

② 参见周清渠《听雨斋诗词吟草》(马六甲:周立训出版,1976),第2页。

《躬耕》（1961年）

躬耕不算苦，投笔且学圃。一椽临水畔，数畦瘦瘠土。
胼胝以耘耨，生活欣有补。扰攘世途中，守拙得其所。
长谢势力客，麋鹿引为伍。①

《秋兴八首用工部韵酬泰马诗人第九届中秋雅集绪友》其三（1973年）

凭栏萧飒对斜晖，芦白枫丹映翠微。
零粉残香蝶款款；辞巢别垒燕飞飞。
故园松菊应无恙；彩舞朝昏愿已违。
省识渊明恬退意，悠然从不羡轻肥。②

《落叶（七律四首用张松谱先生闹墨原韵）》其四（1977年）

惭愧续貂句未工，敢将醉涸比飞鸿。
尚余松菊恋三径，何处姹嫣闹紫红。
却喜门开山更见，不须惆怅翠还空。
高人自是多恬退，化育功深变则通。③

《钟声老友寄示〈心境〉一首一似重有忧者次韵慰之》（1977年）

心境曷如人境烦，浮云落日本无言。
渊明遵宪堪千古，采菊东篱重可论。④

《赏菊》（1983年）

东篱览菊浑无绪，细数年华鬓已苍。

---

① 参见周清渠《听雨斋诗词吟草》，第3页。
② 同上书，第28页。
③ 原载《南州诗词汇刊》第16辑（1977年11月7日），今辑入郑文泉编《周清渠集》（八打灵：拉曼大学中华研究中心汉学组，2014），第109页。
④ 原载《南州诗词汇刊》第16辑（1977年11月7日），今辑入郑文泉编《周清渠集》，第103页。

若问渊明何处所，故园三径早沦荒。①

按白居易《中隐》一诗的"小隐入丘樊（,）丘樊太冷落"说法，他是视陶渊明之"隐"为"小隐"，他自己的"吏隐"则属于"不如作中隐，隐在留司官……唯此中隐士，致身吉且安"的"中隐"，与另一"大隐住朝市……朝市太嚣喧"的"大隐"并为"隐"的三种不同类型。② 陶渊明的"小隐"没有"吏"的成分，周清渠之"省识渊明恬退意"是否意味他也是属于"小隐"而不可归于白居易的"吏隐"？实际上，周清渠并没有选择用陶渊明的弃职方法来达遂自己的"隐"志，而是一直做到退休才告别"吏"场，所以他毋宁仍是白居易的"吏隐"类型的。言下之意，南洲诗社表面上是自觉效仿陶渊明而不是白居易的"隐"，但他们的类型仍然是后者的"吏隐"而不是"小隐"，仍可归之为孟子"穷则独善其身，达则兼济天下"处世观的诗歌表现。

马来西亚孟子热的推展：学术研究与社会传播

承上所述，马来西亚现实有"孟子"的资源，且孟子文化丰沃于孟子学，或属实事。然而，这就能证明孟子或孟子学院与马来西亚现实的相干性吗？实际上，本文孟子文化所提的那些人（陈嘉庚、沈慕羽）与事（"穷则独善其身，达则兼济天下"之"吏隐"诗），并不乏民间基础，如马来西亚陈嘉庚基金、马来西亚陈嘉庚纪念馆、沈慕羽出版基金、金马士沈慕羽纪念馆、沈慕羽书法文物馆，乃至马六甲古城诗社、吉隆坡湖滨诗社、怡保山城诗社、吉打鹤山诗社等各地诗社之存在，即是明证。问题在于，上提陈嘉庚、沈慕羽之"民间热"等，从来不是本文所说的孟子文化意义的陈嘉庚热、沈慕羽热，如前者的"精神特征"也仅止于"忠、公、诚、毅"的德目内涵，其"思欲尽国民一份子之天职"甚至被误植为"思欲尽国民

---

① 原载《南州诗词汇刊》第 32 辑（1983 年 9 月 10 日），今辑入郑文泉编《周清渠集》，第 151 页。

② 参见白居易著，喻岳衡点校《中隐》，《白居易集》，卷五十二，第 799 页。

一份子之大职"①，可见时人敏感之欠。所以，马来西亚民间不是没有陈嘉庚热、沈慕羽热，而是这些"热"是否能进一步升华到孟子文化热的意义，其意义或必要性又为何，恐怕是我们推展孟子之前务必深省的问题。

我们知道，中国江苏师范大学之有孟子学院之举并非孤立现象，而是中国国学热、儒学热具体而微至孟子热的表征。在今天中国，学术性的孟子学团体（如2013年首家设在山东邹城的孟子研究院）和社会性的孟子文化团体（如中国孟子文化推广中心、福建省孟子文化发展促进会等）已日渐趋多，估计将来还会不断增加，孟子热的沸点也可预见。这些热点、热潮是现实马来西亚所不具备的，自然也不是单独一所孟子学院马来西亚拉曼大学分院所能复制和填补的。

换句话说，在一个没有中国国学热、儒学热的马来西亚现实，如何吹热孟子学和孟子文化的热度，可说是我们分析至今的问题点所在。很显然的，除非我们愿意让孟子学院重蹈荀子学院未有营运的覆辙，不然以下措施或可于近期内一推：

（1）学术研究：针对马来西亚或马来西亚以外的孟子课题，展开学术研究，前者课题包括上提马来西亚孟子学和孟子文化所指二事，可暂置其社会效应（如陈嘉庚热得否升华为孟子文化意义之陈嘉庚热）于度外。

（2）社会传播：凡直面社会的孟子学或孟子文化之普及活动（非直接相关之《弟子规》读经、书法竞赛、传统节庆等"国学"活动，暂勿计），如上述陈嘉庚热之升华为孟子文化热，乃至《孟子》读经、《孟子》讲座、孟子故居巡礼、孟母文化节、《孟子》名言书法比赛一直到孟子学与国内其他民族学术文化的对谈与交流等，皆可考虑。

至于中国的孟子学热、孟子文化热能不能因此被复制、移植到马来西亚来，则未可得而知，因为缺的不仅是马、中合作两造需长期精诚合作，还有整个大环境是否变得使人们对孟子学、孟子文化的存在与意义更加完善与支持，此则是一整个时代风气的转移之事，诚非易举。

萨迦1938年（兼公元2016年）10月23日于
竹溪行舍

---

① 参见马来西亚陈嘉庚基金筹委会编《陈嘉庚精神特征》，载《光辉典范、百年照耀：陈嘉庚华侨领袖》（吉隆坡：马来西亚陈嘉庚基金筹委会，无出版年〔估计约2012〕），第11页。

东亚文明中朱子文化的传承与实践

朱茂男[*]

一　前言

朱熹是古代伟大的思想家、哲学家和教育家，朱熹一生从学、著述、传教，集孔子之后历代学术思想之大成，形成儒学思想文化中的朱子理学，为中国古代文化的突出贡献，也为东亚文明乃至世界文明做出贡献。从东亚儒学的发展来看，朱子学影响并涵盖了日本、韩国、越南以及中国台湾等地，对东亚文明发展有其重要意义。朱子是我中华民族自孔、孟以来最重要的思想家。他的著述宏富，思想博大精深，他所编著的《四书集注》自元朝以来成为科举考试的重要依据，对思想、学术及教育乃至一般社会文化之发展，产生了全面性深远的影响。1175年，朱子与吕祖谦合编北宋四子之言论选辑为《近思录》，并以《近思录》为《四书》之阶梯。由于朱子对教育的重视与身体力行，才使他的学问能感召众多弟子，而终能大行于其身后。

儒学在明郑时期传入台湾，主导明郑历史的延平郡王郑成功与晚明儒学有深厚的渊源。因此，明郑时期的台湾儒学，虽刚萌芽，却是上承有明一代儒学，下启清代台湾儒学。延平王郑成功军旅中的一批儒者，则是把中华传统儒学和福建朱子学最早传入台湾的开拓者。台湾儒学的另一来源是清康熙以及此后的理学家。他们在台湾建造学校，开办书院，把福建朱子学即闽学全面系统地传入台湾。闽、台仅一衣带水之隔，荷据时代台湾之汉移民以闽人为主，明郑之时自郑成功以迄下属亦多闽人。清朝时期，

---

[*] 朱茂男，台湾海峡两岸朱子文化交流促进会理事长。

台湾在1885年（光绪十一年）建省之前，也一直是福建辖区。因此，闽学传入台湾乃顺理成章之事。

由于康熙皇帝是朱熹的崇拜者，清代成为台湾儒学的重要发展期。康熙对朱子"最为尊崇，天下士子莫不奉为准绳"，一时朱子学大兴，学者遍及全国。经过二百多年的垦殖，儒学已在台湾的土壤里生根，并开花结果。此期的思想主流是福建朱子学，程明道曾视其大弟子杨龟山归闽为"道南之传"，则朱子学入台可称为"道东之传"。就思想的原创性言，台湾儒学系出福建朱子学；但是就思想的历史性、社会性、文化性而言，台湾朱子学所浮现的问题，诸如与异文化（台湾少数民族文化）的邂逅，与民间信仰（如文昌帝君的信仰）的遭遇，与移民社会的互动，都使台湾朱子学展现奇异缤纷的多元色彩，并彰显其独有的地域文化特色。

二 朱子文化的传承、实践与创新

朱熹的思想理念极具"融旧铸新"之内涵，其融合前人智慧之结晶，以开拓新时代之需求，富有温故知新之效果。朱熹认为读书应"少看熟读，反覆体验"在于重视实践之哲学，主张将所学融入并实行于日常生活之中。

世界朱氏联合会（世朱联）于1993年成立以来，以促进全世界朱氏宗亲之间的亲睦团结、贡献国际亲善及世界和平，承继发扬以朱子为代表的东方优秀传统文化、修复朱子遗迹为宗旨。世朱联作为全球朱氏族裔唯一的世界性组织，自首任会长韩国朱昌均先生创会迄今已走过了二十几年的光辉历程。在二十几年艰辛的开创岁月中，我们有首任会长昌均先生当初创立的辛劳及无私的奉献奠定基础，有第二任会长祥南先生继往开来，2008年10月在婺源第七届会员代表大会上茂男被选为会长，茂男继任会长后，沿着前两任会长所开辟的道路努力前行，力图以三个层次实践推广朱子文化："一以学术研讨学习为视野，二以经典论坛对话为核心，三以文化教育推广为脉络。"

世界朱氏联合会在2010年欣逢纪念朱熹诞辰880周年，举办一系列的庆典活动，获得广大的回响与关注。于一系列多元文化的活动中，包括海峡论坛暨武夷山朱子文化节开幕式、韩国朱子庙大祭。东南亚六国联办庆典活动，以《朱子家训》中英文版的碑文揭牌仪式，及近500位学生默写《朱子家训》的壮观场面令人印象深刻。台湾方面则以新竹朱子学堂的揭牌仪式，开启两岸书院合作的新起点，又以嘉义朱子公庙依照朱子家礼举行的祭朱子大典，最为经典。而接续下来，在大陆南宁举办庆祝活动与北京成立全国朱熹研究会及武夷山朱子文化节闭幕式（涵盖：邮票首发、朱熹铜像落成典礼、朱子文化园启用典礼、朱子林的兴建等重要的仪式）。在学术活动方面，除了内地安徽主办的中国内地与港澳台地区朱子学研讨会，更特地在海外的日本及中国台湾地区举办朱子学学术研讨会，足见朱子学不仅促进东亚文明，更具备全球化的视野与价值，亦为传承朱子文化揭开了新的里程碑。

2008年"朱子之路"的首航，由杨儒宾教授担任领航者的角色，得到了热烈的回响与鼓励，使我们感到这是一项值得推动的文教志业。"朱子之路"即走访一遍朱熹出生成长、求学、讲学、终老的地方，行程中借由学者及学员们读朱子书行朱子路以"走朱子之路，行朱子之道"的精神，累积对于经典中知识的体认，进而发扬朱子学，达其永续传承朱子文化的愿景。2013年新春，台湾举行了为时半个月之久的彪灯会系列活动，"2013台湾彪灯会系列活动——新竹朱子学堂系列讲座暨书院文化论坛"，是台湾彪灯会的卫星（satellite）活动。新竹朱子学堂代表象征新竹之人文特色，更成为推广在地人文、传承朱子文化之重要交流平台。"新竹朱子学堂系列讲座"以"儒家与庶民生活"为主题，扩展朱子文化的社会普及，提高民众的人文素养与社会关怀，进而在2013年秋，成立了"台湾海峡两岸朱子文化交流促进会"，以促进中国内地与台湾地区文化交流的活动。2014年"朱子之路"参与人员，除了中国内地与台湾地区硕博士师生团，还有台湾新竹博爱、关西、新埔国中书法团学员参与此行，并与南平书画社成员于南平市玉屏阁，举办中国内地与台湾地区朱子文化书画交流笔会，以朱熹诗词格言为主轴，于活动中挥毫落纸，借由书画墨宝以增进两岸朱子文化的交流，寓朱子诗文于芳墨之中，为此届"朱子之路"增添书香雅韵。

朱子的许多诗词格言，是弥足珍贵的文化遗产，其中所蕴含的伦理道德、民本思想、治政理念、和谐追求都根深蒂固地存在于民族文化的传统中，为使其广布流传，茂男特敦请福建省歌舞剧院专业作曲家骆季超教授为朱子诗词格言谱曲，融合古乐今声，以合唱、独唱、声乐、演奏等表演方式进行，结合中国内地与台湾地区地域文化、人文历史，打造两岸同声之经典画面。2014 年 10 月在台北中山堂演出的"朱子之歌·道东之传——光复节闽台文化交流音乐会"由南平南词艺术团、台北国乐团及附设合唱团携手合作；在新竹县文化局演艺厅演出的"朱子之歌·两岸同声"则由南平南词艺术团、新竹市立国乐团、新竹县教师合唱团、新竹市立混声合唱团等艺术团体联合演绎，共同谱出朱子心曲，再现圣哲古风！进入 21 世纪全球化的时代，资讯媒体的发达，两岸交流的频繁，促使朱子文化的流布更加普及，相关活动的举办成功见证朱子思想的魅力不分古今。

三 朱子文化走入庶民生活广布四方

在现今全球化的时代，朱熹"理一分殊，存异求同"的思想，及"朱子家训"深化社会伦理的作用，已成为东亚文明之瑰宝，具备当代核心的价值。朱子文化落实在生活之中，且深入在日常生活的日用常行之道，在潜移默化中提升了人民的精神生活，成为一种文化素养的意涵，借由热爱朱子文化的政府、学者专家、宗亲们的热心推动，扩大朱子文化的范畴，推动朱子家训、朱子家礼、朱子之路、社会教育、书法文化、书院文化、茶道文化、闽台文化、儒商文化，并融合学术、庆典、祭祖、商贸交流、宗亲联谊等多元化活动，将朱子的理念与实践推向新的高峰。

为弘扬朱子文化丰富的内涵，我们应将朱子文化促进人文社会的发展，提升生命之层次，继而结合文创产业，打造朱子文化的品牌，达成朱子学研究落实在日常生活并且与地方学术社群结合的愿景。2017 年将追随杨儒宾教授行走"朱子之路"，完成在朱熹墓前许下的心愿，在第 10 年画下完美的句点——"朱子之路 十年有成"。"一带一路"倡议是以有形的基础建设为主，要以王道的思维，把软硬体整合、创新，才能为区域发展做出创造价值的贡献，且有着宏观战略并极具包容与吸纳之特色，我们应同行朱子之礼，同唱朱子之歌，重走朱子之路，结合朱子学院、朱子书院与一带一路成为传统与现代融合的全球品牌之路，建构更美好与和平发展的未来，展现灿烂的朱子文化对于世界文明的影响力，成就"一带一路一朱子"梦想。亦借由明年（2018年）纪念朱熹诞辰888周年之际，举办一系列的活动，让朱子文化成为人民生活的一环，继而推广到全世界，而朱熹"理一分殊、存异求同"之精神将朱子学推向国际，定位其思想为促进东亚文明的发展，在全球化的视野下发挥其当代的价值，促进世界和平发展，也能产生重要作用，引领世人走向更美好的未来。

希冀"在我们的手中，我们拥有今天；在我们的梦里，我们拥有明天；在朱子的领域，我们拥有永远"。